GREEN PLANET BLUES

A project of the Harrison Program on the Future Global Agenda

GREEN
PLANET
BLUES

*Environmental Politics
from Stockholm to Rio*

edited by

KEN CONCA, MICHAEL ALBERTY

& GEOFFREY D. DABELKO

University of Maryland at College Park

WestviewPress

A Division of HarperCollinsPublishers

Copyright © 1995 by Westview Press, Inc., A Division of HarperCollins Publishers, Inc.

Published in 1995 in the United States of America by Westview Press, Inc., 5500 Central Avenue, Boulder, Colorado 80301-2877, and in the United Kingdom by Westview Press, 12 Hid's Copse Road, Cumnor Hill, Oxford OX2 9JJ

Library of Congress Cataloging-in-Publication Data
Green planet blues :   environmental politics from Stockholm to Rio /
    edited by Ken Conca, Michael Alberty, and Geoffrey D. Dabelko.
        p.   cm.
ISBN 0-8133-2596-X—ISBN 0-8133-2597-8 (paperback)
    1. Environmental policy—Political aspects. 2. Sustainable
development. 3. Green movement. I. Conca, Ken. II. Alberty,
Michael. III. Dabelko, Geoffrey D.
HC79. E5G6916 1995
363. 7—dc20   95-14103
                                                                                                            CIP

10   9   8   7   6   5   4

Contents

Part Three: The Prospects for International Environmental Cooperation

Part Four: Institutions as Though the Earth Mattered

Part Five: The Sustainable Development Debate

Part Six: From Ecological Conflict to Environmental Security?

Part Seven: Ecological Justice

Preface

THIS BOOK IS A PROJECT of the Harrison Program on the Future Global Agenda of the University of Maryland at College Park. We are grateful to Horace Harrison for making the program a possibility and to its current director, Dennis Pirages, for logistical, financial, and moral support. We also thank Chris Calwell, Polly Christensen, Peter Goering, Peter Haas, Robert Harper, Jennifer Knerr, Karen Litfin, Connie Oehring, Tim O'Riordan, Dennis Pirages, Marvin Soroos, Peter Taylor, Eric Wright, and Song Zhao for advice and assistance.

Because many of the selections presented in this volume are excerpts, a brief explanation of our editing philosophy is in order. In those cases where space limitations precluded reprinting an entire essay, our goal has been to edit in such a way as to emphasize the underlying ideas and concepts. In many cases, this has meant leaving out some elaborations, trenchant asides, or supporting examples. We have preserved the original notes corresponding to the material reproduced here but left out notes corresponding to passages of text we have not included. We have also preserved the original numbering of all notes to facilitate consulting the original material. For essays with a large number of in-line citations in the original (those by Feeny, Lélé, and Johnston), we have preserved all of the factual citations but removed several of the more general references (to save space and enhance readability). Readers seeking further background, greater detail, or additional references should consult the original material.

Ken Conca
Michael Alberty
Geoffrey D. Dabelko

INTRODUCTION

Two Decades of Global Environmental Politics

Think globally, act locally. Spaceship Earth. The common heritage of humanity. Pollution does not respect national borders. The Earth is one, but the world is not. We have not inherited the Earth from our parents; we have borrowed it from our children. The global commons.

Each of these phrases, well known to environmentalists, invokes similar themes. They remind us of the interconnectedness of the global environment; of the close ties between environmental quality and human well-being; and of the common fate that these realities impose upon all of the planet's occupants, present and future. We live, and have been living for some time, in an era of global environmental politics.

Pollution, ecosystem destruction, and natural resource depletion are not new problems. Many regions and localities were grappling with these issues long before the industrial revolution or even before the emergence of the modern nation-state system in the seventeenth century. And if environmental problems have a long-standing history, so must the political struggles that inevitably accompany those problems. Thus, severe wood shortages led to conservation efforts in Babylonia during the time of Hammurabi.[1] Measures to protect wetlands, in recognition of their importance as sources of fish, game, and fuel, have been traced to the sixth century A.D. in the Huang-Huai-Hai plain of northeastern China.[2] Air-quality crises in London during the early stages of the industrial revolution led to the formation of smoke-abatement societies advocating legislative action.[3] One can easily imagine the political controversies that must have engulfed each of these cases, given the ways in which these measures affected powerful interests and rewrote the rules governing access to the environment and natural resources.

Today, the dramas of environmental politics are ever more frequently being played out on a global stage. It is generally agreed that human transformation of the environment is a global problem. In some cases, this is because the system under stress is globally interconnected in a direct physical sense, as in the case of the Earth's climate, the oceans, or the atmosphere's protective ozone layer. In other cases, local consequences add up to global significance, as in the depletion of the world's fisheries or the reduction of the planet's biological diversity.

One recent study, *The Earth as Transformed by Human Action,* provides the most comprehensive description to date of how human impact on the environment has grown to global proportions.[4] For the purposes of assessment and comparison, the authors divide the world into seven ecological regions;

they then describe for each region the historical "trajectory" by which population growth, technological development, changes in consumption patterns, and different forms of social organization generated profound environmental changes. Although the specific pattern that emerges differs significantly from region to region, the common theme is the expanding scale of human impact, from local to regional to global.

Thus, we speak increasingly of global environmental problems. But what does it mean to speak of global environmental *politics?* To answer this question, consider what people see when they look at a forest. Some see a stock of timber to be exploited for economic gain. Others see a complex ecological system that holds the soil in place, stabilizes the local water cycle, moderates the local climate, and fosters biological diversity. Still others see the forest as a home for people and other living things, or perhaps as an ancestral burial ground. Finally, some see the forest as a powerful cultural symbol: The forest as a living system reflects the potential harmony between humanity and nature and provides a link between the past and the future.

We live in a world that is at once fragmented by the political division into sovereign states and reassembled by the increasingly rapid flows of people, goods, money, ideas, images, and technology across borders.[5] In such a world, conflicting visions of the forest take on international significance. Some see in the forest an important source of international economic power, giving those who control it influence in international markets and a reliable source of foreign exchange. Others see a powerful symbol of global interdependence: The forest reflects the global consequences of local acts in that destruction of the forest may alter the global climate or deplete the global stock of biological diversity. Still others see a very different sort of international symbol: The forest represents national sovereignty in that it confirms the right of a nation to do as it sees fit within its own territory. Such rights may seem to be a luxury that a crowded planet cannot afford. But this is not often the view of those who feel their sovereign rights most immediately threatened—particularly if those rights have been won in a struggle for independence that helped forge the nation itself.

Often these competing visions reflect different interests held by individuals, groups, and perhaps even entire nations. They are also a product, however, of some of the structured patterns that govern world politics. The institution of national sovereignty, the division of labor in the capitalist world economy, the rise of transnational networks of environmentalists, the predominance of powerful beliefs about the links between consumption and "progress"—each of these underlying features of contemporary world politics shapes what people see when they look at the forest. These competing visions, values, and interests often lead to conflict. Actors disagree about the nature of the problem, the effectiveness or fairness of proposed solutions, and the correct place to lay responsibility. Thus, studying global environmental politics means understanding the conflicts of interest that surround environmental issues as well as asking how interests, values, and visions related to the environment are shaped.

The study of global environmental politics also involves the search for cooperative solutions to ecological dilemmas. The idea that global environmental problems require "international cooperation" is widely accepted. But the appropriate scope and content of such cooperation is hotly contested. Does international cooperation mean formal, treaty-based agreements among governments? Does it mean a broader "global bargain" between North and South, linking a number of issues in a single package? Or does it refer to a still broader process of global dialogue, not limited to governments, in which different societies move toward a global convergence of values? Does an increasingly global network of environmental organizations represent an effective new form of international cooperation or is it simply one more way in which the strong impose their will upon the weak? Is the goal to create an increasingly dense web of transnational linkages, one that binds nations to a common future and a common commitment to environmental protection? Or would it be wiser to work toward delinking an already tightly coupled world system, so that various localities and regions have more flexibility to pursue responses appropriate to their unique circumstances?

Finally, an important dimension of the study of global environmental politics is connecting the patterns of international conflict and cooperation over the environment that we see to some of the larger changes that seem to be under way in world politics. If studying the structure of world politics gives us insight into the character of global environmental problems, the reverse is also true. It is no surprise that, as the world stands on the edge of the twenty-first century, environmental problems have emerged as a critical theme in the study of international relations and world politics. At a time when much of the conventional wisdom of international relations is under challenge, studying the politics of the global environment may also give us greater insight into the emerging patterns of world politics as a whole.

Two Decades of Global Environmental Politics

For twelve days in June of 1992, representatives of 178 nations gathered in the city of Rio de Janeiro, Brazil. Diplomats debated the causes of environmental problems, the nature of the linkages between the environment and economic development, and the appropriateness of various policy responses. By the end of the conference, they had produced international agreements on climate change and biological diversity, a statement of general principles on environment and development, and "Agenda 21," an ambitious, 800-page document on a broad array of environmental problems, setting guidelines for action into the twenty-first century.

The political elites gathering in Rio, including more than 100 heads of state, were joined by more than 8,000 journalists from all over the world as well as representatives of more than 1,400 nongovernmental organizations (NGOs).[6] Some of the NGOs, including business groups and mainstream environmental organizations, enjoyed substantial access to the official and unofficial discussions among governments; others, including many grassroots environmental organizations, indigenous peoples' groups, human rights advocates, and women's groups, found themselves relegated to outsider status. Many participated in a parallel "Global Forum" of NGOs, held on the other side of the city. Many activists left Rio frustrated at the relative lack of action on pressing problems, but many also left convinced that the Global Forum was a major step forward in the creation of a global social movement of environmentalism.[7]

The Rio Conference—formally known as the United Nations Conference on Environment and Development (UNCED) and popularly dubbed the Earth Summit—was not the first United Nations conference to discuss the planet's environmental predicaments. Two decades earlier, representatives of many of the world's governments had gathered in Stockholm, Sweden, to discuss a number of the same issues. The 1972 Stockholm Conference—formally known as the United Nations Conference on the Human Environment—did not attract nearly the broad level of participation, public interest, or media attention seen in Rio de Janeiro two decades later. But the fundamental question was the same: How do we respond to urgent environmental problems in a politically, economically, and culturally divided world?[8]

The contrasts between Stockholm and Rio reflect many of the underlying changes that had taken place in the world during the intervening two decades. Stockholm occurred in the shadow of the Cold War; the governments of Eastern Europe and the Soviet Union boycotted the conference after a dispute over the representation of a divided Germany. Rio, in contrast, took place in the relatively optimistic afterglow of the end of the Cold War, amidst a general sense of new opportunities for global cooperation.

The 1992 Earth Summit also reflected the tremendous growth over the past few decades in scientific understanding of environmental problems. Whereas Stockholm had focused attention principally on relatively narrowly defined problems of air and water pollution, Rio embraced a far broader and more complex agenda. This shift reflected, in part, a changing scientific paradigm—one that views the Earth as a single integrated system with complex linkages among the large-scale ecological systems of land, oceans, atmosphere, and biosphere.[9] The discussion at Rio, and in particular the ambitious goals embodied in Agenda 21, also reflected the greater capacity of scientists to measure, monitor, and model complex processes of environmental change.[10]

Another clear change from Stockholm to Rio is the emergence of global public awareness and concern. Many of the participants at Stockholm—and particularly those from the North—framed environmental problems as the by-product of an affluent, industrialized lifestyle. The implication was that the poorer regions of the world neither suffered as much as the industrialized regions from environmental problems nor exhibited similar levels of concern. In the ensuing two decades, however, the notion that there is both a "pollution of affluence" *and* a "pollution of poverty" has gained much broader acceptance. As the environmental causes of poverty have become clearer, what many of those suffering from poverty have presumably known all along has become more generally understood: Environmental concerns are not the exclusive property of the affluent or of the industrialized countries.

Public opinion data support this claim of broad public concern. In a fascinating comparison of polling data from several nations, Riley Dunlap, George Gallup, Jr., and Alec Gallup found a remarkably uniform pattern: Large majorities in each country revealed deep concern about environmental problems, attached significant value to a healthy environment, and expressed very real fears about what the future may hold.[11] The findings (summarized in Table I.1) suggest that even if different peoples, classes, regions, and cultures define the problem somewhat differently, concerns about the environment cut across simplistic distinctions between rich and poor, North and South, overdeveloped and underdeveloped.[12]

Rio also differed from Stockholm in that the governments and other actors gathering to discuss global environmental problems had themselves undergone notable changes in the ensuing two decades. Virtually all of the governments converging on Rio de Janeiro had some form of national environmental bureaucracy; almost none did at the time of the Stockholm Conference. In many cases these agencies enabled governments to take advantage of the growth of environmental knowledge so as to more effectively analyze the causes and consequences of environmental problems. And in some cases the agencies had themselves evolved into advocates for various environmental-protection programs, producing more complex internal debates within national delegations.

Environmental organizations also underwent substantial changes between the Stockholm and Rio Conferences. These changes included growth in num-

Table I.1 Selected Results of the 1992 "Health of the Planet Survey"

Percentage of respondents who say that environmental problems are a "very serious" issue in their nation

Industrialized Nations		*Developing Nations*	
Germany	67	South Korea	67
Switzerland	63	Poland	66
Canada	53	Mexico	66
United States	51	Russia	62
Portugal	51	Turkey	61
Japan	42	Chile	56
Norway	40	Hungary	52
Great Britain	36	India	51
Ireland	32	Brazil	50
Netherlands	27	Nigeria	45
Denmark	26	Uruguay	44
Finland	21	Philippines	37

Percentage of respondents who rate the quality of the world environment as "very" or "fairly" bad

Industrialized Nations		*Developing Nations*	
Denmark	92	Chile	88
Norway	88	Uruguay	74
Germany	86	Poland	73
Switzerland	86	Hungary	71
Netherlands	84	Mexico	70
Canada	79	Russia	66
Great Britain	76	South Korea	65
Portugal	75	Brazil	64
Finland	73	Philippines	58
Ireland	73	Turkey	45
Japan	73	India	42
United States	66	Nigeria	24

SOURCE: Figures 2 and 4 of Riley E. Dunlap, George H. Gallup, Jr., and Alec M. Gallup, "Of Global Concern: Results of the Health of the Planet Survey," *Environment* 35, 9 (November 1993): 7–15, 33–39.

bers (more than 1,400 NGOs were officially accredited participants at Rio, as opposed to 134 at Stockholm) and a shift to greater global representation (one-third of the groups at Rio were from the South, as opposed to only about 10 percent at Stockholm).[13] During the 1970s and 1980s many of these groups turned their attention to the international arena, leading to more effective international coalitions of local- or national-level environmental organizations.[14] Although environmental organizations face many of the same obstacles to North-South cooperation that confront governments, the emergence of this global network fundamentally altered the terms of the debate at Rio.

A final measure of the changes from Stockholm to Rio is growth in the number of international environmental treaties, agreements, and cooperative accords. By one estimate there are now more than 650 such international agreements in operation.[15] Many of the agreements are relatively narrow in scope, including bilateral accords on specific environmental problems or regional agreements involving small numbers of countries and narrow agendas. But the list also includes several major international accords adopted since the Stockholm Conference, including agreements on ocean pollution, acid rain, preservation of the ozone layer, the international trade in endangered species, and environmental protection in Antarctica.[16] The designers of international accords at Rio had a much broader set of examples upon which to draw than did their counterparts at Stockholm; as a result, they also had at least a crude understanding of what makes various approaches to international environmental cooperation more or less effective.[17]

It is equally important to stress what did not change in the twenty years between conferences. Many of the same stumbling blocks to effective global response seen at Stockholm were also in full evidence at Rio. These stumbling blocks include the tremendous mistrust and suspicion governing relations between North and South in world politics; the tenacious embrace of traditional conceptions of national sovereignty by governments, even as they acknowledge the need for a coordinated global response to problems that do not respect borders; and the tensions between the long-term vision necessary for ecologically sane planning and the short-term concern for economic growth and political stability that preoccupies most governments.

Perhaps the most important continuity from Stockholm to Rio is that global environmental change has continued at an alarming rate. Between 1970 and 1990, global commercial energy consumption, a major source of environmental impacts, increased by roughly 62 percent; other global indicators of human impact on the environment, including food production, overall economic activity, and population, increased in roughly similar proportions during the two decades between conferences.[18] To be sure, these very crude indicators of human stress on environmental systems can mask as much as they reveal. They say nothing about how underlying activities actually affect the environment, they tell us nothing about who or what may be responsible, and they give no indication of who suffers the consequences most directly and immediately. But they do indicate the scale of the problem and the enormity of the challenge of reorienting some of the fundamental practices that drive growth, production, consumption, and environmental transformation in the current world system.

This mixed picture of continuity and change raises an obvious question: Compared to where things stood at Stockholm, does the glass appear half empty or half full in the aftermath of Rio? Does the twenty-year period between the two conferences tell an optimistic story of global society moving to meet the challenges of ecological interdependence, or does it chronicle a continued unwillingness or inability to grapple with the root causes of the problem? There are more than enough ways to measure change and more than enough definitions of progress to support either interpretation. Perhaps both are true: Just as some of the differences between Stockholm and Rio may reveal important possibilities for change, learning, and effective global cooperation, so too the enduring patterns and divisions highlight the depth of the political challenge posed by global environmental problems.

Conflicting Views of the Environmental Problematique

Growing scientific understanding and shared levels of public concern do not automatically translate into a shared understanding of the social causes of environmental problems. One of the first challenges facing students of global environmental politics is to sort through a potentially bewildering debate on the causes of pollution and environmental degradation. Some of this uncertainty lies in the realm of science. The physical, chemical, and biological mechanisms involved in processes such as climate change, desertification, and deforestation are sometimes quite poorly understood by leading experts, to say nothing of the general public, policymakers, or interest groups. The global interaction of oceans, atmosphere, land, and biosphere has only recently become a central concern of such separate disciplines as oceanography, atmospheric science, and terrestrial ecology. Although knowledge is expanding rapidly on many fronts, scientific uncertainty remains substantial in the face of the complexity of the processes of environmental change.

These aspects of technical complexity are matched by similar controversies, debates, and uncertainties about the social dimensions of environmental change. In explaining why human populations have had such a substantial impact on planetary ecosystems, different analysts invoke factors as diverse as values, technology, culture, ideology, public policies, demographic change, and social structures of class, race, or gender. Some observers elevate one or a few of these factors to the role of central cause, treating the others as mere symptoms. Others have sought to develop more complex models stressing the interaction of these various forces and processes.

Some see the problem as essentially one of values, and in particular, the value modern societies attach to consumption. Alan Durning of the Worldwatch Institute, a Washington-based environmental policy institute, writes,

> The soaring consumption lines that track the rise of the consumer society are, from another perspective, surging indicators of environmental harm. The consumer society's exploitation of resources threatens to exhaust, poison, or unalterably disfigure forests, soils, water, and air. We, its members, are responsible for a disproportionate share of all the global environmental challenges facing humanity.[19]

Our consumer culture translates wants into needs, stresses material-intensive forms of social gratification, and overwhelms older, more ecologically sustainable traditions that stand in its way. As consumerism spreads through increasingly sophisticated advertising, pop culture, and the global media, more and more regions of the planet adopt the aspirations of the consumer society.

Technology is also a commonly cited culprit. Barry Commoner, a key figure in raising public awareness about environmental problems in the United States through books such as *The Closing Circle* and *Making Peace with the Planet,* uses the simple example of the production of beer bottles in the United States to illustrate the technological dimension.[20] Writing in the mid-1970s, Commoner investigated the impact of three factors commonly cited as a cause of environmental problems—population growth, rising levels of per capita consumption, and technological change. He found that the number of beer bottles produced had increased by a dramatic 593 percent during the study period, even though the population had grown by only 30 percent and per capita beer consumption by only 5 percent. Clearly, a technological change—the replacement of returnable bottles with single-use, throwaway ones—had led to the bulk of the increase and hence to the bulk of the environmental impact in terms of energy use, trash, and so on. Commoner argues that such technological changes, across most of the key sectors of modern society, are at the heart of the environmental crisis.

Some observers argue that prevailing technologies and values are themselves an expression of underlying power dynamics in society. Murray Bookchin, for example, though not necessarily disagreeing with Durning's assessment of the consumer society or Commoner's cautions about technology, stresses the importance of social inequality. He warns against attributing environmental problems to such vague and impersonal formulations as "values," "technology," and "humanity"; such reasoning "serves to deflect our attention from the role society plays in producing ecological breakdown."[21] According to Bookchin,

> A mythic "Humanity" is created—irrespective of whether we are talking about oppressed ethnic minorities, women, Third World people, or people in the First

World—in which everyone is brought into complicity with powerful corporate elites in producing environmental dislocations. In this way, the social roots of ecological problems are shrewdly obscured. A new kind of biological "original sin" is created in which a vague group of animals called "Humanity" is turned into a destructive force that threatens the survival of the living world.[22]

According to Bookchin, the key to understanding lies instead in seeing how social inequality feeds environmental degradation and resource overexploitation. Societies constructed upon hierarchies of race, class, and gender are, in this view, fundamentally based on exploitation. As such, they have an inherent tendency to seek domination over nature rather than a means of living in harmony with it, just as they favor the domination of some people by others.[23]

Vandana Shiva, who has written extensively about forestry issues in postcolonial India, provides a model that seeks to link such diverse causal forces as technology, values, and social structure.[24] For Shiva, the key is historical; technological and demographic change, hierarchical patterns of social structure, and consumption-oriented values are the co-evolutionary products of Indian society's dominant historical experience—the political, economic, and social transformations of Indian society brought about by more than a century of British colonial rule. In Shiva's view, "causes" of environmental degradation in India as diverse as the industrial revolution, the capitalist world economy, and the destructive power of modern science and technology are "the philosophical, technological and economic components of the same process."[25]

Sorting out this diverse array of claims requires carefully detailed, historical study of the ways in which economic, social, and political institutions in society co-evolve over time.[26] Many of the selections in this volume will present their own models of the causes of environmental problems, at varying levels of detail and complexity. It will become apparent to the reader that these various causal claims are based on very different understandings of the sources of power, interest, authority, and legitimacy in society. Sorting out such diverse claims does not guarantee that effective policies and institutions will be designed. Actors may agree on the causes of a problem but still disagree on the appropriate responses; they may see their interests affected differently or hold different views about the fairness or effectiveness of a particular response. But grappling with the complex array of causes does seem to be one necessary step if appropriate responses are to be crafted. Perhaps just as importantly, examining the diversity of claims also helps us to understand the equally diverse beliefs about history, justice, and responsibility that various actors bring to the debate.

How to Use This Book

The material in this book has been selected with three goals in mind. One goal has been to pay particular attention to underlying questions of power, interest, authority, and legitimacy that shape global environmental debates. The challenge of the global environment is often framed as a narrowly technical task of promoting policy coordination among governments. Clearly, rational policies and effective intergovernmental cooperation will be a crucial part of any meaningful response to the challenge. But a narrow focus on governments, treaties, and public policies can blur our understanding of some of the deeper components of the problematique. The environmental problems facing the global community also raise deeper questions of governmental authority and legitimacy; of the relationship between the state and society; and of processes of economic and cultural globalization that challenge state sovereignty.

Second, we have tried to emphasize the ideas that have most powerfully shaped the evolving debate over the global environment. By assembling under one cover some of the most influential voices in the debate, we hope to provide a firsthand sense of how ideas have shaped action, while at the same time stressing the obstacles to changing the world through new ideas. Thus, we examine some of the most powerful paradigms that prevailed at the time of the Stockholm Conference and the controversies engendered by those views. We also explore the emergence of powerful and controversial new paradigms in the two decades since Stockholm, organized around themes of sustainable development, environmental security, and ecological justice. Comparing these sets of ideas over time reveals how many people's thinking has changed and highlights some lasting themes: the enduring obstacles to cooperation in a politically fragmented international system, for example, or the tremendously destructive potential of modern technology and current economic practices.

Our third goal has been to present a broad range of voices in what is, and must be, a global debate. This goal is in some ways in conflict with the just-stated goal of presenting the most powerful and influential ideas. After all, if influence were the only criterion for selecting which voices to include, the result would surely be to shut out those who have the most difficulty being heard.

Even if this narrowing of the debate were not troubling on moral grounds, it would in our view be a serious mistake. The poor and the powerless may lack the ability to shape the ecological future they desire, but they may well have the power to veto "solutions" that exclude considerations of their needs and interests. Thus, although universal agreement awaits a utopia that is difficult even to imagine, durable responses to global environmental problems will require a broadly global consensus. We may be tempted by a sense of urgency to favor a narrowing of the debate, so that it focuses on what the most powerful voices consider to be "feasible" or desirable. In our view, such a narrowing of the debate would be disastrous given the current lack of global consensus on so many fundamental issues. Thus, we have deliberately sought to include essays that broaden the debate: South as well as North, rural as well as urban, female as well as male, critical as well as broadly sympathetic.

The book's organization is meant to serve these goals. We begin with a discussion of some of the dominant paradigms and controversies that shaped debate at the time of the Stockholm Conference, and during the conference itself (Part One). Starting with the views and debates that prevailed in that era provides a useful reference point for measuring what has changed and what has not in the period since Stockholm. The material in Part One focuses in particular on the two most provocative and influential ideas of the Stockholm era: first, the notion that there are inherent "limits to growth" on a planet of finite natural resources and limited ecological resilience; and second, the claim that self-interested individual behavior often adds up to a global "tragedy of the commons."

The second part examines how the structure of the international system shapes the types of problems we face and the types of solutions we can imagine. The discussions focus in particular on the role of national sovereignty, transnational capitalism, and prevailing beliefs about "modernization" and "progress" that shape political and economic institutions. Part Two also examines the phenomenon of environmentalism as a global social movement, asking whether we might be seeing the emergence of new and different forms of political authority that challenge these dominant aspects of system structure.

Parts Three and Four then turn to examine the challenges of international cooperation and institutional reform. Part Three focuses on the question of international cooperation, presenting a range of views on the prospects for cooperation and the appropriate form and substance of such cooperation. Part Four examines the possibilities for reforming existing international institutions so as to foster environmental protection. This section focuses in particular on international trade and international development assistance, two institutionalized practices that have been at the center of the ongoing debate about the relationship between the world economy and the global environment.

The volume concludes with three powerful and controversial new paradigms that crystallized in the two decades between Stockholm and Rio: sustainable development (Part Five), environmental security (Part Six), and ecological justice (Part Seven). For some, these paradigms are complementary parts of a single vision. Others see tensions and trade-offs—perhaps because there are inherent tensions in the simultaneous pursuit of development, security, and justice or perhaps because a particular paradigm favors some values at the expense of others. Or it may be that these visions are sufficiently broad that they can *either* complement or contradict one another, depending on the specific choices made in seeking to implement them. In any case, these paradigms are likely to be the conceptual building blocks for the environmental initiatives of the future.

In compiling this material, we have deliberately avoided organizing the book around a conventional list of environmental "issue areas" (climate change, deforestation, toxics, acid rain, and so on) or generic "classes" of environmental problems (as in the common distinction between local/cumulative processes, transboundary issues, and the global commons). To be sure, these are important and insightful ways to organize one's thinking about a complex, multidimensional set of problems. By focusing on cross-cutting issues of power, authority, and responsibility, we hope this book will provide a useful complement to these other approaches, for which substantial material is already available. However, readers preferring a more conventional, issue-based focus will find several selections corresponding to specific environmental problems, including climate change (see in particular the chapters by Rowlands and Agarwal and Narain), depletion of the Earth's ozone layer (Benedick; Rowlands), deforestation (Mendes; COICA; Rich; MacNeill, Winsemius, and Yakushiji), the oceans (Johnston), and population growth (Hardin; Sen). Similarly, those preferring to organize their thinking in terms of different "classes" of international problems will find some selections particularly useful in the context of the global commons (Hardin; Buck; Feeny; Johnston; Rowlands; Benedick), others for transboundary issues (MacNeill, Winsemius, and Yakushiji; Bhagwati; Daly; Homer-Dixon; Deudney; Myers), and still others for problems such as deforestation, soil erosion, and desertification that have a physically local character but cumulative global implications (Mendes; Rich; Lélé; Homer-Dixon; Myers; COICA; Sen).

PART ONE

The Debate at Stockholm

As discussed in the introductory chapter, the 1972 U.N. Conference on the Human Environment, held in Stockholm, was a seminal event in the history of global environmental politics. Many important international agreements had already been concluded by the time of the Stockholm Conference, including a treaty governing Antarctica (1959), a partial nuclear-test-ban treaty (1963), a treaty governing the exploration and use of outer space (1967), and several international agreements on such ocean-related matters as whaling, the use of marine resources, and ocean pollution.[1] But Stockholm was the first broadly international effort to evaluate and discuss the environment in systematic, comprehensive terms. As such, the conference helped establish the trajectory that followed—the complex array of international diplomatic initiatives and debates, transnational institution-building efforts, and global movements for social change that have unfolded over the past two decades.

Although the Stockholm Conference took place more than twenty years ago, many of its central debates are still with us today. These debates include several key questions that are revisited later in this book: Is global pollution mainly a problem of poverty or a problem of affluence? What is the balance of responsibility between the North and the South in global environmental degradation? Does the institution of national sovereignty help or hinder the effort to construct international responses to environmental problems? Understanding the dominant ideas and controversies at Stockholm provides an important historical perspective on the debates and disputes that dominate contemporary global environmental politics.[2]

In this part we introduce some of the ideas that shaped debate during the Stockholm era. We pay particular attention to three powerful and controversial claims from that era: (1) the idea that there are inherent "limits to growth" facing the international economy, the world's population, and global consumption; (2) the idea that self-interested individual behavior toward the environment adds up to a collective "tragedy of the commons"; and (3) the claim that the environmental crisis demands a firm, even authoritarian, state to deal with the problems facing a "scarcity society."

Although thinking about the environment has evolved considerably in the years since Stockholm, these themes are not just of historical interest. They have strongly influenced the nature of scientific and social-scientific inquiry since Stockholm, with many analysts and activists working to either prove or disprove the existence of limits to growth, a tragedy of the commons, or a political basis for ecological authoritarianism. They have also shaped the political strategies pursued by governments, environmentalists, and other actors seeking to promote or hinder various forms of international environmental cooperation.

For the industrialized countries of the North, the Stockholm Conference was a response to mounting public anxiety over the environmental consequences of industrial society. By the early 1970s, concerns over problems as diverse as air and water pollution, wilderness preservation, toxic chemicals, urban congestion, nuclear radiation, and rising prices for natural-resource commodities began to fuse into the notion that the world was rapidly approaching natural limits to growth. The best-selling book *The Limits to Growth* did much to galvanize public fears. Using a technique known as systems modeling, the authors tried to predict the consequences of unlimited growth in human numbers and consumption. As the passages presented in Chapter 1 indicate, they concluded that the convergence of several trends—accelerating industrialization, rapid population growth, widespread malnutrition, depletion of nonrenewable resources, and a deteriorating environment—was moving the world rapidly toward overall limits on global growth. In order to avoid a potentially catastrophic collapse of the world's economic and social systems, it would be necessary to implement planned restraints on growth in population and resource consumption.

Critics of *The Limits to Growth* argued that the book overstated the urgency of the problem, overlooked the possibility of substituting less-scarce inputs, and underestimated the possibility for technological solutions.[3] (These arguments foreshadowed the emergence in the 1980s of the concept of *sustainable development,* which argues that some forms of economic growth can be compatible with natural limits; see Part Five.) The book's central claims were highly controversial, and most Northern governments were reluctant to fully endorse or embrace its findings. But the fears articulated in *The Limits to Growth* found widespread popular support in industrial societies and converged with the arguments of the growing coalition of environmental organizations found throughout the North.

Not surprisingly, the limits to growth controversy appeared quite differently when viewed from the South. Among the less-industrialized countries, the idea of limits to growth produced not only intellectual skepticism but also political fears. These fears were expressed eloquently in a 1972 essay by João Augusto de Araujo Castro, at that time Brazilian ambassador to the United States and an influential voice in North-South diplomacy. The South has never been monolithic in its views on problems of development and the environment. But as Castro made clear, many in the South linked the North's environmental concerns to the broader pattern of North-South relations. There was widespread agreement among Third World governments at the conference that the North was responsible for the global environmental crisis; that the North, having reaped the fruits of industrialization, was now seeking to close the door on the South; that the environmental problems of poverty differed fundamentally from those of affluence; and that solutions crafted with the North's problems in mind would be ineffective, or worse, if imposed upon the South.

The South's unity at Stockholm made it clear that a global response to environmental problems would require linking the environmental debate to the development concerns of the South and to a broader dialogue about the political and economic rules of the game in the international system. The message was clear: If such connections were not drawn, the South would not participate.

Just as limits to growth dominated the debate over *consequences* of environmental problems, the debate over *causes* crystallized around the powerful and controversial idea of the "tragedy of the commons." This view was popularized by biologist Garrett Hardin in a now-famous 1968 essay in the influential scholarly publication *Science.* According to Hardin, the tragedy occurred when self-interested actors enjoyed open access to, or unlimited use of, natural resources or environmental systems. Because they would benefit fully from additional exploitation but could divide the costs of that exploitation (for example, environmental degradation) with all other users, the overwhelming tendency would be to continue to exploit the resource. But each actor would pursue this logical individual behavior until the result for the system as a whole was the destruction or degradation of the resource in question. Individual logic would produce collective disaster—hence the notion of a tragedy. Hardin suggested that this combination of self-interest and open access was at the root of problems like pollution and overpopulation, just as they had been factors leading to overgrazing of the town commons in medieval England (hence the label "tragedy of the commons"). Hardin's solution was either to replace open access with enforceable private property rights, so that individual users reap the full costs as well as full benefits of their actions, or to impose governmental restrictions on access.

Hardin's model has been enormously influential in shaping thinking about global environmental problems, particularly for the so-called global commons such as the oceans and atmosphere, which fall under the domain of no single government. One reason for its influence is the model's simple elegance: The tragedy of the commons combines a recognizable human motive (self-interest) with a recognizable set of social rules (those allowing open access to natural resources and the environment) to produce a result that most would view as undesirable (rapid depletion or destruction of the resource in question).

Yet Hardin's model is, at heart, just a metaphor—the English commons is invoked as a simplified representation of the complex social rules, customs, goals, and behavioral incentives that shape how people interact with the environment individually and collectively. Whether such a tragedy actually lies at the center of global environmental problems depends on whether this abstraction is in fact an accurate representation of human behavior and social institutions. Even if the tragedy seems plausible conceptually, how widely does it apply as a description of the real world?

Susan J. Buck argues that despite its widespread acceptance, Hardin's tragedy does not even accurately describe the situation of the commons in medieval England on which the metaphor is based. According to Buck, access to the town commons was never unrestrained, but rather governed by a complex set of community rules that ensured sustainable use. The commons system was destroyed not by population growth and self-interested individual behavior, as Hardin asserted, but rather because of changing political and economic conditions in Britain, which gave powerful actors the incentive and ability to privatize the commons or overwhelm community-based systems of property rights. Thus, rather than representing a tragedy, the endurance of the commons system, in some cases for several hundred years, shows that there may be possibilities other than the stark choice Hardin poses between purely private property and state control.

In an article published more than two decades after Hardin's classic essay, David Feeny and his colleagues reviewed a large body of empirical evidence, addressing the question of whether Hardin's tragedy exists in practice. The authors examined a wide range of studies of natural-resource and environmental systems potentially subject to the tragedy, including fisheries, wildlife populations, surface water, groundwater, rangelands, and forests. The authors concluded that Hardin's formulation, though sometimes applicable, is by no means universal. Whether a tragedy of overconsumption ensues depends, in their view, on the type of social rules governing these natural resources or environmental systems. The enforceable private property rights advocated by Hardin are just one such set of rules and not necessarily the most appropriate for all situations. The authors cited numerous examples of societies developing sets of rules to collectively manage local common-property resources.[4]

The work of Buck, Feeny, and others is of critical importance in the effort to craft international responses to environmental problems. If Hardin's tragedy does apply to the global commons, it will be exceedingly difficult to craft effective international responses to global environmental problems. This is so because Hardin's preferred solutions, privatizing the commons or subjecting it to the control of a powerful central authority, are infeasible in the current international system. If these are the only choices, the tragedy seems likely to proceed apace. However, if systems of collective management of the sort identified by Buck, Feeny, and others can be shown to have been effective on the local or regional level, it may also be possible to design such systems to operate on the international level.[5] Under these circumstances there could still be a tragedy of the commons, but it would result from our lack of skill and effectiveness in designing fair and efficient international responses rather than from some iron-clad logic of nature.

What would be the political consequences of the limits to growth and the tragedy of the commons? One provocative answer to this question was provided by William Ophuls in the 1977 book *Ecology and the Politics of Scarcity,* which is summarized in his chapter, "The Scarcity Society." According to Ophuls a new era of scarcity would be marked by an authoritarian political response, just as scarcity in the past acted as the trigger for various forms of violence, oppression, and war. The "scarcity society" that Ophuls described would perceive "the necessity for political control" in order to avoid "ecological self-destruction." The result, as Ophuls foresaw it, would be a political future "much less libertarian and much more authoritarian, much less individualistic and much more communalistic than our present." Ophuls did see an alternative to this grim scenario, which he labeled a "democracy of restraint." He felt it was possible to forge an ecologically rational future, with human gratification decoupled from material consumption, without relying on coercive authority. But a democracy of restraint would demand a prompt response to environmental problems and a broad social consensus on the importance of acting, circumstances that Ophuls deemed unlikely.

Ophuls's notions about the likelihood of authoritarian responses to environmental problems remain controversial.[6] Nor is it clear that authoritarian responses would be effective; Part Seven, on the question of ecological justice, presents a very different interpretation of the links between freedom, democracy, justice, and the environment. But the questions Ophuls raised about the ability of today's governments to respond effectively and in a timely fashion, and the attention he drew to the close link between control of nature and control of people, remain critical themes in environmental politics.

Despite their critics, and despite changes in our understanding in the two decades since Stockholm, the themes of "limits to growth," "the tragedy of the commons," and "the scarcity society" remain powerfully influential in global environmental politics. Not only did they help shape the pathway from Stockholm to Rio, they are also readily seen in contemporary controversies. The limits to growth dispute has reemerged in current debates over the environmental consequences of international trade (see Part Four) and the prospects for sustainable development (see Part Five). Similarly, skeptics about the prospects for effective international cooperation invoke both the logic of self-interested behavior and the commons-like features of global environmental systems (see Part Three)—just as Hardin did more than twenty-five years ago. And the increasingly widespread fear that environmental degradation threatens national and international security raises for some the specter of authoritarian solutions, as posited by Ophuls (see Part Six). The evolution of global environmental politics cannot be understood without examining the history of these ideas; weighing their claims carefully and critically is as important today as it was in the Stockholm era.

DONELLA H. MEADOWS,
DENNIS L. MEADOWS, JØRGEN RANDERS
& WILLIAM W. BEHRENS III

1

The Limits to Growth

Problems and Models

EVERY PERSON APPROACHES HIS problems . . . with the help of models. A model is simply an ordered set of assumptions about a complex system. It is an attempt to understand some aspect of the infinitely varied world by selecting from perceptions and past experience a set of general observations applicable to the problem at hand. . . .

Decision-makers at every level unconsciously use mental models to choose among policies that will shape our future world. These mental models are, of necessity, very simple when compared with the reality from which they are abstracted. The human brain, remarkable as it is, can only keep track of a limited number of the complicated, simultaneous interactions that determine the nature of the real world.

We, too, have used a model. Ours is a formal, written model of the world.* It constitutes a preliminary attempt to improve our mental models of long-term, global problems by combining the large amount of information that is already in

---

Excerpted from Donella H. Meadows, Dennis L. Meadows, Jørgen Randers, and William W. Behrens III, *The Limits to Growth* (Washington, DC: Potomac Associates, 1972). Reprinted with permission.

*The prototype model on which we have based our work was designed by Professor Jay W. Forrester of the Massachusetts Institute of Technology. A description of that model has been published in his book *World Dynamics* (Cambridge, Mass.: Wright-Allen Press, 1971).

human minds and in written records with the new information-processing tools that mankind's increasing knowledge has produced—the scientific method, systems analysis, and the modern computer.

Our world model was built specifically to investigate five major trends of global concern—accelerating industrialization, rapid population growth, widespread malnutrition, depletion of nonrenewable resources, and a deteriorating environment. These trends are all interconnected in many ways, and their development is measured in decades or centuries, rather than in months or years. With the model we are seeking to understand the causes of these trends, their interrelationships, and their implications as much as one hundred years in the future.

The model we have constructed is, like every other model, imperfect, oversimplified, and unfinished. We are well aware of its shortcomings, but we believe that it is the most useful model now available for dealing with problems far out on the space-time graph. To our knowledge it is the only formal model in existence that is truly global in scope, that has a time horizon longer than thirty years, and that includes important variables such as population, food production, and pollution, not as independent entities, but as dynamically interacting elements, as they are in the real world. . . .

In spite of the preliminary state of our work, we believe it is important to publish the model and our findings now. Decisions are being made every day, in every part of the world, that will affect the physical, economic, and social conditions of the world system for decades to come. These decisions cannot wait for perfect models and total understanding. They will be made on the basis of some model, mental or written, in any case. . . .

Our conclusions are:

1. If the present growth trends in world population, industrialization, pollution, food production, and resource depletion continue unchanged, the limits to growth on this planet will be reached sometime within the next one hundred years. The most probable result will be a rather sudden and uncontrollable decline in both population and industrial capacity.

2. It is possible to alter these growth trends and to establish a condition of ecological and economic stability that is sustainable far into the future. The state of global equilibrium could be designed so that the basic material needs of each person on earth are satisfied and each person has an equal opportunity to realize his individual human potential.

3. If the world's people decide to strive for this second outcome rather than the first, the sooner they begin working to attain it, the greater will be their chances of success.

These conclusions are so far-reaching and raise so many questions for further study that we are quite frankly overwhelmed by the enormity of the job that must be done. We hope that this book will serve to interest other people . . . to raise the space and time horizons of their concerns and to join us in understanding and preparing for a period of great transition—the transition from growth to global equilibrium.

. . .

A Finite World

We have mentioned many difficult trade-offs . . . in the production of food, in the consumption of resources, and in the generation and clean-up of pollution. By now it should be clear that all of these trade-offs arise from one simple fact—the earth is finite. The closer any human activity comes to the limit of the earth's ability to support that activity, the more apparent and unresolvable the trade-offs become. When there is plenty of unused arable land, there can be more people and also more food per person. When all the land is already used, the trade-off between more people or more food per person becomes a choice between absolutes.

In general, modern society has not learned to recognize and deal with these trade-offs. The apparent goal of the present world system is to produce more people with more (food, material goods, clean air, and water) for each person. . . . We have noted that if society continues to strive for that goal, it will eventually reach one of many earthly limitations. . . . It is not possible to foretell exactly which limitation will occur first or what the consequences will be, because there are many conceivable, unpredictable human responses to such a situation. It is possible, however, to investigate what conditions and what changes in the world system might lead society to collision with or accommodation to the limits to growth in a finite world.

. . .

Technology and the Limits to Growth

Although the history of human effort contains numerous incidents of mankind's failure to live within physical limits, it is success in overcoming limits that forms the cultural tradition of many dominant people in today's world. Over the past three hundred years, mankind has compiled an impressive record of pushing back the apparent limits to population and economic growth by a series of spectacular technological advances. Since the recent history of a large part of human society has been so continuously successful, it is quite natural that many people expect technological breakthroughs to go on raising physical ceilings indefinitely. These people speak about the future with resounding technological optimism.

. . .

The hopes of the technological optimists center on the ability of technology to remove or extend the limits to growth of population and capital. We have shown that in the world model the application of technology to apparent problems of resource depletion or pollution or food shortage has no impact on the essential problem, which is exponential growth in a finite and complex system. Our attempts to use even the most optimistic estimates of the benefits of technology in the model did not prevent the ultimate decline of population and industry, and in fact did not in any case postpone the collapse beyond the year 2100.

. . .

Applying technology to the natural pressures that the environment exerts against any growth process has been so successful in the past that a whole culture has evolved around the principle of fighting against limits rather than learning to live with them. . . . But the relationship between the earth's limits and man's activities is changing. The exponential growth curves are adding millions of people and billions of tons of pollutants to the ecosystem each year. Even the ocean, which once appeared virtually inexhaustible, is losing species after species of its commercially useful animals. . . .

There may be much disagreement with the statement that population and capital growth must stop *soon*. But virtually no one will argue that material growth on this planet can go on forever. . . . Man can still choose his limits and stop when he pleases by weakening some of the strong pressures that cause capital and population growth, or by instituting counterpressures, or both. Such counterpressures will probably not be entirely pleasant. They will certainly involve profound changes in the social and economic structures that have been deeply impressed into human culture by centuries of growth. The alternative is to wait until the price of technology becomes more than society can pay, or until the side-effects of technology suppress growth themselves, or until problems arise that have no technical solutions. At any of those points the choice of limits will be gone. Growth will be stopped by pressures that are not of human choosing, and that, as the world model suggests, may be very much worse than those which society might choose for itself.

. . . Technological optimism is the most common and the most dangerous reaction to our findings from the world model. Technology can relieve the symptoms of a problem without affecting the underlying causes. Faith in technology as the ultimate solution to all problems can thus divert our attention from the most fundamental problem—the problem of growth in a finite system—and prevent us from taking effective action to solve it.

. . .

The Transition from Growth to Global Equilibrium

We can say very little at this point about the practical, day-by-day steps that might be taken to reach a desirable, sustainable state of global equilibrium. Neither the world model nor our own thoughts have been developed in sufficient detail to understand all the implications of the transition from growth to equilibrium. Before any part of the world's society embarks deliberately on such a transition, there must be much more discussion, more extensive analysis, and many new ideas contributed by many different people. . . .

Although we underline the need for more study and discussion of these difficult questions, we end on a note of urgency. We hope that intensive study and debate will proceed simultaneously with an ongoing program of action. The details are not yet specified, but the general direction for action is obvious. Enough is known already to analyze many proposed policies in terms of their tendencies to promote or to regulate growth.[53] . . . Efforts are weak at the moment, but they could be strengthened very quickly if the goal of equilibrium were recognized as desirable and important by any sizable part of human society. . . .

Taking no action to solve these problems is equivalent to taking strong action. Every day of continued exponential growth brings the world system closer to the ultimate limits to that growth. A decision to do nothing is a decision to increase the risk of collapse. We cannot say with certainty how much longer mankind can postpone initiating deliberate control of his growth before he will have lost the chance for control. We suspect on the basis of present knowledge of the physical constraints of the planet that the growth phase cannot continue for another one hundred years. Again, because of the delays in the system, if the global society waits until those constraints are unmistakably apparent, it will have waited too long.

If there is cause for deep concern, there is also cause for hope. Deliberately limiting growth would be difficult, but not impossible. The way to proceed is clear, and the necessary steps, although they are new ones for human society, are well within human capabilities. Man possesses, for a small moment in his history, the most powerful combination of knowledge, tools, and resources the world has ever known. He has all that is physically necessary to create a totally new form of human society—one that would be built to last for generations. The two missing ingredients are a realistic, long-term goal that can guide mankind to the equilibrium society and the human will to achieve that goal. Without such a goal and a commitment to it, short-term concerns will generate the exponential growth that drives the world system toward the limits of the earth and ultimate collapse. With that goal and that commitment mankind would be ready now to begin a controlled, orderly transition from growth to global equilibrium.

JOÃO AUGUSTO DE ARAUJO CASTRO

2
Environment & Development: The Case of the Developing Countries

Introduction

INTEREST IN THE FIELD OF ecology, which is centered in the developed countries, has recently increased due to the sudden discovery of a possible imbalance between man and earth. Resulting from the population explosion and the misuse of existing and newly developed technologies, this potential imbalance could bring about an environmental crisis menacing the future of mankind. In several countries the emergence of an interest in ecological problems has not been confined to the realm of the scientific community. It has aroused public concern which has expressed itself, although sometimes vaguely, in such initiatives as Earth Week, celebrated in the United States in April 1970, and the mushrooming of a specialized literature.

As would be expected, the methods envisaged to resolve on a world basis the so-called environmental crisis were inspired by the realities of a fraction of that very same world: the family of the developed countries. Furthermore, the bulk of

Originally published in David A. Kay and Eugene B. Skolnikoff, eds., *World Eco-Crisis: International Organizations in Response* (Madison, WI: University of Wisconsin Press, 1972). Reprinted with permission.

the solutions in hand, mainly of a technical nature, seek primarily to make healthier the consequences of the Industrial Revolution without necessarily providing a tool for a further distribution of its benefits among states.

This study seeks to introduce some neglected aspects of the interests of developing countries into discussions about a world ecological policy. The working hypothesis is that the implementation of any worldwide environmental policy based on the realities of the developed countries tends to perpetuate the existing gap in socioeconomic development between developed and developing countries and so promote the freezing of the present international order. . . .

Developed Countries

Although there does not yet exist a systematic body of doctrine, the new ecological policy of the developed countries contains several elements that have already stimulated important developments in academic thought, as indicated by the growing literature on the matter, and attitudes of governments and private sectors in these countries, mainly in their relations with the developing countries.

A short historical digression may help in analyzing the rationale of this ecological policy. As a localized phenomenon in the countries of the Northern Hemisphere, the Industrial Revolution of the eighteenth century was not brought about by one single factor. It was not, for instance, the result of inventions or the coming into operation of new machines. As in the case of other major movements in history, it was the result of the interplay of many factors, some obscure in themselves, whose combined effort laid down the foundations of a new industrial system. Growing organically, cell by cell, new patterns of industrial organization were soon translated into the establishment of a new international order. Around the group of countries enjoying the benefits of the Industrial Revolution there existed an increasing family of countries, trying, mostly unsuccessfully, to modernize their own means of production.

This new international order and the relatively uneven distribution of political power among states, based on the use and monopoly of advanced technologies, may be considered one of the most enduring effects of the Industrial Revolution. And since then, as a normal corollary of the new order, the technologically advanced countries have been endeavoring to maintain their political and economic position in the world while the technologically less endowed countries have been seeking to alter, through development, this global status quo.

This permanent struggle between the two groups of countries persists in the present days and it is unlikely that it will cease in the near future. For this to happen one would have to assume a perfectly homogeneous world community whose conflicts would have been eliminated through a perfect satisfaction, on a homogeneous basis, of all human needs. This condition is most likely to be found only in the realms of utopia. . . .

According to a helpful image taken from academic and governmental sources in the developed countries our planet could be visualized as a "spaceship earth," where life could only be sustained, nay simply possible, through maintenance of a delicate equilibrium between the needs of the passengers and the ability of the craft to respond to those needs. Undisturbed until recently, this equilibrium would now be menaced by an excess of population and the consequences of the use of both previously existing and newly developed technologies. Elaborating the same image, "spaceship earth" would be divided into two classes of passengers, the first coincident with the technologically advanced countries and the second representative of the technologically less endowed countries, which would necessarily have to trade off positions with a view to maintaining the equilibrium of the vessel. . . .

In order to maintain the equilibrium of the vessel the problems created by population explosion and the use of both previously existing and new technologies should, in the view of developed countries, now be dealt with globally, irrespective of the unequal distribution, on a world scale, of the benefits and related destructive effects on the environment engendered by the Industrial Revolution. Germane to such a global ecological policy is the need for world planning for development which, to be successful, might purposely aim at freezing the present relative positions of the two classes inside the vessel.

Provided that the first class already enjoys low average rates of population growth and is unlikely to opt for a slower rate of industrial growth for the sole purpose of guaranteeing a purer atmosphere or cleaner water, the new ecology-saving policy would be more successful if applied in the areas where the environmental crisis has not yet appeared, even in its least acute forms. Actually, these areas would mainly comprise the territory of the second class. Thus: the second class should be taught to employ the most effective and expeditious birth control methods and to follow an orderly pollution-reducing process of industrialization. In the case of industrialization, the mainstream of socioeconomic development, the lesson must be even harsher: The second class must organize production in accordance with environment-saving techniques already tested by the first class or be doomed to socioeconomic stagnation. . . .

Nowadays some ecologists do not hesitate to say that the developing countries can never hope to achieve the consumption patterns of the developed countries. Some seemingly appalling calculations are offered as proof of this. To raise the living standards of the world's existing population to American levels the annual production of iron would have to increase 75 times, that of copper 100 times, that of lead 200 times, and that of tin 250 times. Were a country such as India to make use of fertilizers at the per capita level of the Netherlands, it would consume one-half of the world's total output of fertilizers. Clearly, the parity of the developing countries with the developed ones is no longer compatible with the existing stocks of natural resources. Again, according to those wise men, the increasing expectations in developing countries, which are sometimes associated with something approaching a revolution, are nothing more than expectations of elites and therefore must be curbed. Most of the population of these countries, it is claimed, do not have an ambition to reach Western standards and do not even know that "such a thing as development is on the agenda."

Now, the alleged exhaustion of natural resources is accompanied, in general, by forecasts of the fateful coming of formidable ecological hecatombs. The continuing progress of developed countries would require an economic lebensraum in the Southern Hemisphere. In the name of the survival of mankind developing countries should continue in a state of underdevelopment because if the evils of industrialization were to reach them, life on the planet would be placed in jeopardy. . . .

Very few reasonable people underwrite these fanciful ideas. Yet, it cannot be denied that the environment in developed countries is threatened and that it should be preserved. The difficulty in dealing with environmental problems nowadays is that they have become a myth. . . . From an uttermost neglect of ecological problems public opinion in the United States has swung to an outright "geolatry." The environment has been rediscovered and Mother Earth now has a week dedicated to her in the calendar. School children crusade to clean up the streets; college students organize huge demonstrations; uncivilized industries that dump their wastes in the air, in the water, or on the ground are denounced as public enemies.

. . . The simplistic concepts that ecology is disturbed because there are "too many people" or because they "consume too much" must be discarded as nothing more than fallacies. There is abundant evidence that the earth is capable of supporting a considerably greater population at much higher levels of consumption. The simple fact that in half a century mankind found it possible to wage four major wars, with a terrible waste of wealth, is a clear indication that we are not after all so short of resources although we may be short of common sense. . . .

Environmental problems not only pose a new and compelling argument for disarmament and peace but also call attention to the question of efficiency in the organization of production. It is widely known, but seldom remembered when the availability of natural resources is discussed, that in developed countries billions of dollars are spent every year to purchase so-called farm surpluses. Millions of tons of agricultural products have been regularly stored or destroyed to keep prices up in the world markets. . . . These figures and these facts evidently do not agree with the superficial statements which have been made about the irreparable strain being put on natural resources.

Pollution of the air and water and related damages to the environment are loosely attributed, in general, to faulty technologies, but few have bothered to assess objectively the exact proportions of the problem. According to experts at the Organization for Economic Cooperation and Development (OECD) safeguarding the environment in the United States would require annual expenditures of . . . less than 2 percent of the American GNP [Editors' note: gross national product]. Clearly, there is no real cause for most of the fuzzy agitation about the environment. Put in their proper perspective, environmental problems are little more than a question of the reexamination of national priorities. . . .

When discussing the environment some ecologists and other wise men, as often happens in many other instances, try haphazardly to superimpose peculiar situations prevailing in developed countries onto the realities of the developing countries. . . . If the peculiarities of developing countries are taken into account, it will not be difficult to recognize that, in broad terms, they are still at a prepollu-tion stage or, in other words, have not yet been given the chance to become pol-luted. . . . The 24 countries of Latin America, the least under-developed region in the developing world, have less than one-tenth of the total number of motor vehi-cles in the United States. Only a few ecologists and other wise men would say that Latin Americans should rather have fewer cars and cleaner air.

There is a pollution of affluence and a pollution of poverty. It is imperative to distinguish between the two lest some pollution be prevented at the cost of much economic development. Were it not for the dangers arising from the confusion between the two kinds of pollution, there would be no need for calling attention to the precarious housing conditions, poor health, and low sanitary standards not to mention starvation in developing countries. The linear transposition of eco-logical problems of the developed countries to the context of the developing ones disregards the existence of such distressing social conditions. Wherever these con-ditions prevail, the assertion that income means less pollution is nonsense. It is obvious, or should be, that the so-called pollution of poverty can only be cor-rected through higher incomes, or more precisely, through economic develop-ment.

The most sensible ecologists are of the opinion that the pollution levels can be attributed not so much to population or affluence as to modern technologies. In the United States the economy would have grown enough, in the absence of tech-nological change, to give the increased population about the same per capita amounts of goods and services today as in 1946. The ecological crisis has resulted mainly from the sweeping progress in technologies. Modern technologies have multiplied the impact of growth on the environment and, consequently, gener-ated most of the existing pollution. Those who haphazardly transpose developed countries' situations to the milieu of an underdeveloped country repeatedly warn the latter against the dangers of modern technologies and rapid industrialization. "Don't let happen to your cities what happened to New York; keep your beautiful landscapes." It is ironic that developed countries, which create and sell modern technologies, should caution developing countries against utilizing them. Is this done to justify the second-hand technologies that sometimes accompany foreign direct investments?

Developing Countries

A somewhat apathetic attitude on the part of the developing countries regarding the environmental issue does not imply negation of the relevance of the matter and the need for true international cooperation to solve the problem it poses for the survival of mankind. This apathetic attitude, however, clearly is derived from the developing countries' socioeconomic experience which differs, to a large ex-tent, from that of the developed countries. Consequently, one has to bear in mind that, not having enjoyed the opportunity to experience their own Industrial Revolution, the developing countries have not been stimulated to think about the environmental crisis as posed in the present days. The phenomenon of urbanization in the Southern Hemisphere, even in the countries experiencing a considerable degree of progress, may raise questions about poor living standards in some areas but has not thus far led to industrial congestion.

As indicated in the elements of the ecological policy of the developed countries, the equilibrium of "spaceship earth" would depend on the enforcement of measures bearing on population and on the use of the previously existing and new technologies chiefly in the second class of the vessel or, in other words, in the territory of the developing countries. Even if applied to their full extent, those measures would not result at some foreseeable date in a single-class carrying vessel, preferably closer to the first steerage. This ecological policy, which aims primarily at the equilibrium of the vessel, could better succeed if the relative positions of the classes were maintained, for the emergence of one single class would presuppose a considerable change in the living standards of the first class, something that may not be attained in the light of present global socioeconomic realities. . . .

On the question of the preservation of the environment the passenger's survival would call for the enforcement of a drastic decision, globally applied, to maintain a "green area reserve" which would have to coincide mainly with the territories of the developing countries. This step would safeguard, against complete exhaustion, the natural elements (soil, atmosphere, and water) still available on the planet just to provide some sort of counteraction to the spoilage of the same natural elements used up in the countries where the benefits of the Industrial Revolution were massively concentrated.

Besides the ethical question raised by this policy, as expressed in the ostensive imbalance between responsibility for the damage and obligation for repair, the developing countries, in abiding by its prescriptions, would make a commitment to conservatism rather than to conservation. Furthermore, the possibility of a widespread application of developed countries' ecological policy, theoretically conceived to secure the equilibrium of "spaceship earth," may risk transforming the Southern Hemisphere countries into the last healthy weekend areas for the inhabitants of a planet already saturated with the environment created by the Industrial Revolution. As a token of compensation the Southern Hemisphere countries could claim to have resurrected, and adequately preserved, the environmental milieu for the living and the survival of Rousseau's "happy savage." In expressing their concern over the environmental crisis the developing countries cannot accept, without further refinement, the ecological policy devised by the developed countries whose socioeconomic structure was deeply influenced by the unique phenomenon of the Industrial Revolution.

The first step toward the refinement of that policy may be the rejection of the principle that the ecology issue, taken on a global basis, can be dealt with exclusively through a technical approach, as suggested by the developed countries. Given the implications for the international order, including the freezing of the status quo, any environment-saving policy must necessarily be imbued with a solid and well-informed political approach. This would provide an opportunity for the developing countries, by preserving their national identities, to join safely in the effort of the international community to preserve the equilibrium of "spaceship earth."

As a normal corollary of the political approach, ecological policy should not depart from the broader framework of socioeconomic development. In this regard a second step of refinement would require a corresponding universal commitment to development if the task of preserving the environment is to be shared by the world community. . . .

Evidently, no country wants any pollution at all. But each country must evolve its own development plans, exploit its own resources as it thinks suitable, and define its own environmental standards. The idea of having such priorities and standards imposed on individual countries or groups of countries, on either a multilateral or a bilateral basis, is very hard to accept.

That is why it is disturbing to see the International Bank for Reconstruction and Development (IBRD) set up its own ecological policy. Repercussions on the environment, defined according to IBRD ecologists, have become an important factor in determining whether financial assistance by that institution should be granted for an industrial project in developing countries. It seems reasonable that the preservation of the environment should not exclude the preservation of national sovereignty. Ecological policies should rather be inserted into the framework of national development.

It is perhaps time for the developing countries to present their own views on the framing of an environmental policy in spite of the fact that the developed countries have not yet ended their own controversial debate or furnished definite and convincing data on the issue. In adopting a position the developing countries recognize the existence of environmental problems in the world and the possibility of finding solutions through both national efforts and international cooperation.

The first point to be touched on concerns the question of national sovereignty. In this regard any ecological policy, globally applied, must not be an instrument to suppress wholly or in part the legitimate right of any country to decide about its own affairs. In reality this point would simply seek to guarantee on an operational level the full exercise of the principle of juridical equality of states as expressed, for instance, in the Charter of the United Nations. . . . Sovereignty, in this context, should not be taken as an excuse for isolationism and consequently for escapism in relation to international efforts geared to solving environmental problems. For the developing countries it is crucial to consider, in the light of their own interests, nationally defined, the whole range of alternative solutions devised or implemented in the developed countries. Naturally, it is assumed that all countries can act responsibly and that none is going to deliberately favor policies that may endanger the equilibrium of "spaceship earth."

Closely linked to the problem of sovereignty, the question of national priorities calls for an understanding of the distinction between the developmental characteristics of developed and developing countries. As has been previously pointed out in this article, while the ecological issue came to the forefront of public concern as a by-product of postindustrial stages of development, it is not yet strikingly apparent in the majority of the developing countries. And different realities, of course, should be differently treated or, at least, given the fittest solutions.

In the developing countries the major concern is an urgent need to accelerate socioeconomic development, and a meaningful ecological policy must not hamper the attainment of that goal in the most expeditious way. . . . In this context the developing countries, while rejecting the implementation of any ecological policy which bears in itself elements of socioeconomic stagnation, could only share a common responsibility for the preservation of the environment if it was accompanied and paralleled by a corresponding common responsibility for development.

. . .

Conclusion

This study has probed very briefly some aspects of an ecological policy in the light of the interests of the developing countries. . . . Emphasis has been laid on the undesirability of transposing, uncritically, into the realities of the developing countries the solutions already envisaged by the developed countries to eliminate or reduce the so-called environmental crisis to the extent that those solutions may embody elements of socioeconomic stagnation. . . . Finally, a preliminary and broad picture of a position of the developing countries has stressed the relation between preservation of environment and the urgent need to speed up socioeconomic development and the desirability of a common world effort to tackle both these aspects simultaneously. This common effort, however, should not preclude or trespass on national interest as a departing point for the setting up of concepts and operational guidelines of an ecological policy for the developing countries.

In conclusion, a discussion of any meaningful ecological policy for both developed and developing countries . . . would better reflect a broad socio-economic concern, as tentatively suggested in this article, rather than confine itself to a strictly scientific approach. Man's conceptual environment, and nothing else, will certainly prevail in shaping the future of mankind, for the preservation of the environment presupposes a human being to live in it and a human mind to conceive a better life for man on this planet. From the point of view of man—and we have no other standpoint—Man, Pascal's "roseau pensant," is still more relevant than Nature.

GARRETT HARDIN

3
The Tragedy
of the Commons

Tragedy of Freedom in a Commons

... THE TRAGEDY OF THE COMMONS develops in this way. Picture a pasture open to all. It is to be expected that each herdsman will try to keep as many cattle as possible on the commons. Such an arrangement may work reasonably satisfactorily for centuries because tribal wars, poaching, and disease keep the numbers of both man and beast well below the carrying capacity of the land. Finally, however, comes the day of reckoning, that is, the day when the long-desired goal of social stability becomes a reality. At this point, the inherent logic of the commons remorselessly generates tragedy.

As a rational being, each herdsman seeks to maximize his gain. Explicitly or implicitly, more or less consciously, he asks, "What is the utility to *me* of adding one more animal to my herd?" This utility has one negative and one positive component.

1. The positive component is a function of the increment of one animal. Since the herdsman receives all the proceeds from the sale of the additional animal, the positive utility is nearly +1.

2. The negative component is a function of the additional overgrazing created by one more animal. Since, however, the effects of overgrazing are

Originally published in *Science* 162 (December 13, 1968):1243–1248. Copyright © 1968 by the American Association for the Advancement of Science. Reprinted with permission.

shared by all the herdsmen, the negative utility for any particular decisionmaking herdsman is only a fraction of −1.

Adding together the component partial utilities, the rational herdsman concludes that the only sensible course for him to pursue is to add another animal to
his herd. And another; and another. . . . But this is the conclusion reached by each
and every rational herdsman sharing a commons. Therein is the tragedy. Each
man is locked into a system that compels him to increase his herd without limit—
in a world that is limited. Ruin is the destination toward which all men rush, each
pursuing his own best interest in a society that believes in the freedom of the
commons. Freedom in a commons brings ruin to all.

Some would say that this is a platitude. Would that it were! In a sense, it was
learned thousands of years ago, but natural selection favors the forces of psychological denial.[8] The individual benefits as an individual from his ability to deny
the truth even though society as a whole, of which he is a part, suffers. Education
can counteract the natural tendency to do the wrong thing, but the inexorable
succession of generations requires that the basis for this knowledge be constantly
refreshed. . . .

In an approximate way, the logic of the commons has been understood for a
long time, perhaps since the discovery of agriculture or the invention of private
property in real estate. But it is understood mostly only in special cases which are
not sufficiently generalized. Even at this late date, cattlemen leasing national land
on the western ranges demonstrate no more than an ambivalent understanding,
in constantly pressuring federal authorities to increase the head count to the
point where overgrazing produces erosion and weed dominance. Likewise, the
oceans of the world continue to suffer from the survival of the philosophy of the
commons. Maritime nations still respond automatically to the shibboleth of the
"freedom of the seas." Professing to believe in the "inexhaustible resources of the
oceans," they bring species after species of fish and whales closer to extinction.[9]

The National Parks present another instance of the working out of the tragedy
of the commons. At present, they are open to all, without limit. The parks themselves are limited in extent—there is only one Yosemite Valley—whereas population seems to grow without limit. The values that visitors seek in the parks are
steadily eroded. Plainly, we must soon cease to treat the parks as commons or they
will be of no value to anyone.

What shall we do? We have several options. We might sell them off as private
property. We might keep them as public property, but allocate the right to enter
them. The allocation might be on the basis of wealth, by the use of an auction system. It might be on the basis of merit, as defined by some agreed-upon standards.
It might be by lottery. Or it might be on a first-come, first-served basis, administered to long queues. These, I think, are all the reasonable possibilities. They are
all objectionable. But we must choose—or acquiesce in the destruction of the
commons that we call our National Parks.

Pollution

In a reverse way, the tragedy of the commons reappears in problems of pollution. Here it is not a question of taking something out of the commons, but of putting something in—sewage, or chemical, radioactive, and heat wastes into water; noxious and dangerous fumes into the air; and distracting and unpleasant advertising signs into the line of sight. The calculations of utility are much the same as before. The rational man finds that his share of the cost of the wastes he discharges into the commons is less than the cost of purifying his wastes before releasing them. Since this is true for everyone, we are locked into a system of "fouling our own nest," so long as we behave only as independent, rational, free-enterprisers.

The tragedy of the commons as a food basket is averted by private property, or something formally like it. But the air and waters surrounding us cannot readily be fenced, and so the tragedy of the commons as a cesspool must be prevented by different means, by coercive laws or taxing devices that make it cheaper for the polluter to treat his pollutants than to discharge them untreated. We have not progressed as far with the solution of this problem as we have with the first. Indeed, our particular concept of private property, which deters us from exhausting the positive resources of the earth, favors pollution. The owner of a factory on the bank of a stream—whose property extends to the middle of the stream—often has difficulty seeing why it is not his natural right to muddy the waters flowing past his door. The law, always behind the times, requires elaborate stitching and fitting to adapt it to this newly perceived aspect of the commons.

The pollution problem is a consequence of population. It did not much matter how a lonely American frontiersman disposed of his waste. "Flowing water purifies itself every 10 miles," my grandfather used to say, and the myth was near enough to the truth when he was a boy, for there were not too many people. But as population became denser, the natural chemical and biological recycling processes became overloaded, calling for a redefinition of property rights.

How to Legislate Temperance?

Analysis of the pollution problem as a function of population density uncovers a not generally recognized principle of morality, namely: *the morality of an act is a function of the state of the system at the time it is performed.*[10] Using the commons as a cesspool does not harm the general public under frontier conditions, because there is no public; the same behavior in a metropolis is unbearable. A hundred and fifty years ago a plainsman could kill an American bison, cut out only the tongue for his dinner, and discard the rest of the animal. He was not in any important sense being wasteful. Today, with only a few thousand bison left, we would be appalled at such behavior. . . .

That morality is system-sensitive escaped the attention of most codifiers of ethics in the past. "Thou shalt not . . ." is the form of traditional ethical directives which make no allowance for particular circumstances. The laws of our society follow the pattern of ancient ethics, and therefore are poorly suited to governing a complex, crowded, changeable world. Our epicyclic solution is to augment statutory law with administrative law. Since it is practically impossible to spell out all the conditions under which it is safe to burn trash in the back yard or to run an automobile without smog-control, by law we delegate the details to bureaus. The result is administrative law, which is rightly feared for an ancient reason—*Quis custodiet ipsos custodes?*—"Who shall watch the watchers themselves?" John Adams said that we must have "a government of laws and not men." Bureau administrators, trying to evaluate the morality of acts in the total system, are singularly liable to corruption, producing a government by men, not laws.

Prohibition is easy to legislate (though not necessarily to enforce); but how do we legislate temperance? Experience indicates that it can be accomplished best through the mediation of administrative law. We limit possibilities unnecessarily if we suppose that the sentiment of *Quis custodiet* denies us the use of administrative law. We should rather retain the phrase as a perpetual reminder of fearful dangers we cannot avoid. The great challenge facing us now is to invent the corrective feedbacks that are needed to keep custodians honest. We must find ways to legitimate the needed authority of both the custodians and the corrective feedbacks.

Freedom to Breed Is Intolerable

The tragedy of the commons is involved in population problems in another way. In a world governed solely by the principle of "dog eat dog"—if indeed there ever was such a world—how many children a family had would not be a matter of public concern. Parents who bred too exuberantly would leave fewer descendants, not more, because they would be unable to care adequately for their children. David Lack and others have found that such a negative feedback demonstrably controls the fecundity of birds.[11] But men are not birds, and have not acted like them for millenniums, at least.

If each human family were dependent only on its own resources; *if* the children of improvident parents starved to death; *if*, thus, overbreeding brought its own "punishment" to the germ line—*then* there would be no public interest in controlling the breeding of families. But our society is deeply committed to the welfare state,[12] and hence is confronted with another aspect of the tragedy of the commons.

In a welfare state, how shall we deal with the family, the religion, the race, or the class (or indeed any distinguishable and cohesive group) that adopts overbreeding as a policy to secure its own aggrandizement?[13] To couple the concept of freedom to breed with the belief that everyone born has an equal right to the commons is to lock the world into a tragic course of action. . . .

Conscience Is Self-Eliminating

It is a mistake to think that we can control the breeding of mankind in the long run by an appeal to conscience. . . .

People vary. Confronted with appeals to limit breeding, some people will undoubtedly respond to the plea more than others. Those who have more children will produce a larger fraction of the next generation than those with more susceptible consciences. The difference will be accentuated, generation by generation. . . . The argument has here been stated in the context of the population problem, but it applies equally well to any instance in which society appeals to an individual exploiting a commons to restrain himself for the general good—by means of his conscience. To make such an appeal is to set up a selective system that works toward the elimination of conscience from the race.

Pathogenic Effects of Conscience

. . . To conjure up a conscience in others is tempting to anyone who wishes to extend his control beyond the legal limits. Leaders at the highest level succumb to this temptation. Has any President during the past generation failed to call on labor unions to moderate voluntarily their demands for higher wages, or to steel companies to honor voluntary guidelines on prices? I can recall none. The rhetoric used on such occasions is designed to produce feelings of guilt in noncooperators.

For centuries it was assumed without proof that guilt was a valuable, perhaps even an indispensable, ingredient of the civilized life. Now, in this post-Freudian world, we doubt it.

Paul Goodman speaks from the modern point of view when he says: "No good has ever come from feeling guilty, neither intelligence, policy, nor compassion. The guilty do not pay attention to the object but only to themselves, and not even to their own interests, which might make sense, but to their anxieties."[18]

One does not have to be a professional psychiatrist to see the consequences of anxiety. We in the Western world are just emerging from a dreadful two-centuries-long Dark Ages of Eros that was sustained partly by prohibition laws, but perhaps more effectively by the anxiety-generating mechanisms of education. . . .

Since proof is difficult, we may even concede that the results of anxiety may sometimes, from certain points of view, be desirable. The larger question we should ask is whether, as a matter of policy, we should ever encourage the use of a technique the tendency (if not the intention) of which is psychologically pathogenic. We hear much talk these days of responsible parenthood; the coupled words are incorporated into the titles of some organizations devoted to birth control. Some people have proposed massive propaganda campaigns to instill responsibility into the nation's (or the world's) breeders. But what is the meaning of the word responsibility in this context? Is it not merely a synonym for the word conscience? When we use the word responsibility in the absence of substantial sanctions are we not trying to browbeat a free man in a commons into acting against his own interest? Responsibility is a verbal counterfeit for a substantial quid pro quo. It is an attempt to get something for nothing.

If the word responsibility is to be used at all, I suggest that it be in the sense Charles Frankel uses it.[20] "Responsibility," says this philosopher, "is the product of definite social arrangements." Notice that Frankel calls for social arrangements— not propaganda.

Mutual Coercion
Mutually Agreed Upon

The social arrangements that produce responsibility are arrangements that create coercion, of some sort. Consider bank-robbing. The man who takes money from a bank acts as if the bank were a commons. How do we prevent such action? Certainly not by trying to control his behavior solely by a verbal appeal to his sense of responsibility. Rather than rely on propaganda we follow Frankel's lead and insist that a bank is not a commons; we seek the definite social arrangements that will keep it from becoming a commons. That we thereby infringe on the freedom of would-be robbers we neither deny nor regret.

The morality of bank-robbing is particularly easy to understand because we accept complete prohibition of this activity. We are willing to say "Thou shalt not rob banks," without providing for exceptions. But temperance also can be created by coercion. Taxing is a good coercive device. To keep downtown shoppers temperate in their use of parking space we introduce parking meters for short periods, and traffic fines for longer ones. We need not actually forbid a citizen to park as long as he wants to; we need merely make it increasingly expensive for him to do so. Not prohibition, but carefully biased options are what we offer him. A Madison Avenue man might call this persuasion; I prefer the greater candor of the word coercion.

Coercion is a dirty word to most liberals now, but it need not forever be so. As with the four-letter words, its dirtiness can be cleansed away by exposure to the light, by saying it over and over without apology or embarrassment. To many, the word coercion implies arbitrary decisions of distant and irresponsible bureaucrats; but this is not a necessary part of its meaning. The only kind of coercion I recommend is mutual coercion, mutually agreed upon by the majority of the people affected.

To say that we mutually agree to coercion is not to say that we are required to enjoy it, or even to pretend we enjoy it. Who enjoys taxes? We all grumble about them. But we accept compulsory taxes because we recognize that voluntary taxes would favor the conscienceless. We institute and (grumblingly) support taxes and other coercive devices to escape the horror of the commons.

An alternative to the commons need not be perfectly just to be preferable. . . .
The alternative of the commons is too horrifying to contemplate. Injustice is
preferable to total ruin.

It is one of the peculiarities of the warfare between reform and the status quo
that it is thoughtlessly governed by a double standard. Whenever a reform measure is proposed it is often defeated when its opponents triumphantly discover a
flaw in it. As Kingsley Davis has pointed out,[21] worshippers of the status quo
sometimes imply that no reform is possible without unanimous agreement, an
implication contrary to historical fact. As nearly as I can make out, automatic rejection of proposed reforms is based on one of two unconscious assumptions: (i)
that the status quo is perfect; or (ii) that the choice we face is between reform and
no action; if the proposed reform is imperfect, we presumably should take no action at all, while we wait for a perfect proposal.

But we can never do nothing. That which we have done for thousands of years
is also action. It also produces evils. Once we are aware that the status quo is action, we can then compare its discoverable advantages and disadvantages with the
predicted advantages and disadvantages of the proposed reform, discounting as
best we can for our lack of experience. On the basis of such a comparison, we can
make a rational decision which will not involve the unworkable assumption that
only perfect systems are tolerable.

Recognition of Necessity

Perhaps the simplest summary of this analysis of man's population problems is
this: the commons, if justifiable at all, is justifiable only under conditions of low-
population density. As the human population has increased, the commons has
had to be abandoned in one aspect after another.

First we abandoned the commons in food gathering, enclosing farm land and
restricting pastures and hunting and fishing areas. These restrictions are still not
complete throughout the world.

Somewhat later we saw that the commons as a place for waste disposal would
also have to be abandoned. Restrictions on the disposal of domestic sewage are
widely accepted in the Western world; we are still struggling to close the commons
to pollution by automobiles, factories, insecticide sprayers, fertilizing operations,
and atomic energy installations.

In a still more embryonic state is our recognition of the evils of the commons
in matters of pleasure. There is almost no restriction on the propagation of sound
waves in the public medium. The shopping public is assaulted with mindless mu-
sic, without its consent. Our government is paying out billions of dollars to create
supersonic transport which will disturb 50,000 people for every one person who
is whisked from coast to coast 3 hours faster. Advertisers muddy the airwaves of
radio and television and pollute the view of travelers. We are a long way from outlawing the commons in matters of pleasure. Is this because our Puritan inheri-

tance makes us view pleasure as something of a sin, and pain (that is, the pollution of advertising) as the sign of virtue?

Every new enclosure of the commons involves the infringement of somebody's personal liberty. Infringements made in the distant past are accepted because no contemporary complains of a loss. It is the newly proposed infringements that we vigorously oppose; cries of "rights" and "freedom" fill the air. But what does "freedom" mean? When men mutually agreed to pass laws against robbing, mankind became more free, not less so. Individuals locked into the logic of the commons are free only to bring on universal ruin; once they see the necessity of mutual coercion, they become free to pursue other goals. I believe it was Hegel who said, "Freedom is the recognition of necessity."

The most important aspect of necessity that we must now recognize is the necessity of abandoning the commons in breeding. No technical solution can rescue us from the misery of overpopulation. Freedom to breed will bring ruin to all. At the moment, to avoid hard decisions many of us are tempted to propagandize for conscience and responsible parenthood. The temptation must be resisted, because an appeal to independently acting consciences selects for life disappearance of all conscience in the long run, and an increase in anxiety in the short.

The only way we can preserve and nurture other and more precious freedoms is by relinquishing the freedom to breed, and that very soon. "Freedom is the recognition of necessity"—and it is the role of education to reveal to all the necessity of abandoning the freedom to breed. Only so, can we put an end to this aspect of the tragedy of the commons.

SUSAN J. BUCK

4

No Tragedy
on the Commons

Introduction

IN 1951, JOSEPHINE TEY published her classic detective story *Daughter of Time*. In this defense of Richard III, she coined the term *Tonypandy*, which is the regrettable situation which occurs when a historical event is reported and memorialized inaccurately but consistently until the resulting fiction is believed to be the truth.[1] History is not the only field in which Tonypandy occurs. A prime example of Tonypandy in the field of economics is the "tragedy of the commons."

Academics are often too facile in labeling an article as "seminal," but Garrett Hardin's 1968 article, "The Tragedy of the Commons," deserves the accolade.[2] The article has been reprinted over fifty times,[3] and entire books have been devoted to exploring the meaning and implications of Hardin's memorable title.[4] The phrase "tragedy of the commons" has slipped into common parlance at colleges and universities and is rapidly becoming public property.[5] Discussion of the inevitability of such a tragedy is the lawful prey of economists, sociologists, philosophers, and theologians. Certainly we cannot deny that the phenomenon exists: the ruination of a limited resource when confronted with unlimited access by an expanding population. Where, then, lies Tonypandy in the tragedy of the commons?

Although the tragedy of the commons may occur, that it regularly occurred on the common lands of medieval and post-medieval England is not true; the historical antecedents of the tragedy of the commons as developed by Hardin and oth-

Originally published as Susan Jane Buck Cox, "No Tragedy on the Commons," in *Environmental Ethics* 7 (Spring 1985):49–61. Reprinted with permission.

ers following the 1968 article, and as commonly understood by students and professors, are inaccurate.[6] . . . Decline was not the result of unlimited access, but rather was the result of the historical forces of the industrial revolution, agrarian reform, and improved agricultural practices.

"The Tragedy of the Commons" Defined

. . . [Hardin's original] language is relatively free of cultural phenomena. . . . Later references to Hardin's tragedy of the commons, however, reflect a more explicit historical perspective. In 1977 Hardin used allusions to the Enclosure Acts of the late eighteenth and early nineteenth centuries to explain how the tragedy might be cured.[10] In 1969, Beryl Crowe wrote:

> The commons is a fundamental social institution that has a history going back through our own colonial experience to a body of English common law which antedates the Roman conquest. That law recognized that in societies there are some environmental objects which have never been, and should never be, exclusively appropriated to any individual or group of individuals. In England the classic example of the commons is the pasturage set aside for public use, and the "tragedy of the commons" to which Hardin refers was a tragedy of overgrazing and lack of care and fertilization which resulted in erosion and underproduction so destructive that there developed in the late 19th century an enclosure movement.[11]

. . . Perhaps the most extensive anglicization of the commons is found in *This Endangered Planet* by Richard Falk. He writes that Hardin "has evolved an effective metaphor of [the paradox of aggregation] from a historical experience, the destruction of the common pastures of English country towns in the 1700s and 1800s through overgrazing herds."[13]

Further examples can be found, almost ad infinitum and certainly ad nauseam. Moreover, questioning of graduate students in economics or planning or public administration elicits the same historical background on the tragedy of the commons as described by Falk. Such evidence suggests that there is a general impression among most people today that the tragedy was a regular occurrence on the common lands of the villages in medieval and post-medieval England—a belief which, despite its wide acceptance as fact, is historically false.

The Commons Defined

In order to dispel the myth of the tragedy of the commons, we must first discover the definition of *commons* as it was understood in medieval England. The legal right of common is "a right which one or more persons have to take or use some portion of that which another's soil produces . . . and is a right to part of the profits of the soil, and to part only, the right of the soil lying with another and not with the person who claims common."[14] This right is an ancient one: "Recent archaeological and historical work indicates that in many places nucleated villages did not come into being until the ninth, tenth, or even the eleventh centuries. . . . But whatever their origins, the classic common field system probably developed with them. . . ."[15] These rights "were not something specifically granted by a generous landlord, but were the residue of rights that were much more extensive, rights that are in all probability older than the modern conception of private property. They probably antedate the idea of private property in land, and are therefore of vast antiquity."[16] The right of common was a right granted to specific persons because these persons had some prior claim to the land or because the actual owner of the land granted them that right in return for their services.

Our modern-day notions of *common* as a public right does not accurately describe the medieval commons. Gonner wrote in 1912:

> [Common] now is taken as denoting the claims, somewhat vague and precarious, of the public as against those holding the land and engaged in its cultivation. But this finds no sanction in a time when over very many, if not most, cultivated districts common was a result of claim to land, and formed a necessary condition of its proper management. . . . The early rights of common were anything but vague, and were invariably vested in those employed in cultivation of their representatives; they were anything rather than a general claim on the part of the public. . . . [Common rights] were a necessary element in the agricultural system, they were involved in the ownership and cultivation of the land, and they were largely the source of the profits obtained from the land and the means of rendering its cultivation effective.[17]

Clearly our use of *common* to describe public access to national parks or to deep-sea fishing is at variance with the original use of the term. . . .

We thus have a picture of the legal status of a common. Either by common-law right as freehold tenant or through usage and grants, a villager was entitled to pasture limited numbers of specific animals on the lord's waste. It is important to note that even from the beginning, the use of the common was not unrestricted: "Common pasture of stubble and fallow was a feature of open-field husbandry from the start . . . and with it went communal control."[24] The English common was not available to the general public but was only available to certain individuals who owned or were granted the right to use it. Use of the common even by these people was not unregulated. The types and in some cases the numbers of animals each tenant could pasture were limited, based at least partly on a recognition of the limited carrying capacity of the land.

The Management of the Commons

The earliest records for communal farming regulations are the manor court rolls of the mid-thirteenth century.[25] The earliest record for a village meeting is the fourteenth century. Joan Thirsk writes:

From these dates the evidence points unequivocally to the autonomy of village communities in determining the form of, and the rules governing their field system. . . . In villages which possessed no more than one manor, matters were agreed in the manorial court, and the decisions sometimes, but not always, recorded on the court roll. Decisions affecting villages which shared the use of commons were taken at the court of the chief lord, at which all the villages were represented. In villages where more than one manor existed, agreement might be reached at a village meeting at which all tenants and lords were present or represented.[26]

. . . Such agreements among the neighbors are recorded in the village bylaws. These bylaws "emphasize the degree to which . . . agricultural practice was directed and controlled by an assembly of cultivators, the manorial court, who coordinated and regulated the season-by-season activities of the whole community. Arable and meadowland were normally thrown open for common pasturing by the stock of all the commoners after harvest and in fallow times, and this necessitated some rules about cropping, fencing, and grazing beasts. Similarly, all the cultivators of the intermixed strips enjoyed common pasturage in the waste, and in addition, the rights to gather timber, peat and other commodities were essential concomitants of the possession of arable and meadow shares."[28] There was, however, an extraordinary diversity of bylaws among the various regions of England. In one Lincolnshire fenland village, for example, "strangers coming into the town but having no land could enjoy free common for their cattle for one year. After that they had to abide by the rules governing all other inhabitants. These were generous provisions that reflected the abundance of grazing."[29] In contrast, in 1440, the village of Launton decreed that "any tenant who has a parcel of meadow in East Brokemede shall not mow there now or ever until his neighbors are agreed under pain of 3s.4d."[30], a clear reflection of the need to conserve and to regulate. What is important to note here is the detail with which the open fields were regulated. Ault notes that bylaws covered such points as where field workers were paid (at the granary rather than in the field, where payment in kind might lead to accusations of theft), and at what age boys could begin to pasture sheep on the common (sixteen). The commons were carefully and painstakingly regulated, and those instances in which the common deteriorated were most often due to lawbreaking and to oppression of the poorer tenant rather than to egoistic abuse of a common resource.

Abuses of the Commons

The commons were subject to several forms of abuse. Often the regulations governing the commons were broken, as when greedy farmers took in unauthorized animals, or when wealthy landowners or squatters took grazing to which they were not entitled because of lack of agreement among the tenants. The common thread in these abuses is their illegality.

One of the methods of controlling grazing was "stinting," allocating the number and type of beasts that could be grazed on the waste. Stinting developed more from lack of winter feed when stock was pastured on the arable land than from a desire to protect the summer grazing. This summer grazing "was as carefully controlled as the manorial courts could make it."[31] ... In Westmorland in 1695, "Occasionally, these stinting rules were broken, resulting in the 'Townfield . . . being sore abused and misorderly eaten.' The remedy was to employ a pounder who had to make sure the stints were carefully maintained."[35] Hence, we have one abuse of the common: simple lawbreaking which was remedied by resort to the law.

A similar problem with a less happy solution occurred when the wealthier landholders took advantage of the poorer tenants. In the early sixteenth century, Fitzherbert noted that the rich man benefitted from overcharging the common.[36] According to Gonner, it was "pointed out alike in the sixteenth, seventeenth and eighteenth centuries that the poor owning rights may be largely kept out of their rights by the action of large farmers who exceed their rights and thus surcharge the common to the detriment of all, or by the lack of winter feed in the absence of which summer grazing could be of little worth. . . . The unfortunate poor tenant was denied his remedy at law for the illegal abuses of the more powerful landowners. The ultimate conclusion was the enclosure of the common land, most effective in the parliamentary enclosure acts from 1720 to 1880."[39] Such change was perhaps inevitable, but it is social change and the perennial exploitation of the poor by the less poor rather than Hardin's tragedy.[40]

A third problem arose on unstinted land. In the sixteenth century the "unstinted common was almost invariably overburdened. . . . This state of things was largely to the advantage of rich commoners or the lord of the manor, who got together large flocks and herds and pastured them in the common lands to the detriment of the poorer commoners, who, unlike them, could do little in the way of providing winter feed, and now found themselves ousted even from their slender privileges in the commons."[41] ... By 1800 in the East Riding, "there was a good deal of overstocking. Some of the commons were stinted but others were not, and it was here that overstocking occurred. Many of the commons were frequently waterlogged when a small expenditure would have drained them, but what was everyone's business was nobody's business."[43] Of course, by 1800 parliamentary enclosure was well under way and this report from East Riding was made by an employee of the newly formed board of agriculture, established in response to a "widespread campaign for the more effective use of the land-resources of the country, with particular reference to the large areas of remaining open fields and to the vast areas of common lands and wastes."[44] Sponsored by wealthy landowners, the land reform was frequently no more than a sophisticated land-grab, justified in part by the admittedly striking increase in productivity of enclosed common land.

The Inevitable Decline of the Commons

The increased productivity was often touted by land reformers—wealthy or otherwise—as proof of the evils of the commons system. However, the change was the result of many factors, and not just of enclosure. Some of the increase would probably have occurred without enclosure, but enclosure hastened the process. The common land was not the best land. The lord's waste was often reclaimed land, cultivated from forest and marsh. . . . Enclosure took the better land and subjected it to the new and improved methods of agriculture which had been all but impossible under the common system, for the management of the common could not be changed unless all commoners agreed and, just as important, remained agreed.[46] Improved roads and transportation facilities made marketing easier, and of course, the land had fewer people to support. Economies of scale made it profitable to use improved stock. In 1760, Robert Bakewell, the founder of modern methods of livestock improvement, began selective breeding of farm animals.[47] Previously forbidden by ecclesiastical authorities as incest, inbreeding of animals with desirable qualities soon led to dramatic improvements in stock.[48] Planting the enclosure with nitrogen-fixing crops such as clover improved the soil; drainage improved livestock health. Animals were disturbed less by driving to and from land pasture. All of these factors combined to improve the productivity of the formerly common land.

That enclosure improved productivity is neither a surprise nor a shame to the commons. The commons system "was falling into disuse, a new system was taking its place, and with the change the actual use made of the common or common rights declined. It might indeed have been retorted [to advocates of inclosure] that what was wanted was a stricter enforcement of the whole common right system."[49] A related view was expressed in 1974 by Van Rensselaer Potter:

> When I first read Hardin's article [on the tragedy of the commons], I wondered if the users of the early English commons weren't prevented from committing the fatal error of overgrazing by a kind of 'bioethics' enforced by the moral pressure of their neighbors. Indeed, the commons system operated successfully in England for several hundred years. Now we read that, before the colonial era in the Sahel, 'overpasturage was avoided' by rules worked out by tribal chiefs. When deep wells were drilled to obtain water 'the boreholes threw into chaos the traditional system of pasture use based on agreements among tribal chieftains.' Thus, we see the tragedy of the commons not as a defect in the concept of a 'commons' but as a result of the disastrous transition period between the loss of an effective bioethic and its replacement by a new bioethic that could once again bring biological realities and human values into a viable balance.[50]

Conclusion

Hardin writes that the "view that whatever is owned by many people should be free for the taking by anyone who feels a need for it . . . is precisely the idea of the commons."[51] Why should it matter if this "idea of the commons" is historically inaccurate?

Any academic should feel an aversion to Tonypandy, but the issue is more important than a possible pedantic dislike of inaccuracy. It is beyond dispute that issues such as depletion of limited resources, environmental quality, fisheries economics, and national land management are of great and increasing concern. How those issues are dealt with depends in large part on our perceptions of the disposition of similar issues in the past. If we misunderstand the true nature of the commons, we also misunderstand the implications of the demise of the traditional commons system. Perhaps what existed in fact was not a "tragedy of the commons" but rather a triumph: that for hundreds of years—and perhaps thousands, although written records do not exist to prove the longer era—land was managed successfully by communities. That the system failed to survive the industrial revolution, agrarian reform, and transfigured farming practices is hardly to be wondered at.

Our reexamination of the commons requires a dual focus. The first is to search for the ideas and practices which led to successful commoning for centuries and to try to find lessons and applications for our own times. The second focus is epistemological: are our perceptions of the nature of humankind awry? Since it seems quite likely if "economic man" had been managing the commons that tragedy really would have occurred, perhaps someone else was running the common.

In 1968, Hardin wrote that "'ruin' is the destruction toward which all men rush, each pursuing his own best interest in a society that believes in the freedom of the commons. Freedom in a common brings ruin to all."[52] But the common is not free and never was free. Perhaps in the changed perception of the common lies a remedy for ruin.

DAVID FEENY, FIKRET BERKES,
BONNIE J. MCCAY & JAMES M. ACHESON

5
The Tragedy
of the Commons:
Twenty–two Years Later

Introduction

GARRETT HARDIN'S *The Tragedy of the Commons* was published 22 years ago
(Hardin, 1968). Although it focused attention on overpopulation, the dominant
legacy of the paper has been its metaphor of common-property resource management. In the intervening years, the ideas that Hardin popularized have become
the most widely accepted explanation for overexploitation of resources that are
commonly held. The essential idea was that resources held in common, such as
oceans, rivers, air, and parklands, are subject to massive degradation. . . .

This conclusion has been accorded by some the status of scientific law. The
tragedy of the commons has become part of the conventional wisdom in environ-

Originally published in *Human Ecology* 18, 1 (1990):1–19. Reprinted with permission from
Plenum Publishing Corporation.

The authors acknowledge the helpful comments of Mina Kislalioglu, Donald McCloskey, Stuart
Mestelman, Elinor Ostrom, Henry Reiger, and Darrell Tomkins. Interested readers are referred to *The
Common Property Resource Digest,* available from the International Association for the Study of
Common Property, School of Forestry and Environmental Studies, Yale University, 205 Prospect
Street, New Haven, CT 06511.

mental studies, resource science and policy, economics, ecology, and political science and is featured in textbooks. . . . It has also been used in formulating resource-management policy. . . .

To avoid the tragedy, Hardin concluded that the commons could be privatized or kept as public property to which rights to entry and use could be allocated. Hardin has been widely cited as having said that resource degradation was inevitable unless common property was converted to private property, or government regulation of uses and users was instituted. In a later paper, Hardin (1978) specifically recognized two general solutions, and presumably no others: private enterprise and socialism (control by government). Hardin argued that if we do not act in one of these two ways, we "acquiesce in the destruction of the commons" (Hardin, 1968, p. 1245). . . .

Definitions and Concepts

Common-property resources include fisheries, wildlife, surface and groundwater, range, and forests. It is important to delineate the characteristics shared by these resources, and to distinguish between the resource and the property-rights regime in which the resource is held.

Common-property resources share two important characteristics. The first is excludability (or control of access). That is, the physical nature of the resource is such that controlling access by potential users may be costly and, in the extreme, virtually impossible. Migratory resources such as fish, wildlife, and groundwater pose obvious problems for regulating access. Similarly, range and forest lands typically pose problems of exclusion. For large bodies of water, the global atmosphere, and radio frequency bands, exclusion is even more problematic.

The second basic characteristic of common-property resources is subtractability, that is, each user is capable of subtracting from the welfare of other users. Even if users cooperate to enhance the productivity of their resource, for instance by replanting trees, the nature of the resource is such that the level of exploitation by one user adversely affects the ability of another user to exploit the resource. Subtractability (or rivalry) is the source of the potential divergence between individual and collective rationality. If one user pumps more water from an aquifer, other users will experience an increase in pumping costs as aggregate use approaches or exceeds recharge capacity. If one user harvests fish, the catch per unit of fishing effort of other fishermen declines. Hence, we define common-property resources as *a class of resources for which exclusion is difficult and joint use involves subtractability.* . . . In order to facilitate analysis, we define four categories of property rights within which common-property resources are held: open access, private property, communal property, and state property. These are ideal, analytic types. In practice, many resources are held in overlapping, and sometimes conflicting combinations of these regimes, and there is variation within each. It is nevertheless important to distinguish these four basic property-rights regimes.

Open access is the absence of well-defined property rights. Access to the re-source is unregulated and is free and open to everyone. Many offshore ocean fish-eries before the twentieth century, or the global atmosphere provide examples.

Under *private property,* the rights to exclude others from using the resource and to regulate the use of the resource are vested in an individual (or group of indi-viduals such as a corporation). Private-property rights are generally recognized and enforced by the state. Unlike rights under open access, private-property rights usually are exclusive and transferable. Examples include forests and rangelands that are held privately.

Under *communal property,* the resource is held by an identifiable community of interdependent users. These users exclude outsiders while regulating use by mem-bers of the local community. Within the community, rights to the resource are unlikely to be either exclusive or transferable; they are often rights of equal access and use. Some inshore fisheries, shellfish beds, range lands, and forests have been managed as communal property; similarly, water-users associations for many groundwater and irrigation systems can be included in this category. The rights of the group may be legally recognized. In other cases the rights are de facto, de-pending on the benign neglect of the state. . . .

Finally, under *state property,* or state governance, rights to the resource are vested exclusively in government which in turn makes decisions concerning ac-cess to the resource and the level and nature of exploitation. Examples include forests and rangelands held by the government or crown-owned, and resources such as fish and wildlife that may be held in public trust for the citizenry. . . . The nature of the state property regime also differs from the other regimes in that, in general, the state, unlike private parties, has coercive powers of enforcement.

. . . One theme of the paper is that one must understand a whole host of insti-tutional arrangements governing access to and use of the resource. Knowledge of the property rights is necessary but not sufficient. Many of the misunderstandings found in the literature may be traced to the assumption that common property is the same as open access. Hardin's prediction of the inevitability of over-exploita-tion follows from this assumption. Yet the assumption is inaccurate and it has led to a great deal of confusion. Based on our definition of common property, an ap-proach to testing Hardin's hypothesis is to examine two broad challenges in the management of common-property resources: (1) the exclusion of other potential users, and (2) the regulation of use and users to ameliorate the problems associ-ated with subtractability. . . .

Evidence on Exclusion

Open Access. The evidence supports Hardin's argument concerning degradation due to the inability to regulate access to resources held as open access. Examples are many, and include the classic case of the historical depletion of various whale stocks in the open ocean. Several examples, however, reveal a point not mentioned by Hardin. In many cases, the tragedy occurred only after open-access conditions were created, often as a consequence of the destruction of existing communal land-tenure and marine-tenure systems. A number of these cases involved the imposition of colonial rule, as in sub-Saharan Africa, the Pacific Islands, and northwest North American salmon rivers.

Private Property. The establishment and enforcement of private property rights have frequently provided the institutional arrangements for successful exclusion. Private-property rights may not, however, be sufficiently precise for solving the exclusion problem. A classic example is the exploitation of oil pools in much of the United States. In an 1889 Pennsylvania Supreme Court decision, the doctrine of law of capture was applied to oil. Private property rights in oil were assigned only upon extraction. In practice, this means that each owner of surface rights has the incentive to accelerate their pumping of oil to the surface. The result is a duplication of drilling and other capital costs, substantial reduction in the overall rate of recovery, and dissipation of economic rents. A remedy to the problem has long been recognized—to define property rights in the underground pool as a unit (unitization) before extraction rather than after. In jurisdictions (such as Wyoming) in which unitization is required before drilling on land leased for oil exploration, greater efficiency has been achieved. In spite of the potential gains for all users through unitization, this form of contract is uncommon in other jurisdictions (such as Texas and Oklahoma) because the high cost of private contracting inhibits its adoption. Private property rights and the incentives they afford are not always sufficient to achieve efficient exploitation.

There is an enforcement problem with all types of property rights, including private property. For common-property resources, which by definition pose exclusion problems, such enforcement can be costly. Well recognized de jure rights of the medieval lord, and even contemporary landlords, to fish and game have been routinely violated by poachers. The extent to which the community regards private-property rights as legitimate affects the cost of enforcement. The difficulty of enforcing private claims to common-property resources is exacerbated by competing claims to communal rights in those resources. This is evident in the United States oyster industry, where a private property regime, including leasehold, is not politically acceptable in many areas regardless of the fact that it is logical, feasible, and demonstrably more efficient.

Communal Property. Hardin did not consider the possibility of exclusion under communal-property regimes. By exclusion we mean the power to exclude people other than members of a defined community. Evidence suggests that successful exclusion under communal property is the rule rather than the exception. Well-documented contemporary cases include Amerindian community hunting and fishing lands in James Bay, eastern subarctic Canada. Here, the communal-property regime collapsed as a result of incursions by outsiders and recovered with the re-establishment of exclusion at least twice since the nineteenth century. Other examples come from the Pacific islands where communal-property regimes have collapsed in some areas but continue to be viable in many others.

Communal property is not confined to remote and sparsely populated areas. Cooperative-based coastal fisheries in Japan provide many successful examples of communal-property systems. These fishing communities hold legally guaranteed exclusive fishing rights in coastal areas. One of the major conclusions of the National Research Council conference was that legal recognition of communal rights, as in Japanese coastal fisheries, was crucial for the success of communal-property regimes. . . . Even when there is no legal recognition of communal property, the exclusion of outsiders by local users through such means as threats and surreptitious violence is not uncommon. The persistence of community-based lobster fishing territories in Maine is merely one example, but an important one because it occurs in a country and culture in which the belief in right of free access is deeply held.

The examples given thus far are for fish and wildlife for which exclusion is particularly difficult because of the migratory nature of the resource. Successful exclusion can also be found for other resource types, including grazing lands, forests, and water resources.

Pressure on the resource because of human population growth, technological change, or economic change, including new market opportunities, may contribute to the breakdown of communal-property mechanisms for exclusion. The role of population growth is especially controversial. For example, some argue that in the case of East Africa, the carrying capacity of rangelands under any management regime has been exceeded. Other cases indicate that population is merely one of many interrelated social and economic problems.

Communal-property regimes fail to provide for exclusion for other reasons as well. Many of these failures are associated with the appropriation of the resource by politically or militarily powerful groups, or by other factors such as land reform that disrupt existing communal management systems. Others are associated with problems of scale and internal organization. The social and political characteristics of the users of the resource and how they relate to the larger political system affect the ability of local groups to organize and manage communal property.

State Property. Exclusive state governance of the resource has in many cases been sufficient to provide for adequate exclusion. However, difficulties in exclusion are not necessarily overcome by declaring the resource to be state property. A vivid example comes from Nepal. Alarmed by deforestation, the government nationalized forests in 1957, converting what were often communal forests into de jure state property. But the result more closely approximated the creation of de facto open access. Villagers whose control of nearby forests had been removed often succumbed to the incentives of law of capture. Deforestation accelerated instead of decelerated. In the face of worsening conditions the government began to experiment in 1976 with the re-creation of communal-property rights. . . .

Another problem with state governance is that imperfections in the political process will often be mirrored in resource management. In some cultures, free access to certain resources for citizens at large is viewed as a right. In other cases, the state is especially responsive to the interests of the elite. Some instances of apparent tragedies of the commons are more accurately construed as examples of government failure.

The logic of the argument of *The Tragedy of the Commons* is that we should not observe sustainable management of common-property resources and the exclusion of some uses or users, under regimes other than private or state property. But as we have illustrated, exclusion is feasible, if not always successful, under private, state, *and* communal-property regimes. Furthermore, private or state ownership is not always sufficient to provide for exclusion.

Evidence on Regulations of Use and Users

Open Access. Hardin's predictions that incentives for successful resource management are absent from or weak in open access regimes are in general consistent with the evidence. In such regimes, under conditions in which demand exceeds the capacity of the resource to sustain itself, and where the technology is available to exploit the resource at a high level, many species, including the North American passenger pigeon and the bison, have become extinct, or virtually extinct. In the context of the day, free and unregulated use of resources such as the bison initially made sense. To illustrate the individual rationality that lay behind ecological tragedy, Hardin (1978) invokes the image of Kit Carson shooting bison on the plains, taking only the tongue and leaving the rest. This is not economically irrational if one considers that the game was then abundant but the hunter's time was scarce. Depletion occurred rapidly, before countervailing institutional arrangements or changing cultural values could prevent it.

Private Property. Privatization usually provides incentives for rational exploitation of the resource. If the owner has property rights in the resource and those rights are tradeable, both the costs and benefits will accrue to the same owner and will be reflected in the market price of the resource, giving the owner the pecuniary incentive to refrain from destructive use. These incentives, however, are not necessarily consistent with sustainable use. Suppose a redwood planted for $1 is worth $14,000 at maturity—which may take 2000 years. The implied rate of return would be less than 0.5%, well below the rates of return generally available to investors. Although planting a redwood may make ecological sense, it does not make economic sense under a private-property regime.

More realistically, Clark (1973) has shown that for relatively slow-growing and late-maturing species such as whales, it may be economically optimal to deplete the resource rather than to use it sustainably. . . . [Private property] rights permit the owner to maximize the present value of the resource, yet the resource is not protected from extinction.

Communal Property. There is abundant evidence, contrary to Hardin, on the ability of social groups to design, utilize, and adapt often ingenious mechanisms to allocate use rights among members. The medieval English commons featured in Hardin's paper, like many other historic and contemporary commons, were often subject to comprehensive systems of regulation. For example, stinting was often practiced, that is, limiting the number of head that each owner could graze. Not only was access exclusive to certain members of the village, but their rights were often closely regulated. A plethora of scholars have noted in passing that the commons operated successfully for several hundred years in medieval England, and have questioned if a tragedy of the sort described by Hardin (1968) ever occurred widely.

Forest and meadow commons in Japanese villages were also the subject of elaborate regulations. Village leaders set opening and closing dates for the harvest of certain products. In some villages, thatch was harvested collectively; bundles were then randomly assigned to each household. This device permitted the aggregate level of utilization to be controlled while giving each household an incentive to be reasonably conscientious in its harvesting effort. Guards patrolled the common lands to prevent poaching both by villagers and outsiders. Written rules provided a graduated schedule of fines for violators. Harvesting tools were also regulated. Regulations legislated by villagers ensured sustainable use of common lands for generations.

In the Japanese case, forest and meadow lands and irrigation works were held as communal property while crop lands were held privately. This is not an isolated example of the co-existence of two property-rights regimes. There are other cases indicating the ability of users to match appropriately the resource with the regime. In some societies, the same resource may alternate back and forth between communal and private control seasonally or over the long term.

Not all examples of successful regulation are historic or based on longstanding tradition. In a study of Turkish coastal fisheries, successful regulation was found to have evolved within 15 years in two cases (Alanya, Tasucu), and 9 years in one case. Alarmed by the increasing numbers of users and escalating conflicts, fishermen in Alanya developed a system to regulate use: fishing sites were spaced sufficiently apart to avoid interference, and fisherman agreed among themselves to fish in rotation to ensure equitable access to best sites, with their starting position determined by drawing lots. Although only half of the licensed fishermen belonged to the local marketing cooperative, the authority under which the system was operated, all participated in the process for creating and maintaining it.

Self-regulation of resource use to improve livelihood was also achieved by a local marketing cooperative of New Jersey fishermen. Because large catches depressed prices on the New York fresh fish market, a cooperative was formed to enhance producers' bargaining power. This cooperative decided on total catch levels for the fleet, and provided for the sharing of revenues regardless of the catch levels of individual boats. The pooling of revenues reduced the incentives to over-fish.

Although the system was devised to raise prices, a spillover benefit may have been conservation. . . .

These case studies illustrate that people are not helpless but are able to organize, to monitor resource use by members, to allocate use rights among members, and to adjust aggregate utilization levels to maintain sustainable use of the resource. . . . Under the appropriate circumstances, voluntary collective action is feasible and effective.

State Property. Government ownership (state governance) permits the formulation of appropriate regulations for resource use. It also provides for the expression of public interest and for accountability. But state governance does not necessarily ensure sustainable use. Given that the officials who make decisions do not have the same time horizon or interests as private owners, the general public, or the government itself, this is not surprising.

One of the oft-mentioned problems of state ownership is the proliferation of such regulations. Smith points out, for example, that in a New England regional fishery, the combination of quotas, allocations, and trip limitations generated more than 100 different limits, with the result that there was widespread violation of the law. Noncompliance of users and de facto open access has led to an assertion by some that better protection can be achieved under private- rather than state-property regimes.

State ownership is seldom associated with successful management in less-developed countries. The professional resource-management infrastructure of the state is usually poorly developed and enforcement of regulations problematic. In India, for example, communally-held forests were nationalized before the state had developed the capacity for management. Local communities are, however, starting to re-assert their cultural traditions of conservation. . . . Repetto argues that "villagers who ruthlessly cut trees for firewood and fodder in government forests will zealously nurture and protect groves that belong to them or—if their community is sufficiently strong—to their village" (Repetto, 1986, pp. 30–31).

The logic of the argument of "The Tragedy of the Commons" is that private owners or state managers can and often do manage resources successfully. That is, these two property-rights regimes would provide the incentives to regulate use in a fashion consistent with sustainability. Implicitly Hardin argues that these incentives would be absent or weak for other regimes. However, the evidence indicates that complex interactions among the characteristics of the resource, the property-rights regime and other institutional arrangements, and the socio-economic environment contribute to the degree of management success. Success in the regulation of uses and users is not universally associated with any particular type of property-rights regime. Communal property, private property, and government property have all been associated both with success and failure.

Conclusions

Hardin's model is insightful but incomplete. His conclusion of unavoidable tragedy follows from his assumptions of open access, lack of constraints on individual behavior, conditions in which demand exceeds supply, and resource users who are incapable of altering the rules. Actual common-property situations often do not conform to all four of these assumptions. This leads us to amend Hardin's (1968) heuristic fable. The "tragedy" may start as in Hardin. But after several years of declining yields, the herdsmen are likely to get together to seek ways to (1) control access to the pasture, and (2) agree upon a set of rules of conduct, perhaps including stinting, that effectively limits exploitation. Whether or not the intended self-regulation works depends on a number of factors. Here the simple model breaks down—no single metaphor can tell the full story. The medieval English commons usually were regulated by the community, sometimes effectively, sometimes not. The outcome was never so clear and deterministically predictable as in Hardin's model. . . .

The original Hardin paper did, however, allude to the potential viability of communal property. Hardin's (1968, p. 1247) phrase, "mutual coercion, mutually agreed upon" is consistent with communal-property arrangements, although he appears to have meant state institutions under representative government. Societies have the capacity to construct and enforce rules and norms that constrain the behavior of individuals. In many societies and in many situations, the capacity for concerted social action overcomes the divergence between individual and collective rationality. The cases discussed in this paper provide ample evidence of the ability of groups of users and local communities to organize and to manage local resources effectively. Contrary to assumptions by many common-property analysts, these communal-property arrangements have persisted. A diversity of societies in the past and present have independently devised, maintained, or adapted communal arrangements to manage common-property resources. Their persistence is not an historical accident; these arrangements build on knowledge of the resource and cultural norms that have evolved and been tested over time. . . .

Further, the logic of communal property can also be applied to resources that are global (rather than local) in scope. Here, tragedies are more difficult to prevent. This is perhaps why the World Conservation Strategy (1980) and the World Commission on Environment and Development (1987) both emphasized the global commons. Problems such as ozone depletion and carbon dioxide accumulation in the atmosphere are clearly global tragedies of the commons in the making. The solution of such problems will necessarily involve co-management on a large scale. The 1987 Montreal Protocol to protect the ozone layer is an example of international co-management. The case of oil pollution on the high seas, with various international conventions going back to 1954, and leading to reductions in accidental oil spills in the 1980's, the Alaska spill notwithstanding, demonstrates that international cooperation can be effective.

The problem posed by Hardin over 20 years ago captured the attention of a multi-disciplinary collection of scholars and practitioners, including anthropologists, development planners, ecologists, economists, geographers, political scientists, resource scientists, and sociologists. . . . However, as with many seminal but simple models, Hardin's analysis has been shown by subsequent studies to be overly simplified and deterministic. . . . A new and more comprehensive theory for common-property resources must be able to account for sustainable resource management under communal-property regimes. The theory should be capable of accommodating user self-organization or the lack of it. Such a model can better explain whether and under what conditions sustainable resource management will occur, rather than simply predicting the demise of all resources held in common.

[Editors' note: See the original publication for full references list.]

References

Clark, C. W. (1973). The Economics of Overexploitation. *Science* 181:630–634.

Hardin, G. (1968). The tragedy of the commons. *Science* 162:1243–1248.

Hardin, G. (1978). Political requirements for preserving our common heritage. In Brokaw, H. P. (ed.), *Wildlife and America*. Council on Environmental Quality, Washington, D.C., pp. 310–317.

Repetto, R. (1986). *World Enough and Time*. Yale University Press, New Haven.

World Commission on Environment and Development (1987). *Our Common Future*. Oxford University Press, Oxford.

World Conservation Strategy (1980). *World Conservation Strategy: Living Resource Conservation for Sustainable Development*. IUCN/UNEP/WWF, International Union for the Conservation of Nature and Natural Resources, Gland.

WILLIAM OPHULS

6

The Scarcity Society

. . .

FOR THE PAST THREE CENTURIES, we have been living in an age of abnormal abundance. The bonanza of the New World and other founts of virgin resources, the dazzling achievements of science and technology, the availability of "free" ecological resources such as air and water to absorb the waste products of industrial activities and other lesser factors allowed our ancestors to dream of endless material growth. Infinite abundance, men reasoned, would result in the elevation of the common man to economic nobility. And with poverty abolished, inequality, injustice, and fear—all those flowers of evil alleged to have their roots in scarcity—would wither away. Apart from William Blake and a few other disgruntled romantics, or the occasional pessimist like Thomas Malthus, the Enlightenment ideology of progress was shared by all in the West.* The works of John Locke and Adam Smith, the two men who gave bourgeois political economy its fundamental direction, are shot through with the assumption that there is always going to be more—more land in the colonies, more wealth to be dug from the ground, and so on. Virtually all the philosophies, values, and institutions typical of modern capitalist society—the legitimacy of self-interest, the primacy of the individual and his inalienable rights, economic laissez-faire, and democracy as we know it—are the luxuriant fruit of an era of apparently endless abundance. They cannot continue to exist in their current form once we return to the more normal condition of scarcity.

*Marxists tend to be more extreme optimists than non-Marxists, differing only on how the drive to Utopia was to be organized.

Worse, the historic responses to scarcity have been conflict—wars fought to control resources, and oppression—great inequality of wealth and the political measures needed to maintain it. The link between scarcity and oppression is well understood by spokesmen for underprivileged groups and nations, who react violently to any suggested restraint in growth of output.

Our awakening from the pleasant dream of infinite progress and the abolition of scarcity will be extremely painful. Institutionally, scarcity demands that we sooner or later achieve a full-fledged "steady-state" or "spaceman" economy. Thereafter, we shall have to live off the annual income the earth receives from the sun, and this means a forced end to our kind of abnormal affluence and an abrupt return to frugality. This will require the strictest sort of economic and technological husbandry, as well as the strictest sort of political control.

The necessity for political control should be obvious from the use of the spaceship metaphor: political ships embarked on dangerous voyages need philosopher-king captains. However, another metaphor—the tragedy of the commons—comes even closer to depicting the essence of the ecopolitical dilemma. The tragedy of the commons has to do with the uncontrolled self-seeking in a limited environment that eventually results in competitive overexploitation of a common resource, whether it is a commonly owned field on which any villager may graze his sheep, or the earth's atmosphere into which producers dump their effluents.

Francis Carney's powerful analysis of the Los Angeles smog problem indicates how deeply all our daily acts enmesh us in the tragic logic of the commons:

> Every person who lives in this basin knows that for twenty-five years he has been living through a disaster. We have all watched it happen, have participated in it with full knowledge. . . . The smog is the result of ten million individual pursuits of private gratification. But there is absolutely nothing that any individual can do to stop its spread. . . . An individual act of renunciation is now nearly impossible, and, in any case, would be meaningless unless everyone else did the same thing. But he has no way of getting everyone else to do it.

If this inexorable process is not controlled by prudent and, above all, timely political restraints on the behavior that causes it, then we must resign ourselves to ecological self-destruction. And the new political strictures that seem required to cope with the tragedy of the commons (as well as the imperatives of technology) are going to violate our most cherished ideals, for they will be neither democratic nor libertarian. At worst, the new era could be an anti-Utopia in which we are conditioned to behave according to the exigencies of ecological scarcity.

Ecological scarcity is a new concept, embracing more than the shortage of any particular resource. It has to do primarily with pollution limits, complex trade-offs between present and future needs, and a variety of other physical constraints, rather than with a simple Malthusian overpopulation. The case for the coming of ecological scarcity was most forcefully argued in the Club of Rome study *The Limits to Growth*. That study says, in essence, that man lives on a finite planet containing limited resources and that we appear to be approaching some of these major limits with great speed. To use ecological jargon, we are about to overtax the "carrying capacity" of the planet.

Critical reaction to this Jeremiad was predictably reassuring. Those wise in the ways of computers were largely content to assert that the Club of Rome people had fed the machines false or slanted information. "Garbage in, garbage out," they soothed. Other critics sought solace in less empirical directions, but everyone who recoiled from the book's apocalyptic vision took his stand on grounds of social or technological optimism. Justified or not, the optimism is worth examining to see where it leads us politically.

The social optimists, to put their case briefly, believe that various "negative feedback mechanisms" allegedly built into society will (if left alone) automatically check the trends toward ever more population, consumption, and pollution, and that this feedback will function smoothly and gradually so as to bring us up against the limits to growth, if any, with scarcely a bump. The market-price system is the feedback mechanism usually relied upon. Shortages of one resource—oil, for example—simply make it economical to substitute another in more abundant supply (coal or shale oil). A few of these critics of the limits-to-growth thesis believe that this process can go on indefinitely.

Technological optimism is founded on the belief that it makes little difference whether exponential growth is pushing us up against limits, for technology is simultaneously expanding the limits. To use the metaphor popularized during the debate, ecologists see us as fish in a pond where all life is rapidly being suffocated by a water lily that doubles in size every day (covering the whole pond in thirty days). The technological optimists do not deny that the lily grows very quickly, but they believe that the pond itself can be made to grow even faster. Technology made a liar out of Malthus, say the optimists, and the same fate awaits the neo-Malthusians. In sum, the optimists assert that we can never run out of resources, for economics and technology, like modern genii, will always keep finding new ones for us to exploit or will enable us to use the present supply with ever-greater efficiency.

The point most overlooked in this debate, however, is that politically it matters little who is right: the neo-Malthusians *or* either type of optimist. If the "doomsdayers" are right, then of course we crash into the ceiling of physical limits and relapse into a Hobbesian universe of the war of all against all, followed, as anarchy always has been, by dictatorship of one form or another. If, on the other hand, the optimists are right in supposing that we can adjust to ecological scarcity with economics and technology, this effort will have, as we say, "side effects." For the collision with physical limits can be forestalled only by moving toward some kind of steady-state economy—characterized by the most scrupulous husbanding of resources, by extreme vigilance against the ever-present possibility of disaster should breakdown occur, and, therefore, by tight controls on human behavior. However we get there, "Spaceship Earth" will be an all-powerful Leviathan—perhaps benign, perhaps not.

A Bird in the Bush

The scarcity problem thus poses a classic dilemma. It may be possible to avoid crashing into the physical limits, but only by adopting radical and unpalatable measures that, paradoxically, are little different in their ultimate political and social implications from the future predicted by the doomsdayers.

Why this is so becomes clear enough when one realizes that the optimistic critics of the doomsdayers, whom I have artificially grouped into "social" and "technological" tendencies, finally have to rest their different cases on a theory of politics, that is, on assumptions about the adaptability of leaders, their constituencies, and the institutions that hold them together. Looked at closely, these assumptions also appear unrealistic.

Even on a technical level, for example, the market-price mechanism does not coexist easily with environmental imperatives. In a market system a bird in the hand is always worth two in the bush.* This means that resources critically needed in the future will be discounted—that is, assessed at a fraction of their future value—by today's economic decision-makers. Thus decisions that are economically "rational," like mine-the-soil farming and forestry, may be ecologically catastrophic. Moreover, charging industries—and, therefore, consumers—for pollution and other environmental harms that are caused by mining and manufacturing (the technical solution favored by most economists to bring market prices into line with ecological realities) is not politically palatable. It clearly requires political decisions that do not accord with current values or the present distribution of political power; and the same goes for other obvious and necessary measures, like energy conservation. No consumer wants to pay more for the same product simply because it is produced in a cleaner way; no developer wants to be confronted with an environmental impact statement that lets the world know his gain is the community's loss; no trucker is likely to agree with any energy-conservation program that cuts his income.

We all have a vested interest in continuing to abuse the environment as we have in the past. And even if we should find the political will to take these kinds of steps before we collide with the physical limits, then we will have adopted the essential features of a spaceman economy on a piecemeal basis—and will have simply exchanged one horn of the dilemma for the other.

Technological solutions are more roundabout, but the outcome—greater social control in a planned society—is equally certain. Even assuming that necessity always proves to be the mother of invention, the management burden thrown on our leaders and institutions by continued technological expansion of that famous

---

*Of course, noneconomic factors may temporarily override market forces, as the [1973] Arab oil boycott illustrates.

fishpond will be enormous. Prevailing rates of growth require us to double our capital stock, our capacity to control pollution, our agricultural productivity, and so forth every fifteen to thirty years. Since we already start from a very high absolute level, the increment of required new construction and new invention will be staggering. For example, to accommodate world population growth, we must, in roughly the next thirty years, build houses, hospitals, ports, factories, bridges, and every other kind of facility in numbers that almost equal all the construction work done by the human race up to now.

The task in every area of our lives is essentially similar, so that the management problem extends across the board, item by item. Moreover, the complexity of the overall problem grows faster than any of the sectors that comprise it, requiring the work of innovation, construction, and environmental management to be orchestrated into a reasonably integrated, harmonious whole. Since delays, planning failures, and general incapacity to deal effectively with even our current level of problems are all too obvious today, the technological response further assumes that our ability to cope with large-scale complexity will improve substantially in the next few decades. Technology, in short, cannot be implemented in a political and social vacuum. The factor in least supply governs, and technological solutions cannot run ahead of our ability to plan, construct, fund, and man them.

Planning will be especially difficult. For one thing, time may be our scarcest resource. Problems now develop so rapidly that they must be foreseen well in advance. Otherwise, our "solutions" will be too little and too late. The automobile is a critical example. By the time we recognized the dangers, it was too late for anything but a mishmash of stopgap measures that may have provoked worse symptoms than they alleviated and that will not even enable us to meet health standards without painful additional measures like rationing. But at this point we are almost helpless to do better, for we have ignored the problem until it is too big to handle by any means that are politically, economically, and technically feasible. . . .

Another planning difficulty: the growing vulnerability of a highly technological society to accident and error. The main cause for concern is, of course, some of the especially dangerous technologies we have begun to employ. One accident involving a breeder reactor would be one too many: the most minuscule dose of plutonium is deadly, and any we release now will be around to poison us for a quarter of a million years. Thus, while we know that counting on perfection in any human enterprise is folly, we seem headed for a society in which nothing less than perfect planning and control will do.

At the very least, it should be clear that ecological scarcity makes "muddling through" in a basically laissez-faire socioeconomic system no longer tolerable or even possible. In a crowded world where only the most exquisite care will prevent the collapse of the technological society on which we all depend, the grip of planning and social control will of necessity become more and more complete. Accidents, much less the random behavior of individuals, cannot be permitted;

the expert pilots will run the ship in accordance with technological imperatives. Industrial man's Faustian bargain with technology therefore appears to lead inexorably to total domination by technique in a setting of clockwork institutions. C.S. Lewis once said that "what we call Man's power over Nature turns out to be a power exercised by some men over other men with Nature as its instrument," and it appears that the greater our technological power over nature, the more absolute the political power that must be yielded up to some men by others.

These developments will be especially painful for Americans because, from the beginning, we adopted the doctrines of Locke and Smith in their most libertarian form. Given the cornucopia of the frontier, an unpolluted environment, and a rapidly developing technology, American politics could afford to be a more or less amicable squabble over the division of the spoils, with the government stepping in only when the free-for-all pursuit of wealth got out of hand. In the new era of scarcity, laissez-faire and the inalienable right of the individual to get as much as he can are prescriptions for disaster. It follows that the political system inherited from our forefathers is moribund. We have come to the final act of the tragedy of the commons.

The answer to the tragedy is political. Historically, the use of the commons was closely regulated to prevent overgrazing, and we need similar controls . . . to prevent the individual acts that are destroying the commons today. Ecological scarcity imposes certain political measures on us if we wish to survive. Whatever these measures may turn out to be—if we act soon, we may have a significant range of responses—it is evident that our political future will inevitably be much less libertarian and much more authoritarian, much less individualistic and much more communalistic than our present. The likely result of the reemergence of scarcity appears to be the resurrection in modern form of the preindustrial polity, in which the few govern the many and in which government is no longer of or by the people. Such forms of government may or may not be benevolent. At worst, they will be totalitarian, in every evil sense of that word we know now, and some ways undreamed of. At best, government seems likely to rest on engineered consent, as we are manipulated by Platonic guardians in one or another version of Brave New World. The alternative will be the destruction, perhaps consciously, of "Spaceship Earth."

A Democracy of Restraint

There is, however, a way out of this depressing scenario. To use the language of ancient philosophers, it is the restoration of the civic virtue of a corrupt people. By their standards, by the standards of many of the men who founded our nation (and whose moral capital we have just about squandered), we are indeed a corrupt people. We understand liberty as a license for self-indulgence, so that we exploit our rights to the full while scanting our duties. We understand democracy as a political means of gratifying our desires rather than as a system of government that gives us the precious freedom to impose laws on ourselves—instead of having some remote sovereign impose them on us without our participation or consent. Moreover, the desires we express through our political system are primarily for material gain; the pursuit of happiness has been degraded into a mass quest for what wise men have always said would injure our souls. We have yet to learn the truth of Burke's political syllogism, which expresses the essential wisdom of political philosophy: man is a passionate being, and there must therefore be checks on will and appetite; if these checks are not self-imposed, they must be applied externally as fetters by a sovereign power. The way out of our difficulties, then, is through the abandonment of our political corruption.

The crisis of ecological scarcity poses basic value questions about man's place in nature and the meaning of human life. It is possible that we may learn from this challenge what Lao-tzu taught two-and-a-half millennia ago:

> Nature sustains itself through three precious
> principles, which one does well to embrace and follow.
>
> These are gentleness, frugality, and humility.

A very good life—in fact, an affluent life by historic standards—can be lived without the profligate use of resources that characterizes our civilization. A sophisticated and ecologically sound technology, using solar power and other renewable resources, could bring us a life of simple sufficiency that would yet allow the full expression of the human potential. Having chosen such a life, rather than having had it forced on us, we might find it had its own richness.

Such a choice may be impossible, however. The root of our problem lies deep. The real shortage with which we are afflicted is that of moral resources. Assuming that we wish to survive in dignity and not as ciphers in some ant-heap society, we are obliged to reassume our full moral responsibility. The earth is not just a banquet at which we are free to gorge. The ideal in Buddhism of compassion for all sentient beings, the concern for the harmony of man and nature so evident among American Indians, and the almost forgotten ideal of stewardship in Christianity point us in the direction of a true ethics of human survival—and it is toward such an ideal that the best among the young are groping. We must realize that there is no real scarcity in nature. It is our numbers and, above all, our wants that have outrun nature's bounty. We become rich precisely in proportion to the degree in which we eliminate violence, greed, and pride from our lives. As several thousands of years of history show, this is not something easily learned by humanity, and we seem no readier to choose the simple, virtuous life now than we have been in the past. Nevertheless, if we wish to avoid either a crash into the ecological ceiling or a tyrannical Leviathan, we must choose it. There is no other way to defeat the gathering forces of scarcity.

PART TWO

Ecology and the Structure of the International System

As discussed in the introductory chapter to this volume, environmental problems are the result of a complex array of social forces, including technology, political and economic institutions, social structures, and human values. In this part we are particularly interested in the subset of causes that can be attributed to the structure of the international system. The term *structure* is sometimes used by scholars in international relations to refer to the international distribution of power among states. Thus, during the period of the Cold War, the structure of the system was often said to be bipolar, in that the two superpowers wielded by far the most power in international affairs. Here we use the term more generally to refer to the relatively stable, unchanging characteristics of world politics such as the political division of the world into sovereign states or the capitalist global economy that shapes transactions among those states.[1] These relatively permanent features of the world system give shape and definition to the interactions among governments, international organizations, multinational corporations, nongovernmental organizations, and other agents of world politics.

Three aspects of system structure seem particularly important in shaping the array of global environmental problems we face and the possibilities for responding to those problems. The first is state sovereignty, which many scholars take to be the central feature of world politics. As the World Commission on Environment and Development put it, "The Earth is One but the World Is Not."[2] One of the main reasons is the sovereignty of individual states, which gives them, at least in principle, decisionmaking autonomy over matters falling within their territorial jurisdiction.

The tensions between ecology and sovereignty are to some degree inherent. The poor fit between the boundaries of states and the boundaries of ecosystems means that individual states cannot effectively manage many of their most serious environmental problems. Most large-scale environmental problems cross national borders; many are tied to global systems such as the atmosphere and oceans, which lie inherently beyond the control of individual states. And yet governments have clung tenaciously to the notion that they retain exclusive authority over activities taking place within their territory that affect the global environment. The primacy of state sovereignty was one of the few points on which governments could agree during the contentious Stockholm Conference:

States have . . . the sovereign right to exploit their own resources pursuant to their own environmental policies, and the responsibility to ensure that activities within their jurisdiction or control do not cause damage to the environment of other states or of areas beyond the limits of their national jurisdiction.[3]

Although this principle refers not only to the sovereign rights of states but also to their responsibilities, it has generally been seen as a reinforcement of state sovereignty. In most instances, states have guarded this right emphatically when pressured by the global community—whether the state in question is a tropical rain-forest country such as Brazil or a leading emitter of greenhouse gases such as the United States.

Thus, the tension between sovereignty and ecology is partly due to the inherent conflict between a world of political borders and a world of ecological interconnectedness. But this fundamental tension is reinforced by the behavior of states, in their reluctance to cede their individual sovereign rights when confronted with global problems. This theme is developed by R. J. Johnston in his discussion of the problems of the global commons. Johnston stresses that a system of sovereign states can only manage global environmental problems effectively if a set of enforceable rules can be developed and implemented through international agreements among governments. Johnston reviews the existing body of international law governing the Earth systems of land, oceans, and atmosphere and finds it to fall far short of the task of planetary environmental management. Johnston's conclusion—that, short of "real progress" in international cooperation, the only alternative may be a global "super-state" with concentrated political authority—harkens back to concerns raised in the previous part by William Ophuls. This view is seen by some to be overly pessimistic about international cooperation and by others to be implausible given the historical limits sovereign governments have imposed on international bodies such as the United Nations.[4] But it does highlight the role that sovereignty, as an aspect of system structure, plays in rendering environmental problems "international" and complicating their resolution.

A second crucial feature of system structure is the existence of an increasingly interconnected capitalist world economy. Economic processes do not respect national borders any more than do ecological realities. This has long been the case for international trade, which predates the founding of the modern state system. Today the pattern of economic interconnectedness established by international trade is being deepened by the increasing mobility in the world economy not only of goods and services but also of money, people, technology, and ideas.[5]

Jim MacNeill, Pieter Winsemius, and Taizo Yakushiji develop the concept of "shadow ecologies" to capture the ecological consequences of this economic interconnectedness. The authors point out that the world's major centers of industrial production and consumption, including the United States, Europe, and Japan, are not "ecologically self-contained." These regions rely upon imports of a wide range of commodities, both as raw materials for production and as food for consumption. As a result, the core industrial regions of the world economy draw upon the "ecological capital" of the places that supply those inputs. The production that takes place in the industrialized world casts an ecological shadow far beyond the borders of individual industrialized countries.

The fact that national economies cast ecological shadows beyond their borders has important consequences. Individual states may exert only a limited degree of control over economic processes occurring within their territories and over the environmental consequences of the processes. Pollution and ecosystem destruction may be driven as much by the workings of these transnational economic processes as by the choices of individual governments or local actors. Governments of the South, for example, have long argued that international debt is one of the principal driving forces behind the accelerating pace of resource depletion and environmental degradation in the Third World.[6]

The ecological shadows cast by individual states in an interdependent world economy make the enforcement of international environmental agreements much more difficult. Even when governments are willing to enforce domestically the rules to which they agree internationally, they may simply be unable to do so in the face of powerful transnational economic pressures.

The transnational character of modern capitalism also raises important questions of responsibility. Who is responsible for the destruction of tropical rain forests when the causes of that destruction range from the chain saws in the hands of local timber cutters to the global economic system that creates demand for tropical timber products?

State sovereignty and transnational capitalism have complex implications for the global environment. As discussed in subsequent chapters of this book, some observers see great potential for these structures to be the foundation for solutions to environmental problems, whereas others see them as root causes. What is clear is that just as state sovereignty imposes a pattern of political authority that does not correspond to the underlying ecological reality, so transnational capitalism imposes patterns of economic activity that do not correspond to the prevailing pattern of political authority. Both features of system structure therefore give environmental problems an inherently international dimension, and both greatly complicate the prospects for global cooperation.

Although analyzing the limits imposed by these global structures is crucial, it is important to remember that these structural properties of world politics are not natural or automatic properties of the international system—they are the result of human choices and behavior. This leads us to the question of how ideas, beliefs, and worldviews give structure to the behavior of the various actors in world politics. Obviously, sovereignty and capitalism are two such ideas that have a powerful structuring influence. But some observers argue that these ideas are themselves embedded in a more fundamental idea of "modernity"—a complex set of beliefs that came to dominate European culture in the modern era and subsequently spread to the Americas, Africa, and Asia via colonialism and other manifestations of European power.[7] Some of the principal ideas that compose the "modern" worldview involve beliefs about the autonomy of the individual, the power of science and technology, the desirability of increased consumption, and the inevitability of progress. Thus, it is possible to speak of an ideological structure of modernity alongside the political structure of state sovereignty and the economic structure of global capitalism.[8]

Dennis Pirages argues that such views lie at the core of contemporary world politics, with important environmental implications. Pirages describes a "dominant social paradigm"—a core set of ideas that shapes our understanding in ways that most people never question. Pirages sees underlying technological and economic forces as creating the dominant social paradigm of any given era. The paradigm in turn legitimizes prevailing technological, economic, political, and social practices. For Pirages the current paradigm is a legacy of the industrial revolution and the era of relative resource abundance in which it occurred. Pirages argues that modern industrial society is trapped within this paradigm, even though the paradigm is increasingly unsuited to a world of resource scarcity and environmental vulnerability. Cracks in the paradigm have begun to appear but have not yet allowed replacement by a new paradigm.

Different observers give different weight to the role of ideas in shaping world politics.[9] Pirages sees the dominant social paradigm as a product of underlying economic and technological processes. But he also argues that once in place, the paradigm exerts an independent influence by making other possibilities much harder to imagine.

Not all actors embrace the dominant social paradigm. Indeed, many environmentalists argue that environmentalism is a rejection of several core features of the dominant paradigm. Is this the case? Does environmentalism transcend the limits of state sovereignty, oppose the unfettered operation of global capitalism, and reject many of the central tenets of the modern world-view? Is it possible that the idea of environmentalism is itself building a new global structure: a network of individuals and groups with an "antisystemic" orientation in the sense that they reject many of the values and preferences of the dominant social paradigm?[10] These questions are hotly debated, both by environmentalists and by their critics. There may be no single answer to this question: The environmental movement consists of a patchwork of groups with widely differing goals and views, working at levels ranging from local to global. If environmentalism is to be effective as an "antisystemic force," it will be because of effective collaboration among these diverse groups, on a global scale. For this reason, we conclude this part with three selections focusing on environmental movements operating in three very different contexts—Brazil, the United States, and Eastern Europe.

In his chapter on U.S. environmentalism, Kirkpatrick Sale directly addresses the question of whether U.S. environmental groups are antisystemic in orientation. In Sale's view, success and growing access to political power have led mainstream U.S. environmental groups to behave less like a social movement and more like an institutionalized Washington lobby. Thus environmentalism stands at a crossroads, facing the choice between the paths of a "reformist citizens' lobby" and a social movement working for "structural changes in the system." The debate over the North American Free Trade Agreement exposed the growing rift in the movement, with most of the reformist-minded groups endorsing the agreement and the more radical groups opposing it.[11]

Environmentalism in Eastern Europe presents a strikingly different pattern. Duncan Fisher describes the important role of environmental protest in helping to topple several of the Communist regimes of Eastern Europe. Although opposition to the prevailing political systems involved far more than simply ecological concerns, environmental groups were an important part of civil society rising up against the totalitarian state in several countries throughout the region. Fisher also discusses the difficulties these groups have encountered in maintaining their political influence after the revolutions. The contrast between the U.S. and Eastern European cases is striking in at least two ways. Much more so than in the United States, environmentalism in Eastern Europe effectively merged with other ideological critiques of the prevailing social system. And much more so than anywhere in Eastern Europe, U.S. environmentalism has proven itself able to translate environmental concerns into an institutionalized force in national politics.

The autobiography of Brazilian activist Chico Mendes further extends our sense of the diversity of environmentalism. Mendes was a labor activist and environmentalist working in the western Amazon state of Acre. He led a movement for the preservation of the Amazon forest and the livelihood of its occupants. Mendes advocated a brand of environmentalism that struggled as much against the oppression of people as the destruction of nature. Mendes was killed in 1988, assassinated by powerful local landowning interests who felt threatened by his efforts to organize rural workers in the region. The chapter by Mendes expresses the powerful vision that made him not only an important political leader of the forest peoples' movement in Brazil but also, in death, a martyr and an international symbol. The outcry following his murder greatly enhanced the pressures on the Brazilian government to reverse policies that accelerated deforestation in the Amazon region.[12]

If a sustained global movement of environmentalism is to emerge and exert political power, it will be because movement groups as different as those described here find a way to establish effective, durable international networks to coordinate efforts, exchange information, and pool resources. The barriers to such cooperation are formidable; they include a lack of resources compared to the activities they oppose, the frequent opposition of governments and other powerful actors, conflicting viewpoints on goals and means, and unequal power between relatively well-heeled and influential groups from the North and some of the less institutionalized, grassroots groups of both the North and the South.[13] Despite these obstacles, there have been examples of effective international cooperation among environmentalists, as in the case of the internationally coordinated campaign to change the environmental practices of the World Bank during the late 1980s (see the chapter by Rich in Part Four). In the long run, the catalytic role of both Stockholm and Rio in fostering greater international cooperation among environmental groups may be a more important legacy of those conferences than any of the solemn promises made by governments.

R. J. JOHNSTON

7

Laws, States & Super-States: International Law & the Environment

THE NEED FOR ENFORCEABLE and enforced rules to regulate individual and corporate behaviour in a wide range of circumstances is generally recognized as one of the rationales for the state in capitalism. Garret Hardin's metaphor of 'the tragedy of the commons' is often used to illustrate this need, with its claim that without 'mutual coercion, mutually agreed upon by the majority of the people affected' (1968: 1247) the population problem, involving increased human pressure on the environment, has no solution. The perceived validity of this case sustains state regulation. Unfortunately, as will be argued here, such regulation is so spatially circumscribed that many environmental problems are very unlikely to be effectively tackled, with potential disastrous consequences. . . .

The focus of this paper is thus on the implications of the division of the earth's surface into a large number of separate containers, each controlled by an independent, sovereign state apparatus, for the regulation of environmental use and the prevention of environmental abuse. Environmental systems operate outside those containers, so their use can only be regulated through international agreement. To date, little of real substance has been achieved via this route . . .

Originally published in *Applied Geography* 12 (1992):211–228, Butterworth Heinemann, Oxford, England. Reprinted with permission.

States, Territories, and Laws

The essence of a state apparatus is its ability to mobilize and to exercise power in four spheres—economic, military, political and ideological—*within a defined territory* over which it claims sovereignty. . . . The crucial characteristic of the state, which both defines it and distinguishes it from any other powerful apparatus in capitalist society, is its territorial definition. . . . The widespread exercise of economic, political, ideological and military power, infiltrating almost all aspects of human life, would be virtually impossible if the state could neither claim nor sustain sovereignty over the territory—and hence the resident population and landowners—within which those powers are exercised. . . .

Environmental processes do not recognize socially created state boundaries. The environment comprises a single, complexly interacting, three-dimensional system of very many parts, and laws designed by a state to control environmental use in one territory cannot prevent actions outside that territory from influencing one or more of its own parts of the system. Control of an international system apparently calls for international law.

International Law

The environment is not the only issue for which the division of the earth's land surface into so many separate states—along with large extra-state areas, such as the oceans and the atmosphere—is a major deterrent to effective social, economic and political activity. Thus states have developed means of cooperating among themselves, in a framework of international law and treaty arrangements for regulating a wide range of activities and for structuring the settlement of disputes.

International law differs from national law because it is neither enacted nor implemented by a separate sovereign state. It is the outcome of cooperating states agreeing to abide by the law, which in some situations may involve them agreeing to both the creation of an international regulatory body, with specified powers that override each state's individual sovereignty, and the submission of disputes to an international body whose decisions will be accepted as binding. Entering such agreements is largely voluntary, except when it is imposed upon a relatively weak state—as with post-war inspections and reparations imposed by victors on the vanquished—or when peer group pressure is sufficient to ensure cooperation. Honouring them is also voluntary, unless either military or political pressure (the latter usually linked to economic measures) is such that individual states cannot stand out against the views of the 'international community'.

The operation of international law is dependent on the willingness of individual states to participate in its creation, implementation and enforcement. Those who control sovereign states will thus evaluate whether it is desirable to enter any treaty or other form of international agreement, and then whether to honour it, according to their interpretation of their own state's self-interest (which may well include the potential political and other difficulties which could be created for it by other states if it does not). In the case of the environment, some states, notably the most powerful (economically, politically and militarily), may neither honour nor even agree to international laws unless there is a coercive super-state . . . which requires that. If, as seems possible, this is an eventuality which certain powerful states are unlikely to agree to, one consequence is the severe threat it would pose to the chances of dealing successfully with impending environmental problems.

Types of International Agreement

Laver (1986) has identified the main features of the two dominant types of 'international law'. *Treaty law* is only binding on the parties involved (the signatory states) and cannot be used against others. Regarding regulation of human activity within environmental systems, therefore, it will only be fully effective if all states are signatories—although treaties accepted by all the states in a region may have a very significant impact on their local environment. . . .

Where treaty law does not apply, either because no treaty exists to cover the matter under dispute or because not all states have signed the currently extant treaty(ies), then *general* (or *customary*) *international law* prevails. Its operation depends on 'custom and practice' so that, according to Akehurst (1977: 38), a state can be deemed subject to the operation of a rule unless it can show 'that it has consistently rejected the rule since the earliest days of the rule's existence: dissent expressed after the rule has become well established is too late to prevent the rule binding the dissenting state', although there may be many difficulties in requiring a state to operate within a rule which it no longer accepts. Much customary general international law has evolved through the increasingly widespread acceptance of 'sensible' rules—as with the control of shipping and air lanes.

Not all territory which comprises the earth's environmental system falls within the sovereign territories of recognized states, which requires accepted rules for the treatment of that extra-territorial component. Both treaty and customary international law treat such territory as belonging to one of three categories. . . .

1. *Res nullius* (RN) comprises territory not currently claimed by any state but which is 'susceptible to appropriation' in principle (Laver 1986: 364): sovereignty is claimable but has not yet been claimed.

2. *Res extra commercium* (REC) comprises territory which is beyond national appropriation, because in both customary and/or treaty international law 'national sovereignty can only be claimed on the basis of reasonable proximity to dry land' (Laver 1986: 364): international law precludes it being claimed as part of a state's territory, but does not preclude it being treated as a 'commons' upon which any state (or national thereof) can 'graze' and thereby exploit the resources there for its own ends.

3. *Res communis humanitatis* (RCH) comprises territory recognized not only as REC but also as the common property of all: not only can sovereignty over the territory not be claimed but the principle of common ownership

implies equity (however defined) in the distribution of the fruits of its resources' exploitation. . . .

The relative status of territories within this classification changes over time.
Almost all of the earth's ocean surface was REC until relatively recently, and states
were not concerned to claim sovereignty there because effective control could be
established over no more than a very narrow strip of coastal water. Part of it was
then redefined as RN, by the conception of *territorial sea* introduced in Part II of
the United Nations Convention on the Law of the Sea (UNCLOS) agreed at
Montego Bay, Jamaica, in December 1982. Neither the UK nor the US signed the
Convention, and the majority of signatory states have not since ratified it, so it is
therefore not in force as international treaty law. . . . By defining the territorial sea
as RN the Convention identified the remaining oceans (that is, those areas beyond
its limits) as REC and not claimable as parts of national sovereign territory. . . .
The Convention proposed the establishment of an International Sea-Bed Authority to oversee the area's exploitation and to organize the international allocation
of the benefits obtained.

The distinction between REC and RCH is crucial. The former defines territory
as closed to a claim of sovereignty by any state but open to all to exploit if they
wish and are able to (that is, as a contemporary commons), whereas the latter defines it as collectively owned by all states (that is, a permanent commons, the returns from which are collectively obtained and distributed). Both require international agreement in order for them to be sustained.

. . .

Types of Commons;
Types of Response to Tragedy

Environmental systems are rarely constrained by international boundaries and
environmental processes cross them unhindered. . . . Good laws in one place can
be nullified by bad ones elsewhere, especially, though not necessarily, in neighbouring states. This may discourage states from enacting environmental legislation—a common reaction to the free-rider problem ('if everybody else is exceed-
ing the speed limit then so will I'). If they are convinced of the need for such
legislation, however, they may be encouraged to campaign for international
agreement.

Is such agreement necessary in the face of environmental processes that do not
respect international boundaries? Addressing this question is facilitated by two
stimulating, seminal articles concerning what Laver (1984, 1986) identifies as not
one but several 'tragedies of the commons', in all of which 'none has a private interest in restraining himself yet, if none does restrain himself, all suffer'. Laver
(1984) identifies three separate solutions to such tragedies.

Privatization of the Commons. . . . At the global scale privatization would involve defining all of the relevant territory as RN and would invite states to claim

sovereignty over it. There would then be potential conflict over a myriad claims, with the powerful states undoubtedly winning in the solutions. It would then be possible for each state to privatize its new territory by granting rights over it in the same way that it now does with its land and water surfaces. . . .

Privatization would not necessarily guarantee a solution to the tragedy of the commons, however, since the private owners could still be free to exploit the territory in such a way as to harm its long-term carrying capacity and to damage the territories of others. Laver suggests that this need not be so, but the evidence under capitalism does not offer his case much sustenance. He, and others, argue that landowners (as against the grazers who exploit commons) will see that it is in their own interests to sustain the fertility and productivity of their land (or water, or air), and so will not over-exploit it. This assumes four things. First, it assumes that they know what the carrying capacity of their territory is; many will not (perhaps cannot), and those who discover it by trial and error will do so only when it has been exceeded and when it may be impossible to return it to its previous condition—once over-exploited, some resources at least can never be regained.

The second assumption is that individuals operate as long-term stewards of their territory's productivity rather than as short-term exploiters for whom the longer-term issues, which may only occur long after their own deaths, are at best of trivial importance only: many land-users will give a much higher priority to reaping an immediate gain than to preserving a resource over a long period if the latter involves taking smaller, even if more regular, gains. Thirdly, it assumes that individuals control their own fates: under capitalist systems many agriculturalists identify no alternative to putting greater pressure on the natural resources that they exploit, in order to maintain their incomes and living standards, let alone enhance them. Finally, the argument assumes that a privatized piece of territory is protected from what happens on all others, when it is not. However well some occupiers may act to sustain the productivity of their territorial resource, the actions of others can readily erode that, because of trans-boundary spillover effects. Thus the tragedy of the commons reappears in a different guise: if others are going to ruin your land for you anyway, then you might as well get the most out of it while you can! . . .

Creation of a Collective Regulation System. This overrides national sovereignty by the construction of a 'super-state' whose laws the individual states agree to adopt and implement, subject to sanctions for non-compliance in the same way that individuals are subject to sanctions for law-breaking within a state.

Development of Self-Regulation Within Communities of States. Under this arrangement all the members agree to accept norms of self-restraint. This would be a form of 'international anarchism': states would all sign and honour international treaties and other agreements, recognizing that such action is in their individual and collective best long-term interests. Such self-regulation programmes have involved a proliferation of ad hoc regulatory agencies with very closely constrained powers. An international arbitration system has also been created, using

the International Court of Justice, but its powers are constrained to specified issues (the ultra vires principle) and it lacks the military, economic, political and
ideological power to impose its judgements. . . .

The environment from which humans currently obtain their livelihood is not
inexhaustible if used in many ways. Land privatization through the enclosure
movement in Britain and the forcible expropriation of common rights in many
other parts of the world has neither prevented irreversible deterioration of the resource nor restricted the spillover effects of actions in one state on another—as
with the examples of acid rain, the destruction of the ozone layer and global
warming. The earth's physical environment operates as one large and extremely
complex interacting system and the whole cannot be protected by handing over a
myriad separate parts to individuals who might exploit them for their own immediate ends, which is what the capitalist dynamic requires them to do with privatized land and related resources.

If privatization is not a viable option, then the choice is between an international super-state (to which all individual states must necessarily be subject) or
collective agreement to impose and respect self-regulation and to agree to this
agreement being monitored and its implementation advanced through some kind
of 'police force'.

International Law and the Terrestrial Environment

Laver concludes his analysis of 'outer' space commons by identifying

> . . . a clear and understandable tendency for the strong to favour anarchy and for the
> weak to favour regulation, reflected in the preference of the space powers for REC
> and the fact that the pressure behind anything vaguely resembling RCH comes from
> the non-space powers. Thus, in the case of the space commons, attempts at an enclo-
> sure movement are likely to remain against the interests of the space powers, who
> have no need for a system of property rights over a resource which is, at present,
> firmly under their control (Laver 1986: 373).

But if anarchy is similarly likely to be the preferred option of the powerful with
regard to terrestrial resources, will that be in the long-term interests of humanity
and environmental conservation? . . .

Laver concludes that RCH is the better way forward in the face of potential environmental tragedies, because the environment is easy of access, relatively scarce
(and increasingly so, with population growth), and exhaustible. The potential
gains from cooperation are thus substantial, though the scope for free-riders is
great, especially if power to exploit the environment is unequally distributed
among states. Thus in a critical attack on proponents of anarchy rather than a
strong state, he writes that:

It is noticeable that those who construct arguments for anarchy tend to draw their examples from situations involving reversible tragedies, particularly those involving the social control of private behaviour. Such situations allow scope for the trial and error that tends to form part of the search for self-regulatory solutions. Arguments for government intervention tend to rely more upon situations involving irreversible tragedies (Laver 1984: 70).

The environment clearly falls into the latter category. But has it been defined as an RCH and have international agreements been reached to protect it from exhaustion and permanent tragedy? The following sections look at each of its main components (land, oceans and atmosphere) in turn, using examples in some of which anarchy prevails and in others attempts have been made to institute an RCH.

The Land

Most land has already been privatized and taken out with the realm of international law through the establishment of virtually universal territorial sovereignty. Within most states, land has then been classified as an item of private property with individual owners having the freedom to use it as they see fit. In many countries, that use has been constrained by land-use planning regulations defined to promote the general good of the population by restricting the owners' freedoms, where such regulation can be demonstrated as a necessary part of a coherent policy and not the result of an 'arbitrary whim' (Johnston 1984). Such constraints are generally fewer in rural than in urban areas, although much effort is increasingly being made in some countries (especially the 'developed') to encourage practices that will both protect the land's productivity and ensure that neighbouring land is not affected (through the transfer of pollutants, for example). Elsewhere, the pressure on users to increase the output from their land exacerbates the long-term trend towards its apparent irreversible exhaustion. Thus privatization, sustained by state sovereignty, is insufficient to protect land, and the capitalist mode of production contains within it powerful forces encouraging its destruction.

The major exception to the privatization of land is Antarctica, where the difficulties of exploitation have so far precluded substantial exploration. There is some hope that an RCH regime might be established. The Antarctic Treaty of 1959 was signed by all of the countries with territorial claims there, and they were later joined by others having the potential capacity to exploit Antarctic resources. It was agreed that Antarctica should be used for peaceful purposes only, with no military presence and freedom of scientific investigation. But the contracting parties did not renounce their claims to territorial sovereignty . . . , and other signatories did not prejudice their recognition or otherwise of such territorial claims. . . .

The Antarctic Treaty, plus its associated Commission for the Conservation of Antarctic Marine Living Resources and the Mineral Resources Commission, suggests that states are prepared to define RCH in certain circumstances and, although not explicitly renouncing territorial sovereignty and associated claims, to allow international treaty law to govern activities within the land area that they occupy and control. But Antarctica is very much a special case, because the costs of exploiting mineral resources there would be very high indeed; as yet the need for them has not been established and the technology required has not been developed. The reluctance of some states to sign the Wellington Convention indicates that an RCH was viewed very much as a 'holding operation' only and that future events may see states withdrawing from the Convention, if not from the Treaty, under the two-year notice rule (Article 65). Eventually Antarctica may be privatized, along with the rest of the earth's land surface, and neither treaty nor customary international law will then apply there.

. . .

The international treaty law regarding Antarctica indicates some willingness among states to come to a collective agreement about an REC, and even to legislate for it as an RCH. In terms of the oversight of that law, however, they have been unwilling to move towards the creation of a collective regulation system overriding national sovereignty. There is no super-state, but rather several sets of procedures for self-regulation. It is an anarchic condition which currently suits all interested parties, but they have retained the right to privatize the territory should they see fit.

The Oceans

Privatization of parts of the oceans has been permitted by international agreement in recent decades, recognizing the increased ability of states to occupy and defend wider areas of sea around their shores. As with the occupancy of land, however, this does not guarantee protection of that resource from exhaustion.

Beyond the now-privatized territorial seas, recent experience with UNCLOS, and in particular the putative 1982 Montego Bay Convention, indicates significant resistance to an RCH. The failure of countries such as the US, the UK and West Germany to sign the Convention, and of any of the 'advanced industrial countries' which were signatories during the period 1982–84 to ratify the Convention afterwards, suggests that those with the economic power to exploit and benefit from the high seas . . . preferred anarchy under an REC regime to an RCH involving an International Sea-Bed Authority. . . .

The unwillingness of certain states, mainly in the 'developed' world, to sign UNCLOS III, and so initiate an RCH regime under the proposed International Sea-Bed Authority, reflects their interest in exploiting the mineral resources of the deep sea beds . . . without 'equitable' sharing of the profits from that exploitation with other countries. . . .

Despite the lack of global agreement on defining the high seas as an RCH, there has been substantial progress on establishing regional international treaty law to protect the sea, especially from pollution from neighbouring states. The UN Environment Programme established a Regional Seas Programme in 1976, administered through its Oceans and Coastal Areas Programme. The first agreement was the Convention for the Protection of the Mediterranean Sea against Pollution (ratified by all relevant states except Turkey and Algeria), to which were added a Protocol for the Prevention of Pollution of the Mediterranean Sea by Dumping from Ships and Aircraft and a Protocol concerning Co-operation in Combating Pollution of the Mediterranean Sea by Oil and Other Harmful Substances in Cases of Emergency. Since 1976, 23 further such conventions and protocols have been agreed, involving more than 100 states.

These regional seas agreements indicate a willingness among states to cooperate where the benefits to all are seen as substantial. The sanctions against violators are relatively weak in most cases, however, and there is certainly no evidence of any yielding, or even potential yielding, of sovereignty as would occur if some form of super-state were to be created. Thus the Protocol for the Protection of the South-East Pacific against Pollution from Land-Based Sources . . . contained an Article referring to 'Obligations', which states merely that 'discharges of the substances listed in Annex II to this Protocol shall be subject to a system of self-monitoring and control' (Rummel-Bulska and Osafo 1991: 140). . . .

The relative weakness of international law in this area is exemplified by the International Convention for the Regulation of Whaling, adopted in 1946 and amended several times thereafter. This required that:

> Each Contracting Government shall take appropriate measures to ensure the application of the provisions of this Convention and the punishment of infractions against the said provisions in operations carried out by vessels under its jurisdiction (Kiss 1983: 63).

Those provisions are very stringent, providing substantial barriers to the harvesting of whales for commercial purposes. In 1984, the Commission determined at its annual meeting to introduce a ban on commercial whaling, effective from May 1985. At the 1991 meeting, it agreed by a majority vote to extend the ban. This was opposed by several major fishing countries—Iceland and Norway—and whereas the latter reserved its position the Icelandic Commissioner indicated that he would recommend against his government continuing its membership of the Commission. . . . Clearly, international regulation may not be acceptable to a country with a substantial economic interest in the activity that the majority of countries wish to regulate, and the latter—unless they are prepared to use political, economic and (even?) military sanctions against the recalcitrants—are relatively powerless.

The Atmosphere

The atmosphere has long been both privatized and subject to international agreement for the perceived good of all with regard to the safety of airborne travellers and for the defence of national territory. This is feasible because transgression of defined national air space can be identified by most countries and countered by their own forces.

Most movement of substances through the atmosphere cannot be readily controlled and, if necessary, halted, even though it may be tracked. Emissions into the air in one state are subject to the laws of atmospheric motion: they may become pollutants in the air above another state, and thence in the water that falls on it, or they may contribute to the deterioration of the atmosphere globally, with consequences for environmental quality everywhere. Increased awareness of the latter possibility, through, for example, the appreciation of the destruction of the ozone layer over Antarctica and the growing scientific belief that human activity is stimulating global warming and inducing a 'greenhouse effect', has led to calls for international treaties that will in effect declare the atmosphere an RCH. . . .

. . .

There is . . . little willingness among states to relinquish sovereignty over what is done to the atmosphere above their territories. The international treaties have only weak teeth, and while the nature of the problems of air pollution and ozone layer depletion may have been recognized, there is little evidence of determination to remove them—let alone remove them rapidly—except through relatively anarchistic forms of self-regulation and the power of political persuasion. It is accepted that anarchy is probably insufficient to protect the exhaustible resource of the atmosphere but the yielding of state sovereignty to international control has yet to occur.

Conclusions

There is a widespread belief that in order to tackle the potential environmental tragedies of which we are increasingly aware then 'the state will have to do something about it'. . . . Such state action is difficult, if not impossible, to achieve at present, because no state controls the land, sea and atmospheric resources. Sovereignty over these is divided among a large number of states, which differ in their economic power and their willingness to enter into binding international treaties, with which are associated both sanctions and institutions which can impose them. Anarchy thus rules: most states are prepared to enter international agreements when they are in their interests (or not against their interests—or, really, those of powerful economic groups within their territories), but not to establish bodies with powers over their nationals and their interests. (The main exception to this is the European Community, to which some at least want to transfer a substantial proportion of the sovereignty currently resting with its . . . individual member states, but the main rationale of that transfer of power is not environmental control.) . . .

Individual states can do much to regulate the use of land, water and air within their territories and so contribute to protecting the global environment; many are doing so, at an increasing rate, responding to citizen pressures in many cases, as are many commercial companies. But, as is typical of so much within capitalism, the pursuit by states of individual self-interests . . . is consistent with neither their long-term individual self-interests nor the collective interests of humanity.

In his classic study of sovereign power, Hobbes concluded that if individuals were to avoid lives that were 'solitary, poore, nasty, brutish, and short' (1651: 41) they would have to give up certain freedoms, which they would do so long as all others did too. More recently, Olson (1965: 2) concluded that 'rational self-interested individuals will not act to achieve their common or group interests', and need a coercive power to assist them to realize their goals. Rational individuals will recognize and accept the need for that power, he claims. Our current understanding of the global environmental system and the tragedies it faces (exaggerated many times over by our interference in those systems) is surely a clear example of the need for further yielding of individual state power to a super (or global) state, without which Hobbes's diagnosis of lives that are 'nasty, brutish and short' may well soon come to pass. As yet, however, as has been argued here, there is little evidence of that need being recognized.

Such recognition requires a clear acceptance of the importance of the spatial perspective to an appreciation of the potential for various 'solutions' to environmental problems. Most of these problems are not going to be resolved either by privatization or by small-scale collective self-regulation. The systems to which they refer are global in their operation, and no pollution (including destruction as the ultimate pollution) of the land, the ocean, or the atmospheric component of the environmental system will not eventually affect both other parts of the same component and elements of one or both of the others. Small-scale solutions to small-scale problems are good and desirable, but insufficient, and large-scale problems need to be tackled at large scales.

Tackling large-scale problems at large scales is very substantially hampered by another 'spatial reality'. The world is divided into a large number of independent territorial containers, which we call states. Each is sovereign over its own territory, and tackling the world's environmental problems involves some (probably very considerable) yielding of that sovereignty in order to ensure practices which will protect the environment and sustain its productivity. The creation—or part-creation—of nascent federations such as the EC suggests some willingness to accept that necessity, but there is still a long way to go before a comprehensive international regime is established.

Finally, there are parts of the environmental system which are outside that set of territorial containers, some of which (notably parts of the atmosphere) will probably never come within it. This forms a further arena for international collaboration, for states to agree that enforceable and enforced agreements to treat such resources as the property of humankind, to be exploited and protected for everybody's benefit, are necessary for long-term human survival.

The problems posed in this paper are large, and the apparent solution—an international state, or 'Leviathan-writ-large'—contains within it many dangers of an overweening power. . . . The implicit conclusion here is that, unless real progress can be achieved through international treaties soon, such an overween-ing state may be the only salvation for the environment and for humanity. . . .

References

Akehurst, M. (1977) *A Modern Introduction to International Law* (3rd ed.). London: George Allen and Unwin.

Hardin, G. (1968) The tragedy of the commons: the population problem has no technical solution; it requires a fundamental extension in morality. *Science,* 162, 1243–1268.

Hobbes, T. (1651) *Leviathan.* Harmondsworth: Penguin (1968 ed.).

Johnston, R. J. (1984) *Residential Segregation, the State and Constitutional Conflict in American Urban Areas.* London: Academic Press.

Kiss, A. C. (ed.) (1983) *Selected Multilateral Treaties in the Field of the Environment.* Nairobi: United Nations Environment Programme.

Laver, M. (1984) The Politics of Inner Space: Tragedies of Three Commons. *European Journal of Political Research,* 12, 59–71.

Laver, M. (1986) Public, Private and Common in Outer Space. *Political Studies,* 34, 359–373.

Olson, M. (1965) *The Logic of Collective Action.* Cambridge, MA: Harvard University Press.

Rummel-Bulska, I., and Osafo, S. (eds.) (1991) *Selected Multilateral Treaties in the Field of the Environment, Volume 2.* Cambridge: Grotius Publications.

JIM MACNEILL, PIETER WINSEMIUS

& TAIZO YAKUSHIJI

8

The Shadow Ecologies of Western Economies

MANY NATIONS, BOTH INDUSTRIAL and developing, impose large burdens on the earth's environmental systems. Some do so through wealth, some through poverty; some through large and rapidly growing populations, others through high and rapidly growing levels of consumption of environmental resources per capita. The aggregate impact of any community on the environment can usefully be thought of as the product of three factors: its population, its consumption or economic activity per capita, and its material or energy flow per unit of economic activity. . . . A nation can therefore impose a heavy burden on the environment through any combination of high population growth, high consumption, and the inefficient use of materials and energy.

This simple formulation is complicated by one major factor: the environment and resource content of trade between nations. Economic activity today is concentrated in the world's urban/industrial regions. Few, if any, of these regions are ecologically self-contained. They breathe, drink, feed, and work on the ecological capital of their "hinterland," which also receives their accumulated wastes. At one time, the ecological hinterland of a community was confined to the areas immediately surrounding it, and that may still be true of some rural communities in developing countries. Today, however, the major urban/industrial centers of the world are locked into complex international networks for trade in goods and services of all kinds, including primary and processed energy, food, materials, and other resources. The major cities of the economically powerful Western nations constitute the nodes of these networks, enabling these nations to draw upon the ecological capital of all other nations to provide food for their populations, energy and materials for their economies, and even land, air, and water to assimilate their waste by-products. This ecological capital, which may be found thousands of miles from the regions in which it is used, forms the "shadow ecology" of an economy. The oceans, the atmosphere (climate), and other "commons" also form part of this shadow ecology. In essence, the ecological shadow of a country is the environmental resources it draws from other countries and the global commons.[13] If a nation without much geographical resilience had to do without its shadow ecology, even for a short period, its people and economy would suffocate.

Third World economies seek to be drawn into these trading networks. It is the only way they can hope to attract the investment and technologies needed to develop and trade in world markets. But participation in such networks is a two-edged sword. The economies of most developing countries (and parts of many industrialized countries) are based on their natural resources. . . . Their soils, forests, fisheries, species, and waters make up their principal stocks of economic capital. The overexploitation and depletion of these stocks can provide developing countries with financial gains in the very short term, but can also result in a steady reduction of their economic potential over the medium and long term.[14]

Western nations heavily engaged in global sourcing should be aware of their shadow ecologies and the need to pursue policies that will sustain them. Some countries, of course, are more dependent on them than others. Japan is a case in point. Being a resource-poor country, the world's second largest economy has to import most of its energy and renewable resources as raw materials and export them as finished products. Japan's vast population also depends on access to its shadow ecology. Seventy percent of all cereal (corn, wheat, and barley) consumption and 95 percent of soybean consumption are supplied from abroad. Poor crop yields in exporting countries due to environmental degradation or bad weather could have a grave impact on Japan's food supplies. Japanese imports of round-woods account for one-third of the world total, and more than 50 percent of Japanese consumption is supplied from abroad. . . .

Japan's vulnerability to the effects of global environmental change is not limited to the outsourcing of basic materials; it is also found in the exports of finished products. Nearly 30 percent of Japan's export income is earned by the sale of automobiles, the use of which depends on the availability of sufficient ecological space to handle their waste emissions, especially air pollution, in the cities and towns that form their principal markets. The fact that Japan's automobiles have been more energy and environmentally efficient than those of its competitors has had much to do with their success in export markets. The margin, however, is growing smaller, partly because Japanese firms have begun to produce and export more large, high-consumption automobiles. This should concern the Japanese government. If environment can be used to justify controls on imports of food-stuffs, it can also be used to justify controls on imports of automobiles. Japan must remain sensitive to global environmental trends, lest its exports be limited by stringent measures to protect the "ecological space" available in foreign markets. The same is true of other countries.

. . . These dependencies are large and growing and they apply to North America and Europe as well as to Japan. The figures on exports and imports reveal that the dependencies are also reciprocal. The environment and resource content of trade flows, which is usually hidden in the trade figures, is increased by the global reach of domestic policies, especially policies to increase trade. The agencies that make decisions on trade policies, however, are usually unaware of, and unresponsive to, their environmental connections. Trade in agriculture, energy, forestry, and a range of industrial products suffers from government interventions that are designed to distort markets in ways that protect domestic producers and give exporters an unfair advantage. But, as noted earlier, they also destroy the ecological capital on which prospects for future trade and economic prosperity depend.

Trade in tropical timbers provides a good example. Some industrialized countries impose levies that favor the importation of raw logs rather than processed products from tropical countries. They thus gain the value-added in processing the logs. As a result, the countries exporting the logs, usually developing countries, have to cut far more forest than they otherwise would in order to earn the foreign exchange that they need for development. This overexploitation now threatens the trade itself. Export revenues from tropical timber have been falling for years and are now worth about $8 billion. They are expected to continue to fall to $2 billion by the turn of the century because the resource is simply disappearing.[15] Even the industry concerned now agrees that the trade policies and domestic incentive frameworks which govern the exploitation and trade in tropical forests must be changed. In 1986 a commodity agreement was ratified that incorporated a specific commitment by governments and industry to invest in measures to sustain the growth and production of the forests being traded. It was the first international agreement that attempted to employ novel funding arrangements to address a global issue by bridging the concerns of the importing nations, mainly in the North, and the exporting nations, mainly in the South. The International Tropical Timber Organization (ITTO), based in Yokohama, Japan, was established to implement the agreement, but it is much too early to say whether it will work.

DENNIS PIRAGES

9
Global Technopolitics

. . .

Technology, Revolutions, and Social Paradigms

MANY SCHOLARS INTERPRET the last decades of the twentieth century as a departure from established patterns of social evolution and the beginning of a period of revolutionary change in mature industrial societies.[27] The term *revolution* has a myriad of meanings and is often used loosely. Here it refers to large-scale discontinuities in the structural and value realms of societies. There have been only two such major revolutionary transformations in world history that have impacted the majority of the earth's population. The first large-scale revolutionary transformation of human culture was the agricultural revolution, which apparently began simultaneously in several different places in the Middle East around 8000 B.C. and then subsequently spread slowly outward to the rest of the world. The second was the industrial revolution, which began to gather momentum in the fifteenth and sixteenth centuries in Western Europe and is currently spreading spasmodically to the more remote areas of the world.

Both of these previous revolutions were driven by significant technological innovations and related ecological changes, which created social surplus, or capital over and above what was needed for subsistence.[28] The agricultural revolution was initially driven by innovations in farming that permitted humans to exploit nature more efficiently. These innovations included domestication of plants and animals, and they provided social surplus resulting in enhanced diets, more dependable food supplies, and more sedentary populations. . . . The agricultural revolution eventually produced enough surplus in some countries to support military castes and organized warfare and culminated in the development of several large empires.

The industrial revolution gained much of its impetus from technological innovations that utilized fossil fuels—coal, petroleum, and natural gas—to do the work previously done by human beings and draft animals. This second revolution, which now has moved into advanced stages in much of the world, originally produced social surplus of unprecedented magnitude by enhancing human productivity through a much more intricate division of labor feeding on a generous natural subsidy stored in coal, petroleum, and eventually natural gas.[29] New political, economic, and social institutions were shaped by these technological changes as significant social surplus permitted unprecedented social and political change. . . .

The tumultuous events of the last twenty years are evidence that resource dislocations are pushing and new technologies are pulling the world into a third revolutionary period. But unlike the previous two revolutions, which swept aside tradition on the strength of new technologies and related economic benefits, as yet no positive vision has been articulated by advocates of a new way of life. Thus, the industrial countries seem caught between two ages, experiencing the economic stagnation and political uncertainty brought on by the worldwide slowing of industrial growth while not having yet developed a positive vision and related values appropriate for a new age.

The mental product of these revolutions and related long periods of social evolution, generations of human learning experiences translated into social survival rules, can be called a dominant social paradigm (DSP).[30] These survival rules—individual beliefs, ideas, and values transferred from one generation to the next—are carried as part of the larger culture and transmitted through socialization processes. During normal times of slow change, only simple maintenance learning is required to sustain a dominant social paradigm. Indeed, in the absence of perceived threats to the established ways of doing things, it is very difficult to avoid problems of social stagnation. The industrial paradigm or world view has been shaped by generations of material-intensive economic growth and seemingly gives technological optimists a recipe for future success. But just as natural selection in the biological realm cannot anticipate future environments— witness the fate of the unfortunate dinosaur—the cumulative survival information contained in the present dominant industrial paradigmmay not give relevant guidance for coping with the turmoil of a post-industrial transformation.

. . .

Cracks in the Industrial Paradigm

Change in dominant social paradigms can be slow or rapid, destructive or constructive, minor or major, depending on the rate at which failures and anomalies mount up and the ability of leaders to respond with appropriate policies. Over the course of the industrial period, constant small changes have taken place within the overriding world view that now defines the industrial DSP. But in the last two decades of the twentieth century, considerable evidence is mounting to indicate that the paradigm currently prescribing and shaping behavior within and among nations is not providing adequate guidance for coping with rapidly changing technological and environmental realities.

The current cracks in the industrial paradigm are not easily noticed, because in the early stages of a paradigm shift it is difficult for people caught up in it to realize that a transition is taking place. But such periods are detectable, because they are times when old rules no longer seem to apply and conventional explanations for mounting anomalies no longer make sense. Under such conditions of uncertainty, individuals may return to old ideologies, authority figures, and religious practices in a desperate attempt to cope with an increasingly unexplainable and threatening world. . . .

Harman has suggested four key dilemmas or anomalies within the industrial paradigm that cannot be resolved without a major system transformation.[35] The *growth dilemma* has developed because economic expectations associated with the industrial paradigm require continued rapid growth in material consumption, while on a planetary scale it is impossible to live with the consequences. The *control dilemma* results from a need for more government capacity to control techno-ecological change at the same time that social values portray such control as evil and a brake on progress. The *distribution dilemma* revolves around a growing need for wealthy individuals and nations to develop mechanisms to help those less fortunate while in reality the rich attempt to insulate themselves from the rising expectations among the growing numbers of the world's poor by building walls around their spheres of prosperity. Finally, a *work roles dilemma* results from the fact that not enough industrial jobs can be created to keep unemployment low and meet the expectations of future generations. Harman links these four dilemmas to the emergence of a new scarcity. Old scarcities involved shortages of things needed to meet basic human needs and were overcome by developing new technologies and using more land and resources. The new shortages, however, result from ecological scarcity, approaching technological and resource limits to growth on a planetary scale.[36]

Manifestations of the politics of new scarcity and the approach of ecological limits have been obvious in international relations over the last two decades. The twin oil crises of 1973–74 and 1979–80 and subsequent events in the Persian Gulf have called attention to the longer-term problem of petroleum and natural gas depletion as well as the more immediate problem of reserve location. The food and basic commodity crises of the mid-1970s indicated how rapidly an overheated global economy can exhaust resource inventories and drive up prices. The food crises in Africa in the 1980s highlighted the anomaly of a world in which farmers in industrialized countries hold land out of production while millions starve for lack of food. The global recession, debt crisis, and stock market crash of the 1980s stressed the interdependence of capital markets and the need for careful management of surplus (capital) available for investment on a global scale. . . .

These and many related assessments of the acute problems of advanced industrial societies could well indicate that the industrial revolution has now peaked and that a "third wave," or high-tech revolution focusing on telecommunications, biotechnologies, and information processing, is now under way.[41]

. . .

Theoretical Paradigms in International Relations

Scholarly analysis of international relations has developed within and therefore is difficult to separate from the dominant social paradigm of industrial societies. International relations theory has been very much influenced by a Western industrial world view that is closely related to more general developments in the behavioral and social sciences. Theories, concepts and research are dominated by an exclusionist view of the world that may well lend itself to inappropriate interpretations of current trends and events.

The history of international relations as a discipline, or subdiscipline, has been characterized by a search for a unifying scholarly paradigm. The most commonly accepted explanatory framework within the field is an exclusionist, state-centered, power-politics view of reality. It is firmly anchored in explanations originating in the structural and value domains and depicts nations as frequently in conflict because leaders cannot refrain from attempting to exercise their power within the international hierarchy. According to this view, these industrial-paradigm political "realists" aggressively pursue short-term national interests leading to inevitable conflicts among the nations making up the international system.

Mansbach and Vasquez have characterized the essentials of this exclusionist, state-centered paradigm as follows.

1. Nation-states and/or key decision makers and their motives are the starting point in accounting for international political behavior.

2. Political life is bifurcated into domestic and international spheres, each subject to its own characteristic traits and laws.

3. International relations can be most usefully analyzed as a struggle for power. This struggle constitutes the major issue occurring in a single system and entails a ceaseless and repetitive competition for the single stake of power. Understanding how and why that struggle occurs and suggesting ways for regulating it is the purpose of the discipline.[51]

... These basic ideas have guided generations of international relations scholars and provided policy prescriptions or ideological justifications for political leaders as diverse as Joseph Stalin and Ronald Reagan. The inadequacies of this framework are found in its exclusionist nature, which stresses the autonomy of decision makers and limits causal explanations to leaders and their motives. It assumes that leaders operate in a vacuum rather than an environment of pressures and issues shaped by technological and ecological change. Its basic weaknesses have been illuminated, over time, by numerous scholars, who have contributed pieces of a possible new explanatory paradigm to replace the one now in a state of decay.[53]

The emphasis in this book is on building an inclusionist approach to the theory and practice of international relations that could provide the glue needed to hold many of these new ideas together. . . . Nations are viewed as organized human populations coping with physical laws and resource requirements similar to those confronting other species. Nations compete and cooperate within a system composed of a physical ecosphere, a structured set of practices and rules referred to as the international political economy, and an ideological realm characterized by value conflicts among proponents of different organizational methods. How well nations perform is primarily a function of the ways that they organize internally and the domestic and international policies that they choose to deal with nature's challenges and the imperatives of technology.

Global technopolitics, then, refers to the dynamics of an emerging post-industrial international system increasingly driven by the imperatives of technology. It is different from the expansionist system of the industrial period in a number of ways. There is now no country clearly in charge of maintaining order and prescribing rules of conduct within the international system. The former hegemony of the United States has been repeatedly challenged in different ways by Western Europe, Japan, the Soviet Union, newly industrializing countries such as Korea and Taiwan, and more recently by coalitions of less developed countries. . . .

This contemporary period of transition to a post-industrial international system is not unexpectedly beset with crises: a food and raw materials crisis, two energy crises, a protracted world debt crisis, and a collapse of world economic confidence. . . . Thus, the nature and exercise of power are changing dramatically as "low politics" economic, ethical, and ecological concerns are replacing "high politics" issues involving potential use of military force. . . .

KIRKPATRICK SALE

10
The Green Revolution:
The American Environmental
Movement, 1962–1992

Prospects

...ASSESSING ENVIRONMENTALISM after its first three decades—and considering where it might be heading in the foreseeable future—is a task of great complexity, not only because the movement is so extensive and protean but because there are inter-twined victories and defeats, steps back and steps forward, campaigns successful and strategies not. But there are some measures that can be taken, some signposts that can indicate how much of the road has been traveled and how much is still to come.

o   o   o

To begin with, it is only right to restate the considerable achievements. Within the space of a single generation, environmentalism has become embedded in American life, in law and custom, text and image, classroom and workplace, prac-tice and consciousness, in such a way that suggests that, far from eventually fading away, it will continue to grow, in numbers and impact alike, at least for some time to come. It is embedded in national legislative and administrative institutions—most strikingly the Environmental Protection Act of 1969, the Clean Air and Clean Water acts, and the Endangered Species Act of 1974, all of which have been responsible for regulations now estimated to cost the society $125 billion a year—and in fundamental judicial decisions giving the environmental viewpoint legal standing in countless arenas of public life. It is embedded in the acts of individuals, from schoolchildren to CEOs, in the functions of communities, from villages to block organizations, in the performance of governments, from city water departments to national administrations. It is embedded in political life, where it is both an electoral and nonelectoral force, in economic life, where it now affects billions of dollars' worth of decisions each year, in cultural life, where it is a daily part of journalism, publishing, education, and the arts, and in social life, where it affects habits, vacations, clothing, food, travel, even friendships.

Along with this embedding have come certain home truths, by now well-nigh inescapable. Citizens of the United States (and most other nations) are understood to be vitally concerned about the quality of their physical world, ranging all the way from the importance of clean water, air and food to the sanctity of wilderness and diverse species. Governments at all levels, from local to global, are seen as having a vital role in the protection and preservation of the environment, taken in the very broadest sense, even if this means some impositions on corporate and private behavior. Laws and regulations to carry out that role are regarded as a necessary and proper part of civic life, however inexact and burdensome they may be, and in some sense it can be said that there are even environmental rights of citizens to certain basic natural amenities. Global and national security is threatened by the continuation of ecological abuse and ignorance—including increases in world population, atmospheric alteration, and industrial toxicity—far more than by traditional national and ethnic enmities, and nations have a requirement in some way to address this new reality. Industrial society itself, in both its capitalist and state-socialist variations, both North and South, is a source of much of the eco-peril with its demands for growth, development, consumption, resource exploitation, and progress, as disasters from Bhopal to Chernobyl have made clear. And the stakes are known now to be of the very highest: either the continuing sustenance of the biosphere at virtually every point, on which the fate of the human species inescapably depends, or the destruction of this fragile realm, this earth.

◐   ◐   ◐

Next—and crucial for understanding the future as well as the past—one must consider the shortcomings of environmentalism. Beyond the particular battles lost or crises continuing, there are three general problems, all endemic to the process of social change in America, no doubt, but not the less serious for being familiar.

The first might be called structural. The people in the important mainstream organizations are very largely white and very largely well-off, the more so as you move from membership to board of directors, and there very largely male as well. Whether charges of "racism" and "elitism" against them are quite fair—and those have been leveled with some frequency since the eighties—it is true that their concerns have tended to mirror those of the white suburban well-to-do constituencies and that the kinds of people who have been attracted to the staffs have tended to be college graduates, often professionals, and of the same general milieu as the people they deal with in legislatures and boardrooms. Both because American environmentalism came from a traditional conservationism little concerned with urban problems and because it seemed to ignore immediate social justice issues, very few nonwhites were much interested in it as a primary campaign or have signed on with environmental staffs. (*Audubon* reported in 1991 that Audubon itself had 35 nonwhites in a work force of 320, only 13 in professional positions, the National Wildlife Federation 19 of 283 people in professional jobs, and the Wilderness Society 4 among 80.) This in turn has tended to make these organizations slow to take on certain urban issues (incineration, lead poisoning) even when manifestly environmental—Lois Gibbs started her Citizens' Clearinghouse for Hazardous Wastes in part because she couldn't interest mainstream groups in the Love Canal scandal in 1978—and slow to demand attention to such rural issues as pesticide application and uranium mining that primarily affect people of color.

Along with this has been a practice in some parts of the movement of working with and accepting money from corporate America that seems to compromise its loftier ideals, whether or not this is compensated for by "pragmatic" working arrangements or increased research and lobbying budgets. Though corporate funding is said to be less than 5 percent of most of the organizational budgets, and nowhere more than a fifth, the sources can be somewhat unpleasant: General Electric and Waste Management as donors to Audubon and NWF, oil majors including Amoco, Exxon, and Mobil to Audubon, NWF, and World Wildlife, chemical giants like Dow, Du Pont, and Monsanto to those same three and others. The effects of such bedfellowism are no doubt mixed, but some have raised questions of co-optation and diversion—"We think it dilutes the message," Greenpeace says—and it is hard to imagine that such important donors do not have at least some political influence, however hotly denied, on their beneficiaries.

A second shortcoming can be called institutional, a function of success, and rather neatly exemplified by the Audubon Society in the purposeful new style it chose for itself in early 1991. Already at half a million members, it decided to aim for 1.2 million within five years ("To increase our effectiveness," said president Peter Berle), to broaden its interests from birds and bird habitat to more "people-oriented" issues like toxic wastes and population control, and to become one of the important actors in "bringing about change through the government process." All well and good, but the inevitable trouble with such growth is that, as a *Newsweek* analysis of Audubon put it, it muddies "whatever purity of purpose it once had and, paradoxically, whatever effectiveness it craves"; also, when the organizational identities are thus blurred, style and image become all-important "because when it comes to substance, the groups have become as indistinguishable as sparrows." Moreover, organizations of such size seem to solidify into hierarchy and centralization, becoming "so big, so top-heavy, that to keep the apparatus running they have in many ways become like the institutions they battle." Half a million members there might be, but they had almost no voice in the operations of the New York headquarters, and there was no necessary accountability to them other than occasional reports in the monthly magazine; priorities and policies thus come to be set by the few professionals, with the danger that they are based "on their fundraising campaigns," as one Washington insider said, rather than on important immediate issues.

Nor was Audubon distinctive in this: similar charges were leveled in this period against much of the mainstream movement, particularly the "Beltway biggies" in Washington. Sierra Club activists dissatisfied with their organization's compromises and collaboration even formed a dissident group, the Association of Sierra Club Members for Environmental Ethics, which picketed the national board of directors at their annual meeting in 1991. As one disgruntled member of the new group summed it up: "They've all become just like Queen Victoria—old, fat, and unimaginative."

The third deficiency is, for want of a better word, ideological. By and large both the mainstream majors and the grass-roots NIMBYs [Editors' note: NIMBY stands for "Not in My Backyard"] tend to see environmental problems as isolated aberrations within a functioning system, correctable by regulation and enforcement, and not as inevitable by-products of an economic system based on the imperative of growth and the exploitation of resources, and governments designed to protect it. This means that they tend to confine themselves to piecemeal reforms rather than structural changes and to isolate such problems and their solutions from what might be called a political context. In practical terms, it means concern for the siting of toxic-waste dumps rather than halting the production of toxics, the advocacy of neighborhood recycling centers rather than the vast reduction of packaging, the writing of pollution-control regulations without changing the bureaucracy that failed to carry out the old ones, the campaign to make cars energy-efficient instead of reducing their numbers by millions, to cite a few examples. It means that the great hopes expressed on Earth Day 1990, borne on the rhetoric of how serious the crises are, how urgent the solutions, how committed the homemakers, workers, politicians, and executives, simply cannot be realized within the context of existing norms and givens.

True it is that this is entirely in the American grain, in which special-interest lobbying and electoral lesser-evil-ism are the characteristic ways that hard and serious issues get handled; true, too, that this is entirely characteristic of the American public, which tends by and large not to understand events in a political context or see individual problems as evidence of a failure in the system. But it is also true that this inevitably condemns the environmental movement to a kind of perpetual tinkerism and finger-in-the-dike-ism, a never-ending record of defeats mixed with victories and of victories that are always provisional insofar as they do not alter the values of the prevailing system.

Of course, radical environmentalism, or at least the best of it, does have the various ideological perspectives that allow it to see the perils of reformism, and the need for systemic and structural change, but it, too, is not without problems. In addition to the factionalism endemic to the faithful, it has yet to discover a way to influence the complacent core of the American public except momentarily or to avoid relegation to those fringes of political life where it can be ignored, co-opted, or suppressed. And obviously the more it raises questions about the underlying values of the American system behind the environmental crises, or the civilization on which it rests, the more it is certain to be resisted, in the short run if not the long.

Thus the shortcomings of a movement, even as it became entrenched in the American landscape as few such movements before.

❂   ❂   ❂

To gauge the future of such a movement adequately it is finally necessary to suggest at least the considerable forces ranged against it: an indication of its success, no doubt, but also an indication of its difficulties.

The backlash against environmentalism was naturally initiated by the corporations that had most to lose by its successes. Initially the tactics were essentially duplicates of those of the environmental groups themselves—political lobbying and public relations—in what was estimated in 1990 to be about a $500-million-a-year operation, behind such deceptive and well-funded fronts as the National Wetlands Coalition (oil drillers and developers) and the U.S. Council on Energy Awareness (the nuclear power industry). In the mid-eighties the mass-mail fundraising technique was added, with one such outfit, a direct-mail marketer in Bellevue, Washington, claiming to raise more than half a million dollars a year using the environmental movement as "the perfect bogeyman." Then, in November 1991, 125 business groups and fronts organized under a single flag as the Alliance for America, heavily funded by timber cutters, oil drillers, ranchers, and other anti-environmental corporations who aim, in the words of its chief ideologue, Ron Arnold, "to destroy environmentalists by taking their money and their members." "The tables have turned," says Mary Bernhard of the U.S. Chamber of Commerce, "and there's a renewed commitment now on the part of the business community to be more 'pro-active'" and to "turn things against" the environmental movement.

Where such legitimate efforts have proved inadequate, at least some corporations have turned to tougher tactics, encouraged by such prominent conservatives as former Interior Secretary Watt, who publicly declared in 1990 that "if the troubles from environmentalists cannot be solved in the jury box or at the ballot box, perhaps the cartridge box should be used." Environmental activists coast to coast have reported enough specific examples of violence targeted against them—offices trashed, cars smashed, homes entered, death threats, the home of a Greenpeace researcher burned in Arkansas, the office of a National Toxics Campaign worker burgled in Denver, two Earth First! workers firebombed in California—to leave no doubt that some kind of concerted private crusade was being waged, and at high stakes. One of the most egregious examples surfaced in late 1991 when a congressional committee discovered that the corporate managers of the Trans-Alaska pipeline paid hundreds of thousands of dollars for a nationwide hunt to find and silence critics of the Alaska oil industry—complete with eavesdropping, theft, surveillance, sting operations, and conspiracy—and harassed its own employees to cover up leaks about its environmental and safety errors. "It seems to me to be a very dangerous trend," said Representative George Miller, whose committee exposed the plot.

Corporations often seem to have had a helping hand in their operations from various governmental agencies, and according to investigator Chip Berlet in *The Humanist*, "tactics used to harass activists include obvious surveillance, intimidation, anonymous letters, phony leaflets, telephone threats, police overreaction and brutality, dubious arrests, and other threatening actions." The FBI has targeted environmentalists as legitimate prey, particularly those connected with Earth First!: in addition to the $2 million undercover operation against Dave Foreman and others in Arizona (which ended in a harsh plea bargain in 1991), it cooperated with local police in actions against EF!'s Redwood Summer in 1990 and has regularly visited and harassed EF! activists across the country. The EPA itself has also had a hand in curtailing critics: after a group of environmentalists demonstrated against an EPA-approved incinerator in California, the agency circulated videotapes of the action and forwarded a copy to police in a Phoenix suburb who used it to target the same protesters at an incinerator hearing there, arresting them forcibly and without provocation in the hearing room.

None of this backlash—"in full swing" as of 1992, according to one scholar—has so far derailed the environmental train, but it has undoubtedly taken a toll, particularly among the more radical groups and particularly at the local level. One activist in Fort Bragg, California, who has been vocal against the logging practices of Georgia Pacific, says that a company boycott of her day-care center forced it to close; an anti-toxic worker, harassed by thefts and mysterious power outages, says that with all this "something weird" going on, "we can't build a mass-based movement." Some Earth First!ers have decided to lie low after FBI visits and telephone death threats, and the mood at the EF! national rally in 1991 was said to have been decidedly "paranoid and prickly," according to one participant. There are no signs that environmental activism is waning, even among local groups, but according to one Washington group that monitors reports of environmental harassment, there is a new sense abroad that "the stakes are higher."

●   ●   ●

Ultimately it seems that the prospects of the U.S. environmental movement, after its initial decades of expansion and embeddedness, will depend on just how profound and sweeping a role it sees for itself in the face of the environmental paradox.

It can, on the one hand, continue to operate largely as a reformist citizens' lobby, pressured on the fringes by more radical groups but for the most part willing to work within the system and reap the victories, and rewards, therein. In this role it is likely to put increasing emphasis on scientific breakthroughs and technofixes—Amory Lovins's low-energy light bulbs, hydrogen fuels, photovoltaics, pollution-free coal, deep-ocean waste dumping—and press for a greater proportion of both corporate and government money to be given to environmental research and development. It is apt to make much more of the power of tax policies in changing damaging ecological practices—pollution taxes, for example, as advocated by the Worldwatch Institute, or property taxes tied to corporate environmental performance, as in Louisiana—or starkly new budget priorities to advance the environmentally benign and retard the environmentally destructive. And it is likely also to champion "green power" in the marketplace in new and more extensive ways, such as the Green Seal and Green Cross product-approval ratings, authoritative (perhaps government) "green-labeling" of foods and products, increased pressure on consumer-product industries (particularly for recycled and recyclable goods and packages), and corporate ethics pledges (like the Valdez Principles set up in September 1989) of voluntary environmental good behavior. Wilderness issues will almost certainly remain secondary, except for tropical rainforest protection and the occasional fight over one West Coast timber operation or another.

Or the movement can, on the other hand, deepen and darken its analyses and criticisms, following the lead of the more serious of the radical environmentalists, and try to work for structural changes in the system, with more rapidity or less as the needs arise. In this role it would likely keep up pressure on corporate and bureaucratic malefactors in the Earth First! and Rainforest Action Network style, and might well devote resources toward a strong Green Party that could make an electoral third-party challenge as serious as those in parts of Europe. But its primary emphasis would no doubt be extracorporative and extraparliamentary, aiming to change public opinion in as broad a manner as possible, from weighty tome to flagrant harangue: books and articles, rallies and campaigns, speeches and films, civil disobedience and mass protests. In the eyes of the Institute for Policy Studies, a left-wing think tank in Washington, this sort of path would lead the environmental movement "to confront some of the largest issues of social organization—health, community, political and corporate accountability, jobs, and the future of the economy," and force it "to work toward a common analysis of the system it is attempting to change":

> The promise of environmentalism is that of a society which runs on a safe, sustainable, and democratic use of its resources. The task for environmentalists now is to find or invent the means—economic, technical, and political—to transform this society into that one.

Not an easy task, made all the more difficult by the urgency of the time.

In the fall of 1990 the Public Broadcasting Corporation aired a six-part series called *Race to Save the Planet,* a perhaps belated but elaborate and surprisingly hard-hitting analysis of the ecological perils facing the earth and the extent of the changes that would have to be made to avert them. "Can we change the way we live," it asked as its central, its guiding, question, "in order to save our planet from destruction?" It is the seriousness and the passion with which the environmental movement takes that question that will for the most part determine what shape it takes in the years ahead. For it is the question that goes to the very heart of the American, indeed the industrial, system, its values, its assumptions, its configurations fashioned by five centuries of modern Western civilization.

If it is to be answered in the negative, whether by environmentalists and allies who argue that it is erroneous or alarmist or futile, then it is unlikely that any movement, no matter how powerful and well heeled and popular, will outrace the accumulative forces, from ozone depletion to global warming, toxic pollution to despoliation, resource depletion to overpopulation, that are leading the human species, and with it most other forms of life, to ecocide. If it is to be answered in the affirmative, whether by those environmentalists who believe it possible or only wish it were, then the race to destruction just may be slowed and halted, and the elements of an ecological society, modest and biocentric, attentive to nature's laws and living lightly on the planet as if it were the only one available, might eventually be fashioned. . . .

DUNCAN FISHER

11

The Emergence of the Environmental Movement in Eastern Europe & Its Role in the Revolutions of 1989

Introduction

. . .

The State and Scientists

. . . ENVIRONMENTAL PROTEST EMERGED first from within the scientific establishment.[6] On the one hand, scientists were needed in order to provide the objective assessments necessary for the regime to maintain its legitimacy; access to data was a privilege that could be denied at the state's discretion. But at the same time scientists became increasingly disenchanted with their off-stage consultative role, with no power to determine and implement solutions.[7] The disbursement of information as a privilege could not forever buy the support of the intellectuals. Increasingly, they tended to "abuse" this privilege by allowing information to get

Originally published in Barbara Jancar-Webster, ed., *Environmental Action in Eastern Europe* (Armonk, NY: M. E. Sharpe, 1993). Reprinted with permission.

into the hands of oppositional groups, or speaking out themselves in a manner critical of the state. . . .

The State and Society

Two key features of the political arrangements of the 1960s and 1970s were the exclusion of society from the decision-making process and the necessary corollary of this, the restriction of information flows. The state imposed a paternalistic form of political legitimacy: it would guarantee basic security in return for quiescence and obedience.

Deteriorating environmental conditions in the 1960s and 1970s were one among many areas where the lack of participation and the lack of information emphasized the powerlessness of society to correct the mistakes of the ruling bureaucracy.[12] Demands for the correction of these imbalances were an essential part of the program of many independent East European environmental organizations in the 1980s. In some cases organizations emerged as a direct consequence of increased restrictions on information, as in the case of the Danube Blues in 1985, who responded with a public leafletting campaign.[13] *Ecoglasnost* in Bulgaria specifically demanded open information (hence its name). . . .

Autonomous social activity, however, was one of the fundamental tenets of socialism and was part of the more consensual relationship the regimes were seeking with society as part of the post-Stalinist approach. The regimes, therefore, had to remain formally committed to the creation and support of autonomous social activity. As part of the de-Stalinization process, Khrushchev advocated a "people's state" and supported a greater role for social organizations in nonsensitive areas, including nature conservation.[15] At the same time, it was necessary to deny any real autonomy to the so-called autonomous organizations. The official policy of "controlled autonomous organizations" is expressed clearly in a report to the national conference of the Bulgarian Communist Party in January 1988:

> It would be wrong for us to oppose the creation of autonomous groups, autonomous associations, and other forms of popular self-expression. We are, however, an organized society and cannot accept the creation of conditions that will breed anarchy, chaos, and demagogy. . . . Therefore, it is totally normal and proper to require such autonomous organizations to set themselves up within self-managing public bodies as an inseparable part of them and not as closed and dissociated castes. In this way the autonomous groups will be able to receive the necessary help, to enrich the life of the self-managing organizations, and to be under their control.[16]

The state feared the emergence of independent activity around the environment. . . . Environmental degradation could not be entirely hidden from public view, and so it disrupted the carefully constructed facade of order.[20] At the same time it both undermined the regimes' promises of a good life and questioned the ideology of unlimited growth in an indirect manner that was difficult to repress.[21]

The Environmental Movement in the 1980s

The process of political decay, manifested in increasing environmental deterioration and in a growing alienation among the state, scientists, and society, was one of the primary reasons for the emergence of politically active environmental groups in the 1980s. The influence of the growing environmental movement in the West was also an important factor, partly through hidden contacts between environmentalists in the two halves of Europe.[22]

The Configuration of the Environmental Movement in the 1980s

... There were two categories of environmental organizations: those created "from above" and those created "from below." The exact nature of groups within these two categories and the balance and interaction between the two varied from country to country and over time, and was a function of the degree of tolerance by the regime of uncontrolled social activity. ...

At one end of the spectrum lay Albania and Romania, where independent groups were not tolerated, and state-sponsored social organizations were totally controlled. In both countries there were scientists working on ecological issues at the universities and academies, and in Romania some of the data got into the hands of a loose association of intellectuals under the name of Romanian Democratic Action, which produced an extensive report in 1986.

The situation in Bulgaria was slightly less severe, and the dynamics of protest and suppression were more lively. Ecology had become a focus of protest in 1987 in response to intense pollution floating across the Danube from Romania into the town of Ruse.[23] Increasing press openness at the time elevated the Ruse affair to a national issue. In February 1988 the discussion group "Man, Ecology, Space" started in Sofia and declared its support for the Committee for the Ecological Defense of Ruse. The committee was quickly and effectively suppressed by the Bulgarian authorities, but the problems at Ruse did not disappear.

In 1989 several independent groups emerged,[24] among them Ecoglasnost, which was founded on March 2, 1989. In response to this kind of activity, the Bulgarian state itself became active in creating environmental organizations, most notably the National Committee for Nature Protection.[25] In 1986 the Ecological Youth Club was set up in Sofia, and in 1988, the National Movement for the Protection and Regeneration of the Environment was set up within the Fatherland Front, in response to the social unrest in Ruse.[26] When Ecoglasnost emerged, it was declared unnecessary by the authorities. In October 1989 the Ecology National Youth Club was set up under the guidance of the Komsomol Central Committee.[27]

Next in the spectrum was Czechoslovakia. Control of the constituent parts of state-sponsored social organizations was less total, and the articulation of political alternatives within these sometimes passed without repression. The extent of toleration differed between the Czech Republic and the Slovak Republic; opposition was less tolerated in the former, where the legacy of 1968 was stronger. [Editors' note: The Soviet Union intervened militarily in Czechoslovakia in 1968 to restore the authority of the Communist government.]

In Slovakia the Bratislava city branch of the Slovak Union of Nature and Landscape Protectors became increasingly radical in its criticism of the Gabcikovo-Nagymaros Dam project.[28] Its journal criticized the scheme in 1981 and as a result was suppressed for six months and censorship subsequently tightened. In October 1987 there was further trouble after the publication of *Bratislava nahlas,* a detailed report on environmental conditions in Bratislava.[29] But by 1988 a whole issue of the journal of the Bratislava city branch could be devoted to criticism of the Gabcikovo-Nagymaros Dam scheme, without penalties.

In Prague, on the other hand, opposition was precipitated into unofficial groups. Charter 77 [Editors' note: an organization of human rights dissidents] established a working group on the environment in 1978 and published a number of documents on the subject, some of which contained data obtained from scientists working in state research institutions.[30] . . . Only one samizdat [Editors' note: The term *samizdat* refers to underground, unauthorized publications] journal was published in Czechoslovakia, *Ecological Bulletin.* During the 1980s, it reprinted several texts on the environment, and kept readers informed of environmental activity in Czechoslovakia and the rest of Eastern Europe. In 1989 various loose environmental circles emerged, including the Independent Ecological Society and Children of the Earth. These circles undertook demonstrations in Prague during 1989. One such took place in Stromovka Park, in protest against the proposed construction of a road through it.

Meanwhile, open environmental criticism was emerging from within the Czechoslovak Academy of Sciences. There were a number of criticisms of the Gabcikovo-Nagymaros Dam project. The focus of this activity became the Ecological Section of the Society of Biologists within the academy. As its name suggests, the section lay fairly low in the hierarchical structure of the academy. Primarily due to the political skill of its head, Josef Vavrousek, the section managed to keep the delicate balance of staying in existence within the academy (thereby insuring access to data) at the same time as it maintained a critical distance and informal, hidden contacts with oppositional circles. . . .

The German Democratic Republic provides the prime example of how opposition groups used an already existing resource: the space for independent activity and criticism provided by the Evangelical Church. As a result of this space and the exposure to the environmental politics of West Germany, the environmental movement in the GDR was one of the earliest of those in Eastern Europe to emerge in the 1970s,[33] and was more widespread than might be expected from the low level of toleration of independent social activity. Paradoxically the state-sponsored Society for Nature and Environment, founded in 1980 within the Cultural Union of the GDR, was more restricted than the independent organizations sheltering within the Evangelical Church.[34] . . .

In Hungary in the 1980s there were a wide range of local activities,[42] a number of active conservation clubs,[43] and university groups.[44] Independent environmental activity was not permitted until 1988, when legislation was put in place allowing independent organizations to obtain legal status outside state-sponsored social organizations. In the localities, at a distance from central control exercised in Budapest, state-sponsored mass organizations such as the National Patriotic Front, with local offices throughout the country, did not act to suppress local initiatives from below. Indeed, newly emerging groups made use of state-sponsored structures to improve communication and coordination.[45] Similarly, the Communist Youth League provided the framework for independently minded university groups.[46] Meanwhile, from 1984 onwards, environmental activity in Budapest was dominated by the issue of the Gabcikovo-Nagymaros Dam system[47] and was much more explicitly political. In April 1988, in response to increasing environmental activism in Budapest, the National Patriotic Front set up the Hungarian Society for Nature Conservationists. Its reception was very different in the localities, where it took over the role of the National Patriotic Front, and in Budapest, where it was seen as an extension of Stalinist methods.[48]

Circumstances in Poland were rather exceptional in the early 1980s. Several independent environmental organizations emerged: one within Solidarity [Editors' note: the Polish independent trade-union organization], one within Rural Solidarity, and the most well known, the Polish Ecological Club, closely associated with Solidarity. Founded in September 1980, the club was officially registered as an independent group in May 1981 with 17 branches across the country. Its national reach made it unique at the time in Eastern Europe. After December 1981, however, the situation reverted to that pertaining in other East European countries: There was no room for the Polish Ecological Club in state-sponsored institutions and so it went underground. As conditions became more tolerant through the 1980s, the Polish Ecological Club re-emerged with renewed vigor as part of a rapidly expanding environmental movement. The club held two national conventions in 1983 and 1987. The independent group Freedom and Peace (WiP), founded in 1985, was particularly active in open campaigning during the 1980s.[49]

At the same time the state-sponsored League for the Protection of Nature grew in size, and local groups began to take increasingly independent stands. Formally the league had been a typical state-sponsored organization, boasting large membership and emphasizing education rather than independent participation.[50] The church too responded to environmental issues, focusing on spiritual and moral aspects of environmental concern. A Franciscan Ecology Movement was founded in 1986.

In response to these developments, the Polish state began creating its own social institutions. In 1986 it tried to gather all the various movements into one within the League for the Protection of Nature.[51] But the constituent elements of the league itself quickly became more independent.[52] In 1988 the National Foundation for the Protection of the Environment was created, sponsored by the Social Ecological Movement, an earlier creation of the Patriotic Movement of National Rebirth.[53]

By 1988 there was open and genuine interaction between the authorities and environmental experts in Poland. In October about thirty experts met with Wojciech Jaruzelski to discuss and launch the National Program for the Protection of the Environment until 2010.[54] The environmental experts recommended, among other things, the removal of restrictions on access to information on the environment. In 1989 Solidarity and the government held a round table on ecology, at which the Polish Ecological Club played a leading role.

The Environment and the Revolutions

The only countries where environmental issues played a significant role in precipitating political change were Czechoslovakia, Hungary, and Bulgaria, and in all cases it was not the environmental issues themselves that were crucial, but the fact that they provided a focus for social discontent at the right moment in time.

Czechoslovakia

In Czechoslovakia environmental demonstrations were becoming commonplace, particularly in Prague.[55] The weekend before the revolution occurred, environmental protests took place in Teplice. The authorities promised a public meeting with the inhabitants of the town on Monday, November 20. The meeting turned into a massive celebration of the revolution, which had begun in Prague the preceding Friday, November 17. All the demonstrations in Prague in the days prior to the revolution were focused on the environment.

Hungary

The issue of the Gabcikovo-Nagymaros Dam system provided a focus for political controversy in the process of political change in Hungary.[56] Opposition to the scheme was revitalized in 1988. There were numerous demonstrations, petitions and other actions. New groups emerged. An international conference of environmental groups was organized, the Academy of Sciences stated its opposition to the project openly, and debate within the administration became open. The issue provided a rallying point for the disparate opposition forces. The parliamentary debate in October 1988 turned into a test of the credibility of the Communist Party under Karoly Grosz. When Parliament voted in favor of continuing the project,[57] the dam scheme became the symbol of the old way of government. Reformers, especially Prime Minister Miklos Nemeth, accused the Communist Party, and Karoly Grosz as its leader, of going ahead with the project in an "undemocratic manner." In a speech before Parliament on June 2, 1989, Nemeth attacked the dam scheme, using it as an argument for democratization and greater independence in the fields of economics, culture, and science. A few months later, in October 1989, Parliament voted for the withdrawal of Hungary from the project.

Bulgaria

International environmental conferences were a favorite activity of the Bulgarian state. This policy proved to be the regime's downfall, with the environmental Conference on Security and Cooperation in Europe (CSCE) in October–November 1989. . . . Delegations in Sofia emphasized the extent of public participation in their own countries. Hungary, Poland, the United Kingdom, France, and the United States invited representatives of environmental nongovernmental organizations (NGOs) onto their delegations.[58] The Hungarian Duna Kor, Danube Circle, was largely responsible for drafting the Hungarian proposals on transboundary water pollution, one of the official subjects of the conference.

The other East European delegations were forced to play the same diplomatic game, displaying a commitment in their proposals and speeches to social participation in environmental regulation. Bulgaria's delegation even included Petar Beron, a leading member of Ecoglasnost, but not as a representative of that "illegal" organization. By avoiding the distinction between official and unofficial environmental NGOs, the East European states could wax lyrical about the role of social organizations. The issue of rights, the antithesis of a paternalistic relation between state and society, was studiously avoided. Discussion of rights was replaced with an emphasis on the need for education of society.

Ecoglasnost rose to prominence in Bulgaria in the months preceding the conference, carefully developing a strategy to use the conference to promote its cause.[59] A number of attempts had been made from 1988 onwards to organize oppositional groups, all of which had been met with varying degrees of repression. However, Ecoglasnost did not experience the same degree of repression as did other groups, and as a result became an umbrella for the opposition. It produced two kinds of documents: those solely devoted to environmental and conservation issues (such as "Charter 89"),[60] and those putting forward demands for freedom of information, the right of association, and the need for radical social change, in the language of the forthcoming conference.[61] The conference itself was the scene of intense activity, with extensive interaction between Western delegations and members of Ecoglasnost and other independent NGOs.[62] Ecoglasnost organized two petitions and a series of open meetings. Mass demonstrations began the day after the close of the conference on November 3. On November 10, Todor Zhivkov resigned. Although this change was the result of longer term power struggles within the power elite, only catalyzed, not caused, by the CSCE conference, Ecoglasnost benefitted greatly from the public's association of it with the fall of the former regime.

The Environmental Movement
After the Revolutions

With the rapid disintegration of the Communist regimes in 1989, the situation for environmental NGOs changed completely. The distinction between officially sponsored and independent NGOs evaporated. Formerly unofficial groups came out into the open and were joined by a multitude of new groups. National networks were quickly established.[63] Organizations formerly sponsored by the state either disappeared (in Bulgaria, the GDR, Romania and Serbia) or quickly asserted their independence and began presenting a new image.[64]

Conditions in all the countries favored the creation of green parties.[65] First, and perhaps most obviously, is the example of the West, which was exerting a powerful influence in all sectors, not just the environment. Secondly, the urge to participate in elections was very strong: not only were elections seen as the symbol of the new-found political freedom, but the parliaments were considered the only place where environmental priorities could be advocated effectively at a time of extensive redrafting of legislation. These tendencies coexisted with a strong public distrust of politics per se, a result of the former political system.[66] Along with the articulation of alternative values, the green parties offered a more immediate form of participation, an attractive feature of social movements in general.[67]

. . .

Conclusion: The Future

The situation in Central and Eastern Europe[87] is changing rapidly. With the shift from idealism to pragmatism since the revolutions, the environmental issue has lost much of its former significance as a symbol of the commitment to repairing the damage of the old order and to building a new. Indeed, measures to protect the environment are now often seen as a break in the process of introducing free-market economies, as powerful economic lobbies argue that cleaning up the environment is an unacceptable curb on economic recovery.

The apparent decreasing importance of environmental considerations on the political agenda may be ascribed in part to the lack of a politically powerful advocate of environmental priorities. In the West, environmental NGOs have mobilized and channeled public opinion to the extent that these organizations cannot be ignored. In Central and Eastern Europe, while public opinion is strong, the mechanisms for channeling it into a political lobby are not yet developed. Until strong environmental advocates are established within the countries of Central and Eastern Europe,[88] the political importance of environmental considerations in the corridors of power is likely to be low relative to other issues.

A number of factors will determine the process of development of the environmental movement in Central and Eastern Europe. One factor that will militate against the rapid development of a strong environmental movement is the long tradition throughout the region of state dominance and weak society, reinforced by the experience of the past 40 years. Cultural differences between countries will create big variations. . . .

Another important factor that will hamper the development of a strong environmental movement is the lack of resources. Political and economic instability will heighten this weakness. New NGOs in the West almost always make extensive use of the resources provided by already existing organizations.[89] No such basis yet exists in Central and Eastern Europe. A characteristic feature of Central and East European NGOs is likely to be financial crisis for some years to come. Furthermore, there is little tradition of raising money through membership subscriptions, and a lack of knowledge of the techniques Western NGOs have developed to mobilize public opinion and maintain public support.

This rather gloomy picture should be balanced by some of the advantages enjoyed by Central and East European environmental NGOs that Western organizations did not enjoy in the 1970s. Most important is the fact that public concern for the environment is already strong. In the 1970s, Western environmental NGOs had not only to mobilize public opinion but to a large extent had to create it first. Secondly, there is the possibility of the international transfer of resources, from the wealthy environmental NGOs in Western Europe and North America. This transfer is taking place in a wide variety of ways—provision of capital equipment, joint conferences, internships, provision of documentation, and the execution of joint projects (such as a coordinated response to Western investment). The usual phenomenon of using existing NGO resources is therefore repeating itself, but on an international scale. It is too early to determine how effective this international assistance is.

Lastly, an important factor will be the political priority attached to the environment on the part of Western institutions currently involved in assisting Central and East European countries. Western governments and multilateral banks active in the region are coming under considerable pressure from environmental lobbies within Western Europe, in particular the World Bank and the European Bank for Reconstruction and Development. Western companies investing in Central and Eastern Europe also have an incentive to "impose" environmental standards if and when they do not exist, given that much of the product of such investment is intended for Western markets. . . .

12
Fight for the Forest

Building Bridges

WE REALISED THAT IN ORDER to guarantee the future of the Amazon we had to find a way to preserve the forest while at the same time developing the region's economy.

So what were our thoughts originally? We accepted that the Amazon could not be turned into some kind of sanctuary that nobody could touch. On the other hand, we knew it was important to stop the deforestation that is threatening the Amazon and all human life on the planet. We felt our alternative should involve preserving the forest, but it should also include a plan to develop the economy. So we came up with the idea of extractive reserves.

What do we mean by an extractive reserve? We mean the land is under public ownership but the rubber tappers and other workers that live on that land should have the right to live and work there. I say "other workers" because there are not only rubber tappers in the forest. In our area, rubber tappers also harvest brazil nuts, but in other parts of the Amazon there are people who earn a living solely from harvesting nuts, while there are others who harvest babaçu and jute. . . .

Where did we get the idea of setting up the CNS [Editors' note: National Council of Rubber Tappers]? We discovered there is something called the National Rubber Council which represents the interests of landowners and businessmen but not the interests of the rubber tappers, so we thought, why not create an organisation as a counterweight to all that bureaucracy and try to stop the gov-

Originally published in Chico Mendes with Tony Gross, *Fight for the Forest: Chico Mendes in His Own Words* (London: Latin America Bureau, 1989). Reprinted with permission.

ernment messing the rubber tappers about? The First National Congress set up the CNS and elected a provisional executive committee.

The CNS is not meant to be a kind of parallel trade union, replacing the Xapuri Rural Workers' Union, for example. [Editors' note: Xapuri is the town where Mendes lived and worked until his assassination in December of 1988. It is located in the western Amazonian state of Acre, near the Brazilian border with Bolivia.] It is just an organisation for rubber tappers. The growth of the trade unions was very important for us, but other agricultural workers including day labourers and so on are also members of the same union. Other kinds of agricultural workers have been seen as having particular needs and interests, but not rubber tappers; it's as though we were something that existed only in the past. So one of the reasons for creating the CNS was to recognise the rubber tappers as a particular group of workers fighting for a very important objective—the defence of the Amazon forest. The idea went down very well.

The Indians

We also wanted to seek out the leaders of the Indian peoples in Acre and discuss how to unite our resistance movements, especially since Indians and rubber tappers have been at odds with each other for centuries. In Acre the leaders of the rubber tappers and Indian peoples met and concluded that neither of us was to blame for this. The real culprits were the rubber estate owners, the bankers and all the other powerful interest groups that had exploited us both.

People understood this very quickly, and from the beginning of 1986 the alliance of the peoples of the forest got stronger and stronger. Our links with the Indians have grown even further this year. For example, a meeting of the Tarauacá rubber tappers was attended by 200 Indians and six of them were elected to the Tarauacá Rubber Tappers' Commission. Indians are now beginning to participate in the CNS organising commissions. In Cruzeiro do Sul about 200 Indians are active in the movement and this year they have even joined in our *empates* [Editors' note: The term *empate* means "tie" or "standoff" in Portuguese. It refers here to a common tactic of the movement in which local people physically occupy the area threatened by deforesters. The goals are to create a standoff that inhibits the destruction of the forest and to convince the workers involved in deforestation that their interests lie in forest preservation].

Our proposals are now not just ours alone, they are put forward together by Indians and rubber tappers. Our fight is the fight of all the peoples of the forest.

When the Minister of Agriculture met a joint commission of Indians and rubber tappers in his office, he was really taken aback. "What's going on?", he said, "Indians and rubber tappers have been fighting each other since the last century! Why is it that today you come here together?"

We told him things had changed and this meant the fight to defend the Amazon was stronger. People really took notice of that.

. . .

The Landowners Strike Back

We know we face powerful opposition. As well as the landowners and business-men who dominate the Amazon region, we are up against the power of those who voted against land reform in the Constituent Assembly. The voting power of these people in Congress has been a problem for us and has encouraged the growth of the right-wing landowners' movement, the Rural Democratic Union (UDR). The defeat of the land reform proposal was a big victory for the landowners and land speculators. Now, since the establishment of the UDR in Acre, we've got a real fight on our hands. However, we also believe our movement has never been stronger.

You can already see how strong the UDR is in Acre—it's just organised its first cattle auction to raise funds. We know, through people who have been to UDR meetings here, that their aim is to destroy the Xapuri union by striking at the grassroots organisations of the Xapuri rubber tappers. They think if they can de-feat Xapuri they can impose their terms on the whole state and further afield in the Amazon region as well. The Governor of Acre himself told me this. Just to give you an idea, it was after the UDR's official launch here in Acre that the first drops of blood were spilt in Xapuri. . . .

The Government Takes Sides

There was a time when the state government seemed to be paying a lot of atten-tion to environmental problems and to the rubber tappers.[2] But we soon realised it was just putting on a show of defending the environment so the international banks and other international organisations would approve its development projects.

We can't see how the authorities can say they defend the ecological system while at the same time deploying police to protect those who are destroying the forest. That happened, for example, in the case of the Ecuador rubber estate where there were many nut and rubber trees. The Governor was warned several times about what was going on there. In fact, I personally warned him and sug-gested he go and look at what was happening for himself. I told him he was being very hasty in sending police there. Fifty acres of virgin forest were cut down, but thanks to the pressure, thanks to the hundreds of telegrams sent to the Governor by national and international organisations, we managed to get him to withdraw the police from the area and so saved about 300 hectares of forest.

In the area they destroyed there, the last harvest produced 1,400 cans of brazil nuts,[3] a good crop. We challenged the owner of the land and the Governor himself to work out the annual income per hectare produced by forest products such as brazil nuts and rubber and then compare it with that produced by grazing cattle there. They refused because they knew we could prove the income from one hectare of forest is 20 times greater than when the forest is cleared and given over to cattle.

We quoted decree law 7.511 of 30 July 1986 and regulation 486 of 28 October 1986 which prohibit the cutting down and sale of brazil nut and rubber trees and the deforestation of hillsides. There were two hillsides in the area being cut down on the Ecuador rubber estate and the law was completely flouted. After the second empate, when the rubber tappers managed to stop work going ahead, the local IBDF [Editors' note: Brazilian Forestry Development Institute] representative appeared and without even inspecting what was going on, told the landowner he could go ahead and clear the forest. He gave the landowner a licence even though the landowner did not present, as he should have done, a written plan for managing the area.

Another law—I can't remember its number—says you can only clear up to 50 hectares of forest without presenting a forestry management plan. Further on it adds that it's forbidden to cut down any area of forest on hillsides or where there is a concentration of brazil nut and rubber trees. None of these laws were respected. The Governor himself didn't even consider them and the IBDF certainly didn't.

We do have a good relationship with the Acre Technology Foundation (FUN-TAC) which is a state government agency.[4] They really understand how difficult the lives of rubber tappers are and recognise that deforestation is a problem. But despite the good relationship we've got with FUNTAC, we have no confidence left in the state government. How can we believe a Governor who says he defends the forest, and visits Rio and Japan to talk about defending the forest, but who then orders the police to go and protect the people who are destroying it? He ought to be using the political power that his office gives him. If he used his power in favour of the workers he'd certainly get their support. . . .

The rubber tappers aren't saying that nobody should lay a finger on the Amazon. No. We've got our own proposals for organising production. The rubber tappers and the Indians have always grown their subsistence crops but they've never threatened the existence of the forest. It's the deforestation carried out by the big landowners to open up pasture for their cattle that is threatening the forest. Often, these people are just speculating with the land. What happens in Xapuri and other parts of the Amazon is that these people cut down 10,000 hectares, turn half of it into pasture for their cattle and let the other half grow wild. They are really just involved in land speculation.

The landowners use all the economic power at their disposal. They bribe the authorities; it's common knowledge that they've bought off the IBDF staff in the Amazon region. They also use the law. They request police protection for the workers hired to cut down the trees, saying it is their land so they can do whatever they like with it. They accuse the rubber tappers of trespassing when we try and stop the deforestation. They turn to the courts for support and protection, claiming the land is private property. But the rubber tappers have been here for centuries!

There has been less pressure from the police in the last two years because we are able to present reasoned arguments to them. When we organise an empate, the main argument we use is that the law is being flouted by the landowners and our empate is only trying to make sure the law is respected.

The other tactic the landowners use, and it's a very effective one, is to use hired guns to intimidate us. Our movement's leaders, not just myself but quite a few others as well, have been threatened a lot this year. We are all on the death list of the UDR's assassination squads. Here in Xapuri, these squads are led by Darlí and Alvarino Alves da Silva, owners of the Paraná and other ranches round here. They lead a gang of about 30 gunmen—I say 30 because we've counted them as they patrol the town. Things have changed recently because we managed to get an arrest warrant issued in Umuarama, in the state of Paraná, for the two of them. I don't know whether it was the federal police, but somebody tipped them off. Now they're both in hiding and have said they'll only give themselves up when I'm dead.

We are sure this will be the landowners' main tactic from now on. They are going to fight our movement with violence and intimidation. There's no doubt in our minds about that. The level of violence that has been common in the south of the state of Pará is already spreading to Xapuri, to Acre.

PART THREE

The Prospects for International Environmental Cooperation

Effective responses to global environmental problems clearly require international cooperation. But the barriers to such cooperation are substantial and include uncertainty, mistrust, conflicting interests, different views of causality, complex linkages to other issues, and the myriad problems of coordinating the behavior of large numbers of actors.[1] Effective international cooperation will require both a series of international agreements that respond to specific, pressing environmental problems and a more general commitment to reexamine and restructure existing international practices with destructive environmental consequences. In this part we take up the question of new, issue-specific international agreements; Part Four then turns to the related question of reforming existing practices and institutions.

Barriers notwithstanding, there have been some hopeful signs. International agreements of varying scope and effectiveness now exist on a number of important issues, including the international trade in endangered species, international shipments of toxic waste, ocean dumping, the Antarctic environment, whaling, nuclear safety, and the protection of regional seas.[2] Perhaps the most powerful example of international cooperation is provided by the international agreement on protecting the planet's ozone layer. The successful negotiation of the Montreal Protocol on Substances that Deplete the Ozone Layer in 1987, and its further strengthening in London in 1990, signaled what many hoped would be a new era of increased global environmental cooperation. Certainly that enthusiasm carried over into the 1992 Earth Summit, where governments attempted to hammer out agreements that would slow global warming, protect biological diversity, and reduce rates of deforestation. But effective cooperation on these and related global challenges has been elusive. It is too early to tell whether the Montreal Protocol proves to be an exception to the inability of governments to act collectively or the first of a series of effective new international agreements.

We begin with the question of whether the ozone accords represent a model for future cooperation. Richard Elliot Benedick, a key U.S. negotiator during the crafting of the agreement, provides a glimpse inside the negotiating process. In Benedick's view, skillful diplomacy backed by sound science was able to overcome economic self-interest and bring about a treaty to control the emissions of chlorofluorocarbons (CFCs), the chief culprit in ozone destruction. According to Benedick, not only the substance of the agreement but also the process of negotiation provides a useful model. In the first stage of negotiations participants drafted a framework convention that provided a commitment to investigating the ozone problem without imposing any specific regulations or timetables for curtailing the production or consumption of CFCs. In subsequent meetings of the signatories to the framework convention, more specific regulations to control CFCs were adopted in the form of amendments or "protocols" to the original convention.[3]

The advantage of this "framework-protocol" method was its ability to gradually bring on board the necessary governments, without frightening them away with specific, costly regulations. More stringent regulations were negotiated incrementally, as the scientific evidence needed to support them became available. Also, countries with specific objections were offered inducements, or "side payments," to elicit their support. For example, a special monetary fund, promises of technology transfer, and a special phase-in time period were used to allay the fears of the developing countries that they would have to sacrifice future economic development to meet the provisions of the Montreal Protocol. The economic interests of various governments and their chemical industries were eventually overcome by gearing the initial convention mandates to the lowest common denominator and then allowing the mounting scientific evidence against CFCs to build pressure for tougher controls.

Benedick speaks for many environmentalists, scholars, and diplomats when he suggests that the effective framework-protocol approach on ozone is a model for other global problems. Indeed, elements of the Montreal model can be seen in the treaties on climate and biodiversity signed at the Earth Summit. In a direct challenge to this view, Ian H. Rowlands argues that the preconditions for successful cooperation on climate change differ substantially from the ozone problem. Rowlands cites four conditions that must be met for cooperation to occur: A lack of significant economic costs, a scientific consensus, an equitable agreement, and the ability to monitor and enforce the agreement must all be present. Rowlands argues that these conditions do not currently exist for global warming, which may explain why progress on climate change is stalled at the framework stage.

If Rowlands is correct, there may be scant prospects for effective agreement on complex global problems such as climate, biological diversity, toxic waste, and deforestation. Climate change negotiators, for example, will have to put together a much broader coalition of governments than that needed for the Montreal Protocol and then convince them to accept measures that make the costs of compliance with the Montreal Protocol pale in comparison. It will also be more difficult to reconcile the interests of the North and the South. The negotiators of the Montreal Protocol were able to overcome this problem by, in essence, paying the South to forsake the use and production of CFCs. Because of the South's current rather small reliance on CFCs, this required the relatively small sum of a few hundred million dollars in a multilateral fund. It is difficult to envision a similar compromise on a problem as complex as climate change, where the activities needing restriction are far more central to both Northern and Southern economies and the cost estimates run to tens or even hundreds of billions of dollars.[4]

Even if this complex maze of competing interests can be negotiated, the problem of scientific uncertainty remains. Instead of having the strong support of the scientific community behind them, climate change negotiators face a potentially dizzying variety of scientific theories. Although most theorists now agree that human activities will increase global temperatures, there is a wide variety of opinion as to the amount of temperature change we can expect, how quickly it is likely to occur, and how it will affect different regions of the planet.

This leads to the question of the role of scientific knowledge in fostering or inhibiting international agreements. Is scientific consensus required for international cooperation to occur? Can the sheer power of scientific knowledge spur cooperative action? Sheila Jasanoff argues that although knowledge plays an important role, science alone is an inadequate compass to guide global action. People can examine the same scientific information and still come up with dramatically different interpretations of the cause(s) of a particular natural phenomenon. They may also disagree strongly over the best course of action to remedy the situation even when they agree that a problem exists. Science is inevitably politicized given the high stakes and great uncertainty surrounding environmental change. And Jasanoff makes the provocative claim that too much scientific information can paralyze efforts to achieve cooperation.

Returning again to the climate change example, every new finding regarding the role of some feedback mechanism such as the ocean, every new theory about the influence of solar flares and volcanoes, has led to calls for more research in lieu of moving toward more specific action. Under such circumstances knowledge alone is no substitute for the political will to act, and science requires some value orientation and set of agreed-upon social goals in order to know which questions to ask.

Finally, even if the complex politics of science can be addressed so that new knowledge facilitates rather than inhibits effective international cooperation, there remains the task of crafting agreements that are seen by all sides as reasonably fair, effective, and in their interest. Again, the climate change example illustrates the substantial barriers. In the chapter by Anil Agarwal and Sunita Narain of India's Centre for Science and Environment, we see an example of how different groups can look at the same scientific data—in this case, estimates of how much different countries contribute to the problem of global warming—and come up with radically different interpretations. According to Agarwal and Narain, it is misleading to look at the statistics on greenhouse-gas emissions by each nation. Even if it is true that China, India, and Brazil are now three of the most significant sources of carbon dioxide (the leading greenhouse gas), two important points are ignored by such data. Such gross national figures make no distinction between the "luxury emissions" of the rich and the "survival emissions" of the poor. The data also mask the fact that given their low level of emissions per capita, densely populated countries such as India are using up much less than their "fair share" of the Earth's ability to absorb pollutants. Thus, an act as seemingly neutral as compiling a list of greenhouse-gas emissions on a country-by-country basis is political; it can skew our thinking toward proposed solutions that others see as patently unfair.[5]

Given these diverse barriers, it may seem that the prospects for international cooperation on environmental problems are limited. But perhaps there is more than one way to judge the success of the international system in dealing with environmental issues. Instead of holding up the actual signing of a treaty as the standard of success, there is at least some hope if we see signs that the system appears to be moving in the right direction. This is the view taken by Peter Haas, Marc Levy, and Edward Parson in judging the success of the 1992 Earth Summit. The authors see evidence that the conference laid important groundwork for future efforts to protect the global environment. These include the creation of new international institutions such as the Commission on Sustainable Development within the United Nations; of new financing mechanisms for environmental projects such as the World Bank's Global Environmental Facility; of forums for continued interactions between diplomats, scientists, and environmental activists; and of a global network of environmental organizations that will continue to press for change. These accomplishments could create enough momentum to produce more tangible action by governments in the future. Whether the very real urgency of the problems can sustain such momentum, and whether it will prove adequate to overcome the significant barriers to cooperation discussed by Rowlands and others, remains to be seen.

RICHARD ELLIOT BENEDICK

13
Ozone Diplomacy

ON SEPTEMBER 16, 1987, representatives of countries from every region of the world reached an agreement unique in the annals of international diplomacy. In the Montreal Protocol on Substances that Deplete the Ozone Layer, nations agreed to significantly reduce production of chemicals that can destroy the stratospheric ozone layer (which protects life on earth from harmful ultraviolet radiation) and can also change global climate.

The protocol was not a response to an environmental disaster such as Chernobyl, but rather preventive action on a global scale. That action, based at the time not on measurable evidence of ozone depletion or increased radiation but rather on scientific hypotheses, required an unprecedented amount of foresight. The links between causes and effects were not obvious: a perfume spray in Paris helps to destroy an invisible gas 6 to 30 miles above the earth, and thereby contributes to deaths from skin cancer and extinction of species half a world and several generations away.

The ozone protocol was only possible through an intimate collaboration between scientists and policymakers. Based as it was on continually evolving theories of atmospheric processes, on state-of-the-art computer models simulating the results of intricate chemical and physical reactions for decades into the future, and on satellite-, land- and rocket-based monitoring of remote gases measured in parts per trillion, the ozone treaty could not have occurred at an earlier point in human history.

Another noteworthy aspect of the Montreal Protocol was the negotiators' decision not to take the timid path of controlling through "best available technol-

Excerpted from Richard Elliot Benedick, "Ozone Diplomacy," *Issues in Science and Technology* (Fall 1989):43–50. Copyright © 1989 by the National Academy of Sciences, Washington, D.C. Reprinted with permission.

ogy"—the traditional accommodation to economic interests. Instead, the treaty boldly established firm target dates for emissions reductions, even though the technologies for accomplishing these goals did not yet exist.

The ozone protocol sounded a death knell for an important part of the international chemical industry, with implications for billions of dollars in investment and hundreds of thousands of jobs in related industries such as food, transportation, plastics, electronics, cosmetics, and health care. Here, as in many other areas, international economic competition clashed with the need for international environmental cooperation, but in this case concerns about the environment eventually carried the day. . . .

Environmental Bombshells

In 1974, two theories were advanced that suggested potentially grave damage to the ozone layer. According to the first, chlorine in the atmosphere could continually destroy ozone for a period of decades: A single chlorine atom was capable, through a catalytic chain reaction, of eliminating tens of thousands of ozone molecules. The other theory postulated that man-made chlorofluorocarbons (CFCs) would break down in the presence of radiation in the stratosphere and release dangerously large quantities of chlorine.

These hypotheses were environmental bombshells. Production of CFCs had soared from 150,000 metric tons in 1960 to over 800,000 metric tons in 1974, reflecting their broad usefulness: CFCs are chemically stable and vaporize at low temperatures, which make them excellent coolants in refrigerators and air conditioners, and ideal as propellant gases in spray cans; they are good insulators; they are standard ingredients in the manufacture of such ubiquitous materials as styrofoam; and they are generally inexpensive to produce. The stability of CFCs means that, unlike other man-made gases, they are not chemically destroyed or rained out quickly in the lower atmosphere. Rather, they migrate slowly upward, remaining intact for decades. . . .

Theories about the relationship between the ozone layer, chlorine, and CFCs stimulated tremendous activity in scientific and industrial circles. Although the chemical industry vigorously denied the validity of any linkage between the state of the ozone layer and their growing sales of CFCs, the U.S. scientific community mounted a major research campaign that confirmed the fundamental validity of the chlorine-ozone hypotheses.

But although the theory was sound, making precise measurements of effects was not so easy—especially since growing concentrations of carbon dioxide and methane (originating at least in part from human activities) could greatly offset the projected chlorine impact, and nitrogen compounds could influence the reaction in either direction. Thus, in the years following the initial hypotheses, there were wide fluctuations in the predicted results of CFC emissions. Theoretical-model projections of global average ozone depletion 50 to 100 years in the future began at about 13 percent in 1974, increased to 19 percent in 1979, and dropped to less than 5 percent in 1982–83. For a time, these swings tended to diminish public concern over the urgency of the problem.

But consensus was soon to develop. In 1986, an assessment spearheaded by NASA and sponsored by the United Nations Environment Programme, the World Meteorological Organization, and other agencies concluded that continued CFC emissions at the 1980 rate would reduce global average ozone by about 9 percent by the latter half of the next century, with much larger seasonal and latitudinal decreases. New measurements also indicated that accumulations of CFCs in the atmosphere had nearly doubled between 1975 and 1985, even though production of these chemicals had stagnated over the same period, illustrating the potential long-term danger from these substances.

On the basis of these figures and of projections of continuing, though moderate, CFC emissions, the U.S. Environmental Protection Agency estimated that in the United States alone there could be over 150 million new cases of skin cancer among people currently alive and born by the year 2075, resulting in over 3 million deaths. EPA also projected 18 million additional eye cataract cases in the United States for the same population. Other possible results of CFC emissions included damage to the human immune system, serious impacts on agriculture and fisheries, increased formation of urban smog, and warming of the global climate.

The Great Atlantic Divide

As scientists analyzed the effects of CFCs on the ozone layer and the resultant implications for human health and the environment, the United States and the European Community (EC)—comprising 12 sovereign nations—emerged as the principal protagonists in the diplomatic process that culminated in the Montreal Protocol. Despite their shared political, economic, and environmental orientations, the United States and the European Community, which together accounted for 84 percent of world CFC output in 1974, differed over almost every issue at every step along the route to Montreal.

The U.S. Congress held formal hearings on the ozone layer soon after the theories were published, which led in 1977 to ozone protection legislation that banned use of CFCs as aerosol propellants in all but essential applications. This affected nearly $3 billion worth of sales in a wide range of household and cosmetic products, and rapidly reduced U.S. production of CFCs for aerosols by 95 percent. . . .

In contrast, European parliaments (except for the German Bundestag) showed scant interest in CFCs. The European Community delayed until 1980, and then enacted a 30 percent cutback in CFC aerosol use from 1976 levels and announced a decision not to increase production capacity.

These EC actions, however, were feeble compared to the U.S. regulation. With respect to the 30 percent aerosol reduction, European sales of CFCs for this purpose had, by 1980, already declined by over 28 percent from the 1976 peak year. Moreover, the European Community two years later defined "production capacity" in a manner that would enable current output to increase by over 60 percent. The capacity cap was therefore a painless move, supported by European industry, which gave the appearance of control while in reality permitting undiminished rates of expansion for at least two more decades.

Relative to gross national product, EC production of CFCs was over 50 percent higher than that of the United States. Aerosols, which had virtually disappeared in the U.S., still comprised during the 1980s over half of CFC sales within the European Community. The European Community was also the CFC supplier to the rest of the world, particularly the growing markets in developing countries. EC exports rose by 43 percent from 1976 to 1985 and averaged almost one-third of its production, whereas the United States consumed virtually all it produced.

These developments were reflected in growing differences in attitude between the chemical industries on the two sides of the Atlantic. Shaken by the force of public reaction in the 1970s over the threat to the ozone layer, American producers had quickly developed substitutes for CFCs in spray cans. U.S. chemical companies were also constantly aware of their vulnerability in the environmentally charged domestic atmosphere. . . . The threat of a patchwork of state laws . . . made U.S. industry not only resigned to but even publicly in favor of federal controls, which would at least be uniform and therefore less disruptive.

There was also resentment among American producers that their European rivals had escaped meaningful controls. A constant theme in the U.S. chemical industry during the 1980s was the need to have a "level playing field"—to avoid recurrence of unilateral U.S. regulatory action that was not followed by the other major producers.

In September 1986, the Alliance for Responsible CFC Policy, a coalition of about 500 U.S. producer and user companies, issued a pivotal statement. Following the obligatory reiteration of industry's position that CFCs posed no immediate threat to human health or the environment, the Alliance spokesman declared that "large future increases in . . . CFCs . . . would be unacceptable to future generations," and that it would be "inconsistent with [industry] goals . . . to ignore the potential for risk to those future generations." Thus, only three months before the protocol negotiations began, U.S. industry announced its support for new international controls on CFCs.

This unexpected policy change, which came after much soul-searching within U.S. industry, aroused consternation in Europe. The British and French had been suspicious all along that the United States was using an environmental scare to cloak commercial motivations. Now, some Europeans surmised (incorrectly) that the United States wanted CFC controls because they had substitute products on the shelf with which to enter the profitable EC export markets.

For its part, EC industry's primary objective was to preserve its dominance and to avoid the costs of switching to alternative products for as long as possible. Taking advantage of public indifference and political skepticism, European industrial leaders were able to persuade most EC governments that substitutes for CFCs were neither feasible nor necessary—despite the demonstrated U.S. success in marketing alternative spray propellants. Industry statements were echoed in official EC pronouncements that continually stressed the scientific uncertainties, the impossibility of finding effective substitutes, and the adverse effects of regulations on European living standards.

Self-Serving Positions

Although the United States and the European Community were the major CFC producers, the ozone problem threatened the entire world and therefore could be solved only by international agreement. Filling a catalytic role for such an agreement became the mission of a small and hitherto little publicized United Nations agency, the UN Environment Programme (UNEP). . . . The agency worked to inform governments and world public opinion about the danger to the ozone layer, it provided a nonpoliticized international forum for the negotiations, and it was a driving force behind the consensus that was eventually reached.

In January 1982, representatives of 24 countries met in Stockholm under UNEP auspices to decide on a "Global Framework Convention for the Protection of the Ozone Layer." The following year a group of countries, including the United States, Canada, the Nordic nations, and Switzerland, proposed a worldwide ban on "nonessential" uses of CFCs in spray cans, pointing out that the United States and others had already demonstrated that alternatives to CFC sprays were technically and economically feasible. In late 1984, the European Community countered with a proposal for alternative controls that would prohibit new additions to CFC production capacity.

Each side was backing a protocol that would require no new controls for itself, but considerable adjustment for the other. The United States had already imposed a ban on nonessential uses of CFCs, but U.S. chemical companies were operating at close to capacity and thus would suffer under a production cap. Their European counterparts, on the other hand, had substantial underutilized capacity and could expand CFC production at current rates for another 20 years before hitting the cap.

Despite these disagreements, by March 1985 the negotiators had drafted all elements of a protocol for CFC reductions except the crucial control provisions. Meeting in Vienna, all major producers except Japan signed an interim agreement—the Vienna Convention on Protection of the Ozone Layer—which promoted international monitoring, research, and exchange of data and provided the framework for eventual protocols to control ozone-modifying substances. Over strong objections from European industry representatives, the Vienna Conference passed a separate resolution that called upon UNEP to continue work on a CFC protocol with a target for adoption in 1987.

As formal negotiations began in December 1986, governments were divided into three camps. Despite growing internal strains, the European Community followed the European industry line and mirrored the views of the UK, France, and Italy. The European Community continued to advocate the kind of production capacity cap it had favored during the meetings leading up to the Vienna Convention. Because the scientific models showed there would be at least two decades before any significant ozone depletion would occur, EC negotiators felt there was time to delay production cuts and wait for more evidence. This perspective was initially shared by the USSR and Japan.

Opposing this view were the United States, Canada, Norway, Sweden, Finland, Switzerland, and New Zealand, all favoring stronger new controls. They argued that action needed to be taken well before critical levels of chlorine accumulated: The long atmospheric lifetimes of these compounds meant that future ozone depletion stemming from past and current production was inevitable, and the process could not suddenly be turned off like a faucet. . . .

Complicating the entire process was the fact that the European Community had to achieve internal consensus among its member countries before (and during) international negotiations, which tended to make it a difficult and inflexible negotiating partner. There were deep divisions within the European Community on the ozone issue. Germany, the Netherlands, Belgium, and Denmark were increasingly disposed toward strong CFC controls; but of these, only Germany was a major producer. The UK, supported by France and Italy—all large producers— resisted every step of the way. . . .

Deep Cuts

One of the central disputes of the negotiations was whether restrictions would be placed on the production or consumption of the substances covered by the agreement. This issue, though seemingly arcane, was one of the most important and most difficult to resolve.

The European Community pushed for controls on production, arguing that it was simpler to control output since there were only a small number of producing countries, whereas there were thousands of consuming industries and countless points of consumption. But the United States, Canada, and others who favored a consumption-related formula pointed out that controlling production would confer unusual advantages on the European Community while particularly prejudicing importing nations, including the developing countries. Since about a third of EC output was exported and there were no other exporters in the picture, a production limit essentially locked in the EC export markets. The only way the United States or others could supply those markets would be to decrease their domestic consumption.

The European Community, with no viable competitors, would thus have a virtual monopoly. If European domestic consumption should rise, the European Community could cut back its exports, leaving the current importing countries, with no recourse to other suppliers, to bear the brunt of CFC reductions. Because of this vulnerability, there would be incentives for importing countries to remain outside the treaty and build their own CFC facilities.

To meet the valid EC argument about controlling multiple consumption points, the United States and its allies came up with an ingenious solution: A limit would be placed on production plus imports minus exports to other Montreal Protocol signatories. This "adjusted production" formula eliminated any monopoly based on current export positions, in that producing countries could raise production for exports to protocol parties without having to cut their own domestic consumption. Only exports to nonparties would have to come out of domestic consumption, and this would be an added incentive for importing countries to join the protocol, lest they lose access to supplies. Additionally, an importing signatory whose traditional supplier raised prices excessively or refused to export could either produce on its own or turn to another producer country.

The single most contentious issue was the timing and extent of reductions. Again, the European Community and the United States were the principal opponents. The United States originally called for a freeze to be followed by three phases of progressively more stringent reductions, all the way up to a possible 95 percent cut. But even late into the negotiations, the European Community was reluctant to consider reductions beyond 10 to 20 percent.

The United States and others rejected this as inadequate. In fact, Germany, which had become increasingly concerned over the ozone problem, was already planning an independent 50 percent reduction and early in 1987 it made urgent appeals to the other EC members also to accept deep reductions. Meanwhile, new scientific research was demonstrating that all of the control strategies under consideration would result in some degree of ozone depletion, the extent of which would depend on the stringency of international regulation. These developments helped garner support for deep cuts. . . .

Ultimately, even the most reluctant parties—the European Community, Japan, and the Soviet Union—agreed to a 50 percent decrease. The treaty as signed stipulated an initial 20 percent reduction from the 1986 level of CFCs, followed by 30 percent. Halons were frozen at 1986 levels, pending further research. And one innovative provision—that these reductions were to be made on specific dates regardless of when the treaty should enter into force—removed any temptation to stall enactment of the protocol in the hopes of delaying cuts, and also provided industry with dates upon which to base its planning.

Negotiators at Montreal also faced the difficult task of encouraging developing countries to participate in the treaty. Per capita consumption of CFCs in those countries was tiny in comparison to that of the industrialized world, but their domestic consumption requirements—for refrigeration, for example—were growing, and CFC technology is relatively easy to obtain. The protocol thus had to meet their needs during a transition period while substitutes were being developed, and it had to discourage them from becoming major new sources of CFC emissions.

A formula was developed whereby developing countries would be permitted a 10-year grace period before they had to comply with the control provisions.

During this time they could increase their consumption up to an annual level of 0.3 kilogram per capita—approximately one-third of the 1986 level prevailing in industrialized countries. It was felt that the realistic prospects of growth in CFC use to these levels in the developing countries was not great, as they would not want to invest in a technology that was environmentally detrimental and would soon be obsolete.

Basis for Optimism

. . .

The Montreal Protocol stands as a landmark—a symbol both of fundamental changes in the kinds of problems facing the modern world and of the way the international community can address those problems. . . . But the protocol may also have relevance for dealing with other common dangers, including national rivalries and war. The ozone treaty reflects a realization that nations must work together in the face of global threats, and that if some major actors do not participate, the efforts of others will be vitiated.

In the realm of international relations, there will always be uncertainties—political, economic, scientific, psychological. The protocol's greatest significance may be its demonstration that the international community is capable of undertaking complicated cooperative actions in the real world of ambiguity and imperfect knowledge. The Montreal Protocol can be a hopeful paradigm of an evolving global diplomacy, one wherein sovereign nations find ways to accept common responsibility for stewardship of the planet and for the security of generations to come.

IAN H. ROWLANDS

14

Ozone Layer Depletion
& Global Warming:
New Sources for
Environmental Disputes

Introduction

HISTORICALLY, ENVIRONMENTAL ISSUES have given rise to international disputes at a bilateral, or at most, a regional level. For example, "trans-boundary material flows" from one state to another have caused environmental degradation, which has served as a source of conflict between states. In the past, such environmental issues were thought to be isolated in a physical sense, and therefore they were dealt with individually in a power political sense; the traditional tools of international statecraft (military, economic, diplomacy) were used to address them. Recently, however, a new kind of environmental issue has arisen that can generate international disputes. Consisting of the problems of ozone layer depletion and global warming, it is the issue of "global environmental change." Although the character of the disputes that would be caused by global environmental change resembles the character of previous environmental dis-

Originally published in *Peace and Change* 16, 3 (July 1991):260–284, copyright © 1991 by Sage Publications, Inc. Reprinted by permission of Sage Publications, Inc.

putes, these new challenges are unique, because they are considerable in magnitude and systemic in origin. Because these new environmental problems are not isolated in a physical sense, they cannot be contained in a single narrow issue area politically.

. . .

The Environment as an International Collective Good

. . . In the past, statespeople regarded the environment as a commodity that was to be dominated, conquered, divided among the victors, and put to the service of humankind. Actions reflected such a belief as people dumped, discharged, and discarded wastes into the environment. These processes did not seem to have an effect on the earth in any systemic manner. It is true that there were prices to pay locally, but it was thought that a smoke stack in Liverpool had little effect on the quality of the environment in Ottawa.

Acid rain, common management of a binational lake, and river pollution were all thought to concern only those states that were in the region, because they were the only ones seen to be affected by the environmental action. Hence we believed that these issues could be handled on a local, national, or regional level. Recently, however, this perception has changed.

It is finally being recognized that while we were dumping, discarding, and discharging, we were affecting the earth's natural equilibria. Thus today we are starting to acknowledge that local activities do in fact have global ramifications. Unilateral action can no longer secure a habitable environment; rather, a habitable global environment must be seen as an international collective good.

Much research has been undertaken in the areas of public goods and dilemmas of collective action—much of it is quite controversial.[11] Without entering into that debate, I would simply like to assert that this situation resembles a "tragedy of the commons"[12]—that is, the preservation of a habitable global environment requires worldwide dedication to such a goal.

By claiming that this issue is "systemic in origin," I am not claiming that other environmental concerns are not; they are. But the problems of global environmental change have brought to the international forefront the fact that the environmental damage that we inflict can no longer be confined to certain regions. Instead, the actions of every single state will affect the global environment, and thus will also affect the habitat of every other state.

. . . A proper response to these problems will require worldwide cooperation. Thus, to look at how disputes resulting from global environmental change might be peacefully resolved or altogether avoided, we should look at ways in which international cooperation can be realized. To open such an exploration, an inquiry into the rudiments of international cooperation will first be undertaken.

International Cooperation

"Cooperation" is a term that is used freely in the study of international relations—it seems to be able to encompass a wide range of international associations. Because the word is central to this article's investigation, an accepted definition is required. Therefore I would like to adopt Robert Keohane's explanation:

> Cooperation requires that the actions of separate individuals or organizations—which
> are not in pre-existent harmony—be brought into conformity with one another through
> a process of negotiation . . . [Thus,] cooperation occurs when actors adjust their behav-
> ior to the actual or anticipated preferences of others, through a process of policy coordi-
> nation. To summarize more formally, intergovernmental cooperation takes place when
> the policies actually followed by one government are regarded by its partners as facilitat-
> ing realization of their own objectives, as the result of a process of policy coordination.[15]

By accepting this definition, a couple of key restrictive points are evident. First,
it is clear that cooperation is only a concern in issue areas that can be represented
by positive-sum games. Further, the benefits from these games must be contin-
gent on the actions of other players. Therefore, if cooperation is present, independent decision making will not be undertaken, because the definition stipulates
that communication and consultation take place. Further, it implies that, for the
most part, the cooperating states attempt to coordinate their actions so as to obtain desirable outcomes—in other words, it is anticipated that all players will accrue benefits.

Although the issue of global environmental change is unprecedented, the class
of problem (provision of an international collective good) does have some prece-
dence in the study of international relations. Since the beginning of our present
international political system in 1648 [Editors' note: The treaty of Westphalia,
which put an end to the Thirty Years' War and in the view of many historians
marked the onset of the modern eras of sovereign nation-states, was signed in
1648], states have sometimes entered into mechanisms for international cooperation (e.g., conventions, understandings, and treaties) in order to realize some sort
of order in the anarchical system and in order to escape suboptimal results (e.g.,
human health standards, mail service, transportation regulations, and trading
practices). Recognizing that comparable issues exist can aid our investigation into
the factors that will promote international cooperation on global environmental
change.

Although both issues—ozone layer depletion and global warming—are collective goods problems, there has been markedly different progress on each. There
has been, relatively, considerable success on international attempts to preserve the
ozone layer . . . but there has been little achieved on the issue of global warming.[16]
Such a difference needs to be explained. Therefore, in order to try to understand
the factors that affect international cooperation, I will argue that there are four
major preconditions for international cooperation.[17] These four preconditions

serve as the theoretical framework. I am postulating that "if the four preconditions for cooperation" are realized, then "cooperation will occur."[18] This structure will be applied to the experience of the ozone layer depletion and global warming issues—the former in order to try to validate the theory and the latter in order to try to suggest, quite normatively, what barriers and openings may lie ahead in the international negotiations.

Preconditions for Cooperation

One point of departure for this study involves the use of the rational actor model. This approach . . . assumes that players in the field of international affairs objectively identify the benefits and liabilities associated with particular courses of action. Subsequently, with the help of some set of criteria, each player costs these various options and chooses the route that will yield the greatest gain or, failing that, result in the smallest loss. Although there are many problems with this approach (the work in bureaucratic politics has identified various difficulties), such an assumption of maximizing behavior can highlight an important precondition for cooperation.

In a general sense, a dilemma of collective action will require a state to incur a cost in order to try to realize a larger benefit. With regard to the issue at hand, the larger benefit would be environmental stability. But there obviously would be significant costs associated with any attempt to secure that good. To further complicate the issue, the major benefit—that is, the restoration of a stable, habitable global environment—is one that is not immediately available. Because it will be obtained in the future, there is necessarily some sort of discount rate attached to it.[19] Therefore, rational behavior may dictate that the price of present sacrifice does not justify action to be taken. Thus the basic theoretical proposition being put forward here is that states will not engage in cooperative arrangements if the agreements force them to make large economic sacrifices. The experience in the ozone layer depletion issue goes some way toward validating this hypothesis.

"Solving" the ozone layer depletion issue would obviously involve an economic cost for countries, because emissions of CFCs and other chemicals would have to be reduced and eventually prohibited. But the extent of the cost would be differentiated by one key factor: whether or not substitutes existed for these chemicals. If a ban were implemented without any substitutes available, then there would be a significant price to pay, because many important goods and processes would have to be eliminated. But if appropriate substitutes did exist, then the switch over to alternatives, although still being costly, would pale in comparison to the first scenario. By looking at the history of the ozone layer depletion issue, it is clear that the cost of the former was not acceptable to national governments, but the cost of the latter was, finally, acceptable.

First, when the U.S. imposed regulations on aerosol propellants in 1978 it did not place regulations on those products that did not have existing acceptable substitutes.[20] Second, the Japanese have only recently endorsed a ban on CFCs. Prior to this volte-face, the determining factor seemed to be the fact that such a ban would have had a major economic effect on that country. One of the targeted products—CFC113—is used to clean electronic circuits, and the Japanese were reluctant to agree to any ban that would affect the economic performance of their vital high-technology industry.[21] Third, many of the calls for "near-100%" bans have been cautioned by the issue of substitute availability. For example, when the Canadian government announced a phase-out of CFCs in early 1989, it promised to eliminate the last 1.5% only as soon as the chemicals could be safely replaced.[22] It therefore seems that governments have been willing to cooperate to preserve the ozone layer only if substitute chemicals have been available.

An interesting relationship between government and industry must be noted. For alternative strategies or substitutes to become less costly, major research is needed in order to discover methods that would make them more economically attractive. But private enterprise will not attempt to develop any sort of alternatives to destructive environmental activities unless it is in their economic interest to do so. . . . According to basic economic theory, cost will rise with the threat of scarcity (when either the commodity is being depleted or a regulatory body is threatening its future supply—e.g., an announcement that it will be banned, or its uses restricted, by a cooperative agreement). Therefore, one trigger that accelerates the development of alternatives is the prospect of government regulation.

The ozone layer depletion experience demonstrates that there was a direct correlation between the threat of government regulation and the development of substitute chemicals. For example, the pressure of the "ban the can" campaign in the United States during the mid-1970s meant that, when the ban was finally imposed in 1978, the "CFC industry had received due warning of [the ban] and ha[d] already converted many of its aerosol products to alternative propellants."[23] On the contrary, there was no such threat in the UK. Hence, ICI (the UK's largest chemical manufacturer), despite an investment of 5 million pounds during the 1970s, abandoned its program to develop alternatives. An ICI executive argued that if the company had continued such research into the early 1980s, then it "would have been doing so in a complete vacuum."[24] These statements point to a contradiction that could well place activity in this area in an endless vicious circle—namely, that industry will not develop alternatives until there is a ban in place, but that government will not impose a ban until alternatives are available. Thus it seems that the initiative has to come from government—to let the industry know that regulations will be introduced and therefore allow the manufacturers time to develop safe substitutes. . . . The chemical industry will not have the impetus to fund research and development unless it believes that present inactivity may be sacrificing future profits. Supporting this argument, NASA scientist Robert Watson noted that "industry is looking for a signal from government. It needs to know, before it invests millions, if the replacement gases will be banned in the future. It needs to know how much chlorine can be allowed in the atmosphere."[26] National governments were finally able to send such a message, once a new consensus had emerged in May 1989. At that time, 80 countries agreed to cut out CFCs as soon as possible, with the year 2000 being the latest acceptable date.[27] It is thought that this announcement will motivate the search for alternatives, because increased cooperation in the areas of research and development have been, in the past, triggered by international calls for cuts to CFCs.[28]

Difficulties of this nature will also be a hindrance to the realization of international cooperation on the issue of global warming. Because the release of carbon dioxide is a direct consequence of combustion, the negotiators will have to consider every basic process in industrial society. Once again, the issue for many countries will be to what extent will they be willing to cut back on such industrial emissions—that is, what costs will be acceptable? Although there are no simple substitutes for fossil fuels that could be easily implemented, there are alternatives that could be pursued which would reduce the output of greenhouse gases. Energy conservation, increasing energy efficiency, and developing alternative sources are but three examples. Although some states have pledged to reduce their emission of carbon dioxide, it remains that some states' representatives have employed the economic argument in order to justify the impediment of cooperation. . . .

We are left to wonder how this precondition might be fulfilled so that cooperation on global climatic change might be achieved and so that future disputes in this area might be resolved or altogether avoided. In order to attempt to satisfy this curiosity, let us take a closer look at the costs and benefits. Cooperation will be promoted if either the perceived costs are reduced or the perceived benefits are increased.

With regard to costs, recall the triggering mechanisms that were identified at the beginning of this section. Applying this basic economic argument to the global warming issue, we see that prior to the 1990 Middle East crisis the price of oil was low and the prospect of a restrictive agreement was small. Therefore, these two realities dictate that there is little economic incentive to fund research into substitute and alternative strategies. Thus the costs of alternatives and substitutes remain high.

In order to examine the "benefits" side of the calculation, let us depart from our avowedly rationalistic framework and recognize a contribution of, as Keohane calls them, the reflective writers.[30] This group of scholars argues that, in international society, the prevailing norms and preferences should not be assumed to be fixed. Instead, it should be acknowledged that they are affected by political leadership, by changes in fashion and by learning from experience. With this point in mind, let us look more closely at the two ways in which the benefits could be increased.

First, the discount factor would be reduced if the future benefits were to have more value placed on them—a change in the prevailing norms with respect to the importance set on the future would contribute to this. With regard to the global warming issue, there has recently arisen a greater recognition of the implications that present-day actions will have on future generations. In other words, a new norm has been emerging in the global community—a greater respect for the planet as an integrated earth, rather than viewing it simply as an anthropocentric world. . . . Such a transformation obviously affects the discount rate. Therefore as this norm gains acceptance, the value placed on the future will be to a degree increased. In this way, the future consequences of global warming may have a greater impact on the rational decision maker's economic analysis and calculation.

Second, the sum total of the benefits could be increased by recognizing the value of "secondary" benefits that are captured by laboring toward the primary collective objective. Again, this would require a shift in preferences. The advantages, many of them private in nature, would have to be recognized and valued more highly in order to affect the costing analysis. With respect to the global warming issue, these benefits would include cleaner cities, lower energy expenditures, and less reliance on foreign supplies of energy. . . .

One more point remains to be made with regard to the analysis of costs and benefits. Some players in this issue may not regard global warming as an international collective good. Instead, they may see the developments that would be induced by significant climatic change as being beneficial for their state. For example, the [former] USSR could experience greater agricultural productivity from global warming. I feel that this view is misplaced, because the severe ramifications of global systemic change should cause all states to perceive a stable, habitable global environment as a universal benefit which should be pursued. Nevertheless, until all actors are in agreement with this proposition, cooperation will be hampered. . . .

We must remember that the world is composed of states concerned about their security in the anarchical international society. Although there is some recognition that all countries of the world share a common future, political realities dictate that competition does still exist among states. A government is expected not only to further the interest of its own people (hence the recognition, above, of the role that economic costs play) but it is also not expected to afford other states a disproportionate share of any benefit mutually achieved in an international dealing. If states are to pursue cooperative arrangements, their leaders will expect not only to achieve an absolute gain, but also to avoid a relative loss.

Therefore a second major precondition for cooperation is the presence of fairness, in a system-wide sense. It has been recognized in the literature that in order for a state to enter into an agreement, the terms of the cooperative venture must be seen, by the state, to be equitable.[37] Such equity will not only be based on a comparative analysis of costs and benefits, but it will also be based on less tangible factors, such as history and ideology.

This issue of fairness will continue to play a significant role in the pursuit of a cooperative agreement on issues of global environmental change. Although individual governments have already hinted at reasons why they should be given special consideration in any venture, the largest problem of fairness is, and will continue to be, raised by North-South relations.

Industrialization in the North has resulted in two important consequences: a higher standard of living for these states and an increasingly fragile environment, worldwide. The North is now asking the South to join it in a global effort to stabilize the atmosphere. But the South has not significantly contributed to the deterioration of the atmosphere and therefore does not feel a responsibility to bear the burden of helping to solve this problem. This burden would involve sacrificing the use of certain materials and processes and thereby hampering their attempts to progress toward a higher level of industrialization. It seems that the full cooperation of these states will depend on a satisfactory response from the North to their demand for justice.

The demand for justice was finally met in the ozone layer case in June 1990. At that time, an international fund (valued at U.S. $240 million over 3 years) to help Southern countries to use alternative chemicals was agreed. Such a fund had been a major precondition of participation for states such as India and China.[38] Until that point, concessionary gestures—a 10-year grace period[39] and promises of technological assistance—had not been sufficient. . . .

The negotiations on the ozone layer depletion issue have served, to some extent, as a "dry run" for the larger issue of global warming. The demand for justice has also been articulated in the South's call for a general climate fund to be established in order to help them pursue sustainable methods of industrializing. . . . The dominant consideration in the fairness controversy will continue to be between the North and the South. For if international cooperation is to be achieved on global warming, justice as it applies to North-South relations will have to be agreed.

With regard to dilemmas of collective action, the attainment of the benefit is necessarily dependent on the action of others. Although cooperation may yield the most desirable result for society, each state is also subjected to the temptation to cheat and get a free ride—that is, not pay the cost, but perhaps receive the benefit nevertheless—and therefore realize a higher net gain. Such pressure will be even greater if there is a feeling that others will cheat, because, for a variety of reasons, states would not want to shoulder an inappropriate share of the burden.

Thus another precondition for international cooperation involves expectations—that is, the extent to which participants believe that the developing arrangements are viable and that they will be adhered to. With regard to these environmental issues, this suggests that effective cooperation will require states to publish production and emission figures for a variety of substances and industrial processes. Monitoring and verification will then become important, because no state will want to be making sacrifices while others "cheat." What may seem to be a straightforward matter is hampered by the important consideration of data sovereignty. Keohane has recognized that information can be regarded as "a significant variable in world politics."[41] Indeed, data can be manipulated so to be used as powerful instruments of coercion. Thus many states, especially the weak and the suspicious, may think that the environmental data will be used for other ends—goals which do not bring about worldwide collective benefits, but which instead entrench some sort of neoimperialist dependent relationship. Therefore it would seem that some sort of atmosphere of trust is a precondition for satisfactory expectation, which in turn, is a precondition for cooperation.

With regard to our two issues, it appears that the "expectation" precondition can be much more easily fulfilled in the ozone layer depletion issue. There are a relatively few CFC producers, importers, and exporters in the world. Further, these companies operate in a relatively small number of states. Therefore, the implementation and operation of a monitoring system will not prove to be such a daunting task.[42] There are, however, a vast number of greenhouse gas producers throughout the world. Therefore, because the global warming issue is so wide in scope, the realization of an effective monitoring system will be much more difficult to achieve. Perhaps the experience in arms control (i.e., verification and confidence-building measures) can be an important analogy or precedent. Nevertheless, in both cases, the expectation of compliance will be an important factor in the quest for international cooperation.

The presence of a scientific consensus is another key precondition. International cooperation will remain elusive as long as there is disagreement about the issue being discussed. Consensus will need to include an agreement on the nature and identification of the problem under investigation, an agreement on the data collection process and an agreement on the method of data interpretation.

With regard to the interpretation of the problem under investigation, it has been recognized that "the degree of ideological consensus and agreement over causal relationships, regardless of the nature of the issue, is an important variable in explaining cooperation."[43] Thus the extent to which the actors hold a common perception, interpretation, and understanding of the problem is directly related to the extent of international cooperation.

Also, in order to achieve a cooperative agreement, there must be an acknowledged credible process whereby information is gathered on the issue.[44] Whatever the means, it must be agreed that the raw information being collected is accurate and that the analysis is acceptable to all parties involved. . . .

The ozone layer depletion issue is an important case in point in this regard. The original theory that implicated CFCs was postulated by Sherry Rowland and Mario Molina in 1974.[46] This theory, however, was not generally accepted until 1987. In the interim, a scientific consensus remained elusive for a number of reasons.

During the 1970s, the data that were being collected in this branch of atmospheric chemistry had significant error bars attached to them. . . . It was only with the creation of a more extensive ground monitoring system, the use of satellite monitoring and the development of sensitive solid-state infrared detectors during the 1980s[49] that more faith could be placed in the raw data. With such developments, some sort of agreement on the data collection process was finally realized.

The discovery of a significant "crater" in the ozone layer above the Antarctic in 1985 by the British Antarctic Survey[50] made it clear that the issue of ozone depletion was, indeed, a significant problem. Nevertheless, there was still debate over the interpretation of this phenomenon, and therefore agreement about the cause of the depletion remained elusive. At the time three contending theories—the CFC or chemical theory, the natural or dynamic theory and the solar cycle or "odd-nitrogen" theory[51]—were popular with significant sections of the scientific community. Each theory remained viable until 1987.

In 1987 a major expedition, organized by NASA, traveled to the Antarctic in order to investigate ozone depletion. The journey's results demonstrated "an undoubted chemical cause in the destruction of ozone by atmospheric chlorine."[52] With this pronouncement the cause of ozone depletion was no longer a major point of contention. Thus it is clear that as the scientific method improved— readings became more reliable, a significant problem was identified, and an explanation was agreed on—the scientists were able to provide more reliable information to policymakers. This example highlights the important way in which relations between the scientific and governmental communities affect international cooperation.[53]

. . . The scientific consensus on the global warming issue is by no means concrete. The theory on which the argument is based is accepted by a large portion of the scientific community.[54] It is also agreed that there has not only been an increase in the carbon dioxide levels in the atmosphere,[55] but that there has also been an increase in the observed global average temperature since the beginning of this century.[56] What remains to be resolved is whether or not the observed warming is causally linked to the greenhouse phenomena. Despite all of the attention that has been paid to the case for global warming, there are still a number of questions that need to be answered.

There are those who suggest that the temperature change could well be just a result of the variability of solar output. Further, there has been a suggestion that the effects of alterations on the earth's orbital pattern may be having an effect on the planet's temperatures. Finally, it may simply be that the fluctuations are a reflection of the high noise to signal ratio. Because the current warming trend can only be traced back uninterrupted for 12 years (average global temperatures were stable or decreased from 1940 to the late 1970s), it may be that people are reading something into the data that they should not be. Scientists have noted that it will be at least 10 years before anyone will be uncategorically certain that we are experiencing greenhouse-induced global warming.[57]

Even among those who agree that global warming is upon us, there is no consensus on what the future may hold, because some important questions about the natural processes involved still remain unanswered. At this point, scientists do not know if increased cloudiness will mean that more heat will be reflected back to space before it enters the troposphere or whether more heat will be trapped in the "greenhouse." Obviously, either process would be an important feedback in the system—although the former would be negative and the latter would be positive. Further, it is unclear how the physical, chemical, and biological activities of the ocean will be affected by global warming. Finally, the role of plant life in a carbon-dioxide-enriched atmosphere is not clearly understood. These are just a few examples of the uncertainties which are hampering present efforts to understand the global climate.

It is clear that in order to achieve some sort of cooperative agreement, scientific consensus will be needed. In order to build this consensus, better theory and more data will be required. Such a requirement, however, once again raises the consideration about data sovereignty. For the reasons outlined above, some states may be reluctant to fully participate in the efforts to achieve scientific harmony. Thus the fulfillment of this precondition may be hindered. . . .

Conclusions

This article has examined disputes over environmental issues, focusing on the problems associated with global environmental change. . . . To this end, four preconditions for international cooperation were identified: economic costs, fairness, expectations and commonalities. These preconditions were examined in-depth and applied to the experience of the ozone layer depletion and global warming issues. By applying the evidence to the theory, some insight into the reasons for conflict and cooperation was provided. Further, this framework can be used to examine the potential for future international cooperation, and thus the chances of avoiding and/or resolving future international disputes in these issues.

SHEILA JASANOFF

15

Skinning
Scientific Cats

LET ME BEGIN with the picture that unquestionably accounts for the birth of the modern environmental movement. The World Commission on Environment and Development has this to say in its influential work, *Our Common Future:*

> In the middle of the 20th century, we saw our planet from space for the first time. Historians may eventually find that this vision had a greater impact on thought than did the Copernican revolution of the 16th century. . . . From space we see a small and fragile ball, dominated not by human activity and edifice, but a pattern of clouds, greenery, oceans and soil. Humanity's inability to fit its activities into that pattern is changing boundary systems fundamentally.

The idea of the scientific revolution is never far from the minds of those who comment on the Apollo picture. Many environmentalists have argued that what the picture of the biosphere truly accomplished was a paradigm shift in our ways of thinking about how the world works: the "fourth discontinuity". It was a moment that displaced the human ego by making it conscious of the physical finiteness of the place it inhabits. The effect was on a par with the three great discontinuities of the past: the Copernican revolution, which displaced the earth from the centre of the human universe, the Darwinian revolution, which displaced human beings from the pinnacle of the tree of creation, and the Freudian revolution, which exposed the unconscious, and told humankind that we are not the masters in our own house.

But the scientific paradigm of ecological interconnectedness does not, in fact, provide answers to questions about what we human beings are entitled to do with

---

Originally published in *New Statesman and Society,* 26 February 1993, pp. 29–30. Copyright © *New Statesman and Society.* Reprinted with permission.

our environment. What science is, and how we apply it to our needs, is thus far from straightforward.

The first point I want to make is that scientific inquiry, contrary to expectation, does not always lead to the same explanation for the same observed phenomenon. Consider the seasonal flooding in the plains of northern India, where two competing theories obstinately occupy the field. On the one hand, there is a "mountain theory", preferred by environmental bureaucrats and developers, that holds that population pressure in the foothills of the Himalayas is causing deforestation and soil erosion, and that these effects in turn are responsible for the flooding below.

The contrasting "plains theory", upheld by environmental activists and indigenous people living in the hilly regions, ascribes the flooding to poor resource-management practices lower down. For them, it is the indiscriminate clearing of forests, the damming of rivers, and the resulting siltation of river beds that lead to uncontrollable floods. Uphill tree cutting adds little or nothing in the way of separate environmental stress. So who is to blame? The non-modernised primitive practices of ecologically unconscious indigenous peoples somewhere up in the mountains? Or a model of development dominated by centralised money-lenders, international financial and other institutions?

Controversies of this kind are familiar to many people, and science seems unable to provide satisfying answers. For in the complex systems under study, enough suggestive and even persuasive evidence can be found to sustain very different overall stories about what is *really* going on. Lacking ways of testing or falsification, neither theoretical position is able to deal a body blow to the other. Ideology and politics thus become the primary determinants of choosing among competing scientific accounts of felt reality.

A second point of almost equal importance is that when people reach scientific conclusions about the reasons for a particular natural phenomenon, their explanations are not always the same. To take one case, US public health experts have been convinced for many years that an important reason to reduce lead levels in the environment is the damage the metal causes even at lowest-dose levels to children's learning behavior. When Britain decided to phase out lead additives from petrol, almost ten years after the US, the reasons the British experts provided did not prominently include children's health, an issue regarded as hopelessly uncertain and divisive. Rather their decision was based on findings that lead was toxic, even at very low doses, that it was highly persistent in the environment, and that alternatives to many current uses of lead could be found without damaging the economy. So, in the end, both these countries chose to phase lead additives out of petrol, but the scientific pathways they took to get to these results were very different.

A third point that complicates our initially simplistic connection between science and action is that what compels people to act upon a perceived problem is not necessarily knowledge that is endorsed by science. An example of such an unscientific consensus are the factors that produced agreement on the

Mediterranean Action Plan. Many countries signed on to the treaty because of a mistaken but compelling notion that pollution anywhere in the Mediterranean basin would be equally harmful to all of the coastal states.

By some accounts, UN Environment Programme experts, who participated in the treaty negotiations, apparently knew that the ecological paradigm as applied to the Mediterranean did not in fact drive everybody's pollution up on everybody else's shores. But they withheld this knowledge from the participants, on the theory that it was desirable for the right decision to be taken, in environmental terms, even on the basis of the wrong scientific reason.

In fourth place, just as too little science can sometimes aid decision-making, so too much science sometimes overwhelms the capacity to act. There are many reasons why this can be the case. More information may, to begin with, simply create more grounds for argument, especially when strong enough refereeing agencies cannot be found. Information, too, can outstrip the capacity of our societies to analyse, synthesise and apply to programmes of action. In our own recent past, environmental problems that have reached such a stalemate of knowledge include, prominently, the acid rain controversy, where no new study, however compelling, was likely to change how people believed on that issue. Unless great care is taken, there are signs that at least aspects of the climate-change problem are in danger today of being studied to death in this fashion.

Fifth, and finally, I'd like to mention those instances when states or interest groups agree that a problem exists, but cannot agree about how the problem should be conceptualised for purposes of scientific investigation. To decide what needs to be studied, one needs, in effect, to impose a kind of moral map on the issue in question. And this map may differ from country to country, or even from one scientific organisation to another.

Let's take the so-called problem of human cancer. Now there appears to be good scientific agreement that some fraction of human cancers are caused by environmental factors, such as diet, smoking, certain lifestyle choices *and* by exposure to chemicals. Yet if you look across the spectrum of research-rich nations, the emphasis has not, in fact, been equal on all of these possible areas of explanation. No other country, to my knowledge, can match the US in the richness, intensity, scope and variety of programmes for researching the health effects of industrial chemicals, including their carcinogenicity.

As a result, many have found it difficult to avoid the conclusion that chemicals occupy a different niche in the collective American consciousness of environmental hazards from the niche they occupy in any other country. When it comes to studying the causes of complex environmental problems, there is almost always more than one way to skin the scientific cat. And these choices are not themselves scientific. They're deeply social, cultural, and ethical.

A historical example of this was the mid-century study, funded by the Rockefeller Foundation, to study and solve the problem of world hunger. We all know the miraculous results of that voyage of discovery, the creation of those high-yielding grain varieties that ushered in the green revolution. But students of the green revolution have come in time to ask not merely what was achieved and scientifically celebrated, but also what was not studied, what went unexplored or under-explored, like the environmental consequences of the heavy use of pesticides and fertilisers, which were needed to make the green revolution take root and flourish. The individual life experiences, or even the collective local knowledge of the groups that science was going to help, whose problem of hunger science was going to solve, never figured in the scientific agenda setting.

You will recognise that the implicit hierarchy that the green revolution scientists established is the hierarchy that dominates our western scientific sensibility that some approaches to understanding nature are superior to others. In this hierarchy, not surprisingly, it is the basic physical and biological sciences that occupy the top of the ladder. The social sciences are relegated to some indeterminate middle position. Much lower down, usually disappearing from the frame of inquiry completely, are the unsystematised, or nonprofessionalised ways of knowing nature that are characteristic of the people often living closest to environmental problems.

If more international cooperation in science is necessary to do a better job of understanding and coping with environmental change, then we are not going to get much international cooperation unless we sit down together and address some very important prior questions: What is the problem we are trying to define? From whose point of view is it a problem? Why is it seen as scientific? What do we mean by science? And which areas of science are we going to privilege while we go about seeking solutions?

ANIL AGARWAL & SUNITA NARAIN

16

Global Warming in an Unequal World: A Case of Environmental Colonialism

THE IDEA THAT DEVELOPING countries like India and China must share the blame for heating up the Earth and destabilizing its climate—as espoused in a recent study published in the United States by the World Resources Institute in collaboration with the United Nations Environment Program—is an excellent example of environmental colonialism. India and China may account for more than one-third of the world's population, but are these two nations really responsible for flushing one-third of the muck and dirt into the world's air and oceans?

The report of the World Resources Institute (WRI), a Washington-based private research group, is based less on science than politically motivated mathematics. Its main intention seems to be to blame developing countries for global warming and to perpetuate the current global inequity in the use of the Earth's environment and its resources. . . .

The exercise of blaming developing countries has already begun. Until recently, it was widely accepted that developed countries of the West consume most of the world's fossil fuels and produce most of the carbon dioxide—the main agents of global warming. In recent years, however, Western nations have been carrying out a sustained propaganda campaign alleging that deforestation in developing countries, and the generation of methane through irrigated rice farming and the rais-

Originally published in *Earth Island Journal* (Spring 1991):39–40. Reprinted with permission.

ing of cattle, is also contributing to global warming. This has shifted the onus onto developing countries.

Recently, the World Resources Institute and the United Nations Environment Program released the annual report, *World Resources 1990–91*, that stated for the first time that India, China and Brazil are among the top five countries responsible for the accumulation of these gases in the Earth's atmosphere.

Cooking the Figures

The figures used by the WRI to calculate the quantity of carbon dioxide and methane produced by each country are extremely questionable. Heavy emphasis has been placed on comparisons of carbon dioxide produced by deforestation and methane generated by rice fields and livestock to carbon dioxide produced by burning fossil fuels like oil and coal—an emphasis that tends to underplay the impact of the developed countries.

The methane issue raises further questions of justice and morality. Can we really equate the carbon dioxide contributions of gas guzzling automobiles in Europe and North America (or, for that matter, anywhere in the Third World) with the methane emissions of water buffalo and rice fields of subsistence farmers in West Bengal or Thailand? Do these people not have a right to live? No effort has been made to separate the "survival emissions" of the poor, from the "luxury emissions" of the rich.

Old Numbers; New Recipe

A study conducted by India's Centre for Science and Environment (CSE), which uses WRI's data for each country's gaseous emissions, concludes that developing countries are responsible for only 16 percent of the carbon dioxide accumulating in the Earth's atmosphere. The WRI report claims a Third World share of 48 percent. Similarly, developing countries were not found to be responsible for any excess methane accumulation, although WRI claims a Third World share of 56 percent.

This difference is explained by a simple fact: no country can be blamed for the gases accumulating in the Earth's atmosphere until each country's share in the Earth's cleansing ability has been apportioned on a fair and equitable basis. Since most of the cleansing is done by the oceans and troposphere, the Earth has to be treated as a common heritage of mankind. Good environmental management demands that all nations should learn to live within the Earth's ability to absorb these gaseous wastes.

Since there is no reason to believe that any human being in any part of the world is more or less important than another, CSE has apportioned the world's restoration ability to each country in proportion to its share of the world's population. Thus India, with 16 percent of the world's population, gets 16 percent of the Earth's natural air and ocean "sinks" for carbon dioxide and methane absorption. Describing these emissions as "permissible," CSE finds that India is producing carbon dioxide just equal to six percent of the world's natural sinks and methane equal to 14 of the natural sinks. How, then, can India be blamed for any of the excess carbon dioxide or methane that is accumulating in the Earth's atmosphere?

The same scenario is true for China, Pakistan, Sri Lanka, Egypt, Kenya, Nigeria, Tanzania, Zimbabwe and Chile. Meanwhile, almost all Western countries are emitting well beyond their "permissible shares" of the Earth's carbon dioxide and methane sinks. Clearly, it is Western wastes and willful over-consumption of the world's natural resources that are polluting the Earth and threatening the global environment.

What WRI has done instead is to calculate the percentage of India's total emissions of carbon dioxide and methane before they are absorbed and then hold India responsible for the same quantitative share of the gases actually accumulating in the Earth's atmosphere. This manner of calculating each nation's responsibility is extremely unfair and amounts to a scientific sleight of hand.

According to the WRI-UNEP calculations, the US, which produces 14.4 percent of the world's annual output of the carbon dioxide that is actually accumulating every year, becomes responsible for only 14.4 percent of the carbon dioxide that is actually accumulating every year. The CSE's analysis, however, indicates the United States, with only 4.73 percent of the world's population, emits as much as 26 percent of the carbon dioxide and 20 percent of the methane that is absorbed every year.

It is the production of carbon dioxide and methane by countries like the US and Japan—totally out of proportion to their population and that of the world's absorptive capacity—that is responsible for accumulation of excess, unabsorbed carbon dioxide and methane in the atmosphere. . . . Meanwhile India, with 3.4 times the population of the US, gets less than one fourth of the US' share of the planet's natural sink.

India and China account for less than 0.5 percent of net emissions to the atmosphere, while WRI claims they together contribute about 10 percent. The CSE analysis shows India to be the world's lowest per capita net emitter of greenhouse gases.

. . . Industrialized countries have together exceeded their permissible quotas of carbon dioxide by 2839 million tons of carbon equivalent—50 percent of excess global carbon dioxide emissions. The WRI-UNEP method of calculating pollution is extremely unfair because it favors the biggest polluters—i.e., the bigger the polluter, the larger the share of the sink it gets. . . .

Emissions & Omissions

CSE's method offers a better way of calculating each country's responsibility for global warming. Not only do developing countries get a fair share of the Earth's natural cleansing ability, but several industrialized countries also benefit. Using

CSE's analysis, France's contribution to all greenhouse gases goes down by 43 percent, Japan's and Italy's by 36 percent, the United Kingdom's by 12 percent, and West Germany's by four percent.

On the other hand, Saudi Arabia's share goes up by 131 percent, Canada's by 110 percent, Australia's by 78 percent, and the US share jumps 53 percent. Since the US is the largest emitter of greenhouse gases, this increase overshadows that of all other countries.

The WRI-UNEP figures for methane and carbon dioxide emissions are based on just a handful of Western measurements of cattle and rice field emissions that have then been projected over the entire world. The existing data on deforestation rates are also extremely shaky. Brazil, a frequent target of WRI criticism for deforestation, has accused the organization of inflating its deforestation rates by 300 to 400 percent.

The entire WRI-UNEP study appears designed to bolster both foreign aid and domestic policy interests of Western nations whose governments would like to convince their environmentalists that their nations are not to blame and cannot do much locally unless they rope in the hapless Third World.

. . .

It is time for the Third World to ask the West: "Whose future generations are we seeking to protect—the Western World's or the Third World's?"

PETER M. HAAS, MARC A. LEVY
& EDWARD A. PARSON

17

Appraising the Earth Summit: How Should We Judge UNCED's Success?

WHETHER THE UNITED NATIONS Conference on Environment and Development (UNCED), held from 3 to 14 June 1992 in Rio de Janeiro, Brazil, constitutes cause for hope or for despair is a complex question. Without the benefit of a decade of hindsight, how does one appraise the effectiveness of a meeting that brought together more than 150 nations, 1,400 nongovernmental organizations (NGOs), and 8,000 journalists, as well as thousands of Brazilians?[1]

Instead of being judged against a single conception of what its outcome should have been, the conference, dubbed the Earth Summit, must be judged within the context of a process of increasing attention, sophistication, and effectiveness in the management of environment and development issues.[2] As UNCED Secretary-General Maurice F. Strong said in his opening address to UNCED,

> The Earth Summit is not an end in itself, but a new beginning. The measures you agree on here will be but first steps on a new pathway to our common future. Thus, the results of this conference will ultimately depend on the credibility and effectiveness of its follow-up. . . . The preparatory process has provided the basis for this and

Originally published in *Environment* 34, 8 (October 1992):7–11; 26–32. Reprinted with permission of the Helen Dwight Reid Educational Foundation. Published by Heldref Publications, 1319 Eighteenth St., N.W., Washington, D.C. 20036–1802. Copyright © 1992.

the momentum which has brought us to Rio must be maintained. And institutional changes, as the secretary general has said, to be made within the United Nations must provide an effective and credible basis for its continued leadership of this process.[3]
. . .

Thus, the important question is not how many treaties were signed or what specific actions were agreed on but, rather, how effectively UNCED contributed to this broader process. This more politically sensitive judgment of UNCED should be of greater use both to observers who wish to make sense of the unfolding political activities and to practitioners attempting to enhance the process.

International conferences and institutions are only as effective as governments choose to make them. International efforts to promote environmental protection have been most effective when they enhance governmental concern, provide a forum for governments to harmonize international policies, and improve national capacities to cope with environmental threats.[4] Did UNCED help establish incentives for governments to renew and reinforce their efforts to protect the environment? Did UNCED help governments deal with the unbreakable links between environmental protection and economic development in the Third World? To answer such questions, it is helpful to examine the four central outcomes of the UNCED process—specifically, new international institutions, national reporting measures, financial mechanisms, and heightened public and NGO participation.
. . .

New International Institutions

The agreements signed in Rio created several new international institutions.[9] Agenda 21 created a new United Nations body: the Sustainable Development Commission. The conventions on climate change and biodiversity created new bodies for scientific and technical advice relating to the treaties and their implementation. . . .

Of the formal intergovernmental institutions called for at UNCED, the Sustainable Development Commission is likely to have the greatest impact on global politics. The commission will be responsible for carrying out the objectives in the "Institutions" chapter of Agenda 21. The commission's two broad classes of responsibilities are stated as integrating the United Nations' and other agencies' sector-specific activities relevant to environment and development issues and monitoring progress on UNCED's agenda. Integration and monitoring are vital because of the vast scope of measures in Agenda 21, which will affect activities throughout the entire UN system. The commission . . . [is] a high-level body composed of representatives of the 54 member states of the UN Economic and Social Council (ECOSOC) and . . . [reports] to ECOSOC just as the UN Environment Programme (UNEP) does. . . .

The commission's mandate gives it great potential to raise governmental and public concern for the environment and development agenda by holding regular high-level meetings to monitor progress on Agenda 21. Meetings of the commission, particularly if they include a ministerial session, could focus the attention of the press, public, and activists on global environment and development issues, much as the G-7 summits do for global economic issues or the European environmental summits for environmental issues within Europe. The crucial issue is that such meetings should be conducted at a high enough level to maintain public pressure for compliance. . . .

The commission also could facilitate bargaining aimed at implementing and strengthening Agenda 21 among governments and international organizations. The UNCED agenda presumes that human activities that were once thought unrelated to each other, in fact, have intimate biological, physical, and social connections. Acting on this insight will require both detailed coordination of the agendas of national and international sectorial agencies and political bargains involving linked actions by different nations on environment and development priorities—for example, financial assistance and technology transfer from the North being linked to, or dependent on, increased environmental protection in the South. . . .

It is far from certain, however, that the commission will be given the chance to fulfill this potential. Because of political disagreements and time constraints at UNCED, the commission's mandate is vague on several crucial questions. It does not specifically call for national reports to the commission, for example, but, rather, indicates that the commission will "consider information provided by Governments, including for example in the form of periodic communication or national reports."[12] . . .

The modest institutions created under the two conventions signed in Rio have less potential to foster dramatic change. [Editors' note: Conventions on climate change and biodiversity were negotiated in the Preparatory Committee or PrepCom meetings leading up to UNCED and signed at the conference itself. A third proposed treaty, on forests, collapsed during the preconference negotiating.] Both conventions call for the establishment of "subsidiary bodies" to provide scientific and technical advice to the secretariat and to bodies responsible for administering the conventions. The climate change convention also calls for the monitoring of implementation. These subsidiary bodies are important because they will evaluate the need for regulations and alternative response options. Because, in both conventions, these subsidiary bodies are declared to be open only to "government representatives," each government will decide who may or may not serve from within its borders, and it will be difficult for nongovernmental officials to serve at all. This approach contrasts starkly with the scientific and technical review panels established by the Montreal Protocol on Substances That Deplete the Ozone Layer, which were open to experts without governmental approval. These panels were highly effective at promoting consensus on scientific controversies and at uncovering creative solutions. Because these two conventions give governments more control over choosing the panels, chances are that panel members will be expected to carry specific government briefs and to refrain from the type of open-minded give and take that makes learning and problem-solving possible.[14] . . .

National Reporting

UNCED adopted a number of reporting commitments for national governments. Participating countries were invited to submit national reports on their environment and development as part of their preparations for UNCED. The secretariat produced a series of guidelines that included a "suggestion" that independent sectors of society be involved in the preparation process. Few countries met the submission deadline of July 1991. By November 1991, about 75 reports had been submitted, and 130 were received by mid-April. Thus, the preparations for UNCED and preparations of sectorial papers for the chapters of Agenda 21 were completed without systematic information about the actual conditions and experiences in many countries. A number of NGOs produced "alternative" reports on conditions in their countries and their countries' experiences with policies to promote sustainable development.[18] . . .

In the future, governments will have to report to the Sustainable Development Commission about activities they intend to undertake to implement Agenda 21 and about problems they face regarding financial resources and technology transfer and other relevant environment and development issues. A regular schedule of reporting serves many functions. The UNCED secretariat saw the preparation of national reports as a way to increase public participation in decisionmaking. About 80 to 85 governments formed national committees to prepare the reports, "and quite a few involved NGOs, women's groups, industry, the church, and even the Army."[19] Even though the reports varied widely in quality, their preparation may have led governments to recognize new problems. In addition, the preparation of reports led governments to create new institutional channels through which affected groups can pressure and monitor governmental activities in the area of sustainable development. Ongoing reporting to the commission on follow-up activities should maintain governmental concern. Moreover, reasonably frequent reporting by governments and NGOs could lead governments to learn of new problems and solutions and would make information available to other concerned groups that may hold governments accountable. Such reporting can contribute to both government concern and national capacity to identify environmental problems and assess policies.

The full elaboration of reporting obligations will be one of the early tasks of the commission. UNCED negotiators were divided over how often and in what form these reports ought to be submitted. Third World representatives originally feared that they would be forced to reveal proprietary information (although the nature of this information was never clear), that they may lack the necessary administrative capabilities to gather information and complete such reports, and that such information could be used to require a new form of conditionality in loans from the World Bank and the International Monetary Fund. The Sustainable Development Commission may have to offer both training and funds for governments to learn how to report. . . .

In addition to national reporting, UNCED called for the establishment of a number of monitoring networks. Such networks, if they are fully developed, could reinforce national reporting by providing a nonpartisan counterpart to national reports, as well as another constituency demanding national reporting. Agenda 21 detailed a variety of specific monitoring activities. . . .

Financial Measures

UNCED failed to muster sufficient financial commitments to support all of Agenda 21. After a lengthy North-South deadlock, broken by extremely contentious negotiations by heads of state, UNCED adopted the following text:

> Developed countries reaffirm their commitments to reach the accepted UN target of 0.7% of GNP for ODA [Editors' note: official development assistance] and, to the extent that they have not yet achieved that target, agree to augment their aid programmes in order to reach that target as soon as possible and to ensure a prompt and effective implementation of Agenda 21.[20]

The less developed countries were disappointed with the looseness of this resolution. They saw official development assistance (ODA), consisting of grants and concessionary loans, as a major source of financing activities under Agenda 21. The secretariat initially estimated that the full cost of implementing Agenda 21 in developing countries would be roughly $600 billion per year, of which about $125 billion annually would come from industrial-country sources and the balance from developing-country resources. A major question at the conference was the source of the $125 billion. Present concessionary funding from member countries of the Organization for Economic Cooperation and Development (OECD) totals only $60 billion annually.[21] Third World representatives had hoped to obtain increased OECD unilateral commitments, subsidized technology transfer, debt relief, and an increase in ODA to 0.7 percent of the OECD countries' gross domestic product.[22]

The phrasing accepted at Rio, however, frees countries of any real new financing commitments. Several industrialized countries, including the United States and Switzerland, have not made any commitments to increase ODA levels to 0.7 percent, and many that have made such commitments have not shown signs of fulfilling them. Furthermore, the deadline year of 2000, which had been sought by the group of Third World countries known as G-77, was listed as a suggestion, not a firm target. The OECD countries refused to grant any debt relief.

The mechanisms for financing Agenda 21 remain, therefore, as they were before the Earth Summit: existing aid agencies and ad-hoc unilateral pledges. Unilateral pledges of additional aid for Agenda 21 are unlikely ever to amount to more than a minor percentage of what is required. In Rio, at a time when wealthy governments were under perhaps the greatest pressure to offer significant contributions, the most optimistic estimates tallied only from $6 billion to $7 billion in new commitments. Actual totals may be even lower. Many public commitments during the final days of the conference were oblique; it remains difficult to determine whether leaders were reiterating existing commitments, whether new sums of money were being offered, or whether development assistance was being redirected from other areas to the environment. Japan, for instance, offered $7.7 billion in environmental assistance over the next five years, but, upon closer inspection, that sum included an increase over existing levels of about $500 million per year. Many observers were disappointed that the G-7 economic summit in Munich, held in early July, failed to clarify some of these commitments.

Discussions of using existing aid agencies to finance Agenda 21 focus on the World Bank. The centerpiece of the bank's environmental activity is the Global Environment Facility (GEF), which the bank administers along with UNDP [Editors' note: United Nations Development Programme] and UNEP. GEF was created in 1990 as a three-year pilot program and given the mandate of allocating $1.3 billion for projects related to global warming, biodiversity, international waters, and ozone depletion.

A G-77 initiative to establish an independent "green fund" in lieu of GEF was dismissed by the industrialized countries. G-77 countries distrust the World Bank because they perceive it as intrusive in domestic policymaking and dominated by developed countries (voting at the bank is weighted according to the size of a country's contribution)....

GEF has a tortuous path to follow if it is to play more than its currently nominal role in helping to finance Agenda 21. The facility is under pressure from two conflicting sources. On one hand, the G-77 countries are demanding greater openness in GEF governance and greater decisionmaking power for fund recipients. The April reforms addressed some of these concerns. On the other hand, however, donor countries are insisting that any significant increase in funds be accompanied by strict screening procedures and reliable oversight mechanisms. Running through much of the donor-country opposition to higher aid levels is the view that such aid is likely to be wasted by inefficient economic policies or, worse, corrupt public officials.... Resolving the essential contradiction between open governance and tighter oversight remains a major piece of unfinished business that was not addressed rigorously at UNCED.

Closely related to the discussions about finance was the subject of the transfer of environmentally sound technology because of the significant amount of public funds that might be involved to subsidize the acquisition of technology. Developing countries attempted to obtain commitments that technology would be provided on terms that were preferential and below market prices. Industrialized countries were wary of acceding to a norm that might oblige them to require their firms to turn over technology at a loss. On technology transfer issues, therefore, Agenda 21 uses terms such as "mutually agreed on" measures, or market transactions. Chapter 34 of Agenda 21 affirms the need to promote, facilitate, and finance "as appropriate" access to proprietary technologies through commercial channels. The chapter also states that nations should undertake measures to prevent abuse of intellectual property rights as they are defined under existing international conventions and accepted rules of commerce. . . .

On the questions of financial assistance and technology transfer, then, UNCED moved no further than reiterating prior international norms. The next chance for the issue to be addressed seriously may be during subsequent negotiations for the Climate Change Convention. Many negotiators hope to establish concrete mechanisms for transferring financial resources and energy-efficient technology to developing countries in exchange for greenhouse-gas reduction policies there.

Public and NGO Involvement

The amount and variety of involvement by NGOs at UNCED were striking. Thousands of them participated in the official conference at RioCentro and in parallel events at the Global Forum. Although NGOs have participated in UN conferences for more than 20 years, the scale, variety, and sophistication of NGO involvement at UNCED were unprecedented.

UNCED organizers supported NGO involvement from the outset and accredited NGOs with any substantive claim to being involved in activities related to the environment and development. An extremely broad set of NGOs participated in all formal and some informal UNCED sessions: academic groups, trade unions, business associations, associations of legislators and local authorities, religious groups, and groups representing women, youth, and indigenous peoples, as well as environmental and developmental groups.

NGOs were granted similar standing in the parallel negotiations for the climate and biodiversity treaties, and they used the opportunity effectively. Environmental NGOs at the climate sessions published a sophisticated, irreverent daily newsletter that gained a reputation as the best (and liveliest) source of information on the negotiations. They also developed effective networks, such as the five regional Climate Action Networks, which lobbied national delegations in their regions and coordinated an international strategy in the negotiations. At the New York PrepCom, NGOs formed issue-oriented task forces to coordinate their lobbying, which had substantial success in terms of getting draft proposals to be discussed by delegations and influencing the final content of documents. . . .

In Rio, NGO activity split onto two tracks. At the official conference, there were more than 1,400 NGOs accredited, including NGO observers on 15 national delegations. Environmental NGOs (mostly sophisticated and well-funded North American and European ones) lobbied delegations, talked to the press, and operated a full-time office with daily press briefings.[26] The other main NGO events in Rio were held at the separate Global Forum. . . . The two most significant activities taking place under the forum umbrella were a series of technical, scientific, and policy meetings held at 50 sites around the city and an ambitious exercise in parallel treaty writing conducted by an international network of NGOs called the International Forum of NGOs and Social Movements.

The treaty-writing exercise was organized because of NGO frustration with the lack of progress in the early PrepComs, and it was originally conceived of as an exercise in direct citizen's diplomacy to produce agreements on actions NGOs themselves would undertake. . . . The project was intended to create, in addition to the treaties, an institutional mechanism for coordinating NGO follow-up activity internationally. Although late completion of the treaties left little time to discuss follow-up coordinating mechanisms, NGOs are trying to maintain and solidify the transnational links they built up through the forum. . . .

The connection between the forum and UNCED was much less direct than rhetoric suggested. The two venues were each so intense and consuming and so far apart that few organizations participated significantly in both events. Participants in the forum did not get a chance to present their treaties to the summit and settled instead for a thinly attended press conference at the RioCentro site with, in fact, many more NGO representatives than journalists in attendance. Indeed, there was some suspicion among NGOs that the NGO forum was intentionally hobbled, despite rhetorical support, by a late organizational start and meager funding.

Nevertheless, the forum served three major functions that NGO involvement at the summit did not. First, it helped NGOs to appreciate their different perspectives and agendas and to confront the difficulties of collaboration across lines of language, culture, and wealth. For many organizations, the rationale for their involvement was the edification of their staffs and members. One NGO commentator noted that UNCED may have been "the most expensive adult-education exercise ever undertaken."[27] Preliminary results of a survey of NGOs confirm that many regarded their networking and educational activities in Rio as more important than their lobbying.[28] Many developed-country NGO members said that they would seek to expand their own future agendas to take closer account of the concerns of developing-country NGOs. Although this learning process generated some anger and frustration, it is surely an essential step for developing effective international NGO coordination.

Second, the forum provided an international platform and stature for many organizations that are ignored, starved of resources, or actively oppressed in their countries. Third, it established a set of follow-up measures and nascent international coordinating institutions for NGOs. Such institutions could serve to transfer organizational capacity among NGOs—particularly through such concrete measures as the treaty on NGO sharing of resources—and to promote more effective transnational coordination of NGO activities to raise concern about sustainable development issues in their own countries.

If NGO alliances persist beyond UNCED with some degree of institutionalization, the effect on future global politics could be significant. Institutional links would make it easier for NGOs to share information and expertise, to exchange and coordinate political strategies, and to teach each other about the most press-

ing problems in their home countries. The immediate products of the forum—
the treaties—may be less significant than the learning and capacity building that
occurred through the process of drafting them.

. . .

The impact of NGOs on post-UNCED world politics is still emergent, at best.
The notion of a concerted NGO movement in the area of environment and development dates only to the start of the PrepCom process in 1990, and the extent of
common NGO positions and attitudes toward dealing with governments remains
to be seen.[32] Although NGOs can improve the effectiveness of international decisions made in Rio by holding governments accountable, through public education, and by providing additional sources of information to the public policy
process, a cautionary note is warranted: Unrestricted universal NGO participation can hamper the adoption of reasonable development policies. Such a scenario is already manifested at the national level in the "NIMBY" (not in my back
yard) effect, as a consequence of the growing political influence of environmental
NGOs in a number of industrialized countries. International partnerships could
foreclose some valid development choices by exercising concerted local pressure
in different countries, as well as at the international level.

UNCED's Legacy

With 20 years of hindsight, we have some idea of how the 1972 Stockholm conference affected the political process surrounding environment and development issues. It served to boost concern among governments and other social actors; it
spawned a number of institutional innovations, especially UNEP; and it set in
motion or added momentum to negotiating processes that, by the decade's end,
resulted in numerous measures to reduce marine pollution, control acid rain,
protect the atmosphere, and preserve wetlands.

A comparison of the two conferences suggests that UNCED could play an even
more influential role over the next 20 years. The media attention, the level of participation, and the involvement of NGOs were all much greater in Rio than in
Stockholm, indicating that the issue has become more firmly grounded on the international agenda. UNCED accredited more than 8,000 journalists from 111
countries and received 6 front-page articles in the *New York Times,* as opposed to
3 for the Stockholm conference. More than 100 heads of state attended UNCED,
while only 2 went to Stockholm. Of the more than 1,400 NGOs accredited by
UNCED, about one-third were from the developing world, whereas at Stockholm,
only 134 NGOs attended, about 10 percent of which came from developing countries.[33]

Substantively, UNCED shows more promise as well. Agenda 21 reflects a far
more sophisticated appreciation of the ecological links that must be addressed to
achieve sustainable development than did the Stockholm Action Plan, which was
only 21 pages long. Although Stockholm focused largely on industrial pollution
of air and water, the UNCED agenda was designed to be more sensitive to the sectorial interconnections necessary for effective environmental management.[34] The

Stockholm conferees also paid more attention to the concerns of the developed countries about industrial pollution, whereas UNCED accorded much more attention to the developing countries' agenda of environmental degradation caused by poverty. Some notable developing-country successes included focusing attention on freshwater resources and obtaining a commitment for a future conference on combating desertification. Although at Stockholm only lip service was given to the notion that economic development was the solution to environmental degradation in the Third World, this idea was the bedrock of the Rio conference both in name and as enunciated in principle 3 of the Rio Declaration (despite U.S. resistance) asserting "the right to development."

These comparisons augur well for UNCED's success. If historians in the 21st century have the fortunate task of explaining how global society was capable of solving the intertwined problems of environment and development, UNCED will undoubtedly figure prominently in their accounts. The conference has laid a foundation with which governments and other social actors will be able to pressure each other to maintain a high level of commitment to environmental protection and development; it established institutions and informal networks that will facilitate the striking of effective agreements; and it added momentum to the building of national capacity in weak governments. Moreover, it endorsed a tightly linked policy agenda that reflects the complex ecological and sociopolitical links among various human activities and between human activities and the environment. As governments are swayed by the array of international pressures that UNCED helped to reinforce, more comprehensive and holistic public policies for sustainable development will follow.

But this potential does not constitute grounds for complacency. . . . To realize the potential that UNCED created requires active and ongoing human intervention. To assure UNCED's long-term prospects for success, the Sustainable Development Commission will have to balance participation at high levels, where political embarrassment can be both generated and experienced, and at lower levels, where expertise and creativity can better flourish. And new mechanisms must be developed for transferring financial and technological resources to developing countries—mechanisms that satisfy both industrial countries' legitimate needs for accountability and respect for property rights and developing countries' legitimate demands for democratic decisionmaking.

PART FOUR

Institutions as Though the Earth Mattered

Chris Calwell, NRDC

Most efforts to promote international environmental cooperation have focused on issue-specific agreements for pressing environmental problems. But as more such agreements have come into force, it has become clear that their effectiveness can be limited by the environmentally destructive effects of more fundamental economic and political processes in the world system. Practices such as international trade, foreign investment, technology transfer, and development assistance, for example, can have effects that cut across issue-specific environmental concerns such as soils, forests, or water quality.

Oran Young has defined institutions as "social practices consisting of easily recognized roles coupled with clusters of rules or conventions governing relations among the occupants of these roles."[1] This definition of institutions is not synonymous with organizations, which are "material entities possessing physical locations (or seats), offices, personnel, equipment, and budgets."[2] Many institutions have a formal organizational base; others, such as language systems or the family, endure informally, being reproduced over time by the beliefs and practices of individuals and groups.

International trade, as codified in the General Agreement on Tariffs and Trade (GATT) and regional arrangements such as the European Community and the North American Free Trade Agreement (NAFTA), is an example of an institution—a set of established rules and roles—with important consequences for the global environment. Development assistance, as practiced by the World Bank and the various bilateral programs linking Northern donors and Southern recipients, is another. As the impact on the environment of international institutions such as trade and aid has become more apparent, pressures have mounted for international institutional reform. In this part we examine trade and aid as two central components of this broader debate.

The links between international trade and the global environment are a relatively new concern for environmentalists. Their attention has been engaged by the increasingly apparent environmental consequences of trade (see MacNeill, Winsemius, and Yakushiji in Part Two), the growing importance of trade in the world economy, and the recent flurry of efforts to rewrite the rules of the international trading game through agreements such as NAFTA and GATT. The growing controversies surrounding trade and the environment illustrate that the traditional claims made by neoclassical economists on behalf of free trade will no longer go unchallenged.

167

Two leading voices in this debate, economists Jagdish Bhagwati and Herman Daly, present their cases for and against free trade in Chapters 18 and 19, respectively. Their exchange of views reveals fundamentally different perspectives about the links between free trade and environmental externalities, about fairness in international trade competition, and about the appropriate way to view economic growth. Although Bhagwati and Daly agree on the importance of protecting the environment and promoting prosperity, they disagree strongly on which institutional path to take in order to achieve those goals.

Bhagwati offers the traditional neoclassical defense of free trade. The fewer restrictions on trade, the more efficient the international distribution of resources and the more the parties involved in trade will benefit from increased economic growth. Although many environmentalists argue that increasing economic growth leads to proportionate increases in pollution, Bhagwati suggests that the link between growth rates and environmental degradation is hardly automatic. In fact, Bhagwati claims that economic growth will actually increase the potential for environmental protection by providing the capital for poorer countries to pay for environmental protection programs.[3]

Bhagwati also argues that different environmental standards among countries should not be viewed as unfair trade advantages. Because one country's environmental values may not be universally held by other nations, we should hardly be surprised if different countries choose different paths to environmental protection or different balances between the environment and other values. Moreover, Bhagwati argues, if firms do seek lower environmental standards to reduce their costs and boost their competitiveness, or if they attempt to relocate production to countries with lax standards, governments can respond without resorting to protectionism—for example, by requiring that their businesses adhere to domestic environmental regulations when operating overseas.

Daly, in contrast, argues that the assumptions behind the neoclassical vision of free trade, comparative advantage, and gains from specialization are no longer valid. Now that capital is internationally mobile, it can easily move to those countries with less rigorous environmental, wage, or safety standards. Left behind will be increased unemployment and income inequality. Daly claims that these lower standards are, in essence, a subsidy to the companies in those countries. To combat these unfair subsidies, governments with higher standards should be allowed to "level the playing field" by imposing tariffs on the products coming from those countries.

Daly's central argument, however, is his attack on the neoclassical claim that increased economic growth will redress the inequities and inefficiencies that can arise from unrestricted trade. As one of the founders of the idea of "steady-state economics," Daly argues that traditional neoclassical arguments in favor of increased economic growth and free trade must be seriously reevaluated if the economic growth created by trade increases material throughput in the world economy, thereby threatening the economy beyond the "optimal scale" dictated by ecological realities.

Clearly, Daly and Bhagwati have different visions of the best course for the future. On one hand, Bhagwati, through his chapter in this volume and other writings, has indicated a deep concern for the stability of the international trading system.[4] In his view, we should not risk trade wars by implementing protectionist measures to promote what are often subjective, culturally specific environmental goals. Instead, environmental goals should be accomplished with diplomacy and domestic legislation that minimize the impact on the trading system. Daly, on the other hand, goes far beyond advocating the incorporation of explicit environmental objectives into the rules of international trade. He argues instead that the best way for nations to stay within ecological limits is to move away from free trade and toward domestic production for national markets. Although Daly's is the more radical vision for changing the institution of international trade, it should be noted that even Bhagwati's more limited set of prescriptions for environmental protection would require rewriting some aspects of the rules of international trade. It seems likely that such questions will be taken up in the next round of talks on the GATT agreement, although the outcome remains far from clear.

The case of development assistance provides an interesting contrast to international trade, in that a process of institutional reform for the purposes of environmental protection is already under way. The World Bank in particular, as both the financially and intellectually dominant international organization on the development scene, has felt substantial pressure to change its lending practices. During the 1980s, the Bank's role in distributing tens of billions of dollars annually for development projects that had devastating environmental impacts made it an obvious target for nongovernmental organizations (NGOs) from both the North and the South.[5] As a result, the Bank began to institute a series of internal reforms aimed at increasing the ecological soundness of its projects. The final two chapters in this part present radically different views on the question of how effective these changes have been.

Bruce Rich offers a scathing indictment of the World Bank's purported environmental reforms. He argues that the reforms have failed to change the incentive structures facing the key actors involved in the daily operations of the World Bank. For the country directors who control the loan preparation process, career advancement depends upon the accumulation of large loan portfolios. The fastest way to put those portfolios together is to push large projects, such as dams and coal-fired power plants, which not only require huge amounts of capital but also have significant impacts on the environment. The borrowing countries, besides being unlikely to balk at receiving such sizable amounts of money, are also typically hostile to the idea of having any environmental strings attached to the loans they receive. The Bank's board of executive directors, who have their own reasons for wanting these large loans to move quickly, are too often unwilling or unable to scrutinize the environmental consequences of the loans they approve, regardless of the Environment Department's views.

Kenneth Piddington offers a cautiously optimistic view. From 1988 to 1991 Piddington was the World Bank's first director of environment. His primary task was to oversee the implementation of the environmental reforms initiated by Barber Conable, the president of the Bank during that period. These reforms included the creation of an environment department, new rules mandating environmental assessments on all new lending proposals, new funding mechanisms for environmental protection projects, and an environmental action plan to slow the cutting of tropical forests.

Despite such organizational and procedural changes within the Bank, Piddington acknowledges that change in Bank behavior has been slow and uneven. As with any large organization, reform in the Bank would be painstakingly slow as it collided with bureaucratic inertia and resistance. Piddington believes that despite these barriers, criticisms such as Rich's are misleading, in that they offer a single snapshot view at a fixed point in time. Piddington's optimism lies in his belief that the process of change within the Bank is now irreversible. This optimism is in stark contrast with Rich's belief that the Bank is embedded in a set of institutional and political contradictions, including pressures from governments and the world economic system, that inherently limit the possibilities for reform. Rich believes environmental organizations and other concerned groups from both the North and the South should continue to pressure the Bank instead of waiting for the current reforms to evolve. Their aim should be not only that environmental concerns receive a higher priority but also that the Bank become more open and democratic in its operations. This is clearly a tall order.

International trade and development assistance are but two of the many international institutions that have a profound impact on the global environment. Indeed, one could view national sovereignty in institutional terms, as a longstanding set of roles and rules with profound environmental consequences. But the problems faced in reforming the prevailing trade and aid regimes are specific examples of a more general challenge of institutional change. One clear lesson is that implementing effective reforms will require careful attention to the internal workings of institutions. Failure to take into account the incentive structures of the actors involved, for example, can be devastating to reform efforts, as witnessed in the case of the World Bank. But we must also ask whether internal change of the sort advocated by Pidding-ton can be effective if Rich is correct in concluding that prevailing institutions reflect a larger, structural logic in which environmental concerns are margin-alized.

JAGDISH BHAGWATI

18
The Case for Free Trade

ECONOMISTS ARE RECONCILED to the conflict of absolutes: that is why they invented the concept of tradeoffs. It should not surprise them, therefore, that the objective of environmental protection should at times run afoul of the goal of seeking maximum gains from trade. In fact, economists would be suspicious of any claims, such as those made by soothsaying politicians, that both causes would be only mutually beneficial. They are rightly disconcerted, however, by the passion and the ferocity, and hence often the lack of logic or facts, with which environmental groups have recently assailed both free trade and the General Agreement on Tariffs and Trade (GATT), the institution that oversees the world trading system.

The environmentalists' antipathy to trade is perhaps inevitable. Trade has been central to economic thinking since Adam Smith discovered the virtues of specialization and of the markets that naturally sustain it. Because markets do not normally exist for the pursuit of environmental protection, they must be specially created. Trade therefore suggests abstention from governmental intervention, whereas environmentalism suggests its necessity. Then again, trade is exploited and its virtues extolled by corporate and multinational interests, whereas environmental objectives are embraced typically by nonprofit organizations, which are generally wary of these interests. Trade is an ancient occupation, and its nurture is the objective of institutions crafted over many years of experience and reflection. Protection of the environment, on the other hand, is a recent preoccupation of national and international institutions that are nascent and still evolving.

Originally published in *Scientific American* (November 1993):42–49. Reprinted with permission. Copyright © 1993 by Scientific American, Inc. All rights reserved.

Last year the environmentalists' hostility to trade exploded in outrage when an impartial GATT Dispute Settlement Panel ruled in favor of Mexico and free trade and against the U.S. and the welfare of the dolphin. The U.S. had placed an embargo on the import of Mexican tuna on the grounds that the fish had been caught in purse-seine nets, which kill dolphins cruelly and in greater numbers than U.S. law permits. The GATT panel ruled, in effect, that the U.S. could not suspend Mexico's trading rights by proscribing unilaterally the methods by which that country harvested tuna.

This decision spurred the conservationists' subsequent campaigns against free trade and GATT. GATT has no shortage of detractors, of course. In fact, some of its recent critics have feared its impotence and declared it "dead," referring to it as the General Agreement to Talk and Talk. But the environmentalist attacks, which presume instead GATT's omnipotence, are something else again.

An advertisement by a coalition of environmental groups in the *New York Times* on April 20, 1992, set a new standard for alarmist, even scurrilous, writing, calculated to appeal to one's instincts rather than one's intellect. It talks of "faceless GATT bureaucrats" mounting a "sneak attack on democracy." This veiled reference to Pearl Harbor provides an example of a common tactic in trade controversy: Japan-bashing. The innuendos have continued unabated and are manifest in the endless battles in Congress over the supplemental environmental accords for the North American Free Trade Agreement (NAFTA). The hostility is also intruding on the conclusion of the Uruguay Round of GATT talks, now in their seventh year, with the environmentalists opposing the establishment of the new Multilateral Trade Organization, which is meant to provide effective discipline and a necessary institutional structure for GATT. [Editors' note: The Uruguay Round of multilateral trade negotiations was concluded in early 1994, and the GATT agreement ratified by the U.S. Congress in December of that year.]

It is surely tragic that the proponents of two of the great causes of the 1990s, trade and the environment, should be locked in combat. The conflict is largely gratuitous. There are at times philosophical differences between the two that cannot be reconciled, as when some environmentalists assert nature's autonomy, whereas most economists see nature as a handmaiden to humankind. For the most part, however, the differences derive from misconceptions. It is necessary to dissect and dismiss the more egregious of these fallacies before addressing the genuine problems.

The fear is widespread among environmentalists that free trade increases economic growth and that growth harms the environment. That fear is misplaced. Growth enables governments to tax and to raise resources for a variety of objectives, including the abatement of pollution and the general protection of the environment. Without such revenues, little can be achieved, no matter how pure one's motives may be.

How do societies actually spend these additional revenues? It depends on how getting rich affects the desire for a better environment. Rich countries today have more groups worrying about environmental causes than do poor countries.

Efficient policies, such as freer trade, should generally help environmentalism, not harm it.

If one wants to predict what growth will do to the environment, however, one must also consider how it will affect the production of pollution. Growth affects not only the demand for a good environment but also the supply of the pollution associated with growth. The net effect on the environment will therefore depend on the kind of economic growth. Gene M. Grossman and Alan B. Krueger of Princeton University found that in cities around the world sulfur dioxide pollution fell as per capita income rose. The only exception was in countries whose per capita incomes fell below $5,000. In short, environmentalists are in error when they fear that trade, through growth, will necessarily increase pollution.

Economic effects besides those attributable to rising incomes also help to protect the environment. For example, freer trade enables pollution-fighting technologies available elsewhere to be imported. Thus, trade in low-sulfur-content coal will enable the users of local high-sulfur-content coal to shift from the latter to the former.

Free trade can also lead to better environmental outcomes from a shift in the composition of production. An excellent example is provided by Robert C. Feenstra of the University of California at Davis. He has shown how the imposition of restraints on Japanese automobile exports to the U.S. during the 1980s shifted the composition of those exports from small to large cars, as the Japanese attempted to increase their revenues without increasing the number of units they sold. Yet the large cars were fuel inefficient. Thus, protective efforts by the U.S. effectively increased the average amount of pollution produced by imported cars, making it more likely that pollution from cars would increase rather than diminish in the U.S.

Although these erroneous objections to free trade are readily dismissed (but not so easily eliminated from public discourse), there are genuine conflicts between trade and the environment. To understand and solve them, economists draw a distinction between two kinds of environmental problems: those that are intrinsically domestic and those that are intrinsically transnational.

Should Brazil pollute a lake lying wholly within its borders, the problem would be intrinsically domestic. Should it pollute a river that flows into Argentina, the matter would take on an intrinsically transnational character. Perhaps the most important examples of transnational pollution are acid rain, created when sulfur dioxide emissions in one country precipitate into rain in another, and greenhouse gases, such as carbon dioxide, which contribute to global warming wherever they are emitted.

Why do intrinsically domestic environmental questions create international concern? The main reason is the belief that diversity in environmental standards may affect competitiveness. Businesses and labor unions worry that their rivals in other countries may gain an edge if their governments impose lower standards of environmental protection. They decry such differences as unfair. To level the playing field, these lobbies insist that foreign countries raise their standards up to domestic ones. In turn, environmental groups worry that if such "harmonization up" is not undertaken prior to freeing trade, pressures from uncompetitive businesses at home will force down domestic standards, reversing their hard-won victories. Finally, there is the fear, dramatized by H. Ross Perot in his criticisms of NAFTA, that factories will relocate to the countries whose environmental standards are lowest.

But if the competitiveness issue makes the environmentalists, the businesses and the unions into allies, the environmentalists are on their own in other ways. Two problem areas can be distinguished. First, some environmentalists are keen to impose their own ethical preferences on others, using trade sanctions to induce or coerce acceptance of such preferences. For instance, tuna fishing with purse-seine nets that kill dolphins is opposed by U.S. environmental groups, which consequently favor restraints on the importation of such tuna from Mexico and elsewhere. Second, other environmentalists fear that the rules of free trade, as embodied in GATT and strengthened in the Uruguay Round, will constrain their freedom to pursue even purely domestic environmental objectives, with GATT tribunals outlawing disputed regulation.

Environmentalists have cause for concern. Not all concerns are legitimate, however, and not all the solutions to legitimate concerns are sensible. Worry over competitiveness has thus led to the illegitimate demand that environmental standards abroad be treated as "social dumping." Offending countries are regarded as unfairly subsidizing their exporters through lax environmental requirements. Such implicit subsidies, the reasoning continues, ought to be offset by import duties.

Yet international differences in environmental standards are perfectly natural. Even if two countries share the same environmental objectives, the *specific* pollutions they would attack, and hence the industries they would hinder, will generally not be identical. Mexico has a greater social incentive than does the U.S. to spend an extra dollar preventing dysentery rather than reducing lead in gasoline.

Equally, a certain environmental good might be valued more highly by a poor country than by a rich one. Contrast, for instance, the value assigned to a lake with the cost of cleaning up effluents discharged into it by a pharmaceutical company. In India such a lake's water might be drunk by a malnourished population whose mortality would increase sharply with the rise in pollution. In the U.S. the water might be consumed by few people, all of whom have the means to protect themselves with privately purchased water filters. In this example, India would be the more likely to prefer clean water to the pharmaceutical company's profits.

The consequences of differing standards are clear: each country will have less of the industry whose pollution it fears relatively more than other countries do. Indeed, even if there were no international trade, we would be shrinking industries whose pollution we deter. This result follows from the policy of forcing polluters of all stripes to pay for the harm they cause. To object, then, to the effects our negative valuation of pollution has on a given industry is to be in contradiction: we would be refusing to face the consequences of our environmental preferences.

Nevertheless, there is sentiment for enacting legislation against social dumping. Senator David L. Boren of Oklahoma, the proponent of the International Pollution Deterrence Act of 1991, demanded import duties on the grounds that "some U.S. manufacturers, such as the U.S. carbon and steel alloy industry, spend as much as 250 percent more on environmental controls as a percentage of gross domestic product than do other countries. . . . I see the unfair advantage enjoyed by other nations exploiting the environment and public health for economic gain when I look at many industries important to my own state." Similarly, Vice President Al Gore wrote in *Earth in the Balance: Ecology and the Human Spirit* that "just as government subsidies of a particular industry are sometimes considered unfair under the trade laws, weak and ineffectual enforcement of pollution control measures should also be included in the definition of unfair trading practices."

These demands betray lack of economic logic, and they ignore political reality as well. Remember that the so-called subsidy to foreign producers through lower standards is not given but only implied. According to Senator Boren, the subsidy would be calculated as "the cost that would have to be incurred by the manufacturer or producer of the foreign articles of merchandise to comply with environmental standards imposed on U.S. producers of the same class of merchandise." Anyone familiar with the way dumping calculations are made knows that the Environmental Protection Agency could come up with virtually any estimates it cared to produce. Cynical politics would inevitably dictate the calculations.

Still there may be political good sense in assuaging environmentalists' concerns about the relocation of factories to countries with lower standards. The governments of higher-standards countries could do so without encumbering free trade by insisting that their businesses accede to the higher standards when they go abroad. Such a policy lies entirely within the jurisdictional powers of a higher-standards country. Moreover, the governments of lower standards countries would be most unlikely to object to such an act of good citizenship by the foreign investors.

Environmentalists oppose free trade for yet another reason: they wish to use trade policy to impose their values on other communities and countries. Many environmentalists want to suspend the trading rights of countries that sanction the use of purse-seine nets in tuna fishing and of leg-hold traps in trapping. Such punishments seem an inappropriate use of state power, however. The values in question are not widely accepted, such as human rights, but idiosyncratic. One wonders when the opponents of purse-seine nets put the interests of the dolphin ahead of those of Mexico's people, who could prosper through more productive fishing. To borrow the campaign manifesto of President Bill Clinton: Should we not put people first?

Moreover, once such values intrude on free trade, the way is opened for an endless succession of demands. Environmentalists favor dolphins; Indians have their sacred cows. Animal-rights activists, who do not prefer one species over another, will object to our slaughterhouses.

The moral militancy of environmentalists in the industrialized world has begun to disillusion their closest counterparts in the undeveloped countries. These local environmentalists accuse the rich countries of "eco-imperialism," and they deny that the Western nations have a monopoly on virtue. The most radical of today's proenvironment magazines in India, *Down to Earth*, editorialized recently: "In the current world reality trade is used as an instrument entirely by Northern countries to discipline environmentally errant nations. Surely, if India or Kenya were to threaten to stop trade with the U.S., it would hardly affect the latter. But the fact of the matter is that it is the Northern countries that have the greatest [adverse] impact on the world's environment."

If many countries were to play this game, then repeated suspensions of trading rights would begin to undermine the openness of the trading system and the predictability and stability of international markets. Some environmentalists assert that each country should be free to insist on the production methods of its trading partners. Yet these environmentalists ignore the certain consequence of their policy: a Pandora's box of protectionism would open up. Rarely are production methods in an industry identical in different countries.

There are certainly better ways to indulge the environmentalists' propensity to export their ethical preferences. The U.S. environmental organizations can lobby in Mexico to persuade its government to adopt their views. Private boycotts can also be undertaken. In fact, boycotts can carry much clout in rich countries with big markets, on which the targeted poor countries often depend. The frequent and enormously expensive advertisements by environmental groups against GATT show also that their resources far exceed those of the cash-strapped countries whose policies they oppose.

Cost-benefit analysis leads one to conclude that unilateral governmental suspension of others' trading rights is not an appropriate way to promote one's lesser ethical preferences. Such sanctions can, on the other hand, appropriately be invoked multilaterally to defend universal moral values. In such cases—as in the censure of apartheid, as practiced until recently in South Africa—it is possible to secure widespread agreement for sanctions. With a large majority converted to the cause, GATT's waiver procedure can be used to suspend the offending country's trading rights.

Environmentalists are also worried about the obstacles that the current and prospective GATT rules pose for environmental regulations aimed entirely at domestic production and consumption. In principle, GATT lets a country enforce any regulation that does not discriminate against or among foreign suppliers. One can, for example, require airbags in cars, provided that the rule applies to all automobile makers. GATT even permits rules that discriminate against trade for the purpose of safety and health.

GATT, however, recognizes three ways in which regulations may be set in gratuitous restraint of trade; in following procedures aimed at avoiding such outcomes, GATT upsets the environmentalists. First, the true intention—and effect—of a regulation may be to protect not the environment but local business. Second, a country may impose more restrictions than necessary to achieve its stated environmental objective. Third, it may set standards that have no scientific basis.

The issue of intentions is illustrated by the recently settled "beer war" between Ontario and the U.S. Five years ago the Canadian province imposed a 10-cents-a-can tax on beer, ostensibly to discourage littering. The U.S. argued that the law in fact intended to discriminate against its beer suppliers, who used aluminum cans, whereas local beer companies used bottles. Ontario had omitted to tax the use of cans for juices and soups, a step that would have affected Ontario producers.

The second problem is generally tougher because it is impossible to find alternative restrictions that accomplish exactly the same environmental results as the original policy at lower cost. An adjudicating panel is then forced to evaluate, implicitly or explicitly, the tradeoffs between the cost in trade disruption and the cost in lesser fulfillment of the environmental objective. It is therefore likely that environmentalists and trade experts will differ on which weights the panel should assign to these divergent interests.

Environmentalists tend to be fearful about the use of scientific tests to determine whether trade in a product can be proscribed. The need to prove one's case is always an unwelcome burden to those who have the political power to take unilateral action. Yet the trade experts have the better of the argument. Imagine that U.S. growers sprayed apples with the pesticide Alar, whereas European growers did not, and that European consumers began to agitate against Alar as harmful. Should the European Community be allowed to end the importation of the U.S. apples without meeting *some* scientific test of its health concerns? Admittedly, even hard science is often not hard enough—different studies may reach different conclusions. But without the restraining hand of science, the itch to indulge one's fears—and to play on the fears of others—would be irresistible.

In all cases, the moderate environmentalists would like to see GATT adopt more transparent procedures for adjudicating disputes. They also desire greater legal standing to file briefs when environmental regulations are at issue. These goals seem both reasonable and feasible.

Not all environmental problems are local; some are truly global, such as the greenhouse effect and the depletion of the stratospheric ozone. They raise more issues that require cooperative, multilateral solutions. Such solutions must be both efficient and equitable. Still, it is easy to see that rich countries might use their economic power to reach protocols that maximize efficiency at the expense of poorer countries.

For instance, imagine that the drafters of a protocol were to ask Brazil to refrain from cutting down its rain forests while allowing industrialized countries to continue emitting carbon dioxide. They might justify this request on the grounds that it costs Brazil less to keep a tree alive, absorbing a unit of carbon dioxide every year, than it would cost the U.S. or Germany to save a unit by burning less oil. Such a trade-off would indeed be economically efficient. Yet if Brazil, a poorer country, were then left with the bill, the solution would assuredly be inequitable.

Before any group of countries imposes trade sanctions on a country that has not joined a multilateral protocol, it would be important to judge whether the protocol is indeed fair. Nonmembers targeted for trade sanctions should have the right to get an impartial hearing of their objections, requiring the strong to defend their actions even when they appear to be entirely virtuous.

The simultaneous pursuit of the two causes of free trade and a protected environment often raises problems, to be sure. But none of these conflicts is beyond resolution with goodwill and by imaginative institutional innovation. The aversion to free trade and GATT that many environmentalists display is unfounded, and it is time for them to shed it. Their admirable moral passion and certain intellectual vigor are better devoted to building bridges between the causes of trade and the environment.

HERMAN E. DALY

19

The Perils of Free Trade

No POLICY PRESCRIPTION COMMANDS greater consensus among economists than that of free trade based on international specialization according to comparative advantage. Free trade has long been presumed good unless proved otherwise. That presumption is the cornerstone of the existing General Agreement on Tariffs and Trade (GATT) and the proposed North American Free Trade Agreement (NAFTA). The proposals in the Uruguay Round of negotiations strengthen GATT's basic commitment to free trade and economic globalization. [Editors' note: NAFTA was approved in late 1993 and took effect January 1, 1994. The Uruguay Round of GATT negotiations concluded in early 1994.]

Yet that presumption should be reversed. The default position should favor domestic production for domestic markets. When convenient, balanced international trade should be used, but it should not be allowed to govern a country's affairs at the risk of environmental and social disaster. The domestic economy should be the dog and international trade its tail. GATT seeks to tie all the dogs' tails together so tightly that the international knot would wag the separate national dogs.

The wiser course was well expressed in the overlooked words of John Maynard Keynes: "I sympathize, therefore, with those who would minimize, rather than those who would maximize, economic entanglement between nations. Ideas, knowledge, art, hospitality, travel—these are the things which should of their nature be international. But let goods be homespun whenever it is reasonably and conveniently possible; and, above all, let finance be primarily national." Contrary to Keynes, the defenders of the proposed Uruguay Round of changes to GATT not

Originally published in *Scientific American* (November 1993):50–57. Reprinted with permission. Copyright © 1993 by Scientific American, Inc. All rights reserved.

only want to downplay "homespun goods," they also want finance and all other services to become primarily international.

Economists and environmentalists are sometimes represented as being, respectively, for and against free trade, but that polarization does the argument a disservice. Rather the real debate is over what kinds of regulations are to be instituted and what goals are legitimate. The free traders seek to maximize profits and production without regard for considerations that represent hidden social and environmental costs. They argue that when growth has made people wealthy enough, they will have the funds to clean up the damage done by growth. Conversely, environmentalists and some economists, myself among them, suspect that growth is increasing environmental costs faster than benefits from production—thereby making us poorer, not richer.

A more accurate name than the persuasive label "free trade"—because who can be opposed to freedom?—is "deregulated international commerce." Deregulation is not always a good policy: recall the recent experience of the U.S. with the deregulation of the savings and loan institutions. As one who formerly taught the doctrine of free trade to college students, I have some sympathy for the free traders' view. Nevertheless, my major concern about my profession today is that our disciplinary preference for logically beautiful results over factually grounded policies has reached such lunatical proportions that we economists have become dangerous to the earth and its inhabitants.

The free trade position is grounded in the logic of comparative advantage, first explicitly formulated by the early 19th century British economist David Ricardo. He observed that countries with different technologies, customs and resources will incur different costs when they make the same products. One country may find it comparatively less costly to mine coal than to grow wheat, but in another country the opposite may be true. If nations specialize in the products for which they have a comparative advantage and trade freely to obtain others, everyone benefits.

The problem is not the logic of this argument. It is the relevance of Ricardo's critical but often forgotten assumption that factors of production (especially capital) are internationally immobile. In today's world, where billions of dollars can be transferred between nations at the speed of light, that essential condition is not met. Moreover, free traders encourage such foreign investment as a development strategy. In short, the free traders are using an argument that hinges on the impermeability of national boundaries to capital to support a policy aimed at making those same boundaries increasingly permeable to both capital and goods!

That fact alone invalidates the assumption that international trade will inevitably benefit all its partners. Furthermore, for trade to be mutually beneficial, the gains must not be offset by higher liabilities. After specialization, nations are no longer free *not* to trade, and that loss of independence can be a liability. Also, the cost of transporting goods internationally must not cancel out the profits. Transport costs are energy intensive. Today, however, the cost of energy is frequently subsidized by governments through investment tax credits, federally subsidized research and military expenditures that ensure access to petroleum. The environmental costs of fossil-fuel burning also do not factor into the price of gasoline. To the extent that energy is subsidized, then, so too is trade. The full cost of energy, stripped of these obscuring subsidies, would therefore reduce the initial gains from long distance trade, whether international or interregional.

Free trade can also introduce new inefficiencies. Contrary to the implications of comparative advantage, more than half of all international trade involves the simultaneous import and export of essentially the same goods. For example, Americans import Danish sugar cookies, and Danes import American sugar cookies. Exchanging recipes would surely be more efficient. It would also be more in accord with Keynes's dictum that knowledge should be international and goods homespun (or in this case, homebaked).

Another important but seldom mentioned corollary of specialization is a reduction in the range of occupational choices. Uruguay has a clear comparative advantage in raising cattle and sheep. If it adhered strictly to the rule of specialization and trade, it would afford its citizens only the choice of being either cowboys or shepherds. Yet Uruguayans feel a need for their own legal, financial, medical, insurance and educational services, in addition to basic agriculture and industry. That diversity entails some loss of efficiency, but it is necessary for community and nationhood.

Uruguay is enriched by having a symphony orchestra of its own, even though it would be cost-effective to import better symphony concerts in exchange for wool, mutton, beef and leather. Individuals, too, must count the broader range of choices as a welfare gain: even those who are cowboys and shepherds are surely enriched by contact with countrymen who are not *vaqueros* or *pastores*. My point is that the community dimension of welfare is completely overlooked in the simplistic argument that if specialization and trade increase the per capita availability of commodities, they must be good.

Let us assume that even after those liabilities are subtracted from the gross returns on trade, positive net gains still exist. They must still offset deeper, more fundamental problems. The arguments for free trade run afoul of the three basic goals of all economic policies: the efficient *allocation* of resources, the fair *distribution* of resources and the maintenance of a sustainable *scale* of resource use. The first two are traditional goals of neoclassical economics. The third has only recently been recognized and is associated with the viewpoint of ecological, or steady-state, economics. It means that the input of raw materials and energy to an economy and the output of waste materials and heat must be within the regenerative and absorptive capacities of the ecosystem.

In neoclassical economics the efficient allocation of resources depends on the counting and internalization of all costs. Costs are internalized if they are directly paid by those entities responsible for them—as when, for example, a manufacturer pays for the disposal of its factory wastes and raises its prices to cover that expense. Costs are externalized if they are paid by someone else—as when the public suffers extra disease, stench and nuisance from uncollected wastes. Counting all costs is the very basis of efficiency.

Economists rightly urge nations to follow a domestic program of internalizing costs into prices. They also wrongly urge nations to trade freely with other countries that do not internalize their costs (and consequently have lower prices). If a nation tries to follow both those policies, the conflict is clear: free competition between different cost-internalizing regimes is utterly unfair.

International trade increases competition, and competition reduces costs. But competition can reduce costs in two ways: by increasing efficiency or by lowering standards. A firm can save money by lowering its standards for pollution control, worker safety, wages, health care and so on—all choices that externalize some of its costs. Profit-maximizing firms in competition always have an incentive to externalize their costs to the degree that they can get away with it.

For precisely that reason, nations maintain large legal, administrative and auditing structures that bar reductions in the social and environmental standards of domestic industries. There are no analogous international bodies of law and administration; there are only national laws, which differ widely. Consequently, free international trade encourages industries to shift their production activities to the countries that have the lowest standards of cost internalization—hardly a move toward global efficiency.

Attaining cheapness by ignoring real costs is a sin against efficiency. Even GATT recognizes that requiring citizens of one country to compete against foreign prison labor would be carrying standards-lowering competition too far. GATT therefore allows the imposition of restrictions on such trade. Yet it makes no similar exception for child labor, for uninsured risky labor or for subsistence wage labor.

The most practical solution is to permit nations that internalize costs to levy compensating tariffs on trade with nations that do not. "Protectionism"—shielding an inefficient industry against more efficient foreign competitors—is a dirty word among economists. That is very different, however, from protecting an efficient national policy of full-cost pricing from standards-lowering international competition.

Such tariffs are also not without precedent. Free traders generally praise the fairness of "antidumping" tariffs that discourage countries from trading in goods at prices below their production costs. The only real difference is the decision to include the costs of environmental damage and community welfare in that reckoning.

This tariff policy does not imply the imposition of one country's environmental preferences or moral judgements on another country. Each country should set the rules of cost internalization in its own market. Whoever sells in a nation's market should play by that nation's rules or pay a tariff sufficient to remove the competitive advantage of lower standards. For instance, under the Marine Mammal Protection Act, all tuna sold in the U.S. (whether by U.S. or Mexican fishermen) must count the cost of limiting the kill of dolphin associated with catching tuna. Tuna sold in the Mexican market (whether by U.S. or Mexican fishermen) need not include that cost. No standards are being imposed through "environmental imperialism"; paying the costs of a nation's environmental standards is merely the price of admission to its market.

Indeed, free trade could be accused of reverse environmental imperialism. When firms produce under the most permissive standards and sell their products elsewhere without penalty, they press on countries with higher standards to lower them. In effect, unrestricted trade imposes lower standards.

Unrestricted international trade also raises problems of resource distribution. In the world of comparative advantage described by Ricardo, a nation's capital stays at home, and only goods are traded. If firms are free to relocate their capital internationally to wherever their production costs would be lowest, then the favored countries have not merely a comparative advantage but an absolute advantage. Capital will drain out of one country and into another, perhaps making what H. Ross Perot called "a giant sucking sound" as jobs and wealth move with it. This specialization will increase world production, but without any assurance that all the participating countries will benefit.

When capital flows abroad, the opportunity for new domestic employment diminishes, which drives down the price for domestic labor. Even if free trade and capital mobility raise wages in low-wage countries (and that tendency is thwarted by overpopulation and rapid population growth), they do so at the expense of labor in the high-wage countries. They thereby increase income inequality there. Most citizens are wage earners. In the U.S., 80 percent of the labor force is classified as "nonsupervisory employees." Their real wages have fallen 17 percent between 1973 and 1990, in significant part because of trade liberalization.

Nor does labor in low-wage countries necessarily gain from free trade. It is likely that NAFTA will ruin Mexican peasants when "inexpensive" U.S. corn (subsidized by depleting topsoil, aquifers, oil wells and the federal treasury) can be freely imported. Displaced peasants will bid down wages. Their land will be bought cheaply by agribusinesses to produce fancy vegetables and cut flowers for the U.S. market. Ironically, Mexico helps to keep U.S. corn "inexpensive" by exporting its own vanishing reserves of oil and genetic crop variants, which the U.S. needs to sustain its corn monoculture.

Neoclassical economists admit that overpopulation can spill over from one country to another in the form of cheap labor. They acknowledge that fact as an argument against free immigration. Yet capital can migrate toward abundant labor even more easily than labor can move toward capital. The legitimate case for restrictions on labor immigration is therefore easily extended to restrictions on capital emigration.

When confronted with such problems, neoclassical economists often answer that growth will solve them. The allocation problem of standards-lowering competition, they say, will be dealt with by universally "harmonizing" all standards upward. The distribution problem of falling wages in high-wage countries would only be temporary; the economists believe that growth will eventually raise wages worldwide to the former high-wage level and beyond.

Yet the goal of a sustainable scale of total resource use forces us to ask: What will happen if the entire population of the earth consumes resources at the rate of high-wage countries? Neoclassical economists generally ignore this question or give the facile response that there are no limits.

The steady-state economic paradigm suggests a different answer. The regenerative and assimilative capacities of the biosphere cannot support even the current levels of resource consumption, much less the manyfold increase required to generalize the higher standards worldwide. Still less can the ecosystem afford an ever growing population that is striving to consume more per capita. As a species, we already preempt about 40 percent of the landbased primary product of photosynthesis for human purposes. What happens to biodiversity if we double the human population, as we are projected to do over the next 30 to 50 years?

These limits put a brake on the ability of growth to wash away the problems of misallocation and maldistribution. In fact, free trade becomes a recipe for hastening the speed with which competition lowers standards for efficiency, distributive equity and ecological sustainability.

Notwithstanding those enormous problems, the appeal of bigger free trade blocs for corporations is obvious. The broader the free trade area, the less answerable a large and footloose corporation will be to any local or even national community. Spatial separation of the places that suffer the costs and enjoy the benefits becomes more feasible. The corporation will be able to buy labor in the low-wage markets and sell its products in the remaining high-wage, high-income markets. The larger the market, the longer a corporation will be able to avoid the logic of Henry Ford, who realized that he had to pay his workers enough for them to buy his cars. That is why transnational corporations like free trade and why workers and environmentalists do not.

In the view of steady-state economics, the economy is one open subsystem in a finite, nongrowing and materially closed ecosystem. An open system takes matter and energy from the environment as raw materials and returns them as waste. A closed system is one in which matter constantly circulates internally while only energy flows through. Whatever enters a system as input and exits as output is called throughput. Just as an organism survives by consuming nutrients and excreting wastes, so too an economy must to some degree both deplete and pollute the environment. A steady-state economy is one whose throughput remains constant at a level that neither depletes the environment beyond its regenerative capacity nor pollutes it beyond its absorptive capacity.

Most neoclassical economic analyses today rest on the assumption that the economy is the total system and nature is the subsystem. The economy is an isolated system involving only a circular flow of exchange value between firms and households. Neither matter nor energy enters or exits this system. The economy's growth is therefore unconstrained. Nature may be finite, but it is seen as just one sector of the economy, for which other sectors can substitute without limiting overall growth.

Although this vision of circular flow is useful for analyzing exchanges between producers and consumers, it is actively misleading for studying scale—the size of the economy relative to the environment. It is as if a biologist's vision of an animal contained a circulatory system but not a digestive tract or lungs. Such a beast would be independent of its environment, and its size would not matter. If it could move, it would be a perpetual motion machine.

Long ago the world was relatively empty of human beings and their belongings (man-made capital) and relatively full of other species and their habitats (natural capital). Years of economic growth have changed that basic pattern. As a result, the limiting factor on future economic growth has changed. If man-made and natural capital were good substitutes for one another, then natural capital could be totally replaced. The two are complementary, however, which means that the short supply of one imposes limits. What good are fishing boats without populations of fish? Or sawmills without forests? Once the number of fish that could be sold at market was primarily limited by the number of boats that could be built and manned; now it is limited by the number of fish in the sea.

As long as the scale of the human economy was very small relative to the ecosystem, no apparent sacrifice was involved in increasing it. The scale of the economy is now such that painless growth is no longer reasonable. If we see the economy as a subsystem of a finite, nongrowing ecosystem, then there must be a maximal scale for its throughput of matter and energy. More important, there must also be an optimal scale. Economic growth beyond that optimum would increase the environmental costs faster than it would the production benefits, thereby ushering in an antieconomic phase that impoverished rather than enriched.

One can find disturbing evidence that we have already passed that point and, like Alice in *Through the Looking Glass,* the faster we run the farther behind we fall. Thus the correlation between gross national product (GNP) and the index of sustainable economic welfare (which is based on personal consumption and adjusted for depletion of natural capital and other factors) has taken a negative turn in the U.S.

Like our planet, the economy may continue forever to develop qualitatively, but it cannot grow indefinitely and must eventually settle into a steady state in its physical dimensions. That condition need not be miserable, however. We economists need to make the elementary distinction between growth (a quantitative increase in size resulting from the accretion or assimilation of materials) and development (the qualitative evolution to a fuller, better or different state). Quantitative and qualitative changes follow different laws. Conflating the two, as we currently do in the GNP, has led to much confusion.

Development without growth is sustainable development. An economy that is steady in scale may still continue to develop a greater capacity to satisfy human wants by increasing the efficiency of its resource use, by improving social institutions and by clarifying its ethical priorities—but not by increasing the resource throughput.

In the light of the growth versus development distinction, let us return to the issue of international trade and consider two questions: What is the likely effect of free trade on growth? What is the likely effect of free trade on development?

Free trade is likely to stimulate the growth of throughput. It allows a country in effect to exceed its domestic regenerative and absorptive limits by "importing" those capacities from other countries. True, a country "exporting" some of its carrying capacity in return for imported products might have increased its throughput even more if it had made those products domestically. Overall, nevertheless, trade does postpone the day when countries must face up to living within their natural regenerative and absorptive capacities. That some countries still have excess carrying capacity is more indicative of a shortfall in their desired domestic growth than of any conscious decision to reserve that capacity for export.

By spatially separating the costs and benefits of environmental exploitation, international trade makes them harder to compare. It thereby increases the tendency for economies to overshoot their optimal scale. Furthermore, it forces countries to face tightening environmental constraints more simultaneously and less sequentially than would otherwise be the case. They have less opportunity to learn from one another's experiences with controlling throughput and less control over their local environment.

The standard arguments for free trade based on comparative advantage also depend on static promotions of efficiency. In other words, free trade in toxic wastes promotes static efficiency by allowing the disposal of wastes wherever it costs less according to today's prices and technologies. A more dynamic efficiency would be served by outlawing the export of toxins. That step would internalize the disposal costs of toxins to their place of origin—to both the firm that generated them and the nation under whose laws the firm operated. This policy creates an incentive to find technically superior ways of dealing with the toxins or of redesigning processes to avoid their production in the first place.

All these allocative, distributional and scale problems stemming from free trade ought to reverse the traditional default position favoring it. Measures to integrate national economies further should now be treated as a bad idea unless proved otherwise in specific cases. As Ronald Findley of Columbia University characterized it, comparative advantage may well be the "deepest and most beautiful result in all of economics." Nevertheless, in a full world of internationally mobile capital, our adherence to it for policy direction is a recipe for national disintegration.

BRUCE RICH

20
The Emperor's New Clothes: The World Bank & Environmental Reform

ON OCTOBER 24, 1989, an extraordinary hearing took place in the U.S. Congress. Two and a half years after the president of the World Bank, former congressman Barber Conable, had committed the Bank to sweeping environmental reforms, activists from its most important borrower and donor countries—India and the United States—testified about the Bank's systematic violation of its own environmental and social policies in the Sardar Sarovar dam project in north-central India. The activists objected that the Bank was continuing to finance the project despite five years of noncompliance by project authorities in preparing critical environmental studies and action plans, and in the absence of a resettlement plan for the 90,000 rural poor that the dam's 120-mile long reservoir would displace.... Indeed, the Sardar Sarovar project is only one of literally scores of ongoing and proposed World Bank ecological debacles that have come to congressional and international attention over the past two years—debacles that have occurred despite a tenfold increase in Bank environmental staff and a proliferation of new environmental policies, action plans, and task forces. "[The Bank's] written assurances don't amount to a hill of beans; they don't exist for practical purposes," Scheuer charged. "Where do the pressures come from," he asked, "press-

Originally published in World Policy Journal 7, 2 (Spring 1990):305–329. Reprinted with permission.

ing down on the World Bank to degrade its own procedures and to bring its own integrity into question?"

How has the Bank come to such an impasse, and where indeed do the pressures come from that have led it there?

The answers to these questions have important implications for the fate of the global environment in the 1990s and beyond. Since 1987 the World Bank has been at the forefront of the most important international development institutions— the multilateral development banks (MDBs) and the International Monetary Fund (IMF)—in initiating environmental reform of its lending policies. At the same time, after a period of relative stagnation, the importance of the MDBs and the IMF as international economic and political arbiters has begun to increase dramatically. In 1988 the World Bank's lending capacity was nearly doubled by a $75 billion capital increase, and together the four MDBs are now lending more than $32 billion annually for programs whose total cost is well over $100 billion. . . .

What led the World Bank to undertake environmental reform in the first place was largely the pressures from a coordinated campaign launched by nongovernmental organizations (NGOs) in the United States, Europe, and several developing nations. Starting in 1983, the "MDB Campaign" employed a variety of tactics to pressure the banks, including well-publicized case studies of World Bank–financed ecological disasters in Brazil, India, and Indonesia, congressional and parliamentary hearings in the United States and a number of European nations, and the mobilization of media attention in both the developed and developing world. In May 1987, World Bank President Barber Conable delivered a speech in Washington in which he publicly acknowledged that the Bank had been "part of the problem in the past," and announced that the Bank would mend its ways by greatly increasing its environmental staff and by increasing lending for environmentally beneficial projects.

Environmentalists were guardedly optimistic about Conable's new-found commitment to reform at the time. Now, three years later, it is apparent that the emperor's new clothes bear only faint traces of green. Instead of becoming a leading environmental lender, the Bank has become an arena where the political, practical, and theoretical difficulties of reconciling economic development with ecological sustainability are most glaring. The Bank continues to stress its commitment to the environment, but deep institutional and political contradictions prevent it from implementing reform in any meaningful way. Unless these contradictions are resolved, they will continue to inhibit real environmental change.

The Bank's Environmental Reforms: Appearance and Reality

The Bank's environmental reform program followed in large part the outlines of Conable's May 1987 speech. First, the Bank increased its environmental staff; by 1990, some 60 new positions—representing a tenfold increase—had been created. The Bank also launched a series of environmental issues papers and environmental action plans with the purpose of reviewing and addressing environmental problems in the most vulnerable developing countries. Conable also committed the Bank to financing environmental programs of various kinds, the most important of which was a plan to address tropical deforestation through unprecedented increases in forestry lending. Finally, Conable called for greater involvement of environmental and grass-roots NGOs in both borrowing and donor countries in the Bank's operations.

On the face of it, this program reflected much of what NGOs had pushed for. . . . Beneath its self-proclaimed mission of banker to the poor, and behind its new green facade, the Bank is still essentially doing what it has always done: moving large amounts of money to Third World government agencies for capital-intensive projects or—an innovation of the 1980s—for free-market, export-oriented economic policy changes. Although . . . Conable claimed that a third of Bank projects approved in fiscal year 1989 had "significant environmental components," NGOs now realize that this characterization includes mainly projects whose environmental impacts were so severe to begin with that the Bank felt compelled to incorporate some mitigating measures, as well as ostensibly environmental projects whose hasty design undermines prospects for implementation or, astoundingly, are positively destructive. . . . To their dismay, the NGOs are realizing that their very success in promoting conventional institutional changes has resulted in a proliferation of green rhetoric that hides a reality that is largely unchanged. The Washington-based NGOs that have led the campaign fear that they have inspired the creation of a new Orwellian dialect: greenspeak.

The basis for this fear can be well seen by taking a closer look at two of the most critical areas in the Bank's environmental reform program: the Tropical Forestry Action Plan (TFAP) and the Bank's record in dealing with forced resettlement caused by Bank projects. . . .

The Tropical Forestry Action Plan. Conable's May 1987 speech emphasized that the most important focus of the Bank's new environmental lending would be to contribute to a global program to support tropical forest conservation—the Tropical Forestry Action Plan. To that end he committed the Bank to increase its forestry lending 150 percent by 1989, and in September 1989 he announced a further tripling of forestry lending through the early 1990s.

. . . The TFAP sought to alleviate pressures causing deforestation in the Third World by mobilizing $8 billion from multilateral and bilateral aid agencies over a five-year period for a variety of forestry and agricultural activities that included the building of forestry and environmental institutions, supply of fuelwood needs, conservation of protected areas and vulnerable watershed regions, and support of forest management for industrial uses.

The World Bank's involvement in the TFAP is a revealing and shocking indicator of the gap between rhetoric and reality in the Bank's self-proclaimed greening. Already by 1986, a number of Third World NGOs such as Friends of the Earth in Brazil and the Malaysia-based Asia-Pacific Peoples' Environmental Network (APPEN) were publishing urgent protests maintaining that the TFAP was basically a fraud. It had been prepared, they alleged, without any significant consultation or involvement of NGOs and local communities in tropical forest countries. Worse, it appeared mainly to be a plan to promote traditional, export-oriented timber industry investments camouflaged by small components for environmental purposes. Third World NGOs were particularly outraged because the plan seemed to blame the poor for the destruction of tropical forests while promoting investments to open up large areas of pristine forest for exploitation, rebaptizing such projects as "sustainable forestry."

WRI [Editors' note: the World Resources Institute, a Washington-based environmental think tank] attempted belatedly to address many of the criticisms, but following the Bank's commitment in 1987 to increased funding of the TFAP, the plan gathered seemingly unstoppable momentum to become the most ambitious environmental aid program ever conceived. By the end of 1989, 62 developing nations had requested forestry-sector aid under the TFAP and 21 nations had already completed forestry-sector reviews (pre-investment surveys), with the World Bank as the leader or a major participant in eight. The plan is well on track to mobilize billions of dollars for forestry projects in every country in the world with remaining tropical forests.

Environmentalists around the world now fear that an ecological Frankenstein has been unleashed. The World Rainforest Movement—a Malaysia-based coalition of mainly Third World NGOs—prepared a critique . . . of six completed national TFAP plans—for Peru, Guyana, Cameroon, Tanzania, Nepal, and Colombia. The study concluded that in most of these cases the forestry investments proposed would dramatically accelerate the rate of deforestation through increased logging; in no instance was it found that these investments would actually reduce deforestation. . . .

One of the first TFAP projects to be funded by the Bank (with a sizable contribution from West Germany) is a $23 million forestry and fisheries scheme for Guinea. Yet, as World Wildlife Fund International discovered in late 1989, the so-called "forest management and protection" component of the project actually amounts to a deforestation scheme: the Bank's money will help support the construction of 45 miles of roads in or around two humid forest reserves totalling 150,000 hectares, of which some 106,000 hectares are still pristine rainforest. Worse, hidden in the fine print of the "management and protection" section of the Bank's project document is its real thrust: two-thirds of the remaining 106,000 hectares of rainforest are to be opened for timber production. As a result of these findings, in late 1989 WWF [Editors' note: World Wildlife Fund] mobilized eight national WWF organizations in North America and Europe to lobby the World Bank's executive board against the project. WWF's efforts were too late, however, and the project was approved in January, though minutes of the board meeting reveal the bewilderment of some of the Bank's executive directors. They queried Bank staff on the WWF allegations, which were mostly repetitions of what the Bank's own project appraisal report had stated. The Bank staff replied that deforestation would proceed uncontrolled without the project and that with the project logging could be controlled within "sustainable" limits.

This rationale—that the environmental situation would be worse without Bank intervention—is a particularly specious one, and has been proffered in the past to justify a number of the worst Bank-financed environmental disasters, including rainforest colonization schemes in Brazil and Indonesia. On the contrary, it is often the large infusions of foreign exchange, rapid construction of infrastructure such as roads, and an international stamp of approval provided by the Bank that ensure that a government's environmentally destructive plans become a physical reality within the shortest time possible.

. . .

Forced Resettlement. No single Bank activity has greater immediate social impact than the physical destruction or disruption of rural ecosystems caused by large infrastructure projects such as hydroelectric dams, power plants, and coal mines. The forced resettlement of populations that results from these projects occurs on an enormous scale: as of January [1990] an estimated 1.5 million people were being forcibly displaced by over 70 ongoing Bank projects, and proposed projects currently under consideration may displace another 1.5 million.

The World Bank policy on forced resettlement was established in 1980, predating most other Bank environmental directives. It is the most important of the Bank's environmental policies that deal with the social consequences of ecological destruction. Bank policy requires that when it finances a project that will forcibly displace populations, a resettlement and rehabilitation plan must be prepared and implemented by the borrower in a timely fashion, such that the affected population is at least put in a position where it is no worse off and preferably better off than before. . . .

If anything, since 1987 the situation has worsened. . . . NGOs in the North and South have brought to light more and more examples of the Bank's failure to remedy the plight of populations displaced by ongoing projects, some of which are destitute or on the brink of civil disorder. In Java, where some 20,000 people have been displaced by the Bank-financed Kedung Ombo dam, more than 5,000 "development refugees" still refused to move in early 1990, after the reservoir filled, because there had been no consultations with them regarding resettlement. Rather than ensure that a fair resettlement and rehabilitation plan was being implemented, for years the Bank accepted the Indonesian government's assertion that most of the people affected by the project were volunteering to become rainforest colonists in transmigration (resettlement) sites hundreds of miles away in Indonesia's outer islands. The Bank ignored evidence of coercion and intimidation by project authorities, as reported in numerous newspaper articles and in a letter of protest from a leading Indonesian NGO to the Bank's Jakarta office in 1987.

. . .

Since most of the projects that forcibly displace populations are in the energy sector—large dams and coal-fired power plants, for example—much forced resettlement could be avoided by investments in energy alternatives that are less disruptive environmentally. . . . The Bank again has made rhetorical commitments to increased energy efficiency and conservation investments, but the actual changes have been insignificant. For example, in 1988 and 1989, less than 2 percent of World Bank energy and industry loans were for projects that included end-use efficiency as a component; indeed, the proportion of conservation and efficiency loans in the Bank's energy-sector portfolio was actually higher in the mid-1980s than in more recent years. This gap between rhetoric and reality is one more example that points to deeper institutional problems at the Bank.

The Bank Beset by Contradictions

The Bank's efforts to respond to international pressures for environmental reform have exposed a whole series of contradictions that, when demands on the Bank and multilateral financial institutions were more modest, remained relatively dormant and unexposed. Some of these contradictions are largely internal, others result from conflicting pressures put on the Bank by donors and borrowers, and others appear to be rooted in the nature of the multilateral system itself—especially in its lack of accountability—as well as in current patterns of global economic development, which are often at odds with the requirements of global ecological sustainability.

Internal Contradictions. The first order of Bank contradictions are internal in origin and include a number of classic bureaucratic syndromes, such as a long-standing lack of coordination between the Bank's operations staff, who identify and prepare loans, and its policy, planning and research divisions. The 1987 environmental reforms took place in the context of a larger Bank-wide reorganization that only exacerbated this dichotomy. About half of the new environment staff (approximately 30 positions) was placed in a newly created central Environment Department, but the quality control duties that this department's predecessor had exercised over operations were assigned to four new environmental assessment units that are hampered by limited budgets and staff.

Real power is concentrated even more than in the past in country directors and project officers who actually prepare loans and who have been granted greater autonomy and authority. Thus at times during the past three years the Environment Department has taken on the appearance of a vast paper mill, while the real business of the Bank continued as if on a separate planet called Operations. . . .

The Bank's environmental effectiveness has also been undermined in some cases by the Bank's senior management, which on occasion has overruled the recommendations of its environmental staff. . . . The lack of internal coordination that inhibits environmental effectiveness is compounded by pressures on operations staff to move money rapidly. Bank staff advance their careers by building up large loan portfolios and keeping them moving, not by slowing down the project pipeline to ensure environmental and social quality. Bank-lending priorities appear more understandable in this light. The bias toward large energy infrastructure projects, for instance, is not irrational given that efficiency and conservation loans are harder to prepare and move less money. Vested interests and government bureaucracies in borrowing countries prefer big dam projects for the same reasons. . . .

To some degree the Bank's internal contradictions are amenable to institutional reform. Already more budgetary and staff resources are being channelled into the environmental assessment divisions, which are best placed to influence operations. And with sufficient political will, greater progress could be made in integrating environmental studies and policies into country economic and sector work. But to change priorities from moving money quickly to emphasizing the environmental and social quality of projects requires more than greater political will on the part of senior management. Indeed, such efforts, though they would result in marginal improvements, would probably also have the effect of exacerbating the Bank's environmental schizophrenia. This is because of deeper problems that are linked to fundamentally contradictory pressures exerted on the Bank by its member countries.

Contradictory Pressure of Member Governments. The Bank is subject to a number of simultaneous and contradictory pressures from both its developed and Third World members—pressures that, with respect to the Bank's environmental performance, result not only in contradictory actions but in institutional paralysis.

The pressure to lend more money, for instance, is not only the consequence of the propensity of large bureaucracies to measure success in terms of their own growth and expansion. It also comes from the Bank's major donors, and especially from U.S. efforts to involve the Bank and other multilateral institutions in resolving the Third World debt crisis. . . .

In this regard, there has been a certain convergence of interest between the Bank and the U.S. government. The overall effect of this convergence, however, has been to exacerbate the Bank's tendency to ignore the environmental consequences of its lending. Some of the conditions associated with structural-adjustment loans—such as the reduction of domestic expenditures, currency devaluation, and the increase of exports—often have a negative impact on the environment. They prompt governments to reduce domestic conservation investments and they heighten pressures to exploit resources in an unsustainable fashion in order to increase exports. The Bank has recognized in theory the environmental implications of its adjustment lending, but the exclusion of substantive environmental analysis in its most important economic planning exercises, such as country strategy papers, bodes ill for practical attempts to incorporate environmental concerns into such lending in any systematic way. . . .

Of course borrower countries, too, bear much of the responsibility for the environmental quality of Bank-financed projects. The Bank encounters considerable resistance from some borrowing nations to conditionality of any kind, and particularly to environmental conditionality, which is viewed as both an added cost and as an imposition of the industrialized North's priorities on the South. . . . Not surprisingly, the bigger borrowing nations such as Brazil, India, and Indonesia, which have been subjected to international criticism by the MDB campaign, have been the most vocal opponents of environmental conditionality.

The Bank is acutely sensitive to these pressures, and particularly with respect to its larger borrowers, is reluctant to endanger its "dialogue with host countries" by overly zealous insistence on environmental policies. . . . It is a mistake, however, to assume that either the governments or the societies of developing nations are monolithic. In many governments there are officials who advocate environmental and social measures that equal or even exceed the Bank's standards. And in the civil societies of these countries there can be found even stronger advocates among environmental and social movements, and among disadvantaged minorities such as tribal peoples in India, who suffer a disproportionate share of the adverse effects of large projects and enjoy few of the benefits. Rarely, however, are these advocates able to mount a serious enough challenge to the powerful vested interests inside and outside the government who are often the chief beneficiaries of these projects. . . .

Contradictions of the Multilateral System. While the conflicting pressures of member nations may sometimes hamper the Bank's environmental protection efforts, there is another explanation for its conduct that relates to the fundamental character of the Bank and of the multilateral system generally. The Bank, like other multilateral institutions, is not directly accountable to civil society within borrower and donor countries, or even fully to the representatives of its member nations. Moreover, the Bank heavily restricts access to information concerning details of its activities. These practices make scrutiny of the World Bank and other MDBs—which use *public* monies to lend for *public* purposes—extremely difficult, and place serious constraints on efforts to reform them.

The official avenue of accountability in the World Bank, other MDBs, and the IMF lies with the board of executive directors for each of these institutions. The World Bank's charter, for example, states that "all powers of the Bank are vested in the Board of Governors," who are usually the finance ministers or central bank presidents of each of the Bank's 152 member nations—and most of the powers of the governors are delegated on a day-to-day basis to the Bank's 22 executive directors. The directors approve every loan and every major policy change.

Over the past decade, the executive directors—particularly those representing the United States and a number of European nations—have come under increasing pressure by environmental groups in their countries not only to promote institutional reforms but also to monitor and review individual projects and lending programs of the Bank more closely. But the Bank's management withholds from the executive board access to most of the documents produced by Bank staff in the identification and preparation of projects. Although a project may take over two years to prepare, the directors are given access to appraisal reports on average only two weeks before they are asked to approve a project. . . .

The lack of access to project documents has serious practical consequences. It means that the principal recourse for detailed information on projects are oral briefings by Bank staff. However, there is no assurance that these briefings will include any significant discussion of project risks and problems that can be found in the more candid documents in the project files—information that is obviously necessary for any critical assessment. These briefings often turn out to be little more than confidence-building sessions in which the directors nervously seek reassurances that the projects are under control, and the Bank staff gladly provides them. . . .

If there is a relative lack of Bank accountability to its directors, there is an almost total absence of accountability to the people affected by its projects and to the public in member countries. The Bank withholds all written documents prepared in the planning of projects from the public in both borrower and donor countries, despite the fact that the Bank has been insisting over the past three years that it recognizes the importance of involving local NGOs and community groups in its development activities. . . . Ultimately, the World Bank and other multilateral development institutions justify their lack of transparency and accountability on the grounds that the sole legitimate interlocutor with whom they deal is the nation-state. The Bank, in fact, restricts the channels of communication even further. According to its charter, "Each member shall deal with the Bank only through its treasury, central bank, stabilization fund or other similar fiscal agency, and the Bank shall deal with members only by or through the same agencies." This leaves little room for the substantive involvement of nongovernmental entities of any kind. . . .

The World Bank and other multilateral international institutions are caught in a double bind. The Bank has pledged to incorporate environmental with developmental concerns, but it is constrained to treat these as technical, apolitical matters. Its modus operandi is by definition only with sovereign governments and certain ministries within those governments, but the most crucial environmental challenges are political and social in nature, and call for planning and decision making that give much more legitimacy and empowerment to nongovernmental, civil society.

Contradictions of Global Economic Development. Finally, the World Bank's environmental quandaries are also a reflection of contradictions rooted in the Bank's attempts to reconcile ecological sustainability with global economic development. The most blatant of these contradictions relates to the very slogan that not only the World Bank but most international institutions and governments have adopted as the solution to the environmental dilemma: "sustainable development." The term was popularized by some NGOs in the early 1980s and received multilateral canonization in the 1987 Brundtland Report, the widely cited study by the U.N.'s World Commission on Environment and Development.

Sustainable development is a kind of mother-and-apple-pie formulation that everyone can agree on. The Brundtland Commission defines it as "meet[ing] the needs of the present without compromising the ability of future generations to meet their own needs." Critical to achieving sustainable development, the Commission argues, is the revival of economic growth in both the developing and the industrialized nations. Growth, it maintains, is essential to the alleviation of poverty, which intensifies pressures on the environment and as such is a major cause of environmental degradation in many Third World countries.

The World Bank and other multilateral institutions have enthusiastically embraced this aspect of sustainable development while virtually ignoring many of the Commission's other "strategic imperatives," such as the need to conserve and enhance the resource base and the need to change the quality of growth to one that is less material and energy intensive. The Bank's emphasis on expanding the export capacities of recipient countries thus may be consistent with its own conception of sustainable development, but it is clearly at odds with the requirements of ecological sustainability. . . .

What the World Bank and, for that matter, the Brundtland Commission fail to recognize is that fundamental political, economic, and social changes are required to cope effectively with the intensive use of natural resources that is responsible for so much environmental degradation. Unequal access to natural resources, for instance, must be overcome if per capita pressures on the environment are to be alleviated. Among other things, this means redressing skewed land distribution patterns that, by forcing populations to overwork the land, have resulted in deforestation, soil erosion, siltation of waterways, and other serious environmental problems. Similarly, the Third World and industrialized economies must shift to patterns of development that are less material and energy intensive in order to alleviate future burdens on the environment. These are matters that cannot be solved by economic or technical fixes, but require making difficult political decisions. The formulation and implementation of these decisions will require widespread public support and participation in both the North and South.

. . .

Beyond the Contradictions

When the World Bank announced its environmental reforms in 1987, nongovernmental groups seriously underestimated the barriers to their implementation. Yet while these barriers are formidable, they are not necessarily insurmountable. The Bank's institutional schizophrenia can be remedied, but only if it is forced to choose its identity. If the Bank is truly to be a vehicle of sustainable development, it must place greater emphasis on project quality over the quick disbursement of money. . . . Likewise, if the Bank is to be a democratic institution committed to greater involvement of local people in development planning, it cannot continue to bar the public from access to basic project information. Institutional tinkering is not sufficient for resolving these contradictions; instead, the Bank must be pressured to sort out conflicting priorities.

The growing green movements in the North and South can play a critical role in pushing the Bank to make some of these harder choices. NGOs, for instance,

can and must press for stricter Bank observance of existing environmental policies, for more far-sighted Bank leadership in the formulation of debt-forgiveness
strategies, for greater transparency and accountability on the part of the Bank,
and for greater substantive participation in the Bank's deliberations of those affected by its projects in the Third World. . . .

KENNETH PIDDINGTON

21

The Role
of the World Bank

. . .

Recent History

EARLY APRIL 1987—the Brundtland Report[2] has not yet been published although many are aware of its message; the World Bank is coming up to a painful
process of restructuring and the Development Committee is considering a major
document on the environmental agenda for the Bank.[3] A month later, Mr.
Conable, still a relatively new President, was to spell out this agenda in a public
address to the World Resources Institute in Washington. [Editors' note: Barber
Conable, previously a Republican member of the U.S. House of Representatives
from New York, was president of the World Bank from 1987 to 1991.] His message related to environment and the need for the Bank to give it 'special emphasis'.
The Bank must assist its borrowers to achieve sustainable development, and this
will be done by integrating environmental considerations into the mainstream of
the Bank's country programmes. Mr. Conable acknowledged that failure to do
this had in the past led to errors in project implementation; it was his aim to pre-
side over a reform of the institution's approach.

© Kenneth Piddington 1992. Reprinted from *The International Politics of the Environment*, edited
by Andrew Hurrell and Benedict Kingsbury (1992), by permission of Oxford University Press.

This led to the establishment of the Environment Department in mid-1987, as part of a wider process of reorganization instituted by Mr. Conable when he took office. The Department was placed in the policy and research complex of the Bank, which does not have direct responsibility for the lending programme but which acts as monitor and mentor to the 'regions', the four vice-presidencies which do handle operations. The regions are Latin America, Asia, Africa (south of the Sahara), and 'the rest'—Europe, the Middle East, and North Africa, or EMENA as it is called in the acronymic idiom of the Bank. In each of these 'regions' a small environmental unit was set up in the Technical Department, and this turned out to be a vital element in the overall design, as we shall see.

By 1988, when I arrived in Washington, the bureaucratic foundations were therefore in place and a great deal of work was under way, partly as a follow-up to the programme which Mr. Conable had launched. 'Environmental Issues Papers' for each borrower were being prepared throughout the Bank as a starting point; in several countries in Africa these were to lead quite rapidly to the formulation of environmental action plans.[4] These plans rested on a clear political commitment by the country in question to give priority to key environmental problems. They were similar in concept to the National Conservation Strategies which IUCN [Editors' note: International Union for Conservation of Nature and Natural Resources] had helped to draw up in a number of countries, with the important distinction that the National Environmental Action Plans (which became the standard terminology for the Bank's initiatives) led directly to investment decisions, and also acted as a trigger for the necessary financial flows from the Bank and other sources.

. . .

Not a Facelift . . .

Before accepting this assignment, I made it clear that if the Bank's aim was to have a green frontage, behind which the mode would be 'business as usual', the work would need to be done by a 'façadiste', not an environmental administrator such as myself. The architect of this genre, it is true, works with great elegance to produce the illusion from the outside that the spirit and style of the façade pervades the structure within. The environmental administrator, on the other hand, has a role more akin to that of the plumber or electrician, crawling around the innards of the system to see which pipe is connected where, or how some rewiring might redirect total energy flow.

As we go about the work, what we are really looking for are the command systems in the institution. Unless we can connect with those, we know that environment will be marginalized and will not be seen as central to the purpose and ethic of the organization. This is the shared experience of those who in recent decades have been asked to 'run' environment in corporations, in governments (local, regional, or national) and, increasingly, in international organizations.

President Conable's strong personal commitment, the political interest of our shareholders as reflected in the Executive Board, the new funding initiative which the Bank took in 1990 and which led to the creation of the 'Global Environment Facility' in 1991—all these factors ensured that there was nothing marginal about the environment in the World Bank's policy process. This in turn created sensitivity among colleagues about what should be covered in country programmes, and also meant that by early 1990 the environmental community in the Bank had to deal with a sharp increase in requests for urgent professional advice. Nothing is more welcome, or more demanding, than success in such a tangible form—it triggered the need for an upgrading of Bank in-house resources in many areas of environmental expertise. These increases were (intentionally) concentrated in the Regional Environment Divisions, which grew approximately four-fold between 1988 and 1991.[6]

By early 1991, when it was announced that Mr. Conable would step down and that a prominent merchant banker, Mr. Lewis Preston, would replace him as President on 1 September, it was apparent that the changes introduced in the Bank's structure and its way of doing business were in effect irreversible. Mr. Conable's last few months in office were marked by the adoption of a new policy on tropical forests which removed any ambiguity about the priority to be given to conservation values in future Bank activities in this sector. It stated, for example, that no Bank funding would in future be made available for commercial logging in the remnant tropical forests.[7]

A first principle of environmental administration is to give priority to the establishment of a standard procedure for environmental assessment and to ensure that this is a much more open process than the decision-making sequence followed by most 'closed-circuit' institutions. In practice, this meant that environmental assessment in the Bank would need to bring in the legitimate interest of various groups at the local level. Colleagues therefore worked out how state-of-the-art practice on environmental assessment could be applied to the subtleties of the Bank's relationship with its clients, who . . . are also its shareholders. The Operational Directive on this subject was adopted in October 1989 and there has now been sufficient experience to assess some of the initial results and fine-tune the detailed procedures.

The Directive linked the normal components of an environmental assessment procedure to the project cycle of the Bank. For example, it required a preliminary screening to be carried out as soon as a possible project was identified. It would be rated according to potential environmental impact. Thus, a Category A project would require a full Environmental Assessment (EA), whereas a Category B project might only require limited analysis of specific impacts. A Category C project would be unlikely to have significant environmental impacts and an EA would not therefore be required. A fourth category (D) was assigned to environmental projects, for which separate EAs would not be required—on the grounds that the environment was the major focus of project preparation.[8]

. . . It is clear that some aspects will prove to be of special importance. One is the fact that the assessment (both the documentation and the process) is the responsibility of the borrower, not of the Bank. It is therefore the borrowing government which is asked 'to take fully into account' the views of affected people and local NGOs during the assessment process, which means in effect that it must happen early in the project cycle. The Bank has made it clear that this will be one of the elements to be tested by staff at the appraisal stage, which is the final review of the project by the Bank prior to presentation to the Board.

Linked to this issue is the major boost which the assessment work has given to a more open flow of information about the Bank's activities. Once the forward pipeline has been screened for environmental sensitivity, the results are published in a quarterly supplement to the Monthly Operational Summary, which is the main document through which the Bank conveys information about its future activities to interested parties. I have yet to hear any evaluation by NGOs of the value to them of this (by historical standards) dramatic increase in the Bank's release of information.

. . .

How Does the Ledger Stand?

Reference has already been made to the problem of measuring the Bank's performance. . . . Nevertheless, there are some useful indices of both inputs and outputs which can be derived from the 'dedicated' environmental components of the Bank's work, such as the free-standing environmental projects or trends in staffing the environmental units. Some illustrative examples may be quoted.

(i) **Environmental Lending.** In fiscal 1991, the annual volume of lending for environmental projects had grown to $1.6 billion, approximately 7 per cent of total Bank funding. (The 1991 Annual Report on the Environment states that projects are deemed to be 'primarily' environmental 'if either the costs of environmental protection measures or the environmental benefits accruing from the project exceed 50 per cent of total costs or benefits'.)[11]

(ii) **Special Financing Mechanisms.** The growing interest of donor governments in making funds available for specific aspects of environmental work led to a rapid growth in the number of targeted funds, some of which were managed exclusively within the Bank, while others were operated jointly with agencies such as UNEP [Editors' note: United Nations Environment Programme] and UNDP [Editors' note: United Nations Development Programme]. An example of the latter is the Interim Multilateral Fund established under the Montreal Protocol, which is designed to assist developing countries meet any additional costs they incur by eliminating the use of substances damaging to the ozone layer. Over the initial three-year period, this Fund could account for up to $240 million of grant funding for eligible activities. A similar principle lay behind the Global Environment Facility (GEF), launched in 1991 as a three-year pilot programme to enable actions to be funded in areas where no international agreement had yet been negotiated, such as the limitation of greenhouse gas emissions. GEF funds avail-

able for transfer during the pilot phase could rise to $1.5 billion. Again, the operation is jointly managed by the Bank with UNEP and UNDP.[12] Although these resources do not fall within the criteria for development assistance, they should be seen as additional funds for developing countries to use when they embark on actions which help to protect the global environment.

(iii) **Staff Resources.** The annual report for 1991 gives a Bankwide total of about 270 staff years devoted to environment, or approximately 7 per cent of total Bank effort. This is projected to increase to an average level of 314 staff years over the period 1992–4. These trends should be set alongside the extensive training programmes which have been put in place for 'regular' Bank staff as well as the efforts directed towards officials in borrowing countries, mainly under the aegis of the Bank's Economic Development Institute (EDI).

Conclusion

The above sketch of the Bank's recent history reveals a sizeable redirection of effort and a process which has in effect reached beyond the Bank's façade. Indeed, no institution is completely static. Larger institutions are more likely to appear inert than smaller, less structured groups. But even the most conservative juggernaut will be discovered on closer inspection to be seething with microbial life. The energy in this process will, however, be largely absorbed inside the Kafkaesque corridors, and the outsider may see no external evidence of change in direction.

In the case of the World Bank, which has its quota of corridors, the environmental mission has been as externally directed as any of its major initiatives. As the momentum increases, and as the flow of resources builds up, this means that there will be mutations inside the Bank as well as outside. The process is under way, but the philosophic problem remains. Once an object is moving, it is not possible at a given point in time to have an accurate picture of its position, because it has already changed. It is difficult to present in a freeze frame an assessment of the movement within the Bank, but I would rather face that problem than have to leave unchallenged the mythology of inertia inside or outside the institution.

PART FIVE

The Sustainable Development Debate

Clearly, effective responses to global environmental problems demand both international cooperation and institutional reform. As previous chapters have indicated, these are substantial challenges. The prevailing structures and practices of the international system make attainment of these goals difficult, and they cannot be divorced from the larger struggles over power, wealth, authority, and legitimacy that infuse world politics.

It would be a mistake, however, to chart the course from Stockholm to Rio solely in terms of international treaties and institutional change. Ways of thinking about the global environmental problematique have also changed in important ways. Few would argue that ideas alone have the power to change history. But there is no doubt that paradigms—bundles of fundamental ideas and beliefs—shape the strategies and goals of actors in important ways. They influence how actors understand their interests, how policies are formulated, how resources are allocated, and which actors and institutions are empowered to make the critical decisions that affect global environmental quality.[1]

One powerful but controversial new paradigm that emerged during the 1980s is the idea of sustainable development. As previously discussed, one of the central controversies at Stockholm was the debate over whether economic growth and development are inherently environmentally destructive. This question revealed sharp cleavages between governments of the industrialized North and developing South as well as sharp divisions between growth-oriented governments in general and nongovernmental actors concerned about the negative consequences of continually expanding economic activity.

Sustainable development is an appealing concept to many people because it holds out the promise of reconciling these divergent views. Sustainable development starts with the premise that poverty and economic stagnation are themselves environmentally destructive, and that not all forms of economic organization and activity are equal in their environmental impact. If so, it may be possible to design environmentally friendly forms of production and exchange that simultaneously facilitate economic development, alleviate the pressures of poverty, and minimize environmental damage. This may mean pursuing "development without growth," in the sense of seeking to improve the quality of people's lives without increasing the aggregate level of economic activity.[2] Or it may mean pursuing forms of economic growth that are less ecologically unsound. Whichever path is advocated, reconciling the tension between ecology and economy is the central premise of sustainable development.

The most frequently cited definition of sustainable development is found in *Our Common Future*, the seminal report of the World Commission on Environment and Development. In 1983 the United Nations General Assembly charged the Commission—also known as the Brundtland Commission, after its chairperson, Norwegian Prime Minister Gro Harlem Brundtland—with devising both a conceptual and a practical "global agenda for change."[3] The Commission, which included representatives from twenty-two nations on five continents, conducted a series of hearings around the world before preparing its final report and presenting it to the General Assembly in 1987. The report has had an enormous influence on the shape of the global environmental debate and played a key role in shaping the content and format of the 1992 Earth Summit.

According to the Brundtland Commission, sustainable development is "development that meets the needs of the present without compromising the ability of future generations to meet their own needs."[4] To meet the goal of achieving sustainable development, the Commission set forth a policy blueprint based on enhanced international cooperation, substantial changes in national policies, and a reoriented global economy. The report argues that the problem is not economic growth per se, but rather the environmentally destructive character of many current activities and incentives. Economic growth remains vital, in the Commission's view, given the substantial impact of poverty on the environment. Thus, the Commission combined its recommendations for ecologically sound forms of production and exchange with a call for renewed global growth to solve the problems of Third World poverty.

Some observers see the Commission's advocacy of these positions as inherently contradictory. The continued commitment to a basically unreformed global economic system is, in this view, the biggest impediment to true sustainability, rather than a prerequisite for managing environmental problems more effectively. In an editorial originally published in the British environmental journal *The Ecologist,* Larry Lohmann questions whether the Brundtland Commission has provided an agenda for change or simply a justification for business as usual. In Lohmann's view, the Brundtland proposals would simply put a green face on current practices, while perpetuating unequal relationships of power and wealth—both within countries and between the overdeveloped North and underdeveloped South.[5] As environmental rhetoric, sustainable development is therefore less threatening to powerful interests than some other visions.[6]

Sharachchandra Lélé provides a different, but in some ways equally critical, assessment of the concept of sustainable development. A comprehensive review of the burgeoning literature on sustainability leads Lélé to conclude that the concept lacks a clear, widely accepted definition. There are many different conceptions of sustainable development, not all of which endorse the Brundtland Commission's formulation. Lélé argues that because of the many frequently contradictory uses of the term, "Sustainable development is in real danger of becoming a cliché . . .—a fashionable phrase that everyone pays homage to but nobody cares to define."

Like Lohmann, Lélé writes from the perspective of one who accepts the goal of meeting current needs without compromising the ability of future generations to meet their requirements. His quarrel is with several of the assumptions embedded in mainstream sustainable development thinking. These include a narrowly technical focus on the problem of poverty, while ignoring its fundamentally sociopolitical roots; the neoclassical emphasis on economic growth as an end in itself, rather than a more precise specification of how to meet people's basic needs; and a lack of clarity about exactly what is to be sustained, for whom, and for how long. Definitions that begin instead with the ecological goal of sustaining the conditions for human life and well-being avoid some of these problems, in Lélé's view. But they suffer from an equally debilitating flaw: Too often, they stress the *ecological* conditions required for ecological sustainability but overlook the complex array of *social* conditions that are also required.

Lélé also worries that mainstream notions of sustainable development place an undue burden of structural and value adjustment on the South in order to facilitate the continuation of current consumption practices in the North. In his view, the problem of excessive Northern consumption poses fundamental challenges that are not being adequately addressed with the "managed-growth" model of sustainable development. The idea that the challenge lies primarily in the South is more a reflection of the power of some actors and institutions to set the global agenda than an accurate reflection of the true scope of the problem.

Can the idea of sustainable development break the North-South stalemate on environment and development that emerged at Stockholm? To some extent, it already has; there is no question that the power of the concept—its vision of harmonizing environmental quality and economic well-being—has fundamentally altered the global debate. The next and more difficult step is to clarify whether and how that vision can be attained. Whether this next step is taken, or whether the concept settles into the status of being a contradiction in terms,[7] hinges on its ability to meet several challenges. It must redirect its gaze to encompass the system as a whole and not just the South; it must clarify and reconcile the goals that underlie radically different visions of a sustainable society; and it must broaden its focus to engage the contested issues of power, wealth, and authority that underlie current environmental problems.

22

Towards Sustainable Development

SUSTAINABLE DEVELOPMENT IS development that meets the needs of the present without compromising the ability of future generations to meet their own needs. It contains within it two key concepts:

- the concept of 'needs', in particular the essential needs of the world's poor, to which overriding priority should be given; and
- the idea of limitations imposed by the state of technology and social organization on the environment's ability to meet present and future needs.

Thus the goals of economic and social development must be defined in terms of sustainability in all countries—developed or developing, market-oriented or centrally planned. . . .

Development involves a progressive transformation of economy and society. A development path that is sustainable in a physical sense could theoretically be pursued even in a rigid social and political setting. But physical sustainability cannot be secured unless development policies pay attention to such considerations as changes in access to resources and in the distribution of costs and benefits. . . .

The Concept
of Sustainable Development

The satisfaction of human needs and aspirations is the major objective of development. The essential needs of vast numbers of people in developing countries—for food, clothing, shelter, jobs—are not being met, and beyond their basic needs these people have legitimate aspirations for an improved quality of life. A world in which poverty and inequity are endemic will always be prone to ecological and other crises. Sustainable development requires meeting the basic needs of all and extending to all the opportunity to satisfy their aspirations for a better life.

Living standards that go beyond the basic minimum are sustainable only if consumption standards everywhere have regard for long-term sustainability. Yet many of us live beyond the world's ecological means, for instance in our patterns of energy use. Perceived needs are socially and culturally determined, and sustainable development requires the promotion of values that encourage consumption standards that are within the bounds of the ecological possible and to which all can reasonably aspire.

Meeting essential needs depends in part on achieving full growth potential, and sustainable development clearly requires economic growth in places where such needs are not being met. Elsewhere, it can be consistent with economic growth, provided the content of growth reflects the broad principles of sustainability and non-exploitation of others. But growth by itself is not enough. High levels of productive activity and widespread poverty can coexist, and can endanger the environment. Hence sustainable development requires that societies meet human needs both by increasing productive potential and by ensuring equitable opportunities for all.

An expansion in numbers can increase the pressure on resources and slow the rise in living standards in areas where deprivation is widespread. Though the issue is not merely one of population size but of the distribution of resources, sustainable development can only be pursued if demographic developments are in harmony with the changing productive potential of the ecosystem.

A society may in many ways compromise its ability to meet the essential needs of its people in the future—by overexploiting resources, for example. The direction of technological developments may solve some immediate problems but lead to even greater ones. . . . At a minimum, sustainable development must not endanger the natural systems that support life on Earth: the atmosphere, the waters, the soils, and the living beings.

Growth has no set limits in terms of population or resource use beyond which lies ecological disaster. Different limits hold for the use of energy, materials, water, and land. Many of these will manifest themselves in the form of rising costs and diminishing returns, rather than in the form of any sudden loss of a resource base. The accumulation of knowledge and the development of technology can enhance the carrying capacity of the resource base. But ultimate limits there are, and sustainability requires that long before these are reached, the world must ensure equitable access to the constrained resource and reorient technological efforts to relieve the pressure.

Economic growth and development obviously involve changes in the physical ecosystem. Every ecosystem everywhere cannot be preserved intact. . . . In general, renewable resources like forests and fish stocks need not be depleted provided the rate of use is within the limits of regeneration and natural growth. But most renewable resources are part of a complex and interlinked ecosystem, and maximum sustainable yield must be defined after taking into account system-wide effects of exploitation.

As for non-renewable resources, like fossil fuels and minerals, their use reduces the stock available for future generations. But this does not mean that such resources should not be used. In general the rate of depletion should take into account the criticality of that resource, the availability of technologies for minimizing depletion, and the likelihood of substitutes being available. . . . Sustainable development requires that the rate of depletion of non-renewable resources should foreclose as few future options as possible.

Development tends to simplify ecosystems and to reduce their diversity of species. . . . The loss of plant and animal species can greatly limit the options of future generations; so sustainable development requires the conservation of plant and animal species.

So-called free goods like air and water are also resources. . . . Sustainable development requires that the adverse impacts on the quality of air, water, and other natural elements are minimized so as to sustain the ecosystem's overall integrity.

In essence, sustainable development is a process of change in which the exploitation of resources, the direction of investments, the orientation of technological development, and institutional change are all in harmony and enhance both current and future potential to meet human needs and aspirations.

Equity and the Common Interest

. . . How are individuals in the real world to be persuaded or made to act in the common interest? The answer lies partly in education, institutional development, and law enforcement. But many problems of resource depletion and environmental stress arise from disparities in economic and political power. An industry may get away with unacceptable levels of air and water pollution because the people who bear the brunt of it are poor and unable to complain effectively. . . .

Ecological interactions do not respect the boundaries of individual ownership and political jurisdiction. . . . Traditional social systems recognized some aspects of this interdependence and enforced community control over agricultural practices and traditional rights relating to water, forests, and land. This enforcement of the 'common interest' did not necessarily impede growth and expansion though it may have limited the acceptance and diffusion of technical innovations.

Local interdependence has, if anything, increased because of the technology used in modern agriculture and manufacturing. Yet with this surge of technical progress, the growing 'enclosure' of common lands, the erosion of common rights in forests and other resources, and the spread of commerce and production for the market, the responsibilities for decision making are being taken away from both groups and individuals. This shift is still under way in many developing countries.

It is not that there is one set of villains and another of victims. All would be better off if each person took into account the effect of his or her acts upon others. But each is unwilling to assume that others will behave in this socially desirable fashion, and hence all continue to pursue narrow self-interest. Communities or governments can compensate for this isolation through laws, education, taxes, subsidies, and other methods. . . . Most important, effective participation in decision-making processes by local communities can help them articulate and effectively enforce their common interest. . . .

The enforcement of common interest often suffers because areas of political jurisdictions and areas of impact do not coincide. . . . No supranational authority exists to resolve such issues, and the common interest can only be articulated through international cooperation.

In the same way, the ability of a government to control its national economy is reduced by growing international economic interactions. . . . If economic power and the benefits of trade were more equally distributed, common interests would be generally recognized. But the gains from trade are unequally distributed, and patterns of trade in, say, sugar affect not merely a local sugar-producing sector, but the economies and ecologies of the many developing countries that depend heavily on this product.

The search for common interest would be less difficult if all development and environment problems had solutions that would leave everyone better off. This is seldom the case, and there are usually winners and losers. Many problems arise from inequalities in access to resources. . . . 'Losers' in environment/development conflicts include those who suffer more than their fair share of the health, property, and ecosystem damage costs of pollution.

As a system approaches ecological limits, inequalities sharpen. Thus when a watershed deteriorates, poor farmers suffer more because they cannot afford the same anti-erosion measures as richer farmers. . . . Globally, wealthier nations are better placed financially and technologically to cope with the effects of possible climatic change.

Hence, our inability to promote the common interest in sustainable development is often a product of the relative neglect of economic and social justice within and amongst nations.

Strategic Imperatives

The world must quickly design strategies that will allow nations to move from their present, often destructive, processes of growth and development onto sustainable development paths. . . .

Critical objectives for environment and development policies that follow from the concept of sustainable development include:

- reviving growth;
- changing the quality of growth;
- meeting essential needs for jobs, food, energy, water, and sanitation;
- ensuring a sustainable level of population;
- conserving and enhancing the resource base;
- reorienting technology and managing risk; and
- merging environment and economics in decision making.

Reviving Growth

. . . Development that is sustainable has to address the problem of the large number of people who . . . are unable to satisfy even the most basic of their needs. Poverty reduces people's capacity to use resources in a sustainable manner; it intensifies pressure on the environment. . . . A necessary but not a sufficient condition for the elimination of absolute poverty is a relatively rapid rise in per capita incomes in the Third World. It is therefore essential that the stagnant or declining growth trends of . . . [the 1980s] be reversed.

While attainable growth rates will vary, a certain minimum is needed to have any impact on absolute poverty. It seems unlikely that, taking developing countries as a whole, these objectives can be accomplished with per capita income growth of under 3 per cent. . . .

Growth must be revived in developing countries because that is where the links between economic growth, the alleviation of poverty, and environmental conditions operate most directly. Yet developing countries are part of an interdependent world economy; their prospects also depend on the levels and patterns of growth in industrialized nations. The medium-term prospects for industrial countries are for growth of 3–4 per cent. . . . Such growth rates could be environmentally sustainable if industrialized nations can continue the recent shifts in the content of their growth towards less material- and energy-intensive activities and the improvement of their efficiency in using materials and energy.

As industrialized nations use less materials and energy, however, they will provide smaller markets for commodities and minerals from the developing nations. Yet if developing nations focus their efforts upon eliminating poverty and satisfying essential human needs, then domestic demand will increase for both agricultural products and manufactured goods and some services. Hence the very logic of sustainable development implies an internal stimulus to Third World growth. . . .

Changing the Quality of Growth

Sustainable development involves more than growth. It requires a change in the content of growth, to make it less material- and energy-intensive and more equitable in its impact. These changes are required in all countries as part of a package of measures to maintain the stock of ecological capital, to improve the distribution of income, and to reduce the degree of vulnerability to economic crises.

The process of economic development must be more soundly based upon the realities of the stock of capital that sustains it. . . . For example, income from forestry operations is conventionally measured in terms of the value of timber and other products extracted, minus the costs of extraction. The costs of regenerating the forest are not taken into account, unless money is actually spent on such work. Thus figuring profits from logging rarely takes full account of the losses in future revenue incurred through degradation of the forest. . . . In all countries, rich or poor, economic development must take full account in its measurements of growth of the improvement or deterioration in the stock of natural resources. . . .

Yet it is not enough to broaden the range of economic variables taken into account. Sustainability requires views of human needs and well-being that incorporate such non-economic variables as education and health enjoyed for their own sake, clean air and water, and the protection of natural beauty. . . .

Economic and social development can and should be mutually reinforcing. Money spent on education and health can raise human productivity. Economic development can accelerate social development by providing opportunities for underprivileged groups or by spreading education more rapidly.

Meeting Essential Human Needs

The satisfaction of human needs and aspirations is so obviously an objective of productive activity that it may appear redundant to assert its central role in the concept of sustainable development. All too often poverty is such that people cannot satisfy their needs for survival and well-being even if goods and services are available. At the same time, the demands of those not in poverty may have major environmental consequences.

The principal development challenge is to meet the needs and aspirations of an expanding developing world population. The most basic of all needs is for a livelihood: that is, employment. Between 1985 and 2000 the labour force in developing countries will increase by nearly 900 million, and new livelihood opportunities will have to be generated for 60 million persons every year.[5] . . .

More food is required not merely to feed more people but to attack undernourishment. . . . Though the focus at present is necessarily on staple foods, the projections given above also highlight the need for a high rate of growth of protein availability. In Africa, the task is particularly challenging given the recent declining per capita food production and the current constraints on growth. In Asia and Latin America, the required growth rates in calorie and protein consumption seem to be more readily attainable. But increased food production should not be based on ecologically unsound production policies and compromise long-term prospects for food security.

Energy is another essential human need, one that cannot be universally met unless energy consumption patterns change. The most urgent problem is the requirements of poor Third World households, which depend mainly on fuelwood.

By the turn of the century, 3 billion people may live in areas where wood is cut faster than it grows or where fuelwood is extremely scarce.[7] Corrective action would both reduce the drudgery of collecting wood over long distances and preserve the ecological base. . . .

The linked basic needs of housing, water supply, sanitation, and health care are also environmentally important. Deficiencies in these areas are often visible manifestations of environmental stress. In the Third World, the failure to meet these key needs is one of the major causes of many communicable diseases such as malaria, gastro-intestinal infestations, cholera, and typhoid. . . .

Ensuring a Sustainable Level
of Population

The sustainability of development is intimately linked to the dynamics of population growth. The issue, however, is not simply one of global population size. A child born in a country where levels of material and energy use are high places a greater burden on the Earth's resources than a child born in a poorer country. . . .

In industrial countries, the overall rate of population growth is under 1 per cent, and several countries have reached or are approaching zero population growth. The total population of the industrialized world could increase from its current 1.2 billion to about 1.4 billion in the year 2025.[8]

The greater part of global population increase will take place in developing countries, where the 1985 population of 3.7 billion may increase to 6.8 billion by 2025.[9] The Third World does not have the option of migration to 'new' lands, and the time available for adjustment is much less than industrial countries had. Hence the challenge now is to quickly lower population growth rates, especially in regions such as Africa, where these rates are increasing.

Birth rates declined in industrial countries largely because of economic and social development. Rising levels of income and urbanization and the changing role of women all played important roles. Similar processes are now at work in developing countries. These should be recognized and encouraged. Population policies should be integrated with other economic and social development programmes—female education, health care, and the expansion of the livelihood base of the poor. . . .

Developing-country cities are growing much faster than the capacity of authorities to cope. Shortages of housing, water, sanitation, and mass transit are widespread. A growing proportion of city-dwellers live in slums and shanty towns, many of them exposed to air and water pollution and to industrial and natural hazards. Further deterioration is likely, given that most urban growth will take place in the largest cities. Thus more manageable cities may be the principal gain from slower rates of population growth. . . .

Conserving and Enhancing
the Resource Base

. . . Pressure on resources increases when people lack alternatives. Development policies must widen people's options for earning a sustainable livelihood, particularly for resource-poor households and in areas under ecological stress. . . .

The conservation of agricultural resources is an urgent task because in many parts of the world cultivation has already been extended to marginal lands, and fishery and forestry resources have been overexploited. These resources must be conserved and enhanced to meet the needs of growing populations. Land use in agriculture and forestry should be based on a scientific assessment of land capacity, and the annual depletion of topsoil, fish stock, or forest resources must not exceed the rate of regeneration.

The pressures on agricultural land from crop and livestock production can be partly relieved by increasing productivity. But shortsighted, short-term improvements in productivity can create different forms of ecological stress, such as the loss of genetic diversity in standing crops, salinization and alkalization of irrigated lands, nitrate pollution of ground-water, and pesticide residues in food. Ecologically more benign alternatives are available. Future increases in productivity, in both developed and developing countries, should be based on the better controlled application of water and agrochemicals, as well as on more extensive use of organic manures and non-chemical means of pest control. These alternatives can be promoted only by an agricultural policy based on ecological realities. . . .

The ultimate limits to global development are perhaps determined by the availability of energy resources and by the biosphere's capacity to absorb the by-products of energy use.[11] These energy limits may be approached far sooner than the limits imposed by other material resources. First, there are the supply problems: the depletion of oil reserves, the high cost and environmental impact of coal mining, and the hazards of nuclear technology. Second, there are emission problems, most notably acid pollution and carbon dioxide build-up leading to global warming.

Some of these problems can be met by increased use of renewable energy sources. But the exploitation of renewable sources such as fuelwood and hydropower also entails ecological problems. Hence sustainability requires a clear focus on conserving and efficiently using energy.

Industrialized countries must recognize that their energy consumption is polluting the biosphere and eating into scarce fossil fuel supplies. Recent improvements in energy efficiency and a shift towards less energy-intensive sectors have helped limit consumption. But the process must be accelerated to reduce per capita consumption and encourage a shift to non-polluting sources and technologies. The simple duplication in the developing world of industrial countries' energy use patterns is neither feasible nor desirable. . . .

The prevention and reduction of air and water pollution will remain a critical task of resource conservation. Air and water quality come under pressure from such activities as fertilizer and pesticide use, urban sewage, fossil fuel burning, the use of certain chemicals, and various other industrial activities. Each of these is expected to increase the pollution load on the biosphere substantially, particularly in developing countries, Cleaning up after the event is an expensive solution. Hence all countries need to anticipate and prevent these pollution problems. . . .

Reorienting Technology and Managing Risk

The fulfillment of all these tasks will require the reorientation of technology—the key link between humans and nature. First, the capacity for technological innovation needs to be greatly enhanced in developing countries. . . . Second, the orientation of technology development must be changed to pay greater attention to environmental factors.

The technologies of industrial countries are not always suited or easily adaptable to the socio-economic and environmental conditions of developing countries. To compound the problem, the bulk of world research and development addresses few of the pressing issues facing these countries. . . . Not enough is being done to adapt recent innovations in materials technology, energy conservation, information technology, and biotechnology to the needs of developing countries. . . .

In all countries, the processes of generating alternative technologies, upgrading traditional ones, and selecting and adapting imported technologies should be informed by environmental resource concerns. Most technological research by commercial organizations is devoted to product and process innovations that have market value. Technologies are needed that produce 'social goods', such as improved air quality or increased product life, or that resolve problems normally outside the cost calculus of individual enterprises, such as the external costs of pollution or waste disposal.

The role of public policy is to ensure, through incentives and disincentives, that commercial organizations find it worthwhile to take fuller account of environmental factors in the technologies they develop. . . .

Merging Environment and Economics in Decision Making

The common theme throughout this strategy for sustainable development is the need to integrate economic and ecological considerations in decision making. They are, after all, integrated in the workings of the real world. This will require a change in attitudes and objectives and in institutional arrangements at every level.

Economic and ecological concerns are not necessarily in opposition. For example, policies that conserve the quality of agricultural land and protect forests improve the long-term prospects for agricultural development. . . . But the compatibility of environmental and economic objectives is often lost in the pursuit of individual or group gains, with little regard for the impacts on others, with a blind faith in science's ability to find solutions, and in ignorance of the distant consequences of today's decisions. Institutional rigidities add to this myopia. . . .

Intersectoral connections create patterns of economic and ecological interdependence rarely reflected in the ways in which policy is made. Sectoral organizations tend to pursue sectoral objectives and to treat their impacts on other sectors as side effects, taken into account only if compelled to do so. . . . Many of the environment and development problems that confront us have their roots in this sectoral fragmentation of responsibility. Sustainable development requires that such fragmentation be overcome.

Sustainability requires the enforcement of wider responsibilities for the impacts of decisions. This requires changes in the legal and institutional frameworks that will enforce the common interest. Some necessary changes in the legal framework start from the proposition that an environment adequate for health and well-being is essential for all human beings—including future generations. . . .

The law alone cannot enforce the common interest. It principally needs community knowledge and support, which entails greater public participation in the decisions that affect the environment. This is best secured by decentralizing the management of resources upon which local communities depend, and giving these communities an effective say over the use of these resources. . . .

Changes are also required in the attitudes and procedures of both public and private-sector enterprises. Moreover, environmental regulation must move beyond the usual menu of safety regulations, zoning laws, and pollution control enactments; environmental objectives must be built into taxation, prior approval procedures for investment and technology choice, foreign trade incentives, and all components of development policy.

The integration of economic and ecological factors into the law and into decision-making systems within countries has to be matched at the international level. The growth in fuel and material use dictates that direct physical linkages between ecosystems of different countries will increase. Economic interactions through trade, finance, investment, and travel will also grow and heighten economic and ecological interdependence. Hence in the future, even more so than now, sustainable development requires the unification of economics and ecology in international relations. . . .

Conclusion

In its broadest sense, the strategy for sustainable development aims to promote harmony among human beings and between humanity and nature. In the specific context of the development and environment crises of the 1980s, which current national and international political and economic institutions have not and perhaps cannot overcome, the pursuit of sustainable development requires:

- a political system that secures effective citizen participation in decision making,
- an economic system that is able to generate surpluses and technical knowledge on a self-reliant and sustained basis,
- a social system that provides for solutions for the tensions arising from disharmonious development,

- a production system that respects the obligation to preserve the ecological base for development,
- a technological system that can search continuously for new solutions,
- an international system that fosters sustainable patterns of trade and finance, and
- an administrative system that is flexible and has the capacity for self-correction.

These requirements are more in the nature of goals that should underlie national and international action on development. What matters is the sincerity with which these goals are pursued and the effectiveness with which departures from them are corrected.

LARRY LOHMANN

23
Whose Common Future?

NEVER UNDERESTIMATE the ability of modern elites to work out ways of coming through a crisis with their power intact.

From the days of the American populists through the Depression, postwar reconstruction, the end of colonialism and the age of 'development', our contemporary leaders and their institutions have sought to turn pressures for change to their advantage. The New Deal, the Marshall Plan, Bretton Woods, multilateral lending—all in their turn have taken challenges to the system and transformed them into ways of defusing popular initiatives and developing the economic and political domains of the powerful.

Now comes the global environmental crisis. Once again those in high places are making solemn noises about "grave threats to our common security and the very survival of our planet". Once again their proposed solutions leave the main causes of the trouble untouched. As ordinary people try to reclaim local lands, forests and waters from the depredations of business and the state, and work to build democratic movements to preserve the planet's health, those in power continue to occupy themselves with damage control and the containment of threats to the way power is currently distributed and held. The difference is important to keep in mind when listening to the calls to arms from the new statesmen and women of 'environmentalism'.

Excerpted from *The Ecologist* 20, 3 (May/June 1990):82–84. Used by permission of The Ecologist, Agriculture House, Bath Road, Sturminster Newton, Dorset DT10 1DU, UK, and MIT Press Journals, 55 Hayward Street, Cambridge, MA 02142.

Political Management
of the Crisis

Two of the most prominent of these, former Norwegian Prime Minister Gro Harlem Brundtland and Canadian businessman Maurice Strong, . . . Secretary General of the 1992 United Nations Conference on Environment and Development (UNCED), were in Vancouver in March [1990] to reiterate the message that we all share a 'common future' in environmental preservation and 'sustainable development'. Their speeches at the 'Globe 90' conference and 'green' trade fair gave valuable clues about how the more progressive global elites are organizing themselves for the political management of the environment crisis.

The first instinct of those in high places when faced with a problem is to avoid analyzing its causes if doing so would put the current power structure in an unfavourable light. In Vancouver, Brundtland averted her gaze from the destruction brought about through economic growth, technology transfer and capital flows from North to South and vice versa, and instead rounded up the usual suspects of 'poverty', 'population growth' and 'underdevelopment', without exploring the origins of any of them. She spoke of global warming, a declining resource base, pollution, overexploitation of resources and a 'crushing debt burden' for the South, but omitted mentioning who or what might be responsible. Environmental problems, she implied, were mainly to be found in the South. Admittedly the North had made some mistakes, she said, but luckily it knows the answers now and can prevent the South from making the same errors as it toddles along behind the North on the path to sustainable development.

Whose Security?

The stress of a crisis also tends to drive those in power to the use of vague code words that can rally other members of the elite. In Vancouver the word was 'security'. Brundtland and Strong warned of the "new (environmental) threats to our security" and dwelt on the ideas of a 'global concept of security', a 'safe future' and a new 'security alliance' with an obsessiveness worthy of Richard Nixon.

What was all this talk of 'security' about? In the rural societies where most of the world's people live, security generally means land, family, village and freedom from outside interference. Had the ex-Prime Minister of Norway and the Chairman of Strovest Holdings, Inc. suddenly become land reform activists and virulent opponents of the development projects and market economy expansion which uproot villagers from their farms, communities and livelihoods? Or were they perhaps hinting at another kind of security, the security that First World privilege wants against the economic and political chaos that would follow environmental collapse? In the atmosphere of Globe 90, where everyone was constantly assured that all humanity had 'common security' interests, it was not al-

ways easy to keep in mind the distinction between the first, which entails devolu-
tion of power, and the second, which requires the reverse.

A third instinct of crisis managers in high places is to seek the 'solution' that requires the least change to the existing power structure. Here Brundtland and Strong,
as befits two contenders for the UN Secretary-Generalship, repeated a formula to be
found partly in UN General Assembly documents relating to UNCED. This is:

1. reverse the financial flows currently coursing from South to North, using
   debt relief, new lending, and new infusions of aid possibly augmented by
   taxes on fossil fuels and transfers from military budgets;
2. transfer technology, particularly 'green' technology, from North to South;
   and
3. boost economic growth, particularly in the South.

This scheme has obvious attractions for the world's powerful. For one thing, a re-
sumption of net North-South capital flows would provide a bonanza for Northern
export industries. Funds from the West and Japan would be sent on a quick round
trip through a few institutions in other parts of the world before being returned,
somewhat depleted by payoffs to elites along the way, to the coffers of Northern
firms. Third World income freed up by debt relief would add immensely to corporate profits. Buoyed up by a fresh flow of funds, Southern leaders would become
more receptive to the advice of Northern-dominated institutions and more dependent on Northern technology and aid. Injections of remedial technology, in addition, might well provide an incentive for the South to follow the strategy of dealing
with the effects rather than the causes of environmental degradation. That would
mean more money for both polluting and pollution-correcting industries.

The scheme also shores up the present industrial and financial system by suggesting that the solution to the environmental crisis lies within that system. . . . It
implies that environmental issues are technological and financial and not matters
of social equity and distribution of power—discussion of which would call much
of the system into question. The scheme invokes and reinforces the superstitions
that it is lack of capital that leads to environmental crisis; that capital flows are going to 'expand the resource base', replace soil fertility and restore water tables and
tropical forests lost to commercial exploitation; that poverty will be somehow relieved rather than exacerbated by economic growth; and that capital flows 'naturally' in large quantities from North to South.[1]

Weighing Up the Costs

Admittedly, the UNCED plan has costs for those in power. Bankers may not be
overjoyed at the prospect of debt relief, but since the alternatives seem to be either
continued insupportable and destabilizing South-North net financial transfers or
the perpetuation of the process of servicing Third World debts with new loans,
they may agree in the end. Northern countries will also have to spend massively

on 'green' technology now in order to be in a position to put pressure on the South to do the same later.[2] But this is not necessarily a bad thing for industry, which can 'clean up' the mess it itself makes around the world, perhaps in the process creating new problems which will require further business solutions. As one of Globe 90's organizers put it, "a solution to most environmental issues is a business opportunity".[3] Another obstacle to the UNCED scheme is that it may stir resistance among its Southern 'beneficiaries'. . . .

Perhaps a bigger problem for the UNCED scheme is that it does not actually address the environmental crisis in either North or South. By tailoring solutions not to the problems but to the interests of those who created them, the plan is in fact likely to make things worse. . . . The UNCED plan will reinforce Southern dependence on environmentally destructive models of development imposed by the North and increase the power of Southern elites over their societies. It will promote technology most of which, like the tree-planting machine on display at Globe 90, has only a spurious claim to being 'green' and which will have to be paid for eventually by cashing in resources. It does not examine the effects of importing large amounts of capital into the South and endorses the continuing devastating economization of the natural and social heritage of both North and South. It is, however, probably as far as elites can go at present without challenging their own position. As for the future, there is always the hope that, as the brochure of one Japanese organization present at Globe 90 put it, the problems of global warming, ozone depletion, acid rain, desertification and tropical forest destruction can someday be solved "through technological innovations".[4]

The 'New' Alliance

A fourth tendency among elite crisis managers is to identify the executors of the solution with the existing power structure. . . .

The technical fixes of the UNCED agenda are to be promoted and implemented by a 'new global partnership' or environmental quadruple alliance consisting of industry, government, scientists and non-governmental organizations—"the most important security alliance we have ever entered into on this planet" according to Strong. . . .

Seasoned observers . . . may wonder what is supposed to distinguish the new environmental alliance from the familiar sort of elite ententes that helped land the world in its current environmental mess—the old-boy networks and clubs typified by the military-industrial complex, the World Bank's web of clients, consultants and contractors, the Trilateral Commission, and so on.

Co-opting the NGOs

The answer is non-governmental organizations (NGOs). . . . Why the interest in NGOs? One reason is that they might be used to push business and government in a slightly less destructive direction. Another is that official or corporate environmental initiatives need credibility. Establishment political strategists have not failed to note the growing role of NGOs in recent popular movements from Latin America to South and Southeast Asia and Eastern and Central Europe. . . . 'New alliance' leaders are thus courting and manipulating NGOs, particularly tame NGO umbrella groups, groups with establishment links, and groups with jet-set ambitions, in the hope of being able to use their names to say that UNCED initiatives have the backing of environmentalists, youth, trade unions, women's groups, the socially concerned and "all the nations and peoples of the world".

These manoeuvres, however, cannot conceal the fact that grassroots NGO 'participation' in UNCED and other 'new alliance' activities, to say nothing of the participation of ordinary people, is a fraud. . . . It is governments who decide who is allowed to say what, just as it is governments who will be signing agreements. . . . NGOs are expected to carry governments' message to the people and help them stay in power.[5]

A Common Interest?

Outside official meetings, of course, it is business whose voice will inevitably carry above that of all others in the 'new alliance'. If Globe 90 is any indication, it is not likely to be a voice urging environmental and political sanity. Nor are grassroots-oriented environmental activists likely to be excited about joining a coalition carrying the industry agenda. . . .

Many environmentalists, nevertheless, will feel that joining the 'new global alliance' can do no harm if it presents an opportunity for nudging business and government in a more 'green' direction. Such a conclusion is questionable. It is one thing to pressure business and government into changing their ways with all the means at one's disposal. It is quite another to pledge allegiance in advance to a new elite coalition with a predetermined or unknown agenda which one will have little power to change.

Any alliance which tells us that we *must* seek consensus, that no opposition is to be brooked to Brundtland as Our Common Leader, or that there is a perfect potential community of interest between, say, a UN bureaucrat and a Sri Lankan subsistence fisherman, is one that deserves suspicion at the outset. Consensus-seeking is neither good nor necessary in itself—it may, after all, function merely to conceal exploitation—but only when it is agreed by all parties after full discussion to be possible and fruitful.

This is not to denigrate the ambitious professionals associated with the UNCED, but merely to state a fact. To seek genuine solutions it is necessary to accept, respect and explore differences, to face causes, and to understand the workings of power. It may well be that parties with wildly divergent interests can come to agreements on the crisis confronting the planet. Come the millennium, we may all even be able to form one grand coalition. But until then, it is best to remember the lesson of history: that no matter how warmly it seems to have embraced the slogans of the rebels, the Empire always strikes back.

SHARACHCHANDRA M. LÉLÉ

24
Sustainable Development: A Critical Review

Introduction

THE LAST FEW YEARS HAVE SEEN a dramatic transformation in the environment-development debate. The question being asked is no longer "Do development and environmental concerns contradict each other?" but "How can sustainable development be achieved?" All of a sudden the phrase Sustainable Development (SD) has become pervasive. . . . It appears to have gained the broad-based support that earlier development concepts such as "ecodevelopment" lacked, and is poised to become the developmental paradigm of the 1990s.

But murmurs of disenchantment are also being heard. "What *is* SD?" is being asked increasingly frequently without, however, clear answers forthcoming. SD is in real danger of becoming a cliché like appropriate technology—a fashionable phrase that everyone pays homage to but nobody cares to define. . . . Agencies such as the World Bank, the Asian Development Bank and the Organization for Economic Cooperation and Development have been quick to adopt the new rhetoric. The absence of a clear theoretical and analytical framework, however, makes it difficult to determine whether the new policies will indeed foster an environmentally sound and socially meaningful form of development. . . .

The persuasive power of SD (and hence the political strength of the SD movement) stems from the underlying claim that new insights into physical and social

Originally published in *World Development* 19, 6 (June 1991):607–621. Reprinted with permission from Elsevier Science Ltd., Pergamon Imprint, Oxford, England.

phenomena force one to concur with the operational conclusions of the SD platform almost regardless of one's fundamental ethical persuasions and priorities. I
argue that while these new insights are important, the argument is not inexorable,
and that the issues are more complex than is made out to be. Hence . . . many of
the policy prescriptions being suggested in the name of SD stem from subjective
(rather than consensual) ideas about goals and means, and worse, are often inadequate and even counterproductive. . . .

Interpreting Sustainable Development

The manner in which the phrase "sustainable development" is used and interpreted varies so much that while O'Riordan (1985) called SD a "contradiction in
terms," Redclift suggests that it may be just "another development truism"
(Redclift, 1987, p. 1). These interpretational problems, though ultimately conceptual, have some semantic roots. Most people use the phrase "sustainable development" interchangeably with "ecologically sustainable or environmentally sound
development" (Tolba, 1984a). This interpretation is characterized by: (a) "sustainability" being understood as "ecological sustainability"; and (b) a conceptualization of SD as a process of change that has (ecological) sustainability added to its
list of objectives.

In contrast, sustainable development is sometimes interpreted as "sustained
growth," "sustained change," or simply "successful" development. Let us examine
how these latter interpretations originate and why they are less useful than the
former one. . . .

Contradictions and Trivialities

Taken literally, sustainable development would simply mean "development that
can be continued—either indefinitely or for the implicit time period of concern".
But what is development? Theorists and practitioners have both been grappling
with the word and the concept for at least the past four decades. . . . Some equate
development with GNP growth, others include any number of socially desirable
phenomena in their conceptualization. The point to be noted is that development
is *a process of directed change*. Definitions of development thus embody both (a)
the objectives of this process, and (b) the means of achieving these objectives.

Unfortunately, a distinction between objectives and means is often not made in
the development rhetoric. This has led to "sustainable development" frequently
being interpreted as simply a process of change that can be continued forever. . . .
This interpretation is either impossible or trivial. When development is taken to
be synonymous with growth in material consumption—which it often is even today—SD would be "sustaining the growth in material consumption" (presumably
indefinitely). But such an idea contradicts the general recognition that "*ultimate*
limits [to usable resources] exist"[4] (WCED, p. 45, emphasis added). At best, it

could be argued that growth in the per capita consumption of certain basic goods is necessary in certain regions of the world in the short term. To use "sustainable development" synonymously with "sustain[ing] growth performance" (Idachaba, 1987) or to cite the high rates of growth in agricultural production in South Asia as an example of SD is therefore a misleading usage, or at best a short-term and localized notion that goes against the long-term global perspective of SD.

One could finesse this contradiction by conceptualizing development as simply a process of socio-economic change. But one cannot carry on a meaningful discussion unless one states what the objectives of such change are and why one should worry about continuing the process of change indefinitely.

. . .

Sustainability

. . . The concept of sustainability originated in the context of renewable resources such as forests or fisheries, and has subsequently been adopted as a broad slogan by the environmental movement. Most proponents of sustainability therefore take it to mean "the existence of the ecological conditions necessary to support human life at a specified level of well-being through future generations," what I call *ecological sustainability*. . . .

Since ecological sustainability emphasizes the constraints and opportunities that nature presents to human activities, ecologists and physical scientists frequently dominate its discussion. But what they actually focus on are the ecological conditions for ecological sustainability—the biophysical "laws" or patterns that determine environmental responses to human activities and humans' ability to use the environment. The major contribution of the environment-development debate is, I believe, the realization that in addition to or in conjunction with these ecological conditions, there are social conditions that influence the ecological sustainability or unsustainability of the people-nature interaction. To give a stylized example, one could say that soil erosion undermining the agricultural basis for human society is a case of ecological (un)sustainability. It could be caused by farming on marginal lands without adequate soil conservation measures—the ecological cause. But the phenomenon of marginalization of peasants may have social roots, which would then be the social causes of ecological unsustainability.

. . .

The Concept of Sustainable Development

Evolution of Objectives

The term sustainable development came into prominence in 1980, when the International Union for the Conservation of Nature and Natural Resources (IUCN) presented the World Conservation Strategy (WCS) with "the overall aim of achieving sustainable development through the conservation of living resources" (IUCN, 1980). Critics acknowledged that "By identifying Sustainable Development as the basic goal of society, the WCS was able to make a profound contribution toward reconciling the interests of the development community with those of the environmental movement" (Khosla, 1987). They pointed out, however, that the strategy restricted itself to living resources, focussed primarily on the necessity of maintaining genetic diversity, habits and ecological processes. . . . It was also unable to deal adequately with sensitive or controversial issues—those relating to the international economic and political order, war and armament, population and urbanization (Khosla, 1987). . . .

The United Nations Environment Program (UNEP) was at the forefront of the effort to articulate and popularize the concept. UNEP's concept of SD was said to encompass

(i)   help for the very poor, because they are left with no options but to destroy their environment;

(ii)   the idea of self-reliant development, within natural resource constraints;

(iii)   the idea of cost-effective development using nontraditional economic criteria;

(iv)   the great issues of health control [sic], appropriate technology, food self-reliance, clean water and shelter for all; and

(v)   the notion that people-centered initiatives are needed (Tolba, 1984a).

This statement epitomizes the mixing of goals and means, or more precisely, of fundamental objectives and operational ones, that has burdened much of the SD literature. While providing food, water, good health and shelter have traditionally been the fundamental objectives of most development models (including UNEP's), it is not clear whether self-reliance, cost-effectiveness, appropriateness of technology and people-centeredness are additional objectives or the operational requirements for achieving the traditional ones. . . .

In contrast to the aforementioned, the currently popular definition of SD—the one adopted by the World Commission on Environment and Development (WCED)—is quite brief:

> Sustainable development is development that meets the needs of the present without compromising the ability of future generations to meet their own needs (WCED, 1987; p. 43).

The constraint of "not compromising the ability of future generations to meet their needs" is (presumably) considered by the Commission to be equivalent to the requirement of some level of ecological and social sustainability.[5]

While the WCED's statement of the fundamental objectives of SD is brief, the Commission is much more elaborate about (what are essentially) the operational objectives of SD. It states that "the critical objectives which follow from the concept of SD" are:

(1) reviving growth;

(2) changing the quality of growth;

(3) meeting essential needs for jobs, food, energy, water, and sanitation;

(4) ensuring a sustainable level of population;

(5) conserving and enhancing the resource base;

(6) reorienting technology and managing risk;

(7) merging environment and economics in decision making; and

(8) reorienting international economic relations (WCED, 1987, p. 49).

Most organizations and agencies actively promoting the concept of SD subscribe to some or all of these objectives with, however, the notable addition of a ninth operational goal, viz.,

(9) making development more participatory.[6]

This formulation can therefore be said to represent the mainstream of SD thinking. This "mainstream" includes international environmental agencies such as UNEP, IUCN and the World Wildlife Fund (WWF), developmental agencies including the World Bank, the US Agency for International Development, the Canadian and Swedish international development agencies, research and dissemination organizations such as the World Resources Institute, the International Institute for Environment and Development, the Worldwatch Institute (1984–88), and activist organizations and groups such as the Global Tomorrow Coalition.

. . .

The Premises of SD

The perception in mainstream SD thinking of the environment-society link is based upon the following premises:

(i) *Environmental degradation:*

- Environmental degradation is already affecting millions in the Third World, and is likely to severely reduce human well-being all across the globe within the next few generations.

- Environmental degradation is very often caused by poverty, because the poor have no option but to exploit resources for short-term survival.

- The interlinked nature of most environmental problems is such that environmental degradation ultimately affects everybody, although poorer individuals/nations may suffer more and sooner than richer ones.

(ii) *Traditional development objectives:*

- These are: providing basic needs and increasing the productivity of all resources (human, natural and economic) in developing countries, and maintaining the standard of living in the developed countries.

- These objectives do not necessarily conflict with the objective of ecological sustainability. In fact, achieving sustainable patterns of resource use is necessary for achieving these objectives permanently.
- It can be shown that, even for individual actors, environmentally
sound methods are "profitable" in the long run, and often in the short
run too.

(iii) *Process:*

- The process of development must be participatory to succeed even in
the short run).

Given these premises, the need for a process of development that achieves the traditional objectives, results in ecologically sustainable patterns of resource use, and
is implemented in a participatory manner is obvious.

Most of the SD literature is devoted to showing that this process is also feasible
and can be made attractive to the actors involved. SD has become a bundle of neat
fixes: technological changes that make industrial production processes less polluting and less resource intensive and yet more productive and profitable, economic
policy changes that incorporate environmental considerations and yet achieve
greater economic growth, procedural changes that use local non-governmental organizations (NGOs) so as to ensure grassroots participation, agriculture that is less
harmful, less resource intensive and yet more productive, and so on. In short, SD is
a "metafix" that will unite everybody from the profit-minded industrialist and
risk-minimizing subsistence farmer to the equity-seeking social worker, the pollu-
tion-concerned or wildlife-loving First Worlder, the growth-maximizing policy
maker, the goal-oriented bureaucrat, and therefore, the vote-counting politician.

Weaknesses

The major impact of the SD movement is the rejection of the notion that environmental conservation necessarily constrains development or that development
necessarily means environmental pollution—certainly not an insignificant gain.
Where the SD movement has faltered is in its inability to develop a set of concepts, criteria and policies that are coherent or consistent—both externally (with
physical and social reality) and internally (with each other). The mainstream formulation of SD suffers from significant weaknesses in:

- its characterization of the problems of poverty and environmental
degradation;
- its conceptualization of the objectives of development, sustainability
and participation; and
- the strategy it has adopted in the face of incomplete knowledge and
uncertainty.

Poverty and Environmental Degradation: An Incomplete Characterization

The fundamental premise of mainstream SD thinking is the two-way link between poverty and environmental degradation. . . .

In fact, however, even a cursory examination of the vast amount of research that has been done on the links between social and environmental phenomena suggests that both poverty and environmental degradation have deep and complex causes. . . .

To say that mainstream SD thinking has completely ignored [this complexity] would be unfair. But . . . inadequate technical know-how and managerial capabilities, common property resource management, and pricing and subsidy policies have been the major themes addressed, and the solutions suggested have been essentially techno-economic ones. . . . Deeper socio-political changes (such as land reform) or changes in cultural values (such as overconsumption in the North) are either ignored or paid lip-service. . . .

Conceptual Weaknesses

Removal of poverty (the traditional developmental objective), sustainability and participation are really the three fundamental objectives of the SD paradigm. Unfortunately, the manner in which these objectives are conceptualized and operationalized leaves much to be desired. On the one hand, economic growth is being adopted as a major operational objective that is consistent with both removal of poverty and sustainability. On the other hand, the concepts of sustainability and participation are poorly articulated, making it difficult to determine whether a particular development project actually promotes a particular form of sustainability, or what kind of participation will lead to what kind of social (and consequently, environmental) outcome.

The Role of Economic Growth. By the mid-1970s, it had seemed that the economic growth and trickle-down theory of development had been firmly rejected, and the "basic needs approach" (Streeten, 1979) had taken root in development circles. Yet economic growth continues to feature in today's debate on SD. In fact, "reviving [economic] growth" heads WCED's list of operational objectives quoted earlier. Two arguments are implicit in this adoption of economic growth as an operational objective. The first, a somewhat defensive one, is that there is no fundamental contradiction between economic growth and sustainability, because growth in economic activity may occur simultaneously with either an improvement or a deterioration in environmental quality. Thus, "governments concerned with long-term sustainability need not seek to limit growth in economic output so long as they stabilize aggregate natural resource consumption" (Goodland and Ledec, 1987). But one could turn this argument around and suggest that, if economic growth is not correlated with environmental sustainability, there is no reason to have economic growth as an operational objective of SD.[8]

The second argument in favor of economic growth is more positive. The basic premise of SD is that poverty is largely responsible for environmental degradation. Therefore, removal of poverty (i.e., development) is necessary for environmental sustainability. This, it is argued, implies that economic growth is absolutely necessary for SD. The only thing that needs to be done is to "change the quality of [this] growth" (WCED, 1987, pp. 52–54) to ensure that it does not lead to environmental destruction. In drawing such an inference, however, there is the implicit belief that economic growth is necessary (if not sufficient) for the removal of poverty. But was it not the fact that economic growth per se could not ensure the removal of poverty that led to the adoption of the basic needs approach in the 1970s?

Thus, if economic growth by itself leads to neither environmental sustainability nor removal of poverty, it is clearly a "non-objective" for SD. The converse is a possibility worth exploring, viz., whether successful implementation of policies for poverty removal, long-term employment generation, environmental restoration and rural development will lead to growth in GNP, and, more important, to increases in investment, employment and income generation. This seems more than likely in developing countries, but not so certain in developed ones. In any case, economic growth may be the fallout of SD, but not its prime mover.

Sustainability. The World Conservation Strategy was probably the first attempt to carry the concept of sustainability beyond simple renewable resource systems. It suggested three ecological principles for ecological sustainability (see the nomenclature developed above), viz., "maintenance of essential ecological processes and life-support systems, the preservation of genetic diversity, and the sustainable utilization of species and resources" (IUCN, 1980). This definition, though a useful starting point, is clearly recursive as it invokes "sustainability" in resource use without defining it. Many subsequent attempts to discuss the notion are disturbingly muddled. There is a very real danger of the term becoming a meaningless cliché, unless a concerted effort is made to add precision and content to the discussion. . . .

Any discussion of sustainability must first answer the questions "What is to be sustained? For whom? How long?" The value of the concept (like that of SD), however, lies in its ability to generate an operational consensus between groups with fundamentally different answers to these questions, i.e., those concerned either about the survival of future human generations, or about the survival of wildlife, or human health, or the satisfaction of immediate subsistence needs (food, fuel, fodder) with a low degree of risk. It is therefore vital to identify those aspects of sustainability that do actually cater to such diverse interests, and those that involve tradeoffs.

Differentiating between ecological and social sustainability could be a first step toward clarifying some of the discussion. Further, in the case of ecological sustainability, a distinction needs to be made between renewable resources, nonrenewable resources, and environmental processes that are crucial to human life, as well as to life at large. The few researchers who have begun to explore the idea of ecological sustainability emphasize its multidimensional and complex nature. . . .

In the rush to derive ecological principles of (ecological) sustainability, we cannot afford to lose sight of the social conditions that determine which of these principles are socially acceptable, and to what extent. Sociologists, eco-Marxists and political ecologists are pointing out the crucial role of socioeconomic structures and institutions in the pattern and extent of environmental degradation globally. Neoclassical economists, whose theories have perhaps had the greatest influence in development policy making in the past and who therefore bear the responsibility for its social and environmental failures, however, have been very slow in modifying their theories and prescriptions. The SD movement will have to formulate a clear agenda for research in what is being called "ecological economics" and press for its adoption by the mainstream of economics in order to ensure the possibility of real changes in policy making.

Social sustainability is a more nebulous concept than ecological sustainability. Brown et al. (1987), in a somewhat techno-economic vein, state that sustainability implies "the existence and operation of an infrastructure (transportation and communication), services (health, education, and culture), and government (agreements, laws, and enforcement)." Tisdell (1988) talks about "the sustainability of political and social structures" and Norgaard (1988) argues for cultural sustainability, which includes value and belief systems. Detailed analyses of the concept, however, seem to be nonexistent.[9] Perhaps achieving desired social situations is itself so difficult that discussing their maintainability is not very useful; perhaps goals are even more dynamic in a social context than in an ecological one, so that maintainability is not such an important attribute of social institutions/structures. There is, however, no contradiction between the social and ecological sustainability; rather, they can complement and inform each other.

Participation. A notable feature of . . . some of the earlier SD literature was the emphasis placed on equity and social justice. . . . Subsequently, however, the mainstream appears to have quietly dropped these terms (suggesting at least a deemphasizing of these objectives), and has instead focused on "local participation."

There are, however, three problems with this shift. First, by using the terms equity, participation and decentralization interchangeably, it is being suggested that participation and decentralization are equivalent, and that they can somehow substitute for equity and social justice. . . .

Second, the manner in which participation is being operationalized shows up the narrow-minded, quick-fix and deceptive approach adopted by the mainstream promoters of SD. . . . Mainstream SD literature blithely assumes and insists that "involvement of local NGOs" in project implementation will ensure project success (Maniates, 1990; he dubs this the "NGOization" of SD).

Third, there is an assumption that participation or at least equity and social justice will necessarily reinforce ecological sustainability. Attempts to test such assumptions rigorously have been rare. But preliminary results seem to suggest that equity in resource access may not lead to sustainable resource use unless new institutions for resource management are carefully built and nurtured. . . . This should not be misconstrued as an argument against the need for equity, but rather as a word of caution against the tendency to believe that social equity automatically ensures environmental sustainability (or vice-versa).

. . .

Concluding Remarks: Dilemmas and Agendas

The proponents of SD are faced with a dilemma that affects any program of political action and social change: the dilemma between the urge to take strong stands on fundamental concerns and the need to gain wide political acceptance and support. . . . SD is being packaged as the inevitable outcome of objective scientific analysis, virtually an historical necessity, that does not contradict the deep-rooted normative notion of development as economic growth. In other words, SD is an attempt to have one's cake and eat it too.

It may be argued that this is indeed possible, that the things that are wrong and need to be changed are quite obvious, and there are many ways of fixing them without significantly conflicting with either age-old power structures or the modern drive for a higher material standard of living. . . . If, by using the politically correct jargon of economic growth and development and by packaging SD in the manner mentioned above, it were possible to achieve even 50% success in implementing this bundle of "conceptually imprecise" policies, the net reduction achieved in environmental degradation and poverty would be unprecedented.

I believe, however, that (analogous to the arguments in SD) in the long run there is no contradiction between better articulation of the terms, concepts, analytical methods and policy-making principles, and gaining political strength and broad social acceptance—especially at the grassroots. In fact, such clarification and articulation is necessary if SD is to avoid either being dismissed as another development fad or being coopted by forces opposed to changes in status quo. More specifically, proponents and analysts of SD need to:

(a) clearly reject the attempts (and temptation) to focus on economic growth as means to poverty removal and/or environmental sustainability;

(b) recognize the internal inconsistencies and inadequacies in the theory and practice of neoclassical economics, particularly as it relates to environmental and distributional issues; in economic analyses, move away from arcane mathematical models toward exploring empirical questions such as limits to the substitution capital for resources, impacts of different sustainability policies on different economic systems, etc.;

(c) accept the existence of structural, technological and cultural causes of poverty and environmental degradation; develop methodologies for estimating relative importance of and interaction between these causes in specific situations; and explore political, institutional and educational solutions to them;

(d) understand the multiple dimensions of sustainability, and attempt to develop measures, criteria and principles for them; and

(e) explore what patterns and levels of source demand and use would be compatible with different forms or levels of ecological and social sustainability, and with different notions of equity and social justice.

There are, fortunately, some signs that a debate on these lines has now begun.

In a sense, if SD is to be really "sustained" as a development paradigm, two apparently divergent efforts are called for: making SD more precise in its conceptual underpinnings, while allowing more flexibility and diversity of approaches in developing strategies that might lead to a society living in harmony with the environment and with itself.

References

Brown, B. J., M. Hanson, D. Liverman, and R. Merideth, Jr. "Global Sustainability: Toward Definition," *Environmental Management,* Vol. 11, No. 6 (1987), pp. 713–719.

Brown, L. R., *Building a Sustainable Society* (New York: W. W. Norton, 1981).

Chambers, R., *Sustainable Livelihoods: An Opportunity for the World Commission on Environment and Development* (Brighton, UK: Institute of Development Studies, University of Sussex, 1986).

Daly, H., *Economics, ecology, ethics: Essays toward a steady-state economy* (San Francisco: W. H. Freeman, 1980).

Goodland, R., and G. Ledec, "Neoclassical Economics and Principles of Sustainable Development," *Ecological Modelling,* Vol. 38 (1987), pp. 19–46.

Idachaba, F. S., "Sustainability Issues in Agriculture Development," in T. J. Davis and I. A. Schirmer (Eds.), *Sustainability Issues in Agricultural Development* (Washington, DC: World Bank, 1987), pp. 18–53.

IUCN, *World Conservation Strategy: Living Resource Conservation for Sustainable Development* (Gland, Switzerland: International Union for Conservation of Nature and Natural Resources, United Nations Environment Program and World Wildlife Fund, 1980).

Khosla, A., "Alternative Strategies in Achieving Sustainable Development," in P. Jacobs and D. A. Munro (Eds.), *Conservation with Equity: Strategies for Sustainable Development* (Cambridge, England: International Union for Conservation of Nature and Natural Resources, 1987), pp. 191–208.

Maniates, M., "Organizing for Rural Energy Development: Local Organizations, Improved Cookstoves, and the State in Gujarat, India," Ph.D. thesis (Berkeley: Energy & Resources Group, University of California, 1990).

Norgaard, R. B., "Sustainable Development: A Coevolutionary View," *Futures,* Vol. 20, No. 6 (1988), pp. 606–620.

———, "Three Dilemmas of Environmental Accounting," *Ecological Economics,* Vol. 1, No. 4 (1989), pp. 303–314.

O'Riordan, T., "Future Directions in Environmental Policy," *Journal of Environment and Planning,* Vol. 17 (1985), pp. 1431–1446.

Peskin, H. M., "National Income Accounts and the Environment," *Natural Resources Journal,* Vol. 21 (1981), pp. 511–537.

Redclift, M., *Sustainable Development: Exploring the Contradictions* (New York: Methuen, 1987).

Repetto, R., *World Enough and Time* (New Haven, CT: Yale University Press, 1986a).

Riddell, R., *Ecodevelopment* (New York: St. Martin's Press, 1981).

Sachs, I., *Environment and Development—A New Rationale for Domestic Policy Formulation and International Cooperation Strategies* (Ottawa: Environment Canada and Canadian International Development Agency, 1977).

Streeten, P., "Basic Needs: Premises and Promises," *Journal of Policy Modelling,* Vol. 1 (1979), pp. 136–146.

Tisdell, C., "Sustainable Development: Differing Perspectives of Ecologists and Economists, and Relevance to LDCs," *World Development,* Vol. 16, No. 3 (1988), pp. 373–384.

Tolba, M. K., "The Premises for Building a Sustainable Society. Address to the World Commission on Environment and Development," October 1984 (Nairobi: United Nations Environment Programme, 1984).

World Commission on Environment and Development, *Our Common Future* (New York: Oxford University Press, 1987).

Worldwatch Institute, *State of the World* (New York: Norton, various years).

PART SIX

From Ecological Conflict to Environmental Security?

Chris Calwell, NRDC

As seen in the previous part, the concept of sustainability has emerged as a powerful new paradigm, shaping the interpretations, goals, and behavior of a broad range of actors on the global environmental stage. But the global environmental debate of the past two decades has engaged not only economic issues of welfare, production, and livelihood but also political questions of international conflict, violence, and geopolitics. It is not surprising that paradigms focused on the conflictual dimensions of environmental problems have also begun to emerge.

One attempt to grapple with these intensely political themes is the emerging paradigm of "environmental security." Like sustainability, environmental security offers a potentially powerful but also controversial new way to think about the social dimensions of environmental problems. The environmental security paradigm rests on a series of claims: that environmental change is an important source of social conflict; that many societies face graver threats from environmental change than from traditional military threats; and that security policies must be redefined to take these new realities into account.

The chapter by Thomas Homer-Dixon addresses the connection between environmental change and violent conflict. Homer-Dixon argues that environmental change is becoming an increasingly important source of social instability, civil strife, and violence among, and especially within, societies. The growing scarcity of renewable resources—principally water, fish stocks, forests, and fertile land—already promotes such conflict and is likely to cause a surge in violence in the future. Homer-Dixon stresses that political and economic institutions remain central to determining specific patterns of conflict. But "environmental scarcity"—which he suggests is caused by environmental change, population growth, and the unequal social distribution of natural resources—is an increasingly important factor.

Given such conflict potential, proponents of environmental security have argued that there is an urgent, compelling need to redefine the concept of security.[1] Environmental threats must become central concerns of the security policies of states. In the second chapter in this part, environmentalist Norman Myers calls for such a redefinition. Myers argues that security should be conceptualized in terms of individual human well-being as well as the territorial integrity of the state. Environmental problems such as soil erosion, water pollution, and ozone depletion pose immediate and significant threats to the in-

241

dividual, the state, and human society as a whole. Just as economic considerations have become increasingly important in security policy deliberations, so too must environmental concerns be raised to the level of "high politics."[2] Myers's conception of security also stresses that cooperation, and not defensive preparations for conflict, is the most effective way to address such non-military security threats.

Myers's arguments make clear that environmental security is more than just an effort to reconceptualize the nature of the threats societies face today and in the future. It is also a tangible political agenda, seeking to mobilize the state and society toward a new set of goals and, in the process, redirect resources and energies currently dedicated to highly militarized security policies. Some proponents argue that only by framing the environmental problematique in security terms can the necessary level of governmental attention and social mobilization be ensured.[3] Others argue that security institutions could contribute directly to environmental protection, given their financial resources, monitoring and intelligence-gathering capabilities, and scientific and technological expertise.[4]

Thus, although the origins of the environmental security paradigm can be traced at least to the early post–World War II period,[5] it is surely no accident that the idea of rethinking security policy in ecological terms has flourished in the post–Cold War era. Policymakers, military institutions, and entire societies have begun to reconsider the character of the threats they face. Many proponents of environmental security are driven by the practical belief that these changes have opened a window of opportunity for fundamental changes in security policies and a reordering of social priorities.

Among the many controversies surrounding the paradigm of environmental security, two are central. First, is there enough strong evidence to support the claim that ecological change is, or will be, a major new source of conflict? Although a growing body of research points to specific cases in which environmental change seems to have played a role in promoting or exacerbating social conflict, many questions remain. Why does environmental stress produce such conflict in some cases but not in others? Is it possible that environmental problems are a *symptom* of conflict-prone social systems, and not themselves a root cause of conflict? Such questions have led some to doubt whether environmental change is itself an important, independent source of conflict. A second question involves the more nebulous concept of "security." Are the advantages of linking environmental problems to security concerns worth the risk of militarizing a society's responses to environmental problems?

The chapter by Daniel Deudney raises both sets of questions. Deudney is skeptical that environmental change precipitates acute conflict, at least in the form of war; he argues that environmental problems have little in common with the traditional security problem of interstate violence. Deudney is also wary of evoking the powerful concept of security in order to mobilize society: "For environmentalists to dress their programs in the bloodsoaked garments of the war system betrays their core values and creates confusion about the real tasks at hand." Others have voiced stronger criticisms, suggesting that the powerful association between the concept of security and the use of military force creates the danger of turning environmental problems into sources of military tension and conflict.[6] Matthias Finger argues, "The military must be addressed as a cause and not a cure of global environmental problems." In Finger's view, worldwide militarization wastes scarce resources that could be deployed in the struggle against environmental degradation and is itself a source of massive amounts of pollution.[7] These critics share Deudney's view that the conflictual mind-set and military tools of security institutions are poorly suited to the global environmental problematique.

The environmental security debate is further complicated by the way in which it intersects the North-South axis in world politics. The focus of ecological conflict research tends to be on less economically developed regions of the planet; most analysts emphasize these regions when identifying likely sites of environmentally induced conflicts. There are many reasons for this focus on the South: limited financial and technological resources, high population growth rates, preexisting political instability, and the day-to-day struggles for survival engulfing large segments of the population. However, even if it is plausible to claim that the South will be the site of environmental conflicts, this concern cannot be divorced from the broader pattern of North-South relations. The chapter by Egyptian diplomat Somaya Saad reflects the deep suspicion with which many Southern governments view the North's concern for security in the South, environmental or otherwise. She sees the rhetoric of environmental security as an excuse to continue the North's long-standing practice of military and economic intervention. She also suggests that the extensive focus on the South is a way for the North to deny its own overwhelming responsibility for the deteriorating state of the planet. Saad's concerns emphasize the importance of history and context. In a world where many people feel their security is threatened mainly by other people, calls for change in security policies may seem like a way to break the cycle of violence, suspicion, and zero-sum thinking. But given the purposes that security policies have served in the past, such calls also raise deep suspicions about ulterior motives.

Social science may lack the tools to tell us exactly when and where environmental problems will produce violence. Nevertheless, the capacity of environmental change to disrupt people's lives, erode standards of living, and threaten established interests tells us that the possibility of widespread violent conflict must be taken seriously. Research that helps us understand when and where such conflict is more or less likely to occur could be an important tool for conflict avoidance, international confidence building, and nonviolent conflict resolution. But the paradigm of environmental security remains controversial because it links plausible claims about conflict to the symbolically powerful and highly charged concept of security. At its best, linking environment and security could be a way to build trust among nations and make security a cooperative, global endeavor, while steering resources and public energy toward the resolution of environmental problems. But at its worst, tying environmental concerns to militarized approaches to social conflict could itself be a recipe for greater violence in the future.

THOMAS F. HOMER-DIXON

25

Environmental Scarcities and Violent Conflict: Evidence from Cases

WITHIN THE NEXT FIFTY YEARS, the planet's human population will probably pass nine billion, and global economic output may quintuple. Largely as a result, scarcities of renewable resources will increase sharply. The total area of high-quality agricultural land will drop, as will the extent of forests and the number of species they sustain. Coming generations will also see the widespread depletion and degradation of aquifers, rivers, and other water resources; the decline of many fisheries; and perhaps significant climate change.

If such "environmental scarcities" become severe, could they precipitate violent civil or international conflict? I have previously surveyed the issues and evidence surrounding this question and proposed an agenda for further research.[1] Here I report the results of an international research project guided by this agenda.[2] . . .

In brief, our research showed that environmental scarcities are already contributing to violent conflicts in many parts of the developing world. These conflicts are probably the early signs of an upsurge of violence in the coming decades that will be induced or aggravated by scarcity. The violence will usually be subnational, persistent, and diffuse. Poor societies will be particularly affected since they are less able to buffer themselves from environmental scarcities and the social crises they cause. These societies are, in fact, already suffering acute hardship from shortages of water, forests, and especially fertile land.

Social conflict is not always a bad thing: mass mobilization and civil strife can produce opportunities for beneficial change in the distribution of land and wealth and in processes of governance. But fast-moving, unpredictable, and complex environmental problems can overwhelm efforts at constructive social reform. Moreover, scarcity can sharply increase demands on key institutions, such as the state, while it simultaneously reduces their capacity to meet those demands. These pressures increase the chance that the state will either fragment or become more authoritarian. The negative effects of severe environmental scarcity are therefore likely to outweigh the positive.

General Findings

Our research was intended to provide a foundation for further work. We therefore focused on two key preliminary questions: does environmental scarcity cause violent conflict? And, if it does, how does it operate?

The research was structured as I proposed in my previous article. Six types of environmental change were identified as plausible causes of violent inter-group conflict:

- greenhouse-induced climate change;
- stratospheric ozone depletion;
- degradation and loss of good agricultural land;
- degradation and removal of forests;
- depletion and pollution of fresh water supplies; and
- depletion of fisheries.

We used three hypotheses to link these changes with violent conflict. First, we suggested that decreasing supplies of physically controllable environmental resources, such as clean water and good agricultural land, would provoke interstate "simple-scarcity" conflicts or resource wars. Second, we hypothesized that large population movements caused by environmental stress would induce "group-identity" conflicts, especially ethnic clashes. And third, we suggested that severe environmental scarcity would simultaneously increase economic deprivation and disrupt key social institutions, which in turn would cause "deprivation" conflicts such as civil strife and insurgency. . . .

Resource Depletion and Degradation

Of the major environmental changes facing humankind, degradation and depletion of agricultural land, forests, water, and fish will contribute more to social turmoil in coming decades than will climate change or ozone depletion.

When analysts and policymakers in developed countries consider the social impacts of large-scale environmental change, they focus undue attention on climate change and stratospheric ozone depletion.[4] But vast populations in the developing world are already suffering from shortages of good land, water, forests, and fish; in contrast, the social effects of climate change and ozone depletion will probably not be seen till well into the next century. If these atmospheric problems do eventually have an impact, they will most likely operate not as individual environmental stresses, but in interaction with other, long-present resource, demographic, and economic pressures that have gradually eroded the buffering capacity of some societies.

Mexico, for example, is vulnerable to such interactions. People are already leaving the state of Oaxaca because of drought and soil erosion. Researchers estimate that future global warming could decrease Mexican rainfed maize production up to 40 percent. This change could in turn interact with ongoing land degradation, free trade (because Mexico's comparative advantage is in water-intensive fruits and vegetables), and the privatization of communal peasant lands to cause grave internal conflict.[5]

Environmental Scarcity

Environmental change is only one of three main sources of scarcity of renewable resources; the others are population growth and unequal social distribution of resources. The concept "environmental scarcity" encompasses all three sources.

Analysts often usefully characterize environmental problems as resource scarcities. Resources can be roughly divided into two groups: non-renewables, like oil and iron ore, and renewables, like fresh water, forests, fertile soils, and the earth's ozone layer. The latter category includes renewable "goods" such as fisheries and timber, and renewable "services" such as regional hydrological cycles and a benign climate.

The commonly used term "environmental change" refers to a human-induced decline in the quantity or quality of a renewable resource that occurs faster than it is renewed by natural processes. But this concept limits the scope of environment-conflict research. Environmental change is only one of three main sources of renewable-resource scarcity. The second, population growth, reduces a resource's per-capita availability by dividing it among more and more people.[6] The third, unequal resource distribution, concentrates a resource in the hands of a few people and subjects the rest to greater scarcity.[7] The property rights that govern resource distribution often change as a result of large-scale development projects or new technologies that alter the relative values of resources.

In other words, reduction in the quantity or quality of a resource shrinks the resource pie, while population growth divides the pie into smaller slices for each individual, and unequal resource distribution means that some groups get disproportionately large slices.[8] Unfortunately, analysts often study resource depletion and population growth in isolation from the political economy of resource distribution.[9] The term "environmental scarcity," however, allows these three distinct sources of scarcity to be incorporated into one analysis. Empirical evidence suggests, in fact, that the first two sources are most pernicious when they interact with unequal resource distribution.

We must also recognize that resource scarcity is, in part, subjective; it is determined not just by absolute physical limits, but also by preferences, beliefs, and norms. This is illustrated by a debate about the role of population growth and resource scarcity as causes of the conflict between the Sandinista government and the Miskito Indians in Nicaragua.[10] Bernard Nietschmann argues that the Nicaraguan state's need for resources to sustain the country's economic and agricultural development caused environmental degradation to spread from the Pacific to the Atlantic coast of the country. As this happened, indigenous Miskitos in the east came into conflict with the central government. Sergio Diaz-Briquets responds that the Sandinistas expropriated Miskito lands because of ideology, not scarcity. The Atlantic coastal region was largely ignored by the Nicaraguan state under Somoza. Following the revolution, the Sandinistas had ample newly expropriated land to distribute to their followers; but the new government—guided by Marxism—saw the Miskitos as a backward people with a competing worldview and a precapitalist mode of production, whose land rightfully belonged to a state that was removing impediments to the historical progress of the working class.

The gap between the two views can be bridged by noting that scarcity is partly subjective. Marxist ideology encouraged the Sandinistas to adopt a strategy of state-directed industrialization and resource-use; this led them to perceive resources as more scarce than had the Somoza regime.

Interaction of Sources
of Environmental Scarcity

The three sources of environmental scarcity often interact, and two patterns of interaction are particularly common: "resource capture" and "ecological marginalization." . . .

A fall in the quality and quantity of renewable resources can combine with population growth to encourage powerful groups within a society to shift resource distribution in their favor. This can produce dire environmental scarcity for poorer and weaker groups whose claims to resources are opposed by these powerful elites. I call this type of interaction "resource capture." Unequal resource access can combine with population growth to cause migrations to regions that are ecologically fragile, such as steep upland slopes, areas at risk of desertification, and tropical rain forests. High population densities in these areas, combined with a lack of knowledge and capital to protect local resources, causes severe environmental damage and chronic poverty. This process is often called "ecological marginalization."[11]

. . .

Hypothesis 1: Simple-Scarcity
Conflicts Between States

There is little empirical support for the first hypothesis that environmental scarcity causes simple-scarcity conflicts between states. Scarcities of renewable resources such as forests and croplands do not often cause resource wars between states. This finding is intriguing because resource wars have been common since the beginning of the state system. For instance, during World War II, Japan sought to secure oil, minerals, and other resources in China and Southeast Asia, and the 1991 Gulf War was at least partly motivated by the desire for oil.

However, we must distinguish between non-renewable resources such as oil, and renewable resources. Arthur Westing has compiled a list of twelve conflicts in the twentieth century involving resources, beginning with World War I and concluding with the Falklands/Malvinas War.[28] Access to oil or minerals was at issue in ten of these conflicts. Just five conflicts involved renewable resources, and only two of these—the 1969 Soccer War between El Salvador and Honduras, and the Anglo-Icelandic Cod War of 1972–73—concerned neither oil nor minerals (cropland was a factor in the former case, and fish in the latter). However, the Soccer War was not a simple-scarcity conflict between states; rather it arose from the ecological marginalization of Salvadorean peasants and their consequent migration into Honduras.[29] It is evidence in support, therefore, of our second and third hypotheses (below), but not for the first. And, since the Cod War, despite its name, involved very little violence, it hardly qualifies as a resource war.

States have fought more over non-renewable than renewable resources for two reasons, I believe. First, petroleum and mineral resources can be more directly converted into state power than can agricultural land, fish, and forests. Oil and coal fuel factories and armies, and ores are vital for tanks and naval ships. In contrast, although captured forests and cropland may eventually generate wealth that can be harnessed by the state for its own ends, this outcome is more remote in time and less certain. Second, the very countries that are most dependent on renewable resources, and which are therefore most motivated to seize resources from their neighbors, also tend to be poor, which lessens their capability for aggression.

Our research suggests that the renewable resource most likely to stimulate interstate resource war is river water.[30] Water is a critical resource for personal and national survival; furthermore, since river water flows from one area to another, one country's access can be affected by another's actions. Conflict is most probable when a downstream riparian is highly dependent on river water and is strong in comparison to upstream riparians. Downstream riparians often fear that their upstream neighbors will use water as a means of coercion. This situation is particularly dangerous if the downstream country also believes it has the military power to rectify the situation. The relationships between South Africa and Lesotho and between Egypt and Ethiopia have this character.[31] . . .

However, our review of the historical and contemporary evidence shows that conflict and turmoil related to river water are more often internal than international. The huge dams that are often built to deal with general water scarcity are especially disruptive. Relocating large numbers of upstream people generates turmoil among the relocatees and clashes with local groups in areas where the relocatees are resettled. The people affected are often members of ethnic or minority groups outside the power hierarchy of their society, and the result is frequently rebellion by these groups and repression by the state. Water developments can also induce conflict over water and irrigable land among a country's downstream users, as we saw in the Senegal River basin.[33]

Hypothesis 2: Population Movement and Group-Identity Conflicts

There is substantial evidence to support the hypothesis that environmental scarcity causes large population movement, which in turn causes group-identity conflicts. But we must be sensitive to contextual factors unique to each socio-ecological system. These are the system's particular physical, political, economic, and cultural features that affect the strength of the linkages between scarcity, population movement, and conflict.

For example, experts emphasize the importance of both "push" and "pull" factors in decisions of potential migrants.[34] These factors help distinguish migrants from refugees: while migrants are motivated by a combination of push and pull, refugees are motivated mainly by push. Environmental scarcity is more likely to produce migrants than refugees, because it usually develops gradually, which means that the push effect is not sharp and sudden and that pull factors can therefore clearly enter into potential migrants' calculations.

Migrants are often people who have been weak and marginal in their home society and, depending on context, they may remain weak in the receiving society. This limits their ability to organize and to make demands. States play a critical role here: migrants often need the backing of a state (either of the receiving society or an external one) before they have sufficient power to cause conflict, and this backing depends on the region's politics. Without it, migration is less likely to produce violence than silent misery and death, which rarely destabilizes states.[35] We must remember too that migration does not always produce bad results. It can act as a safety valve by reducing conflict in the sending area. Depending on the economic context, it can ease labor shortages in the receiving society, as it sometimes has, for instance, in Malaysia. Countries as different as Canada, Thailand, and Malawi show the astonishing capacity of some societies to absorb migrants without conflict.

. . .

Hypothesis 3: Economic Deprivation, Institutional Disruption, and Civil Strife

Empirical evidence partially supports the third hypothesis that environmental scarcity simultaneously increases economic deprivation and disrupts key social institutions, which in turn causes "deprivation" conflicts such as civil strife and insurgency. Environmental scarcity does produce economic deprivation, and this deprivation does cause civil strife. But more research is needed on the effects of scarcity on social institutions.

Resource degradation and depletion often affect economic productivity in poor countries and thereby contribute to deprivation. For example, erosion in upland Indonesia annually costs the country's agricultural economy nearly half a billion dollars in discounted future income.[45] The Magat watershed on the northern Filipino island of Luzon—a watershed representative of many in the Philippines—suffers gross erosion rates averaging 219 tons per hectare per year; if the lost nutrients were replaced by fertilizer, the annual cost would be over $100 per hectare.[46] Dryland degradation in Burkina Faso reduces the country's annual gross domestic product by nearly 9 percent annually because of fuelwood loss and lower yields of millet, sorghum, and livestock.[47] . . .

I originally hypothesized that scarcity would undermine a variety of social institutions. Our research suggests, however, that one institution in particular—the state—is most important. Although more study is needed, the multiple effects of environmental scarcity, including large population movements and economic decline, appear likely to weaken sharply the capacity and legitimacy of the state in some poor countries.

First, environmental scarcity increases financial and political demands on governments. For example, to mitigate the social effects of loss of water, soil, and forest, governments must spend huge sums on industry and infrastructure such as new dams, irrigation systems, fertilizer plants, and reforestation programs. Furthermore, this resource loss can reduce the incomes of elites directly dependent on resource extraction; these elites usually turn to the state for compensation. Scarcity also expands marginal groups that need help from government by producing rural poverty and by displacing people into cities where they demand food, shelter, transport, energy, and employment. In response to swelling urban populations, governments introduce subsidies that drain revenues, distort prices, and cause misallocations of capital, which in turn hinders economic productivity. Such large-scale state intervention in the marketplace can concentrate political and economic power in the hands of a small number of cronies and monopolistic interests, at the expense of other elite segments and rural agricultural populations.

Simultaneously, if resource scarcity affects the economy's general productivity, revenues to local and national governments will decline. This hurts elites that benefit from state largesse and reduces the state's capacity to meet the increased demands arising from environmental scarcity. A widening gap between state capacity and demands on the state, along with the misguided economic interventions such a gap often provokes, aggravates popular and elite grievances, increases rivalry between elite factions, and erodes the state's legitimacy.

Key contextual factors affect whether lower economic productivity and state weakening lead to deprivation conflicts. Civil strife is a function of both the level of grievance motivating challenger groups and the opportunities available to these groups to act on their grievances. The likelihood of civil strife is greatest when multiple pressures at different levels in society interact to increase grievance and opportunity simultaneously. Our third hypothesis says that environmental scarcity will change both variables, by contributing to economic crisis and by weakening institutions such as the state. But numerous other factors also influence grievance and opportunity.

. . .

A Combined Model

There are important links between the processes identified in the second and third hypotheses. For example, although population movement is sometimes caused directly by scarcity, more often it arises from the greater poverty caused by this scarcity. Similarly, the weakening of the state increases the likelihood not only of deprivation conflicts, but of group-identity conflicts.

It is useful, therefore, to bring the hypotheses together into one model of environment-conflict linkages. . . . Decreases in the quality and quantity of renewable resources, population growth, and unequal resource access act singly or in various combinations to increase the scarcity, for certain population groups, of cropland, water, forests, and fish. This can reduce economic productivity, both for the local groups experiencing the scarcity and for the larger regional and national economies. The affected people may migrate or be expelled to new lands. Migrating groups often trigger ethnic conflicts when they move to new areas, while decreases in wealth can cause deprivation conflicts such as insurgency and rural rebellion. In developing countries, the migrations and productivity losses may eventually weaken the state which in turn decreases central control over ethnic rivalries and increases opportunities for insurgents and elites challenging state authority. . . .

South Africa and Haiti illustrate this combined model. In South Africa, apartheid concentrated millions of blacks in some of the country's least productive and most ecologically sensitive territories, where population densities were worsened by high natural birth rates. In 1980, rural areas of the Ciskei homeland had 82 people per square kilometer, whereas the surrounding Cape province had a rural density of 2. Homeland residents had little capital and few resource-management skills and were subject to corrupt and abusive local governments. Sustainable development in such a situation was impossible, and wide areas were completely stripped of trees for fuelwood, grazed down to bare dirt, and eroded of top soil. A 1980 report concluded that nearly 50 percent of Ciskei's land was moderately or severely eroded, and nearly 40 percent of its pasturage was overgrazed.[70]

This loss of resources, combined with a lack of alternative employment and the social trauma caused by apartheid, created a subsistence crisis in the homelands. Thousands of people have migrated to South African cities, which are as yet incapable of adequately integrating and employing these migrants. The result is the rapid growth of squatter settlements and illegal townships that are rife with discord and that threaten the country's move to democratic stability.[71]

In Haiti, the irreversible loss of forests and soil in rural areas deepens an economic crisis that spawns social strife, internal migration, and an exodus "boat people." When first colonized by the Spanish in the late fifteenth century and the French in the seventeenth century, Haiti was treasured for abundant forests. Since then, Haiti has become one of the world's most dramatic examples of environmental despoliation. Less than two percent of the country remains forested, and the last timber is being felled at four percent per year.[72] As trees disappear, erosion follows, worsened by the steepness of the land and by harsh storms. The United

Nations estimates that at least 50 percent of the country is affected by topsoil loss that leaves land "unreclaimable at the farm level."[73] So much soil washes off the slopes that the streets of Port-au-Prince have to be cleared with bulldozers the rainy season.

Unequal land distribution was not a main cause of this catastrophe. Haiti gained independence in 1804 following a revolt of slaves and ex-slaves against the French colonial regime. Over a period of decades, the old plantation system associated with slavery was dismantled, and land was widely distributed in small parcels.[74] As a result, Haiti's agricultural structure, unique to Latin America, has 73 percent of cropland in private farms of less than 4 hectares.[75]

But inheritance customs and population growth have combined to produce scarcity, as in Bangladesh. Land has been subdivided into smaller portions with each generation. Eventually the plots cannot properly support their cultivators, fallow periods are neglected, and greater poverty prevents investment in soil conservation. The poorest people leave for steeper hillsides, where they clear the forest and begin farming anew, only to exhaust the land in a few years.[76] Many peasants try to supplement their falling incomes by scavenging wood for charcoal production, which contributes to further deforestation.

These processes might have been prevented had a stable central government invested in agriculture, industrial development, and reforestation. Instead, since independence Haiti has endured a ceaseless struggle for power between black and mulatto classes, and the ruling regimes have been solely interested in expropriating any surplus wealth the economy generated. Today, over 60 percent of the population is still engaged in agriculture, yet capital is unavailable for agricultural improvement, and the terms of exchange for crop production favor urban regions.[77] The population growth rate has actually increased, from 1.7 percent in the mid-1970s to over 2 percent today: the UN estimates that the current population of 6.75 million will grow to over 13 million by 2025.[78] As the land erodes and the population grows, incomes shrink: agricultural output per capita has decreased 10 percent in the last decade.[79]

Analysts agree that rising rural poverty has caused ever-increasing rural-rural and rural-urban migration. In search of work, agricultural workers move from subsistence hillside farms to rice farms in the valleys. From there, they go to cities, especially to Port-au-Prince, which now has a population of over a million. Wealthier farmers and traders, and even those with slimmer resources, try to flee by boat. . . .

Implications for International Security

Environmental scarcity has insidious and cumulative social impacts, such as population movement, economic decline, and the weakening of states. These can contribute to diffuse and persistent sub-national violence. The rate and extent of such conflicts will increase as scarcities worsen.

This sub-national violence will not be as conspicuous or dramatic as inter-state resource wars, but it will have serious repercussions for the security interests of both the developed and the developing worlds. Countries under such stress may fragment as their states become enfeebled and peripheral regions are seized by renegade authorities and warlords. Governments of countries as different as the Philippines and Peru have lost control over outer territories; although both these cases are complicated, it is nonetheless clear that environmental stress has contributed to their fragmentation. Fragmentation of any sizeable country will produce large outflows of refugees; it will also hinder the country from effectively negotiating and implementing international agreements on collective security, global environmental protection, and other matters.

Alternatively, a state might keep scarcity-induced civil strife from causing its progressive enfeeblement and fragmentation by becoming a "hard" regime that is authoritarian, intolerant of opposition, and militarized. Such regimes are more prone to launch military attacks against neighboring countries to divert attention from internal grievances. If a number of developing countries evolve in this direction, they could eventually threaten the military and economic interests of rich countries.

A state's ability to become a hard regime in response to environmentally induced turmoil depends, I believe, on two factors. First, the state must have sufficient remaining capacity—despite the debilitating effects of scarcity—to mobilize or seize resources for its own ends; this is a function of the internal organizational coherence of the state and its autonomy from outside pressures. Second, there must remain enough surplus wealth in the country's ecological-economic system to allow the state, once it seizes this wealth, to pursue its authoritarian course. Consequently, the countries with the highest probability of becoming "hard" regimes, and potential threats to their neighbors, are large, relatively wealthy developing countries that are dependent on a declining environmental base and that have a history of state strength. Candidates include Indonesia and, perhaps, Nigeria.

. . .

Conclusions

Our research shows that environmental scarcity causes violent conflict. This conflict tends to be persistent, diffuse, and sub-national. Its frequency will probably jump sharply in the next decades as scarcities rapidly worsen in many parts of the world. Of immediate concern are scarcities of cropland, water, forests, and fish, whereas atmospheric changes such as global warming will probably not have a major effect for several decades, and then mainly by interacting with already existing scarcities.

The degradation and depletion of environmental resources is only one source of environmental scarcity; two other important sources are population growth and unequal resource distribution. Scarcity often has its harshest social impact when these factors interact. As environmental scarcity becomes more severe, some societies will have a progressively lower capacity to adapt. Of particular concern is the decreasing capacity of the state to create markets and other institutions that promote adaptation. The impact of environmental scarcity on state capacity deserves further research.

Countries experiencing chronic internal conflict because of environmental stress will probably either fragment or become more authoritarian. Fragmenting countries will be the source of large out-migrations, and they will be unable to effectively negotiate or implement international agreements on security, trade and environmental protection. Authoritarian regimes may be inclined to launch attacks against other countries to divert popular attention from internal stresses. Any of these outcomes could seriously disrupt international security. The social impacts of environmental scarcity therefore deserve concerted attention from security scholars.

NORMAN MYERS

26

Environmental Security: How It Works

ENVIRONMENTAL PROBLEMS can figure as causes of conflict. If we continue on our road to environmental ruin worldwide, they will likely become predominant causes of conflict in the decades ahead. . . . Environment has become a fundamental factor in security issues in many regions already, and in the future will increasingly lie at the heart of security concerns of nations around the world.[1]

Example: water in the Middle East. This vital liquid is the cause of much pushing and shoving among countries of the region. . . . For instance, Israel and Jordan depend on the Jordan River for much of their water. The two countries' need for the river's water in the year 2000 is expected to be 150 percent of the total flow. Somebody is going to run badly short of what is ultimately the most precious of all resources in the Middle East. . . . Of more than 200 major river systems, around 150 are shared by two nations, and more than 50 by three to ten nations. All in all, they supply nearly 40 percent of the world's population with water for domestic use, agriculture, hydropower, and similar purposes. Between 1940 and 1980, water consumption around the world has more than doubled, and it can be expected to double again within another twenty years. Note, too, that two-thirds of the water will be used to produce that basic commodity of people everywhere, food. . . . As many as 80 countries, with two-fifths of the world's population, already suffer serious water deficits. So water, scarce and precious water, could soon become a cause célèbre of conflict between nations as fast-growing numbers of people make ever-increasing demands on this crucial resource. . . .

We can discern other linkages between environment and conflict with respect to deforestation. In the Ganges River system, . . . monsoonal flooding has become so widespread that it regularly imposes damages to crops, livestock, and property worth $1 billion a year among downstream communities of India and Bangladesh, even though the main deforestation occurs in another country altogether, Nepal. The result is deteriorating relations among the three governments. . . .

In the instances listed, the linkages are readily apparent. In other cases, the impact is more deferred and diffuse. . . . Probably the most deferred and diffuse impact of all, although the most consequential all around, will prove to be that of climatic dislocation. Buildup of carbon dioxide and other greenhouse gases in the global atmosphere will, if continued as projected, engender far-reaching disruptions for temperature and rainfall patterns. As a result of probably warmer and drier weather in its established grain belt, leading to severe drought persisting year in and year out, the United States could well become less capable of growing food. Conversely, Russia and Ukraine, possibly enjoying more favorable circumstances in a good part of their territories, could become major suppliers of surplus food. India could conceivably find itself better off in agricultural terms and Pakistan worse off, which in turn could affect the relations between these two traditional adversaries. There will be many other "winners" and "losers" in a greenhouse affected world, with all manner of destabilizing repercussions for a world already experiencing other types of environmental turmoil—hence we shall have a world in which we all end up losers.

The New Security

In short, there is an array of environmental factors that contribute to problems of security—security in its proper all-round sense, security for all, security forever. . . . Each environmental factor serves, to one degree or another, as a source of economic disruption, social tension, and political antagonism. For sure, certain of the linkages are diffuse in their workings and hence difficult to discern in their immediate operation. But they are real and important already, and they are fast growing in their number and extent. While they may not always trigger outright confrontation, they help to destabilize societies in an already unstable world—a world in which we can expect this destabilizing process to become more common as growing numbers of people seek to sustain themselves from declining environments.

. . . Security concerns can no longer be confined to traditional ideas of soldiers and tanks, bombs and missiles. Increasingly they include the environmental resources that underpin our material welfare. These resources include soil, water, forests, and climate, all prime components of a nation's environmental foundations. If these foundations are depleted, the nation's economy will eventually decline, its social fabric will deteriorate, and its political structure will become destabilized. The outcome is all too likely to be conflict, whether in the form of disorder and insurrection within a nation or tensions and hostilities with other nations.

This is not to deny that natural resources have often been important for the security of individual nations in the past, even to the extent of generating conflict.[2] . . . [But] environmental factors look likely to become pervasive and even predominant as sources of conflict. So there is a quantum advance in the scale of environment's role in conflict. Nations everywhere will likely suffer if much of the world is impoverished through environmental ills of myriad sorts. . . .

All in all, then, national security is no longer about fighting forces and weaponry alone. It relates increasingly to watersheds, croplands, forests, genetic resources, climate, and other factors rarely considered by military experts and political leaders, but that taken together deserve to be viewed as equally crucial to a nation's security as military prowess. . . .

What Also Counts

Of course we must be careful not to overstate the case. Not all environmental problems lead to conflict, and not all conflicts stem from environmental problems. Far from it. But there is enough evidence . . . for the central thesis to stand. Similarly, while environmental phenomena contribute to conflicts, they can rarely be described as exclusive causes. There are too many other variables mixed in, such as inefficient economies, unjust social systems, and repressive governments, any of which can predispose a nation to instability (and thus, in turn, make it especially susceptible to environmental problems) . . . .

In developing countries there often are a number of further factors that undermine security. They include faulty economic policies, inflexible political structures, oligarchical regimes, oppressive governments, and other adverse factors that have nothing directly to do with environment. . . . These deficiencies often aggravate environmental problems, and are aggravated by environmental problems in turn.

The biggest factor of all in many developing countries is the population explosion, still to enter its most explosive phase. There are now 4.5 billion people in developing countries, half as many again as just thirty-five years ago. The number is projected to surge to 7.2 billion, 67 percent more than today, by the year 2025. . . . Population pressures already generate discord and strife of multiple forms, often erupting in violence. Equally to the point, these pressures encourage the overexploitation of environments such as farmlands and water stocks, a process that fosters the spread of poverty among the "bottom billion" people.

These poorest of the poor cause a disproportionate share of environmental degradation. They find they have no alternative. Their concern is not tomorrow's world, it is tonight's supper. Constituting 20 percent of the world's population, they enjoy about 1 percent of global income, trade, investment, and bank lending. . . .

While these bottom billion often cause more environmental decline than the other three billion developing-world people put together, the world's top billion also cause an undue amount of environmental decline. With less than one-quarter of the world's population, and through their excessively consumerist and wasteful life-styles, they are responsible for most of the overuse of raw materials: they account for 70 to 85 percent of the world's consumption of fossil fuel and the manufacture of chemicals, as well as military spending. Most important of all in the long run, they cause the great bulk of ozone layer depletion and global warming. . . .

In short, there is a growing connection between environment and conflict. Environmental deficiencies engender conditions which render conflict all the more likely. These deficiencies can serve to determine the source of conflict, they can act as multipliers that aggravate core causes of conflict, and they can help to shape the nature of conflict. Moreover, not only can they contribute to conflict, they can stimulate the growing use of force to repress disaffection among those who suffer the consequences of environmental decline. . . .

Collective Security

. . . What can nations do to meet the new challenges? Primarily they can recognize that many forms of environmental impoverishment constitute a distinctive category of international problems, unlike any of the past. These new problems lie beyond the scope of established diplomacy and international relations. While impinging on the strategic interests of individual nations, they prove altogether immune to the standard response to major threats, namely, military force. We cannot launch fighter planes into the sky to resist global warming, we cannot dispatch tanks to counter the advancing desert, we cannot fire the smartest missiles against the rising sea.

These problems require a response different in yet another sense. This response must emphasize cooperation rather than confrontation within the international arena. No nation can meet the challenges of global change on its own. Nor can any nation protect itself from the actions—or inaction—of others. . . . It postulates as big a change for the nation-state as any since the emergence of the nation-state four hundred years ago. To cite Sir Crispin Tickell, former British ambassador to the United Nations, "No man is an island, no island is an island, no continent is an island. Yet nation-states still think principally if not almost entirely in terms of islands—economic, political, environmental islands." . . . Hitherto we have adopted a stance that essentially says that what I gain must be what you lose, and vice versa. Today, for the first time and for all time henceforth, we face situations where we shall all win together or we shall all lose together.

Developed Nations
and Developing Nations

Certain of the instances cited—notably water shortages, agricultural decline, and deforestation—are located mainly in developing nations. Why, then, . . . should security analysts in developed nations be concerned with water disputes in the Indian subcontinent, food shortages in Africa, and deforestation in Amazonia? There are several reasons.

First is that the developed world has a decisive stake in the wellbeing of the developing world—little though that connection may be recognized in certain councils of power. In particular, the United States finds that its prime hope for expanding its exports lies with developing countries. By the mid-1980s a full two-fifths of exports were going to those countries (and they were accounting for one in three of American manufacturing jobs). The proportion of exports to developing countries could swell to one-half as soon as the year 2000.[4] . . . But this latter prospect depends upon the capacity of developing countries' economies to keep on growing. In turn, this depends in major measure upon the environmental-resource base in which the economies of many developing countries are grounded. If that base becomes depleted, the economies will falter and fail, becoming less able to afford America's exports. . . .

To this extent, the economic health of the United States is tied to the environmental health of developing countries. . . . (Much the same applies to developed nations generally.) . . .

A second security linkage arises with respect to political stability in developing countries. To cite a 1988 report [on long-term strategy][6] . . . "Violence in the Third World threatens our interests in a variety of ways. It can imperil a fledgling democracy (as in El Salvador), increase pressures for large-scale migration to the United States (as in Central America), jeopardize important U.S. bases (as in the Philippines), and threaten vital sea lanes (as in the Persian Gulf)." Again, these security linkages between the United States and developing nations apply to other developed nations, albeit with differences in accord with particular strategic relationships.

A third linkage between the developed world and the developing world lies with the fact that environmental problems in one country often spill way beyond its borders. As Brazilian Amazonia goes up in flames, we might recall that a full 50 percent of the chief greenhouse gas, carbon dioxide, already comes from the burning of tropical forests—and the proportion is rising rapidly. . . . Thus everyone in the developed world has an emphatic interest, whether they are aware of it or not, in what goes on in developing countries around the back of the Earth. . . .

Fourth, we are finding that environmental degradation in developing countries, accentuated by population growth and poverty, sometimes triggers mass migrations of people who can no longer sustain themselves in their erstwhile homelands. Already these desperate throngs total well over 10 million people, as many as all political and other conventional refugees combined. This could be small potatoes, however, as compared with the multitudes that could feel driven to flee their environmentally ravaged homelands in the future, notably as a result of global warming. . . . Indeed, whole waves of destitute humanity washing around the world could soon start to pose entirely new threats to international stability. . . .

Our Global Experiment

We do not know that all these unfortunate environmental outcomes will come to pass. Nor do we know that they will not come to pass. What we do know is that we are now intervening in the most basic of our planet's workings, and doing it with increasing ingenuity and vigor. At the time of the Stockholm Conference on the Human Environment in 1972, the scientific experts and the political leaders of the world came up with a lengthy list of environmental problems that merited urgent action. If we did not get on top of these problems before they got on top of us, there would be a hefty price to pay. Yet missing from that list were such altogether unrecognized items as acid rain, ozone-layer depletion, and global warming. What new items are we overlooking today? What fresh threats are rolling away under the surface, working their disruptive way, building up momentum until, by the time they make themselves all too plain, we shall find it difficult to come to grips with them, if indeed we can come to grips with them at all except at exceptional cost and after much irreversible injury? . . .

No doubt about it, we are conducting a global-scale experiment with Planet Earth. . . . Our experiment . . . is entirely unplanned, and we know next to nothing about its outcome except that probably it will be irreversible and certainly it will be adverse. . . . In a situation of such overwhelming ignorance, the prudent course is to play safety first. As in other circumstances where the central factor is uncertainty, it will be better for us to find we have been roughly right than precisely wrong.

Our New Departure

So, we stand on the verge of an entirely new set of security issues. . . . What is most critically needed as we head into unknown territory is the vision to sense the fundamentally new dimensions of one-world living. If we accept the revolution that is under way, a revolution that can bring peace beyond dreams, we shall avoid the many violent revolutions that will surely erupt through default. Fortunately, we enjoy a "thinking dividend" with the end of the Cold War, heralding an era when old patterns are willy-nilly giving way to fresh approaches, as witness the collective response to the Gulf War. Can we expand our vision to take in the far larger problems and opportunities supplied by the far larger demands of environmental security? . . .

What Is This Thing Called Security?

Just as health is more than the absence of disease, so security—let alone peace—is more than the absence of hostilities. Yet while a nation knows what insecurity is, it cannot say so readily what it means by security—just as disease is more readily recognizable than health in the full and proper sense of the term. We need a clear-cut idea of what security is: what it amounts to, where we get it, and, most of all, what it means to *feel secure* whether on the part of governments, global society, communities, or individuals. At the same time, we need to determine how we can gain security without resorting to force.

In essence, and little though this is generally recognized by governments, security applies most at the level of the individual citizen. It amounts to human well-being: not only protection from harm and injury but access to water, food, shelter, health, employment, and other basic requisites that are the due of every person on Earth. It is the collectivity of these citizen needs—overall safety and quality of life—that should figure prominently in the nation's view of security.

As conventionally understood, a nation's view of security entails ensuring its territorial integrity and maintaining its position in the world beyond its borders. So a nation must enjoy assured access to raw materials and energy, to trading opportunities wherever available, and to scope for its government, large enterprises, and other major institutions to pursue their activities without let or hindrance. In addition, a nation also generally needs to foster its political ideals and its cultural outlook, both within its own land and further afield. Without these essentials, a nation has no security.

So, too, the entire community of nations, indeed all humankind, needs to enjoy security in the form of acceptably clean (unpolluted) environments, supplies of environmental goods such as water and food, and a stable atmosphere and climate. In short, all nations need a planetary habitat that is secure in every down-to-Earth respect—which means, in turn, that "we" are only as safe as "they" are. . . .

DANIEL DEUDNEY

27

The Case Against Linking Environmental Degradation and National Security

Introduction

... ENVIRONMENTAL ISSUES are likely to become an increasingly important dimension of political life at all levels—locally, inside states, as well as internationally. How institutions respond to these emerging constraints is likely to shape politics in a profound manner. Because state and interstate conflict are such central features of both world politics and geopolitical theory, there is a strong tendency for people to think about environmental problems in terms of national security and to assume that environmental conflicts will fit into the established patterns of interstate conflict.

The aim of this essay is to cast doubt upon this tendency to link environmental degradation and national security. Specifically, I make three claims. First, it is analytically misleading to think of environmental degradation as a national security threat, because the traditional focus of national security—interstate violence—has little in common with either environmental problems or solutions. Second, the effort to harness the emotive power of nationalism to help mobilise environmental awareness and action may prove counterproductive by undermining glob-

Originally published in *Millennium: Journal of International Studies* 19, 3 (Winter 1990):461–476. Reprinted with permission.

alist political sensibility. And third, environmental degradation is not very likely to cause interstate wars.

The Weak Analytical Links Between Environmental Degradation and National Security

One striking feature of the growing discussion of environmental issues in the United States is the attempt by many liberals, progressives and environmentalists to employ language traditionally associated with violence and war to understand environmental problems and to motivate action. Lester Brown, Jessica Tuchman Matthews, Michael Renner and others have proposed 'redefining national security' to encompass resource and environmental threats.[2] More broadly, Richard Ullman and others have proposed 'redefining security' to encompass a wide array of threats, ranging from earthquakes to environmental degradation.[3] Hal Harvey has proposed the concept of 'natural security',[4] and US Senator Albert Gore has spoken extensively in favour of thinking of the environment as a national security issue.[5] During the renewed Cold War tensions of the late 1970s and early 1980s, such concepts were advanced to prevent an excessive focus on military threats. As the Cold War winds down, such links are increasingly popular among national security experts and organisations looking for new missions. . . .

Historically, conceptual ferment of this sort has often accompanied important changes in politics.[7] New phrases are coined and old terms are appropriated for new purposes. Epochal developments like the emergence of capitalism, the growth of democracy and the end of slavery were accompanied by shifting, borrowing and expanding political language. The wide-ranging contemporary conceptual ferment in the language used to understand and act upon environmental problems is therefore both a natural and an encouraging development.

But not all neologisms and linkages are equally plausible or useful. Until this recent flurry of reconceptualising, the concept of 'national security' (as opposed to national interest or well-being) has been centred upon *organised violence.*[8] As is obvious to common sense and as Hobbes argued with such force, security from violence is a primal human need, because loss of life prevents the enjoyment of all other goods. Of course, various resource factors, such as access to fuels and ores, were understood as contributing to states' capacities to wage war and achieve security from violence.

Before either 'expanding' the concept of 'national security' to encompass both environmental and violence threats, or 're-defining' 'national security' or 'security' to refer mainly to environmental threats, it is worth examining just how much the national pursuit of security from violence has in common with environmental problems and their solutions.

Military violence and environmental degradation are linked directly in at least three major ways. First, the pursuit of national-security-from-violence through military means consumes resources (fiscal, organisational and leadership) that could be spent on environmental restoration. Since approximately one trillion US dollars is spent worldwide on military activities, substantial resources are involved. However, this relationship is not unique to environmental concerns, and unfortunately there is no guarantee that the world would spend money saved from military expenditures on environmental restoration. Nor is it clear that the world cannot afford environmental restoration without cutting military expenditures.

Second, war is directly destructive of the environment. In ancient times, the military destruction of olive groves in Mediterranean lands contributed to the long-lasting destruction of the lands' carrying capacities. More recently, the United States' bombardment and use of defoliants in Indochina caused significant environmental damage. Further, extensive use of nuclear weapons could have significant impacts on the global environment, including altered weather (i.e., 'nuclear winter') and further depletion of the ozone layer. Awareness of these environmental effects has played an important role in mobilising popular resistance to the arms race and in generally de-legitimising use of nuclear explosives as weapons.

Third, preparation for war causes pollution and consumes significant quantities of resources. In both the United States and the Soviet Union, significant quantities of radioactive waste have been produced as a by-product of the nuclear arms race, and several significant releases of radiation have occurred—perhaps most disastrously when a waste dump at a Soviet nuclear weapons facility exploded and burned, spreading radioactive materials over a large area near the Urals. Military activities have also produced significant quantities of toxic wastes.

In short, war and the preparation for war are clearly environmental threats and consume resources that could be used to ameliorate environmental degradation. In effect, these environmental impacts mean that the war system has costs beyond the intentional loss of life and destruction. Nevertheless, most of the world's environmental degradation is not caused by war and the preparation for war. Completely eliminating the direct environmental effects of the war system would leave most environmental degradation unaffected. Most of the causes and most of the cures of environmental degradation must be found outside the domain of the traditional national security system related to violence.

The war system is a definite but limited environmental threat, but in what ways is environmental degradation a threat to 'national security'? Making such an identification can be useful if the two phenomena—security from violence and security from environmental threats—are similar. Unfortunately, they have little in common, making such linkages largely useless for analytical and conceptual purposes. Four major dissimilarities . . . deserve mention.

First, environmental degradation and violence are very different types of threats. Both violence and environmental degradation may kill people and may reduce human well-being, but not all threats to life and property are threats to security. Disease, old age, crime and accidents routinely destroy life and property, but we do not think of them as 'national security' threats or even threats to 'security'. (Crime is a partial exception, but crime is a 'security' threat at the individual level, because crime involves violence.) And when an earthquake or hurricane strikes with great force, we speak about 'natural disasters' or designate 'national disaster areas', but we do not speak about such events threatening 'national security'. If everything that causes a decline in human well-being is labelled a 'security' threat, the term loses any analytical usefulness and becomes a loose synonym of 'bad'.

Second, the scope and source of threats to environmental well-being and national-security-from-violence are very different. There is nothing about the problem of environmental degradation which is particularly 'national' in character. Since environmental threats are often oblivious of the borders of the nation-state, they rarely afflict just one nation-state. Nevertheless, this said, it would be misleading to call most environmental problems 'international'. Many perpetrators and victims are within the borders of one nation-state. Individuals, families, communities, other species and future generations are harmed. A complete collapse of the biosphere would surely destroy 'nations' as well as everything else, but there is nothing distinctively national about either the causes, the harms or the solutions that warrants us giving such privileged billing to the 'national' grouping.

A third misfit between environmental well-being and national-security-from-violence stems from the differing degrees of *intention* involved. Violent threats involve a high degree of intentional behaviour. Organisations are mobilised, weapons procured and wars waged with relatively definite aims in mind. Environmental degradation, on the other hand, is largely unintentional, the side-effects of many other activities. No one really sets out with the aim of harming the environment (with the so far limited exception of environmental modification for military purposes).

Fourth, organisations that provide protection from violence differ greatly from those in environmental protection. National-security-from-violence is conventionally pursued by organisations with three distinctive features. First, military organisations are secretive, extremely hierarchical and centralised, and normally deploy vastly expensive, highly specialised and advanced technologies. Second, citizens typically delegate the goal of achieving national security to remote and highly specialised organisations that are far removed from the experience of civil society. And third, the specialised professional group staffing these national security organisations are trained in the arts of killing and destroying.

In contrast, responding to the environmental problem requires almost exactly opposite approaches and organisations. Certain aspects of virtually all mundane activities—for example, house construction, farming techniques, sewage treatment, factory design and land use planning—must be reformed. The routine everyday behaviour of practically everyone must be altered. This requires behaviour modification in situ. The professional ethos of environmental restoration is husbandmanship—more respectful cultivation and protection of plants, animals and the land.

In short, national-security-from-violence and environmental habitability have little in common. Given these differences, the rising fashion of linking them risks creating a conceptual muddle rather than a paradigm or world view shift—a *de-definition* rather than a *re-definition* of security. If we begin to speak about all the forces and events that threaten life, property and well-being (on a large-scale) as threats to our national security, we shall soon drain the term of any meaning. All large-scale evils will become threats to national security. To speak meaningfully about actual problems, we shall have to invent new words to fill the job previously performed by the old spoiled ones.

The Risks in Harnessing the Rhetorical and Emotional Appeals of National Security for Environmental Restoration

Confronted with these arguments, the advocate of treating environmental degradation as a national security problem might retort:

> Yes, some semantic innovation without much analytical basis is occurring, but it has a sound goal—to get people to react as urgently and effectively to the environmental problem as they have to the national-security-from-violence problem. If people took the environmental problem as seriously as, say, an attack by a foreign power, think of all that could be done to solve the problems!

In other words, the aim of these new links is not primarily descriptive, but polemical. It is not a claim about fact, but a rhetorical device designed to stimulate action. Like William James, these environmentalists hope to find a 'moral equivalent to war' to channel the energies behind war into constructive directions. . . .

At first glance, the most attractive feature of linking fears about environmental threats with national security mentalities is the sense of urgency engendered, and the corresponding willingness to accept great personal sacrifice. If in fact the basic habitability of the planet is being undermined, then it stands to reason that some crisis mentality is needed. Unfortunately, it may be difficult to engender a sense of urgency and a willingness to sacrifice for extended periods of time. . . . A second apparently valuable similarity between the national security mentality and the environmental problem is the tendency to use worse case scenarios as the basis for planning. However, the extreme conservatism of military organisations in responding to potential threats is not unique to them. The insurance industry is

built around preparations for the worst possibilities, and many fields of engineer-
ing, such as aeronautical design and nuclear power plant regulation, routinely
employ extremely conservative planning assumptions. These can serve as useful
models for improved environmental policies.

Third, the conventional national security mentality and its organisations are
deeply committed to zero-sum thinking. 'Our' gain is 'their' loss. Trust between
national security organisations is extremely low. The prevailing assumption is
that everyone is a potential enemy, and that agreements mean little unless con-
gruent with immediate interests. If the Pentagon had been put in charge of negotiating an ozone layer protocol, we might still be stockpiling chlorofluorocarbons
as a bargaining chip.

Fourth, conventional national security organisations have short time horizons.
The pervasive tendency for national security organisations to discount the future
and pursue very near-term objectives is a poor model for environmental problem
solving.

Finally, and perhaps most importantly, is the fact that the 'nation' is not an
empty vessel or blank slate waiting to be filled or scripted, but is instead pro-
foundly linked to war and 'us vs. them' thinking. The tendency for people to identify themselves with various tribal and kin groupings is as old as humanity. In the
last century and a half, however, this sentiment of nationalism, amplified and manipulated by mass media propaganda techniques, has been an integral part of to-
talitarianism and militarism. Nationalism means a sense of 'us vs. them', of the
insider vs. the outsider, of the compatriot vs. the alien. The stronger the nationalism, the stronger this cleavage, and the weaker the transnational bonds.
Nationalism reinforces militarism, fosters prejudice and discrimination, and feeds
the quest for 'sovereign' autonomy. . . .

Thus, thinking of national security as an environmental problem risks undercutting both the globalist and common fate understanding of the situation and the
sense of world community that may be necessary to solve the problem. In short, it
seems doubtful that the environment can be wrapped in national flags without
undercutting the 'whole earth' sensibility at the core of environmental awareness.

If pollution comes to be seen widely as a national security problem, there is also
a danger that the citizens of one country will feel much more threatened by the
pollution from other countries than by the pollution created by their fellow citizens. This could increase international tensions and make international accords
more difficult to achieve, while diverting attention from internal cleanup. Citizens
of the United States, for example, could become much more concerned about deforestation in Brazil than in reversing the centuries of North American deforestation. Taken to an absurd extreme—as national security threats sometimes are—
seeing environmental degradation in a neighboring country as a national security
threat could trigger various types of interventions, a new imperialism of the
strong against the weak.

Instead of linking 'national security' to the environmental problem, environmentalists should emphasise that the environmental crisis calls into question the

national grouping and its privileged status in world politics. The environmental crisis is not a threat to national security, but it does challenge the utility of thinking in 'national' terms. . . .

Environmental Degradation
and Interstate War

Many people are drawn to calling environmental degradation a national security problem, in part because they expect this phenomenon to stimulate interstate conflict and even violence. States often fight over what they value, particularly if related to 'security'. If states begin to be much more concerned with resources and environmental degradation, particularly if they think environmental decay is a threat to their 'national security', then states may well fight resource and pollution wars. . . . In general, I argue that interstate violence is not likely to result from environmental degradation, because of several deeply rooted features of the contemporary world order—both material and institutional—and because of the character of environmental and resource interests.

Few ideas seem more intuitively sound than the notion that states will begin fighting each other as the world runs out of usable natural resources. The popular metaphor of a lifeboat adrift at sea with declining supplies of clean water and rations suggests there will be fewer and fewer opportunities for positive-sum gains between actors. . . .

There are, however, three strong reasons for concluding that the familiar scenarios of resource war are of diminishing plausibility for the foreseeable future. First, the robust character of the world trade system means that states no longer experience resource dependency as a major threat to their military security and political autonomy. During the 1930s, the world trading system had collapsed, driving states to pursue autarkic economies. In contrast, the resource needs of contemporary states are routinely met without territorial control of the resource source, as Ronnie Lipschutz has recently shown.[17]

Second, the prospects for resource wars are diminished, since states find it increasingly difficult to exploit foreign resources through territorial conquest. Although the invention of nuclear explosives has made it easy and cheap to annihilate humans and infrastructure in extensive areas, the spread of small arms and national consciousness has made it very costly for an invader, even one equipped with advanced technology, to subdue a resisting population—as France discovered in Indochina and Algeria, the United States in Vietnam and the Soviet Union in Afghanistan. . . .

Third, the world is entering what H. E. Goeller and Alvin M. Weinberg have called the 'age of substitutability', in which industrial civilisation is increasingly capable of taking earth materials such as iron, aluminum, silicon and hydrocarbons (which are ubiquitous and plentiful) and fashioning them into virtually everything needed.[19] The most striking manifestation of this trend is that prices for virtually every raw material have been stagnant or falling for the last several decades, despite the continued growth in world output. In contrast to the expectations voiced by many during the 1970s—that resource scarcity would drive up commodity prices to the benefit of Third World raw material suppliers—prices have fallen, with disastrous consequences for Third World development.

In a second scenario, increased interstate violence results from internal turmoil caused by declining living standards. . . . Faced with declining living standards, groups at all levels of affluence can be expected to resist this trend by pushing the deprivation upon other groups. Class relations would be increasingly 'zero-sum games', producing class war and revolutionary upheavals. Faced with these pressures, liberal democracy and free-market systems would increasingly be replaced by authoritarian systems capable of maintaining minimum order.[20]

The international system consequences of these domestic changes may be increased conflict and war. If authoritarian regimes are more war-prone because of their lack of democratic control and if revolutionary regimes are more war-prone because of their ideological fervour and lack of socialisation into international norms and processes, then a world political system containing more such states is likely to be an increasingly violent one. The historical record from previous economic depressions supports the general proposition that widespread economic stagnation and unmet economic expectations contribute to international conflict.

Although initially compelling, this scenario has flaws as well. First, the pessimistic interpretation of the relationship between environmental sustainability and economic growth is arguably based on unsound economic theory. Wealth formation is not so much a product of cheap natural resource availability as of capital formation via savings and more efficient ways of producing. The fact that so many resource-poor countries, like Japan, are very wealthy, while many countries with more extensive resource endowments are poor, suggests that there is no clear and direct relationship between abundant resource availability and national wealth. Environmental constraints require an end to economic growth based on increasing raw material through-puts, rather than an end to growth in the output of goods and services.

Second, even if economic decline does occur, interstate conflict may be dampened, not stoked. . . . How societies respond to economic decline may in large measure depend upon the rate at which such declines occur. An offsetting factor here is the possibility that as people get poorer, they will be less willing to spend increasingly scarce resources for military capabilities. In this regard, the experience of economic depressions over the last two centuries may not be relevant, because such depressions were characterised by under-utilised production capacity and falling resource prices. In the 1930s, increased military spending had a stimulative effect, but in a world in which economic growth had been retarded by environmental constraints, military spending would exacerbate the problem. . . .

Environmental degradation in a country or region could become so extreme that the basic social and economic fabric comes apart. Should some areas of the world suffer this fate, the impact of this outcome on international order may not, however, be very great. If a particular country, even a large one like Brazil, were tragically to disintegrate, among the first casualties would be the capacity of the industrial and governmental structure to wage and sustain interstate conventional war. As Bernard Brodie observed in the modern era, 'the predisposing factors to military aggression are full bellies, not empty ones'.[22] The poor and wretched of the earth may be able to deny an outside aggressor an easy conquest, but they are themselves a minimal threat to outside states. Offensive war today requires complex organisational skills, specialised industrial products and surplus wealth.

In today's world everything is connected, but not everything is tightly coupled. Regional disasters of great severity may occur, with scarcely a ripple in the rest of the world. After all, Idi Amin drew Uganda back into savage darkness, the Khmer Rouge murdered an estimated two million Cambodians and the Sahara has advanced across the Sahel without the economies and political systems of the rest of the world being much perturbed. Indeed, many of the world's citizens did not even notice.

A fourth possible route from environmental degradation to interstate conflict and violence involves pollution across state borders. It is easy to envision situations in which country A dumps an intolerable amount of pollution on a neighboring country B (which is upstream and upwind), causing country B to attempt to pressure and coerce country A into eliminating its offending pollution. We can envision such conflict of interest leading to armed conflict.

Fortunately for interstate peace, strongly asymmetrical and significant environmental degradation between neighboring countries is relatively rare. Probably more typical is the situation in which activities in country A harm parts of country A and country B, and in which activities in country B also harm parts of both countries. This creates complex sets of winners and losers, and thus establishes a complex array of potential intrastate and interstate coalitions. In general, the more such interactions are occurring, the less likely it is that a persistent, significant and highly asymmetrical pollution 'exchange' will result. The very multitude of interdependency in the contemporary world, particularly among the industrialised countries, makes it unlikely that intense cleavages of environmental harm will match interstate borders, and at the same time not be compensated and complicated by other military, economic or cultural interactions. Resolving such conflicts will be a complex and messy affair, but the conflicts are unlikely to lead to war.

Finally, there are conflict potentials related to the global commons. Many countries contribute to environmental degradation, and many countries are harmed, but since the impacts are widely distributed, no one country has an incentive to act alone to solve the problem. Solutions require collective action, and with collective action comes the possibility of the 'free rider'. . . .

It is difficult to judge this scenario, because we lack examples of this phenomenon on a large scale. 'Free-rider' problems may generate severe conflict, but it is doubtful that states would find military instruments useful for coercion and compliance. . . .

Conclusion

The degradation of the natural environment upon which human well-being depends is a challenge of far-reaching significance for human societies everywhere. But this challenge has little to do with the national-security-from-violence problem that continues to plague human political life. Not only is there little in common between the causes and solutions of these two problems, but the nationalist and militarist mindsets closely associated with 'national security' thinking directly conflict with the core of the environmentalist world view. Harnessing these sentiments for a 'war on pollution' is a dangerous and probably self-defeating enterprise. And fortunately, the prospects for resource and pollution wars are not as great as often conjured by environmentalists.

The pervasive recourse to national security paradigms to conceptualise the environmental problem represents a profound and disturbing failure of imagination and political awareness. If the nation-state enjoys a more prominent status in world politics than its competence and accomplishments warrant, then it makes little sense to emphasise the links between it and the emerging problem of the global habitability.[23] Nationalist sentiment and the war system have a long-established logic and staying power that are likely to defy any rhetorically conjured 're-direction' toward benign ends. The movement to preserve the habitability of the planet for future generations must directly challenge the tribal power of nationalism and the chronic militarisation of public discourse. Environmental degradation is not a threat to national security. Rather, environmentalism is a threat to 'national security' mindsets and institutions. For environmentalists to dress their programmes in the bloodsoaked garments of the war system betrays their core values and creates confusion about the real tasks at hand.

SOMAYA SAAD

28
For Whose Benefit? Redefining Security

. . .

The Quest for a Redefinition of Security

TODAY, THE NORTH is preoccupied by environmental threats. Indeed, since the Stockholm Conference of 1972, a very different approach to the environment has become evident.

Twenty years ago, the emphasis was on ending the pollution that the industrialized North had been inflicting on the nations of the South. The goals were clean air and water and arable land—the requisites of a decent life; and the modality was international cooperation.

Today, however, the North has seized hold of environmental issues by using them to cloak its own security concerns. The new ideology—or, to some, religion—of the environment allows its proponents to ignore nationalities and national boundaries.

Earth Rights or National Rights?

For some, a parallel meeting of non-government organizations at the ... [1992] United Nations Conference on Environment and Development could be the forum for redefining security and sovereignty. The aim is to exert pressure on the participating national governments.

Originally published in *Eco-Decisions*, September 1991, pp. 59–60. Reprinted with permission.

The call for such a meeting is highly revealing. For those making it, the cause of the environment is to be used as a tool that can efface national boundaries and uproot national affiliations. They appeal instead to wider concepts: the sovereignty of the earth, the Global Commons, humanity or universal rights.

That approach could undermine national solidarity, stir up local conflicts, put individuals at odds with their governments, and cause governments to be judged without due consideration for the particular conditions that they face.

Such an approach might distort the issue. After all, it is the comparatively weaker states—who also happen to be developing nations—that have the bulk of the world's remaining natural resources. And it is these same countries that have relatively clean environments. Now these nations are being told to limit their military expenditures for the sake of development.

The Tilt Toward the "Haves"

Even in the boundary-free global utopia that some imagine lies ahead, a form of administration would still be required. Very likely, that "administration" would cover not territory but rather particular aspects of human activity.

Of these, most important is the domain of development. Within this area falls the entire range of environmental concerns: population, migration, poverty, the use of resources, patterns of production and consumption, and finally pollution. All these are shaped by the asymmetry in the global distribution of power.

That imbalance has political and military aspects. As a result, certain nations, cultures and lifestyles exert dominance over others. If those not favoured by the current arrangement try to redress the balance, their efforts are met with resistance which can escalate into conflict.

In consequence, the present division of power is likely to be maintained. The balance—whether military, economic or technological—is tilted in favour of the nations of the North, who now are seeking international cooperation in their bid to put their own house in order. Outside the North, there are strict limits on the amount of permitted national or regional power.

Redefining the Environment

Some nations are redefining the environment as a territory-free, non-geographical issue in which supranational institutions may intervene. They seek to mediate when necessary between other nations, and to force them to follow particular policies. Apparently their aim is to impose the economic and political norms and lifestyles of the North on the rest of the world, instead of allowing other nations to develop their own norms. The outcome will be a still greater tilt in favour of those that already hold economic and political power.

This trend will produce a new division of labour between nations. The powerful will gain more power, while the weak will lose what little power they have.

What Kind of Future?

Such a development naturally arouses questions. For instance, what does the brave talk of global security mean? Security, after all, implies the protection of a particular territory by one group against another. We need to know who will define the new concept of security. And herein lies the danger.

There are indications that now that the Cold War is ended, the larger countries consider the environment as a major field of security concern. Defined in those terms, the environment will present an ugly face particularly to the developing world.

In the new order taking shape, who or what will be sacrificed? There are several possible scenarios.

One is that weak nations will be subjugated to powerful ones. Some analysts point to the inadequacy of a world order based on state sovereignty. According to these thinkers, the passing of the Cold War may mark the passing of the nation states created by the earlier great wars of this century, replacing them with an order having a new basis. The tool used will be the economic leverage which the North exerts over the rest of the world.

Another possibility is an increase in tensions within and between nations. Environmental concerns could provoke disagreements that would exacerbate internal problems. Further, if sovereignty, regional and international legal standards and instruments are all swept away, the new so-called environmental rights could serve as a pretext for more conflicts.

Still another outcome might be the imposition of the norms, cultures and lifestyles of powerful nations on the others. Evidence for such a development is provided by the move to attach conditions to international assistance, and the banding together of the powerful nations in such groupings as the Enterprise of the Americas (starting with the United States, Canada and Mexico) and Europe 1992. Nations that refuse to accept this domination might be subjected to restrictions that could endanger their growth and even their survival.

It would be highly ironic if the move to protect the environment ended up thus destroying some cultures and peoples. Are the interests of humanity to be sacrificed to the interests of the earth?

PART SEVEN

Ecological Justice

Some of the main controversies surrounding the paradigms of sustainable development and ecological security involve questions of justice. Critics have raised concerns that these paradigms can blur questions of fairness, power, and distribution. Worse, it is argued, environmental arguments may even be used to justify measures that worsen aspects of social inequality, promote authoritarian measures, or otherwise concentrate power in the hands of elites. Thus, questions of justice are raised not only by the unequal effects of pollution and ecosystem destruction but also by the socially unequal effects of environmental policy responses.

Concerns about the relationship between environmental protection and social equity have been voiced since the Stockholm Conference first placed the environment on the international agenda.[1] As the pace of environmental degradation has accelerated, and as policy responses to environmental problems have grown more complex and ambitious, the question of how various forms of environmental change affect different social groups has become increasingly central to environmental debates.

Today the link between ecology and justice is being articulated by a diverse array of voices: people of color in cities throughout the United States challenging the "environmental racism" of concentrating toxic facilities in minority communities; rural women in India protesting the impact of deforestation on their lives and communities; Green party activists in Europe drawing links between militarism, patriarchy, and environmental destruction; Third World activists arguing that the North seeks to solve its environmental problems at the expense of the South, particularly in ways that harm the poorest of the poor; indigenous peoples of both the North and the South organizing to reclaim their lands and their traditions as an alternative to the ecological onslaught of modernity.[2]

Given this diversity, is it possible to identify a single paradigm of ecological justice based on a common set of core arguments? Although there are many different visions of an ecologically just world, a handful of themes lies at the heart of the ecological justice paradigm. First, violence against nature and violence against human beings are said to be closely linked. Second, ecological justice stresses the links between the power to control nature and the power to control people. Third is the observation that not all people or groups are affected equally by environmental problems or by the responses to those problems. Fourth, advocates of ecological justice stress that environmentalism must pursue solutions that are both ecologically sound *and* socially just, because neither can endure in the absence of the other. Finally, the need for a fundamental transformation of politics, economics, and society is stressed.

Because the call for ecological justice often comes from groups that lack the power to set policy, these arguments are often presented as a critique of prevailing policies and institutions. One common theme among the selections in this part, however, is that ecological justice also contains an alternative vision for society and for the human-nature relationship.

The call for an alternative vision is reflected in the first chapter in this part. Petra Kelly, the author, was a founder of the Green movement in Germany and, until her death in 1992, a longtime activist in German and European politics. Although the Greens are often labeled an "environmental party," their platforms have consistently sought to *link* environmental problems to aspects of social inequality and oppression, including patriarchy, militarism, violence, and corporate power. In this chapter Kelly stresses in particular the need to *combine* ecological balance with a system of economic justice and a transformation in the way modern consumer societies measure their well-being. The tactics Kelly invokes—a combination of personal transformation and social struggle—are also common themes in the ecological justice literature.

The paradigm can be used to analyze questions of ecology and justice on many different social levels. The question of justice among nations, with a particular focus on North-South inequality, was a central dispute at Stockholm in 1972 (see the chapter by Castro in Part One). As the comments by Malaysian Prime Minister Dr. Mahathir Mohamad at the 1992 Earth Summit make clear, the issue was not fully resolved in the two decades between Stockholm and Rio. Despite the promise that "sustainable development" can merge conflicting concerns of North and South with regard to environment and development, distributional issues remain central to the North-South environmental debate. Mahathir stresses that the question of justice applies not only to who should pay the costs of environmental protection in poor societies but also to the debate over who holds decisionmaking power and who bears historical responsibility for the planet's predicament.

Although the North-South gap is a central concern of the ecological justice literature, it would be wrong to conclude that the focus of the paradigm is limited to the debates between governments of the North and South. Important questions have also been raised about the links among ecology, justice, and power within societies. Power is distributed unequally not only among nations but also in social divisions based on race, class, gender, ethnicity, and region. The chapter by Gita Sen illustrates one such division—gender. Sen's work shows some of the complex ways that the construction of gender roles in society empowers men and disempowers women. In her chapter, Sen focuses on the population debate. Failure to grasp the link between gender and power—which operates at the interpersonal level of the household as well as at the national or international level—produces flawed understandings of the forces driving population growth. This in turn can lead to unjust and ineffective responses to the very real problem of rapid population growth.

The links among gender, ecology, and power on which Sen focuses are the concern of a rapidly growing body of thought that is often referred to as *ecofeminism.*[3] Karen Warren summarizes the central tenets of ecofeminist perspectives:

> Ecological feminism is the position that there are important connections—historical, symbolic, theoretical—between the domination of women and the domination of nonhuman nature. . . . Any feminist theory with any environmental ethic which fails to take seriously the interconnected dominations of women and nature is simply inadequate.[4]

Some ecofeminists see an inherent difference in how men and women relate to and interact with nature. Environmentally destructive societies are in their opinion an inherent consequence of male dominance. Other ecofeminists have pointed out that gender is in many important ways a socially constructed set of roles and rules and not just a biological fact. These "social" ecofeminists tend to see patriarchy and environmental destruction as stemming from a common source: the hierarchical concentration of power in society.[5]

The final chapter in this part, which focuses on indigenous peoples, links questions of justice at the local and global levels. COICA, the Coordinating Body for the Indigenous Peoples' Organizations of the Amazon Basin, published two letters in 1989 arguing that the future of the Amazon and the fate of its indigenous occupants are inherently linked. The rampant quest for modernization, colonization, territorial occupation, and economic development of the Amazon has been destructive of both natural ecosystems and indigenous communities. The destruction has been driven by governments of the Amazon Basin countries, which have excluded indigenous communities from decisionmaking about the region. Much of the destructive activity has been funded by external sources, including multinational corporations and multilateral development agencies such as the World Bank. Both at the national and international levels, decisions about the fate of the Amazon forest and its people have been made over the heads of those most directly affected.[6]

COICA addressed the first letter to the multilateral development banks that fund so many of the projects and policies threatening indigenous peoples. The second letter is addressed to the international environmental movement, which is also taken to task for its lack of attention to indigenous concerns. Although they acknowledge the efforts of environmentalists and the potential for common cause between the environmental and indigenous peoples' movements, COICA points out that governments, international organizations, and Northern environmental groups have struck bargains that leave out the people most directly and immediately affected. COICA defends an alternative vision: Given the long history of sustainable interaction between indigenous peoples and the region's ecology, the best way to ensure an ecologically sound future is to restore and protect the land rights and lifestyles of indigenous peoples.

In this regard the struggles of indigenous peoples bear much in common with the movement against "environmental racism" that has flourished over the past decade in the United States.[7] This movement has both an urban and a rural component: the struggle of urban communities of color against the practice of siting toxic facilities in the inner city, and the struggle of rural communities to combat the health and safety risks of environmentally unsound agricultural practices (in particular the heavy use of toxic agricultural chemicals)—risks borne disproportionately by low-paid agricultural workers. In both the North and South American cases, the goal is not merely to change environmental outcomes but also to return greater decisionmaking power to the community. And in both cases the notion that current practices are inherently unjust has been an important weapon in the struggle.

Advocates of ecological justice have played a crucial role in pointing out how environmental problems often cause greater harm to the poor and powerless. Perhaps their greatest contribution, however, has been to show that "solutions" to environmental problems can also be unjust, both locally and globally—and that such outcomes may not be solutions at all. Thus, one of the principal challenges facing ecological justice advocates and the environmental movement as a whole is to use these insights in the effort to design responses to environmental problems that are both ecologically effective and socially just.

PETRA KELLY

29
The Need for
Eco-Justice

WHEN WE ARE FACED WITH such critical issues as nuclear experiments and cancer from food poisoning, we find that, like it or not, we are deeply embedded in the natural world. Human beings pollute the natural environment and human beings, assuming a new sense of responsibility to one another and to generations to come, can also restore the natural environment. The question remains: where are the political leaders of the established political parties in the Western world who understand so far what the politics of "environmental ethics" are all about? I stress the established parties: the Conservatives, the Liberals, the Labour Governments. None has yet understood what it means to contain aggressive economic growth in order to save this planet. E.F. Schumacher admirably has pointed out that a non-violent and gentle attitude toward nature must be the ecological basis of all politics.[1] Anyone analyzing Western economics will realize how violent and aggressive the Western approach has been until now. Western economic thinking depends upon insatiable consumption—demanding more and more and larger and larger goods and services, to be available at all times. But where is the basic ethic of restraint? Schumacher was right when he declared that small is beautiful. We must develop a consciousness of limits to enable people to act without degrading themselves and their environment. We need eco-justice—ecological balance in the context of economic justice and economic justice in the context of ecological sustainability.

As human beings we have taken the earth for granted. We have never hesitated to exploit it in order to gratify our immediate wants. We have felt free to abuse

Originally published in *Fletcher Forum of World Affairs* 14 (Summer 1990):327–331. Reprinted with permission.

our fellow humans as well as the earth and its inhabitants and its living things. We must learn that, as the motto of the German Green Party, we have only *borrowed* the earth from our children. We are, in fact, our own best resource for solving the problems we have created. Thus we must become our own best experts and begin to understand how we live, how we work, how we consume, how we produce and how we exploit the Third World.

What will it take to turn things around in this present ecological state of crisis? Are we losing the battle to save the earth? The World Climate Conference in Toronto concluded that the dangers threatening us from our own atmosphere are as great as those of a nuclear war. When the earth's climate warms up, deserts will expand, the polar ice caps will melt and the seas will rise up, flooding entire countries. If industry and agriculture continue to develop as they have so far in the West, this dramatic heating of the earth's climate may come in a mere fifty years. In fact, it has started already. Scientists talk of a first-rate non-military threat to international security. The end of life on this planet, I believe, has become conceivable. Creation is slowly dying.

One example of the egoism of the Western industrialized countries is garbage imperialism. Industrial countries, including those in the European Economic Community (EEC), account for 70 percent of carbon dioxide emissions and 84 percent of CFC production. We in the Western countries who over-produce, over-consume and then dump highly poisonous hazardous wastes in developing countries are practicing garbage imperialism. Between 1986 and 1988, over 3.1 million tons of wastes were shipped from industrialized to developing countries. The cash payments for accepting our wastes are often large enough to tempt poor nations to consider mortgaging their public health and ecological integrity for needed currency. Grossly unequal distribution of wealth and power threatens our immediate future. The deepening poverty for two-thirds of humanity and environmental degradation are not separate problems, although our politicians treat them as such.

It is we the rich in the Western economies who are making the world poorer because of our use of disproportionate amounts of the world's energy and resources. For example, 16 million Australians have the same impact on world resources as 1.2 billion Africans. The earth is losing 24 billion tons of top soil per year and yet the world's farmers are trying to feed 86 million more people each year. Western economic policies are trapping poor countries in a cycle of poverty as their incomes fall and their debts rise. Often it is we who exclude the poor from their traditional land so that our multinational companies can grow cash crops for export. Is it then surprising that the world's poorest end up living on land that is most seriously environmentally degraded?

Our first priority in the industrialized countries must be to transform our consumer mentality and our industrial economic growth system and move to ecologically sustainable economies. Conservation must replace consumption as the driving force of our economy. We can only take and use what we really need; ecological green politics is about "enough," not "more and more."

Measuring well-being in terms of good health, clean air, pure water, unpoisoned food and a variety of plants and animals sharing our environment must become the basis of our Western political and economic thinking so that others far less privileged have a real chance. No official economic policy in the West today has taken the global damage resulting from human activity into consideration. The opposite is true. Parts of our natural base have been destroyed and other parts are seriously threatened by manufacturing decisions made solely on the grounds of economic gain and growth. In the end, this economic system will pull the rug out from underneath its own feet. We feel that what is ecologically necessary is also economically sound.

An ecologically based economy does not measure the prosperity of a society in terms of the greatest possible number of goods and services produced (i.e. the GNP), but rather in production methods which can serve the environment, protect human health and result in durable, useful consumer goods. In an ecological society, lifestyles and consumer expectations are characterized by consideration of human health and environment. Present lifestyles and present Western economic policies of the industrial societies endanger the natural conditions of human existence. At present, these lifestyles can be maintained only by an increased exploitation of Third World countries.

Environmental problems cannot be understood outside of an economic context. The poor, for example, are financing the rich at a scale never before known in history. Between 1982 and 1987 Third World countries, as a group, experienced a net negative flow of $220 billion, including interest payments on development loans and payments for imports.

Rainforests are turning into desert. Every minute 21.5 hectares—forty-three football fields—of tropical forest are destroyed. Two-fifths of the world's people must cook with wood they gather themselves whereas in parts of Southeast Asia, the Pacific and South America tropical rainforests are being cut down to meet the appetite of rich countries for paper and timber. This vicious cycle continues since revenue from the sale of tropical forest timber is needed to meet the interest on debt repayments from poor countries to rich countries. In the Amazon basin last year 6.4 million hectares of jungle were burned to make way for farmland and development. In Costa Rica, where 40 percent of the forest has been destroyed to provide beef for fast food markets created by McDonald's and Burger King, foods like corn and beans as well as US cattlefeed must be imported at high prices. The only ones benefitting from "Big Macs" are rich landowners, grain exporters and fast food merchants.

We can respond personally with non-violent transformations in lifestyle. We can begin by reducing our consumption of goods to a point at which we only use our share of the world's resources. Perhaps an international boycott of fast food chains could constitute a first step. As a part of the problem, we must be part of the solution.

What are the results of our present economic growth policies? Every year the European Community produces 2 billion tons of waste, including 160 million tons of industrial waste of which 25 million is highly poisonous. Existing facilities for treating industrial waste can handle only 10 million tons per year. The resultant illegal dumping and incineration mocks EEC directives on toxic waste disposal. We must reduce our rubbish mountains drastically by outlawing waste packaging and using recyclable containers. We must press for local waste management plans on ecological lines and encourage recycling and the use of recyclable waste to create energy. We must work for an EEC ban on the shipment of hazardous waste from one country to another—in particular to Third World countries—and seek an early halt to dumping of waste at sea. The real present danger of all environmental problems has little to do with any superpower polarities or even with rich-poor polarities on the North-South axis. It has more to do with polarities between human activities and the life-sustaining capacities of the earth—polarities that threaten the ecological security of East and West and North and South alike. In seeking effective environmental solutions, economic imbalances must be redressed, but in an ecologically sound way. What is needed is sustainable development that simultaneously supports an ecological economic system, a more just distribution within and among nations, political reforms and access to knowledge and resources without compromising the ecosystem.

Two hopeful signs have emerged recently. Jubilant environmentalists and ecologists celebrated an unprecedented victory for the Green movement in Eastern Europe: Hungary decided to scrap a multi-billion dollar hydroelectric dam project on the Danube River in Nagymaros, thirty miles from Budapest. [Editors' note: See the chapter by Duncan Fisher in Part Two]. Additionally, in the Indian town of Harsud, a town facing imminent destruction by the Narmada dam project, over 60,000 tribal people, landless laborers and peasants gathered in September 1989 in a show of strength to press the message that the people will no longer keep quiet when projects are forced on them in the name of progress.

On other fronts, the people of Baliapal have been fighting their battle against the missile-testing range at Orissa for the past seven years. Agitation has begun against five-star hotels in Goa, India. The message coming from these green movements in the Third World and eastern Europe is very clear: cease assaulting the earth. Let us not forget the arms race and underdevelopment—two sides of the same problem. The arms race continues to kill though the weapons themselves may never be used; by their cost alone armaments can kill the poor by causing them to starve. One fifth of the international expenditure on armaments could abolish world hunger by 2000. The arms race, the production of weapons and military equipment are all a waste of money and talent. We should think instead of how these resources—money and skills—could be used for environmental protection, alternative energy and prevention of disease and poverty.

We must learn to live on the earth with consciousness. We must realize that the future is increasingly a matter of human choice and human freedom. There must be a fundamental change of politics and economics if the planet is to stay alive. We must learn to address the economic and ecological dimensions together in order to achieve just, realistic and sustainable results. Eco-justice is nothing less than taking seriously the destiny of humanity and the planet on which we live. If there is a future, it will be Green.

MAHATHIR MOHAMAD

30
Statement to the
U.N. Conference on
Environment & Development

IT IS CLAIMED THAT ONE of the causes of environmental degradation is the size of the population of some developing countries. We dispute this assumption.

However, we note that rich developed communities tend to have low birth rates. If we want to reduce population growth then we must help poor communities to become developed. Yet we hear from the rich, proposals which would result in stopping the development of poor countries in order to reduce population. You may be able to reduce pollution but you will end up with massive overpopulation in the poorest developing countries.

We know that the 25 per cent of the world population who are rich consume 85 per cent of its wealth and produce 90 per cent of its waste. Mathematically speaking, if the rich reduce their wasteful consumption by 25 per cent, worldwide pollution will be reduced by 22.5 per cent. But if the poor 75 per cent reduce consumption totally and disappear from this earth altogether the reduction in pollution will only be by 10 per cent.

It is what the rich do that counts, not what the poor do, however much they do it. That is why it is imperative that the rich change their life-styles. A change in the life-styles of the poor only, apart from being unfair, is quite unproductive environment-wise. But the rich talk of the sovereignty of the consumers and their

Originally published in *Environmental Policy and Law* 22, 4 (1992):232. Reprinted with permission.

right to their life-styles. The rich will not accept a progressive and meaningful cutback in their emissions of carbon dioxide and other greenhouse gases because it will be a cost to them and retard their progress. Yet they expect the poor people of the developing countries to stifle even their minute growth as if it will cost them nothing.

The other issue before us is bio-diversity. The poor countries have been told to preserve their forests and other genetic resources on the off-chance that at some future date something is discovered which might prove useful to humanity. This is the same as telling these poor countries that they must continue to be poor because their forests and other resources are more precious than themselves. Still they are not rejecting the value of bio-diversity, at least not totally.

Denying them their own resources will impoverish them and retard their development. Surely, if something is discovered in their forests, they should be entitled to some returns.

But now we are told that the rich will not agree to compensate the poor for their sacrifices. The rich argue that the diversity of genes stored and safeguarded by the poor are of no value until the rich, through their superior intelligence, release the potential within. It is an intellectual property and must be copy-righted and protected.

Developing countries which met in Kuala Lumpur in April have agreed on a plan to reafforest the whole world. A Fund for this Greening of the World was proposed. But the North are resisting this proposal. Perhaps it is considered to be yet another attempt by the developing countries to squeeze the rich using the environmental issue. The rich North can only see the chiseling ways of the South and is determined that they will not be squeezed. Yet the North demands a forest convention.

Obviously the North wants to have a direct say in the management of forests in the poor South at next to no cost to themselves. The pittance they offer is much less than the loss of earnings by the poor countries and yet it is made out as a generous concession.

We will accept the Global Environmental Facility, and we will accept that it be administered by the OECD dominated World Bank. But can we not have a little say; can we not have more transparency in the administration of this Fund? Surely, this does not amount to the South squeezing the North.

The poor is not asking for charity. When the rich chopped down their own forests, built their poison-belching factories and scoured the world for cheap resources, the poor said nothing. Indeed, they paid for the development of the rich. Now the rich claim a right to regulate the development of the poor countries. And yet any suggestion that the rich compensate the poor adequately is regarded as outrageous. As colonies we were exploited. Now as independent nations we are to be equally exploited.

Malaysia was disillusioned about these inequities long before we reached Rio. In a world that has been won for democracy, we find powerful nations laying down terms even for participating in a democratic process. We find scant regard for the principles of fairness and equity. We find that even the Rio Declaration and Agenda 21 have been watered down upon insistence from the powerful and the rich.

Notwithstanding all these, we still have high expectations of this conference and we would consider this Conference on the Environment and Development a success if there emerged a better understanding of the enormity of the problems we face and the need for us to cooperate on an equitable basis. Malaysia will do what can reasonably be expected of it for the environment.

GITA SEN[1]

31

Women, Poverty & Population: Issues for the Concerned Environmentalist

Introduction

DIFFERENCES IN PERCEPTIONS regarding the linkages between population and environment became particularly acute during the preparatory build-up to the UN Conference on Environment and Development, variously known as the Earth Summit and Rio 92. Disagreement between Southern and Northern countries on the extent of attention to be given to population received considerable publicity. At the non-governmental level too, the issue of population has been, of late, a subject of considerable debate among environmentalists (especially those from the North), feminists and population lobbyists.

The basis of these differences often appears baffling; the apparent lack of willingness to compromise, or to acknowledge the obvious merits of opposing views seems to indicate a lack of analytical rigour. The debate appears, to some at least, to be based on passionately held but ultimately ephemeral differences. I wish to argue that, although the positions taken in the policy debate have been exaggerated at times, some of the oppositions have deeper roots. They arise from conceptual and possibly paradigmatic differences rather than from disagreements regarding the 'truth-value' of particular scientific propositions. These shape the protagonists'

Originally published in Wendy Harcourt, ed., *Feminist Perspectives on Sustainable Development* (London: Zed Books, 1994). Reprinted with permission.

perceptions of problems, the analytical methods used, and weights assigned to different linkages and relationships. In particular, varying views regarding development strategies, the linkages between poverty and population growth, and the role of gender relations in shaping those links colour the positions taken in the debate.

This chapter is an attempt to examine the different perspectives on these issues held by environmental scientists and environmental activists[2] on one hand, and women's health researchers and feminist activists on the other. Its motivation is twofold: first, to identify the positions taken by these two broad groupings within the larger discourses on development and on population; secondly to propose a possible basis for greater mutual understanding.[3]

Gender in the Population Field

In the history of population policy, women have been viewed typically in one of three ways. The narrowest of these is the view of women as principal 'targets' of family planning programmes; of women's bodies as the site of reproduction, and therefore as the necessary locus of contraceptive technology, and reproductive manipulation. The early history of population programmes is replete with examples of such views; but even more recently, the 'objectification' of women's bodies as fit objects for reproductive re-engineering, independent of a recognition of women as social subjects, continues apace. (Hubbard, 1990)

A second view of women which gained currency after the Bucharest Population Conference in 1983 was women as potential decision-makers whose capabilities in managing childcare, children's health in particular, could be enhanced through greater education. Women began to be viewed as social subjects in this case, but the attention given to women's education has not spun off (in the population policy literature) into a fuller consideration of the conditions under which the education of girls takes hold in a society, and therefore the extent to which education is embedded within larger social processes and structures. While this view represented a step away from objectification, women were still perceived as a means to a demographic end, with their own health and reproductive needs becoming thereby incidental to the process.

A third view which grew in the 1980s focused on maternal mortality as an important health justification for family planning. This view, which was at the core of the Safe Motherhood Initiative, attempted to claim a health justification for family planning on the basis of rates of maternal mortality. In practice, the initiative has received relatively little funding or support.

Conceptual Approaches

Economic theories of fertility are closely associated with the 'new' household economics. Premised on the belief that children are a source of both costs and benefits to their parents, such theories argue that parents determine their 'optimum' number of children based on a balancing of costs and benefits at the margin. As a description of differences between societies where children are viewed as a source of both present and future streams of income vs. those where children are essentially a cost to parents (balanced by a measure of psychological satisfaction but not by a significant flow of money income), the theory has an appealing simplicity. It purports to explain why the former societies may be more pro-natalist than the latter. It also suggests that shifting children away from child labour (a source of parental income) towards schooling (a parental cost) might work to reduce fertility.

Such theories have been criticized on a number of grounds. (Folbre, 1988) The main criticism centres on the assumption that actual fertility is the result of choices made by a homogenous household unit innocent of power and authority relations based on gender and age. Once such relations are acknowledged, and there is enough anthropological and historical evidence of their existence, the basis of decision-making within households has to be rethought in terms of differential short-term gains and losses for different members, as well as strategic choices by dominant members which will protect and ensure their continued dominance. For example, if the costs of child-raising increase, ceteris paribus, there may be little impact on fertility if the increased costs are largely borne by subordinate members of the household (such as younger women) who do not have much say in household decision-making.

Traditionally, in many societies the costs of high fertility in terms of women's health and work-burdens are rarely acknowledged as such, as long as the benefits in terms of access to a larger pool of subordinate children's labour or the social prestige inherent in being the father of many sons continue to accrue to men. Such authority relations are further cemented by ideologies which link woman's own personal status within the authoritarian household to her fertility. Newer game-theoretic models of household behaviour (Sen, 1987) provide more interesting and complex theories that take better account of the differential distribution of types of assets as well as gains and losses within the household. These have not thus far, however, generated adequate explanations of fertility outcomes.[4]

Against the Stream: Gender Relations and Reproductive Rights

Many of the influential approaches to theory and policy within the population field have been less than able or equipped to deal with the complexity and pervasiveness of gender relations in households and the economies and societies within which they function. Both feminist researchers and activists within women's health movements have been attempting to change the terms of the debate and to expand its scope. An important part of this challenge is the critique of population policy and of family-planning programmes as being biased (in gender, class and race terms) in their basic objectives and in the methods that they predominantly use.

The definition of a social objective of population limitations[5] which does not recognize that there may be costs to limiting family size that are differential across social classes and income groups, has long been criticized.[6] In particular, such costs are likely to be less than transparent in non-democratic polities or even within democratic states where the costs are disproportionately visited on groups that are marginal on ethnic or racial bases and therefore do not have sufficient voice.[7]

Population policy has also been criticized by some as being a substitute for rather than complementary to economic development strategies that are broad-based in their allocation of both benefits and costs. For example, if impoverished peasants were persuaded or coerced to limit family size on the premise that their poverty is a result of high fertility, independent of the possible causal impact of skewed land-holding patterns, commercialization processes, or unequal access to development resources, then it is questionable whether smaller families would make them more or less poor.

The critique becomes more complicated once the gender dimension is introduced. Critics of population policy on class grounds have sometimes been as gender blind as the policy itself. Having many children may be an economic imperative for a poor family in certain circumstances, but the costs of bearing and rearing children are still borne disproportionately by the women of the household. Gender concerns cannot be subsumed under a notion of homogeneous national or global concerns. For feminist critics of population policy, development strategies that otherwise ignore or exploit poor women, while making them the main target of population programmes, are highly questionable. But they do not believe that the interests of poor women in the area of reproduction are identical to those of poor men.

In general terms, the feminist critique agrees with many other critics that population control cannot be made a surrogate for directly addressing the crisis of economic survival that many poor women face. Reducing population growth is not a sufficient condition for raising livelihoods or meeting basic needs.[8] In particular, the critique qualifies the argument that reducing fertility reduces the health risks of poor women and therefore meets an important basic need. This would be true provided the means used to reduce fertility did not themselves increase the health hazards that women face, or were considerably and knowably less than the risks of childbearing. If family-planning programmes are to do this, critics argue, they will have to function differently in the future than they have in the past.

The most trenchant criticism questions the objectives (population control rather than, and often at the expense of, women's health and dignity), the strategies (family planning gaining dominance over primary and preventive health care in the budgets and priorities of departments), the methods (use of individual incentives and disincentives for both 'target' populations and programme personnel, targets and quotas for field personnel, overt coercion, the prevalence of 'camps' and absence of medical care either beforehand or afterwards, inadequate monitoring of side-effects), and the birth-control methods (a narrow range of birth prevention methods, technology that has not been adequately tested for

safety, or which has not passed regulatory controls in Northern countries) advocated and supplied through population programmes. A now extensive debate
around the 'quality of care' has focused particularly on the implications of alternative programme methods and birth-control techniques for the quality of family
programme services. (Bruce, 1989) More broad-ranging evaluations of population policy objectives and strategies have found them guilty of biases of class,
race/ethnicity and gender. (Hartmann, 1987)

Viewed as a development strategy, the critics see population policies as usually
falling within a class of strategies that are 'top-down' in orientation, and largely
unconcerned with (and often violating) the basic human rights needs of target
populations. Even the developmentalist concern with improving child health and
women's education has received little real support from population programmes
despite the extensive research and policy debate it has generated.

The critical perspective argues that ignoring co-requisites, such as economic
and social justice and women's reproductive health and rights, also makes the
overt target of population policies (a change in birth rates) difficult to achieve.
Where birth rates do fall (or rise as the case may be) despite this, the achievement
is often predicated on highly coercive methods, and is antithetical to women's
health and human dignity. The women's health advocates argue for a different approach to population policy—one that makes women's health and other basic
needs more central to policy and programme focus, and by doing so increases human welfare, transforms oppressive gender relations, and reduces population
growth rates. (Germain and Ordway, 1989)

Around the world there is a growing emergence of positive statements about
what human rights in the area of reproduction might encompass. (Petchesky and
Weiner, 1990) Many of these statements are culturally and contextually specific,
but they usually share a common critique of existing population programmes,
and a common understanding of alternative principles. Many of them prioritize
the perspective of poor women, although they recognize that the reproductive
rights of all women in most societies are less than satisfactory. Their attempt to
recast population policies and programmes is also, therefore, a struggle to redefine development itself to be more responsive to the needs of the majority.

Enter the Environmentalists

Environmentalist concern with population growth pre-dates the public debate
sparked by the UN Conference on Environment and Development (UNCED).
Probably some of the most influential early documents were the Club of Rome's
Limits to Growth and Ehrlich and Ehrlich's *The Population Bomb*. (Ehrlich, 1969)
The interest in global and local carrying capacity, vis-à-vis growing human population sizes and densities, stimulated the production of considerable literature,
both scientific and popular. Unfortunately, the popular and activist literature has
tended to ignore some of the important anthropological debates about carrying
capacity, as well as to disregard the inconclusiveness of empirical evidence linking

environmental change to population growth.[9] It tends, furthermore, to treat the population-environment linkages as simple mathematical ones, linking numbers of people to their environments through technology.

But the argument of both developmentalists in the population field and women's health and rights advocates has been precisely that population is not just an issue of numbers, but of complex social relationships which govern birth, death and migration. People's interactions with their environments can be only partially captured by simple mathematical relationships which fail to take the distribution of resources, incomes and consumption into account; such mathematical relationships by themselves may therefore be inadequate as predictors of outcomes or as guides to policy.[10]

Furthermore, from a policy point of view, more precise modelling of population-environment interactions has not, thus far, provided much better guidance about appropriate population policy programmes. Ignoring the wide disparities in the growth rates of consumption between rich and poor within developing countries and hence their relative environmental impacts, as well as the critiques of women's health advocates outlined in previous sections, leads to single-minded policy prescriptions directed once more simply to increasing family-planning funding and effort. The leap from over-aggregated population-environmental relations to policy prescriptions favouring increased family planning becomes an implicit choice of politics, of a particular approach to population policy, to environmental policy, and to development. Because it glosses over so many fundamental issues of power, gender and class relations, and of distribution, and because it ignores the historical experience of population programmes, it has come to be viewed by many as a retrograde step in the population-development discourse.

Population Actors

The preceding discussion suggests that important actors in the population field are as follows.

First come those population specialists who traditionally have focused on the size and growth of populations, on age structures, migration and population composition. In general, they enter the development discourse primarily through their concern with what impact population growth might have on rates of economic growth. In addition, population projections are mapped onto planning needs in areas such as food production, energy, and other infrastructures, as well as health, education, and so on. These mappings can be said to belong to a class of simple mathematical planning models which usually ignore problems of distribution (based as they tend to be on per capita needs and availabilities), as well as the social and institutional aspects of making a plan actually work.

The second group are the developmentalists who focus less on the impact of demographic change, and more on the prerequisites of sustained decline in mortality and fertility rates. In particular they stress the importance of improving health and women's education. They thus represent a major revision of traditional population approaches, but all too often stop short of addressing the problem of sustainability or of livelihoods.

A third group, the fundamentalists, has become increasingly important in the population field during the 1980s, gaining political legitimacy through their links to mainstream political organizations. Their primary interest is not the size or growth of populations, but rather control over reproduction and a conservative concern to preserve traditional family structures and gender rules. The moral overtones of the US abortion debate notwithstanding, their interest in procreation appears to derive largely from an opposition to changing gender relations in society.

The fourth group are the Northern environmentalists. At the risk of oversimplification, one might argue that many of these individuals and groups focus mainly on the links between economic growth and ecological sustainability on the one hand, and the size and growth of population on the other.

The fifth important group of actors are the women's health groups which have evolved either out of the feminist movement or out of other social movements or population organizations. Their understanding of the population problem is distinctive in that they define it as primarily a question of reproductive rights and reproductive health, in the context of livelihoods, basic needs and political participation. They often acknowledge that economic growth and ecological sustainability are concerns, but believe these ought to be viewed in the co text of reproductive rights and health. In particular, many of them give priority to the needs and priorities of poor women in defining issues, problems and strategies.

Each of these sets of population actors has a view of the population question that is consistent with a particular view of development; as such they tend to overlap with particular sets of development actors, and find a niche within a particular set of development ideas. For example, population specialists are attracted to problems of economic growth, developmentalists to basic needs issues, and women's health activists to the problems of livelihoods, basic needs and political empowerment. Many Northern environmentalists, on the other hand, tend to view population solely through the lens of ecological sustainability, and this accounts for a considerable amount of the dissonance between their views and those of grassroots groups in the South.

Towards More Synergy Between Environmentalists and Feminists

Despite the dissonance provoked by the population-environment debate, there is much in common between feminists and environmentalists in their visions of society and in the methods they use. Both groups (or at least their more progressive wings) have a healthy critical stance towards ecologically profligate and inequitable patterns of economic growth, and have been attempting to change mainstream perceptions in this regard. Both use methods that rely on grassroots mobilization and participation, and are therefore sensitive to the importance of political openness and involvement. As such, both believe in the power of widespread knowledge and in the rights of people to be informed and to participate in decisions affecting their lives and those of nations and the planet. Indeed, there are many feminists within environmental movements (North and South) and environmentalists within feminist movements.

Greater mutual understanding on the population question can result from a greater recognition that the core problem is that of development within which population is inextricably meshed. Privileging the perspective of poor women can help ground this recognition in the realities of the lives and livelihoods of many within the South.

Economic growth and ecological sustainability must be such as to secure livelihoods, basic needs, political participation and women's reproductive rights, not work against them. Thus, environmental sustainability must be conceptualized so as to support and sustain livelihoods and basic needs, and not in ways that automatically counterpose 'nature' against the survival needs of the most vulnerable. Where trade-offs among these different goals exist or are inevitable, the costs and burdens must not fall on the poorest and most vulnerable, and all people must have a voice in negotiating resolutions through open and genuinely participatory political processes. Furthermore, environmental strategies that enhance livelihoods and fulfill needs can probably help lay the basis for reduced rates of mortality and fertility.

Population and family-planning programmes should be framed in the context of health and livelihood agendas, should give serious consideration to women's health advocates, and be supportive of women's reproductive health and rights. This has to be more than lip service; it requires reorienting international assistance and national policy, reshaping programmes and rethinking research questions and methodologies. Using the language of welfare, gender equity or health, while continuing advocacy for family planning as it is at present practised will not meet the need.

Reproductive health strategies are likely to succeed in improvimg women's health and making it possible for them to make socially viable fertility decisions if they are set in the context of an overall supportive health and development agenda. Where general health and social development are poorly funded or given low priority, as has happened in the development agendas of many major development agencies and countries during the last decade, reproductive rights and health are unlikely to get the funding or attention they need. Reproductive health programmes are also likely to be more efficacious when general health and development are served. A poor female agricultural wage-labourer, ill-nourished and anaemic, is likely to respond better to reproductive health care if her nutritional status and overall health improve at the same time.

The mainstream Northern environmental movement needs to focus more sharply on gender relations and women's needs in framing its own strategies, as well as on the issues raised by minority groups. These issues (such as those raised by native peoples and African Americans in the US) tend to link environmental issues with livelihoods and basic needs concerns in much the same way as do the people's organizations in the South.[11] Greater sensitivity to the one, therefore, might bring greater awareness of the other.

Wide discussion and acknowledgement of these principles could help to bridge some of the current gaps between feminists and environmentalists, and make it possible to build coalitions that can move both agendas forward.

References

Bruce, J. (1989) 'Fundamental Elements of the Quality of Care: A Simple Framework'. The Population Council, Programmes Division Working Papers No. 1, May, New York.

Caldwell, J., and P. Caldwell (1987) 'The Cultural Context of High Fertility in Sub-Saharan Africa', in *Population and Development Review*, 13:3, September, pp 409–38.

Ehrlich, P. (1969) *The Population Bomb*. Ballantine Books, New York.

Folbre, N. (1988) 'The Black Four of Hearts: Towards a New Paradigm of Household Economics', in J. Bruce and D. Dwyer (eds.), *A Home Divided: Women and Income in the Third World*. Stanford University Press, Stanford.

Germain, A., and J. Ordway (1989) *Population Control and Women's Health: Balancing the Scales*. International Women's Health Coalition, New York.

Hartmann, B. (1987) *Reproductive Rights and Wrongs: The Global Politics of Control and Contraceptive Choice*. Harper and Row, New York.

Hubbard, R. (1990) *The Politics of Women's Biology*. Rutgers University Press, New Brunswick.

Little, P. (1992) 'The Social Causes of Land Degradation in Dry Regions' (manuscript). Institute of Development Anthropology, Binghamton.

Mamdani, M. (1974) *The Myth of Population Control*. Monthly Review Press, New York.

Petchesky, R., and J. Weiner (1990) *Global Feminist Perspectives on Reproductive Rights and Reproductive Health*. Report on the Special Sessions at the Fourth International Interdisciplinary Congress on Women, Hunter College, New York, NY.

Scott, J. (n.d.) 'Norplant: Its Impact on Poor Women and Women of Color'. National Black Women's Health Project Public Policy/Education Office, Washington, DC.

Sen, A. K. (1987) 'Gender and Cooperative Conflicts'. Discussion Paper No. 1342. Harvard Institute of Economic Research, Cambridge.

Shaw, R. P. (1989) 'Population Growth: Is It Ruining the Environment?', in *Populi*, 16:2, pp. 21–9.

32

Two Agendas on Amazon Development

For Bilateral and Multilateral Funders

(This document is addressed to the World Bank, the Inter-American Development Bank, the US Agency International Development, and the European Economic Community.)

WE, THE INDIGENOUS PEOPLES, have been an integral part of the Amazon Biosphere for millennia. We have used and cared for the resources of that biosphere with a great deal of respect, because it is our home, and because we know that our survival and that of our future generations depends on it. Our accumulated knowledge about the ecology of our home, our models for living with the peculiarities of the Amazon Biosphere, our reverence and respect for the tropical forest and its other inhabitants, both plant and animal, are the keys to guaranteeing the future of the Amazon Basin, not only for our peoples, but also for all of humanity.

What COICA Wants

1. The most effective defense of the Amazonian Biosphere is the recognition and defense of the territories of the region's Indigenous Peoples and the promotion of their models for living within that Biosphere and for managing its re-

Originally published in *Cultural Survival Quarterly* 13, 4 (1989):75–78. Reprinted with permission.

sources in a sustainable way. The international funders of Amazonian development should educate themselves about the Indigenous Peoples' relationship with
their environment, and formulate new concepts of Amazonian development together with new criteria for supporting Amazonian development projects which
would be compatible with the Indigenous Peoples' principles of respect and care
for the world around them, as well as with their concern for the survival and well-
being of their future generations.

2. The international funders must recognize the rights of Indigenous Peoples
as those are being defined within the Working Group on Indigenous Peoples, established by the UN Human Rights Commission. These rights should form the
basis of the institution's policy towards the Indigenous Peoples and their territories who live in those areas where the funder is supporting development work.
The funders should consult directly with the organizations of the Indigenous
Peoples throughout the process of establishing this policy and should distribute
that policy widely among governments and the organizations of Indigenous
Peoples.

3. There can be no development projects in indigenous areas without the informed consent of the Indigenous Peoples affected. The funders must make every
effort, through field research conducted by personnel of the funding institution,
to verify the existence of an indigenous population, or the possible negative impact on an indigenous population, in areas where they are considering the implementation of a project. If either is the case, the funder must openly recognize the
existence of this population or the negative impact on them, and then should establish as a condition for further funding the project

- that the government responsible for implementing the project also
  recognize the existence of the population and/or the negative impact;
- that the affected population be informed of the plans and impact of
  the plans; and
- that the affected population consent to the implementation of the
  plans.

These conditions should be monitored by both the funder and the organization which represents the affected population.

4. If the indigenous population has given its informed consent to the implementation of a development project within its territory, the project must be designed in such a way that it respects the territories of the population as they define
them, their economy and their social organization, according to the institutional
policy as described in Point One. There should be special components of the project which lend support directly to the indigenous population for their own needs
and for the development proposals which they may have. The organization which
represents the affected population should participate in the design of the project.

5. The international funders should enter into a direct relation of collaboration and mutual respect with the organizations of Indigenous Peoples, through their representatives. This relation should establish the basis for:

- *consultations* on all aspects of projects implemented in areas with an indigenous population or which have an impact on an indigenous population;
- *participation* of representatives of Indigenous Peoples in the planning, implementation, and evaluation of projects;
- *exchange* of information of mutual interest on plans, projects, activities, and needs of both.

  . . .

Indigenous Peoples' Alternatives for Amazonian Development

An important task of the Coordinating Body is to present to the international community the alternatives which we indigenous peoples offer for living with the Amazonian Biosphere, caring for it and developing within it. This is one of our important contributions to a better life for humankind. The following represent, in general terms, our program for the defense of the Amazonian Biosphere.

1. The best defense of the Amazonian Biosphere is the defense of the territories recognized as homeland by Indigenous Peoples, and their promotion of our models for living within that biosphere and for managing its resources. This implies:

- education for the national and international communities regarding the Indigenous Peoples' concept of the unity between people and territory, and regarding our models for managing and caring for our environment.
- work with national governments, environmental organizations, and in ternational institutions which fund Amazon development to develop-new concepts and models for occupying and using the Amazon Basin in keeping with our long-term perspective (future generations), our respect for the interdependence between humankind and our environments, and our need to improve the wellbeing of the entire community; further work with the same institutions to translate these new concepts into concrete programs for developing and caring for the Amazon Basin and its inhabitants.
- work with national governments, environmental organizations, and international funders to reorganize the occupation of supposedly empty

Amazonian territories by combining indigenous territories, with forest, wildlife, and extractive reserves in favor of the indigenous and other current inhabitants; by discouraging the "conquest and colonization" of our homeland; and by recuperating those vast areas devastated by state policies of conquest and colonization.

- research on the natural resources and traditional crops used by Indigenous Peoples, on the traditional systems for utilizing and conserving resources, and on models for the extraction of renewable resources.
- evaluation and systematization of the development projects implemented by Indigenous Peoples which attempt to combine the demands of the market with a respect for indigenous principles of development.

2. The defense of the Amazon Biosphere/Indigenous territories must go hand-in-hand with the recognition of and respect for the territorial, political, cultural, economic, and human rights of the Indigenous Peoples. This implies:

- continued participation and support for the UN process for establishing an international instrument recognizing the rights of Indigenous Peoples.
- education for the national and international communities regarding the rights of Indigenous Peoples.
- establishment of mechanisms at both the national and international level for defending the rights of Indigenous Peoples in cases of violations of or conflicts over those rights.

3. The right of self-determination for Indigenous Peoples within their environment/territory is fundamental for guaranteeing the well-being of the indigenous population and of the Amazonian Biosphere. This implies:

- respect for our autonomous forms of community, ethnic, and regional government.
- indigenous control over the economic activities within the indigenous territories, including the extraction of mineral reserves.
- respect for indigenous customary law and the indigenous norms for social control.

4. Concrete Proposals for International Cooperation: For many decades now, most of our peoples have been experimenting with ways to participate in the encroaching market economies of our respective countries while trying to survive as peoples intimately linked to the Amazonian forest. We have done this despite the hostility shown us by the frontier society and despite the fact that, within the con-

text of the market economy, we are desperately poor. For these reasons, we have organized ourselves in new ways and developed and managed a variety of small programs to improve our health, education, and economy. . . . It is these small scale, locally controlled initiatives which should be the cornerstone of future Amazonian development.

. . .

To the Community of Concerned Environmentalists

We, the Indigenous Peoples, have been an integral part of the Amazonian Biosphere for millennia. We use and care for the resources of that biosphere with respect, because it is our home, and because we know that our survival and that of our future generations depend on it. Our accumulated knowledge about the ecology of our forest home, our models for living within the Amazonian Biosphere, our reverence and respect for the tropical forest and its other inhabitants, both plant and animal, are the keys to guaranteeing the future of the Amazon Basin. A guarantee not only for our peoples, but also for all of humanity. Our experience, especially during the past 100 years, has taught us that when politicians and developers take charge of our Amazon, they are capable of destroying it because of their shortsightedness, their ignorance and their greed.

We are pleased and encouraged to see the interest and concern expressed by the environmentalist community for the future of our homeland. We are gratified by the efforts you have made in your country to educate your peoples about our homeland and the threat it now faces as well as the efforts you have made in South America to defend the Amazonian rain forests and to encourage proper management of their resources. We greatly appreciate and fully support the efforts some of you are making to lobby the US Congress, the World Bank, USAID, and the InterAmerican Development Bank on behalf of the Amazonian Biosphere and its inhabitants. We recognize that through these efforts, the community of environmentalists has become an important political actor in determining the future of the Amazon Basin.

We are keenly aware that you share with us a common perception of the dangers which face our homeland. While we may differ about the methods to be used, we do share a fundamental concern for encouraging the long-term conservation and the intelligent use of the Amazonian rain forest. We have the same conservation goals.

Our Concerns

We are concerned that you have left us, the Indigenous Peoples, out of your vision of the Amazonian Biosphere. The focus of concern of the environmental community has typically been the preservation of the tropical forest and its plant and animal inhabitants. You have shown little interest in its human inhabitants who are also part of that biosphere.

We are concerned about the "debt for nature swaps" which put your organizations in a position of negotiating with our governments for the future of our homelands. We know of specific examples of such swaps which have shown the most brazen disregard for the rights of the indigenous inhabitants and which are resulting in the ultimate destruction of the very forests which they were meant to preserve.

We are concerned that you have left us Indigenous Peoples and our organizations out of the political process which is determining the future of our homeland. While we appreciate your efforts on our behalf, we want to make it clear that we never delegated any power of representation to the environmentalist community nor to any individual or organization within that community.

We are concerned about the violence and ecological destruction of our homeland caused by the increasing production and trafficking of cocaine, most of which is consumed here in the US.

What We Want

We want you, the environmental community, to recognize that the most effective defense of the Amazonian Biosphere is the recognition of our ownership rights over our territories and the promotion of our models for living within that biosphere.

We want you, the environmental community, to recognize that we Indigenous Peoples are an important and integral part of the Amazonian Biosphere.

We want you, the environmental community, to recognize and promote our rights as Indigenous Peoples as we have been defining those rights within the UN Working Group for Indigenous Peoples.

We want to represent ourselves and our interests directly in all negotiations concerning the future of our Amazonian homeland.

What We Propose

We propose that you work directly with our organizations on all your programs and campaigns which affect our homelands.

We propose that you swap "debt for indigenous stewardship" which would allow your organizations to help return areas of the Amazonian rain forest to our care and control.

We propose establishing a permanent dialogue with you to develop and implement new models for using the rain forest based on the list of alternatives presented with this document.

We propose joining hands with those members of the worldwide environmentalist community who:

- recognize our historical role as caretakers of the Amazon Basin.

- support our efforts to reclaim and defend our traditional territories.
- accept our organizations as legitimate and equal partners.

We propose reaching out to other Amazonian peoples such as the rubber tappers, the Brazil-nut gatherers, and others whose livelihood depends on the non-destructive extractive activities, many of whom are of indigenous origin.

We propose that you consider allying yourselves with us, the Indigenous Peoples of the Amazon, in defense of our Amazonian homeland.

Notes

Introduction: Two Decades of Global Environmental Politics

1. John Perlin, *A Forest Journey: The Role of Wood in the Development of Civilization* (Cambridge, MA: Harvard University Press, 1991), p. 46.

2. Zuo Dakang and Zhang Peiyuan, "The Huang-Huai-Hai Plain," in B. L. Turner II, William C. Clark, Robert W. Kates, John F. Richards, Jessica T. Mathews, and William B. Meyer, eds., *The Earth as Transformed by Human Action* (New York: Cambridge University Press, 1990).

3. Peter Brimblecombe, *The Big Smoke: A History of Air Pollution in London Since Medieval Times* (London: Methuen, 1987).

4. Turner et al., *The Earth as Transformed by Human Action.*

5. For a range of views on this theme, see James Rosenau, *Turbulence in World Politics: A Theory of Change and Continuity* (Princeton: Princeton University Press, 1990); Robert Cox, *Production, Power and World Order* (New York: Columbia University Press, 1987); Benjamin R. Barber, "Jihad vs. McWorld," *The Atlantic Monthly,* March 1992, pp. 53–63; Arjun Appadurai, "Disjuncture and Difference in the Global Cultural Economy," in Mike Featherstone, ed., *Global Culture: Nationalism, Globalization and Modernity* (London: Sage, 1990).

6. Peter M. Haas, Marc A. Levy, and Edward A. Parson, "Appraising the Earth Summit: How Should We Judge UNCED's Success?" *Environment* 34, 8 (October 1992):7–11, 26–32.

7. On the political implications of such a global network, see Ronnie D. Lipschutz, "Reconstructing World Politics: The Emergence of Global Civil Society," *Millennium: Journal of International Studies* 21, 3 (Winter 1992):389–420; Leslie Paul Thiele, "Making Democracy Safe for the World: Social Movements and Global Politics," *Alternatives* 18 (Summer 1993):273–305; Eric Laferrière, "Environmentalism and the Global Divide," *Environmental Politics* 3, 1 (Spring 1994):91–113.

8. For an overview of the Stockholm Conference, see Lynton Caldwell, *International Environmental Policy: Emergence and Dimensions,* 2nd ed. (Durham, NC: Duke University Press, 1990).

9. See National Academy of Sciences, *One Earth, One Future: Our Changing Global Environment* (Washington, DC: National Academy Press, 1990), especially pp. 15–19.

10. On the growth of scientific knowledge about the environment, see Mostafa K. Tolba, Osama A. El-Kholy, E. El-Hinnawi, M. W. Holdgate, D. F. McMichael, and R. E. Munn, *The World Environment 1972–1992: Two Decades of Challenge* (London: Chapman & Hall, 1992), chapter 20.

11. Riley E. Dunlap, George H. Gallup, Jr., and Alec M. Gallup, "Of Global Concern: Results of the Health of the Planet Survey," *Environment* 35, 9 (November 1993):6–15, 33–39.

12. On public opinion, perceptions, and attitudes, see also Tolba et al., *The World Environment 1972–1992,* chapter 21.

13. Haas, Levy, and Parson, "Appraising the Earth Summit."

14. One example of such a coalition in action can be seen in the campaign to change World Bank lending practices; see the chapter by Bruce Rich in Part Four.

15. Karen Litfin, "Eco-Regimes: Playing Tug of War with the Nation-State," in Ronnie D. Lipschutz and Ken Conca, *The State and Social Power in Global Environmental Politics* (New York: Columbia University Press, 1992).

16. Tolba et al., *The World Environment 1972–1992,* chapter 23; Helge Ole Bergesen, Magnar Norderhaug, and Georg Parmann, eds., *Green Globe Yearbook* (New York: Oxford University Press, 1992).

17. On the effectiveneess of international environmental regimes, see Peter M. Haas, Robert O. Keohane, and Mark A. Levy, eds., *Institutions for the Earth: Sources of Effective International Environmental Protection* (Cambridge, MA: MIT Press, 1993).

18. Tolba et al., *The World Environment 1972–1992,* p. 374.

19. Alan Durning, *How Much Is Enough? The Consumer Society and the Future of the Earth* (New York: W. W. Norton, 1992), p. 23.

20. Barry Commoner, *Making Peace with the Planet,* 5th ed. (New York: The New Press, 1992), pp. 148–150.

21. Murray Bookchin, *Remaking Society: Pathways to a Green Future* (Boston: South End Press, 1990), p. 9.

22. Bookchin, *Remaking Society,* pp. 9–10.

23. This theme is central to much of the literature on ecological justice; see Part Seven.

24. Vandana Shiva, "People's Ecology: The Chipko Movement," in Saul Mendlovitz and R.B.J. Walker, *Towards a Just World Peace* (London: Butterworths, 1987). See also Vandana Shiva, *Ecology and the Politics of Survival: Conflicts Over Natural Resources in India* (Newbury Park, CA: Sage, 1991); Ramachandra Guha, *The Unquiet Woods: Ecological Change and Peasant Resistance in the Himalayas* (Berkeley: University of California Press, 1989).

25. Shiva, "People's Ecology," p. 262.

26. On the concept of co-evolution, see Richard B. Norgaard, "Sociosystem and Ecosystem Coevolution in the Amazon," *Journal of Environmental Economics and Management* 8 (181):238–254.

Part One: The Debate at Stockholm

1. Mostafa K. Tolba, Osama A. El-Kholy, E. El-Hinnawi, M. W. Holdgate, D. F. Mc Michael, and R. E. Munn, *The World Environment 1972–1992: Two Decades of Challenge* (London: Chapman & Hall, 1992), chapter 23.

2. Lynton Caldwell, *International Environmental Policy: Emergence and Dimensions,* 2nd. ed. (Durham, NC: Duke University Press, 1990).

3. Several of these criticisms are summarized in W. D. Nordhaus, "World Dynamics: Measurement Without Data," *Economic Journal* 83, 332 (December 1973):1156–1183. See also Julian Simon and Herman Kahn, *The Resourceful Earth* (Oxford: Basil Blackwell, Ltd., 1984). For an overview of the limits to growth debate, see John McCormick, *Reclaiming Paradise: The Global Environmental Movement* (Bloomington, IN: Indiana University Press, 1989), chapter 4.

4. See also Eleanor Ostrom, *Governing the Commons: The Evolution of Institutions for Collective Action* (Cambridge, England: Cambridge University Press, 1990).

5. This theme is developed in Ronnie D. Lipschutz and Ken Conca, *The State and Social Power in Global Environmental Politics* (New York: Columbia University Press, 1992).

6. Robert L. Heilbroner presents a similar set of arguments in *An Inquiry into the Human Prospect* (New York: W. W. Norton, 1974). For a more recent debate on whether environmental degradation may lead to more authoritarian governmental systems, see the chapters by Thomas Homer-Dixon and Daniel Deudney in Part Six.

Chapter 1

53. See, for example, "Fellow Americans Keep Out!" *Forbes,* June 15, 1971, p. 22, and *The Ecologist,* January 1972.

Chapter 3

8. G. Hardin, ed., *Population, Evolution, and Birth Control* (Freeman, San Francisco, 1964), p. 56.

9. S. McVay, *Sci. Amer.* 216 (No. 8), 13 (1966).

10. J. Fletcher, *Situation Ethics* (Westminster, Philadelphia, 1966).

11. D. Lack, *The Natural Regulation of Animal Numbers* (Clarendon Press, Oxford, 1954).

12. H. Girvetz, *From Wealth to Welfare* (Stanford Univ. Press, Stanford, Calif., 1950).

13. G. Hardin, *Perspec. Biol. Med.* 6, 366 (1963).

18. P. Goodman, *New York Rev. Books* 10(8), 22 (23 May 1968).

20. C. Frankel, *The Case for Modern Man* (Harper, New York, 1955), p. 203.

21. J. D. Roslansky, *Genetics and the Future of Man* (Appleton-Century-Crofts, New York, 1966), p. 177.

Chapter 4

1. Tonypandy was a Welsh mining town where, in 1910, Winston Churchill sent un-armed London policemen to quell rioting strikers. The version popularly believed in Wales is that government troops shot Welsh miners who were striking for their workers' rights. In precise Tey-usage, *Tonypandy* exists when such a fiction is allowed to persist even by those people who know better. An example of Tonypandy in American history is the Boston Massacre. Josephine Tey, *Daughter of Time* (New York: Macmillan, 1951).

2. Garrett Hardin, "The Tragedy of the Commons," *Science* 162 (1968):1243–48.

3. Gordon Foxall, "A Note on the Management of 'Commons,'" *Journal of Agricultural Economics* 30 (1979):55.

4. For example, Garrett Hardin and John Baden, eds., *Managing the Commons* (San Francisco: Freeman, 1977).

5. Who could mistake the content—or inspiration—of articles such as "The Use of the Commons Dilemma in Examining the Allocation of Common Resources" (R. Kenneth Godwin and W. Brace Shepard, Resources for the Future Reprint 179), or "Legislating Commons: The Navajo Tribal Council and the Navajo Range" (Gary D. Libecap and Ronald N. Johnson, *Economic Inquiry* 18 [1980]:69–86), or Hardin and Baden, *Managing the Commons.* See also basic American government texts such as Robert Lineberry, *Government in America,* 2nd ed. (Boston: Little, Brown, 1983), in which he identifies the tragedy of the commons as "a parable about sheep overgrazing a common meadow" (pp. 579–80).

6. This is not to imply that the tragedy of the commons *never* occurred in those centuries; records are incomplete and to assert positively that something never occurred is to court contradiction and exposure.

10. Garrett Hardin, "Denial and Disguise," in Hardin and Baden, *Managing the Commons,* pp. 45–52. Hardin acknowledges the injustice of the Enclosure Acts but applauds the increase in agricultural productivity that they entailed.

11. Beryl Crowe, "The Tragedy of the Commons Revisited," in Hardin and Baden, *Managing the Commons,* 54–55.

13. Richard A. Falk, *This Endangered Planet* (New York: Random, 1971), p. 48.

14. E. C. K. Gonner, *Common Land and Inclosure,* 2nd ed. (London: Cass, 1966). The first portion of this quote is quoted by Gonner without attribution. This is not, however, an outmoded or esoteric definition: basic American college dictionaries provide the same definition.

15. C. C. Taylor, "Archaeology and the Origins of Open-Field Agriculture," in Trevor Rowley, ed., *The Origins of Open-Field Agriculture* (London: Groom Helm, 1981), p. 21. See also Della Hooke, "Open-field Agriculture—The Evidence from the Pre-Conquest Charters of the West Midlands," ibid., p. 58: "Land held in common by a community is clearly in evidence by the tenth century."

16. W. G. Hoskins and L. Dudley Stamp, *The Common Lands of England and Wales* (London: Collins, 1965), p. 6.

17. Gonner, *Common Land,* pp. 3–4.

24. W. O. Ault, *Open-Field Farming in Medieval England* (London: Allen and Unwin, 1972), p. 17.

25. Ibid., p. 18. Ault gives 1246 as the earliest manor court rolls; the earliest manorial reeve's accounts are for 1208–9.

26. Joan Thirsk, "Field Systems of the East Midlands," in Alan R. H. Baker and Robin A. Butlin, eds., *Studies of Field Systems in the British Isles* (Cambridge, England: Cambridge University Press, 1973), p. 232.

28. B. K. Roberts, "Field Systems of the West Midlands," in Baker and Butlin, *Studies,* p. 199.

29. Thirsk, "Field Systems," p. 251.

30. Westminster Muniments, 1550; quoted in Ault, *Open-Field Farming,* p. 26.

31. G. Elliot, "Field Systems of Northwest England," in Baker and Butlin, *Studies,* p. 67. As an example, in Denwick in 1567 the stint of "each husbandland was 6 old beasts above two years old, 37 sheep above one year old besides lambs and other young cattle, four pigs above one year old, two geese and one horse or mare" (R. A. Butlin, "Field Systems of Northumberland and Durham," in Baker and Butlin, *Studies,* p. 138).

35. Elliot, "Field Systems," p. 83. The internal quote is from the Westmorland Record office, Musgrave D. P., Court Rolls 1695.

36. Edward Scrutton, *Commons and Common Fields* (1887; reprint ed., New York: Lenox Hill, 1970), p. 122.

39. Roberts, "Field Systems," p. 190.

40. A classic example of exploitation is the Statute of Merton (1236), which allowed "chief tenants to assart land for their own or their villeins' exclusive use, provided that 'sufficient' common land was left for the needs of the village community." June A. Sheppard, "Field Systems of Yorkshire," in Baker and Bullin, *Studies,* pp. 176–77.

41. Gonner, *Common Land,* p. 103.

43. Hoskins and Stamp, *Common Lands,* p. 55.

44. Ibid., p. 54.

46. Scrutton, *Commons,* pp. 120–21. For example, all the farmers might agree to let one field lie fallow against custom for two years. If, in the second year, one tenant decided to return to the customary management and to graze his cattle in the field, the rest were powerless to stop him, and of course, the result would be the use of the field by all the tenants.

47. Victor Rice, Frederick Andrews, Everett Warwick, and James Legates, *Breeding and Improvement of Farm Animals* (New York: McGraw-Hill, 1957), p. 16.

48. For example, between 1710 and 1790, the weight at Smithfield of cattle changed from 370 pounds to 800 pounds, of calves from 50 to 148, of sheep from 28 to 80, and of lambs from 18 to 50. This weight change is of course due to a multitude of causes. Scrutton, *Commons,* p. 121.

49. Gonner, *Common Land*, pp. 306–07.

50. Van Rensselaer Potter, *Science* 185 (1974):813.

51. Garrett Hardin, "Denial and Disguise," in Hardin and Baden, *Managing the Commons*, p. 47.

52. Hardin, "Tragedy of the Commons," in Hardin and Baden, *Managing the Commons*, p. 20.

Part Two: Ecology and the Structure of the International System

1. The term *structure* is used in this sense in Ken Conca, "Environmental Change and the Deep Structure of World Politics," in Ronnie D. Lipschutz and Ken Conca, eds., *The State and Social Power in Global Environmental Politics* (New York: Columbia University Press, 1993).

2. World Commission on Environment and Development, *Our Common Future* (New York: Oxford University Press, 1987).

3. Mostafa K. Tolba, Osama A. El-Kholy, E. El-Hinnawi, M. W. Holdgate, D. F. McMichael, and R. E. Munn, *The World Environment 1972–1992: Two Decades of Challenge* (London: Chapman & Hall, 1992), p. 808. This principle was reiterated twenty years later at the Earth Summit; see "Rio Declaration on Environment and Development," United Nations Conference on Environment and Development, U.N. Doc. A/CONF.151/5/Rev. 1(1992).

4. For a more optimistic view of the possibilities of tempering the more ecologically destructive aspects of sovereignty through international cooperation, see Peter M. Haas, Robert O. Keohane and Mark A. Levy, eds., *Institutions for the Earth: Sources of Effective International Environmental Protection* (Cambridge, MA: MIT Press, 1993).

5. On international trade prior to the founding of the modern state system, see Barry Buzan and Richard Little, "The Idea of 'International System': Theory Meets History," *International Political Science Review* 15, 3 (1994):231–255. On the dilemmas states face as a result of deepening economic interdependence, see Robert Gilpin, *The Political Economy of International Relations* (Princeton, NJ: Princeton University Press, 1987).

6. See, for example, Latin American and Caribbean Commission on Development and Environment, *Our Own Agenda* (Washington, DC: Inter-American Development Bank and UNDP, 1991).

7. On the role of colonialism in promoting the spread of European values, see Edward Said, *Culture and Imperialism* (New York: Random House, 1993).

8. This theme is developed in Conca, "Environmental Change and the Deep Structure of World Politics."

9. Judith Goldstein and Robert O. Keohane, eds., *Ideas and Foreign Policy: Beliefs, Institutions, and Political Change* (Ithaca, NY: Cornell University Press, 1993).

10. The term "antisystemic movement" is taken from G. Arrighi, T. K. Hopkins, and I. Wallerstein, *Antisystemic Movements* (London: Verso, 1989).

11. On divisions within the U.S. environmental community over NAFTA, see John Audley, *Environmental Interests and Trade Policy*, Ph.D. thesis, Department of Government and Politics, University of Maryland at College Park, forthcoming 1995.

12. On the international pressures surrounding deforestation in the Amazon, see Susanna Hecht and Alexander Cockburn, *The Fate of the Forest: Developers, Destroyers, and Defenders of the Amazon* (New York: HarperCollins, 1990).

13. On the problems and prospects for North-South coalitions among environmental groups, see Nancy Peluso, "Coercing Conservation," in Lipschutz and Conca, *The State and Social Power in Global Environmental Politics;* Bob Ostertag, "Greenpeace Takes Over the World," *Mother Jones,* March/April 1991; World Resources Institute, "Policies and Insti-

tutions: Nongovernmental Organizations," *World Resources 1992–93* (New York: Oxford University Press, 1992); Eric Laferrière, "Environmentalism and the Global Divide," *Environmental Politics* 3, 1 (Spring 1994):91–113.

Chapter 8

13. Although a measured activity (say, consumption of a hamburger) may occur in one place, its associated impact can be spread over many places: the rangeland where the beef was fed (maybe sustainable, maybe not; maybe on land deforested for grazing, maybe not), the rural landfill where the packaging waste will be discarded, the region where a dammed river provided the energy for cooking, the oil field depleted for energy and petrochemical feedstocks to make the plastics used in packaging, and worldwide damage from ozone depletion caused by the CFC blowing agent used to manufacture the packaging.

14. See "The Problem of Interregional Trade" in William E. Rees, "A Role for Environmental Assessment in Achieving Sustainable Development," *Environmental Impact Assessment Review* 8 (1988):271–72.

15. World Resources Institute, *World Resources 1988–89: An Assessment of the Resource Base That Supports the Global Economy.* New York: Basic Books, 1989.

Chapter 9

27. See Willis Harman, *An Incomplete Guide to the Future* (New York: Norton, 1979); Alvin Toffler, *The Third Wave* (New York: Morrow, 1980); Daniel Bell, *The Coming of Post-Industrial Society* (New York: Basic Books, 1973); Peter Drucker, *The Age of Discontinuity* (New York: Harper and Row, 1968).

28. The role of social surplus in growth and development is discussed in A. S. Boughey, "Environmental Crises—Past and Present," in Lester Bilsky, ed., *Historical Ecology* (Port Washington, NY: Kennikat Press, 1980).

29. Earl Cook, *Man, Energy, Society* (San Francisco: W. H. Freeman, 1976), p. 19.

30. The dominant social paradigm concept was developed by Willis Harman, op. cit., chap. 2; see also Dennis Pirages and Paul Ehrlich, *Ark II: Social Response to Environmental Imperatives* (New York: Viking, 1974), chap. 2.

35. Willis Harman, op. cit., pp. 25–28.

36. Willis Harman, "The Coming Transformation," *The Futurist* (February 1977).

41. See Alvin Toffler, op. cit.

51. Richard Mansbach and John Vasquez, *In Search of Theory: A New Paradigm for Global Politics* (New York: Columbia University Press, 1981), p. 5.

53. See ibid. [Mansbach and Vasquez], chapter 1.

Chapter 11

6. The most thorough analysis of this development is in the Soviet Union, e.g., T. Gustafson, *Reform in the Soviet Politics: Lessons of Recent Policies on Land and Water* (Cambridge: Cambridge University Press, 1981), pp. 231–38; J. DeBardeleben, *The Environment and Marxism-Leninism: The Soviet and East European Experience* (Boulder, CO: Westview Press, 1985), p. 60. Waller notes that specialist debate also became a legitimate part of the political process in Eastern Europe (M. Waller, "The Ecology Issue in Eastern Europe: Protest and Movements," *Journal of Communist Studies* 5, no. 3 [September 1989]: 309).

7. In the case of the Soviet Union, this frustration is described by C. E. Ziegler, *Environmental Policy in the USSR* (London: Pinter, 1987), p. 66.

12. The situation in Eastern Europe in this respect was different only in degree from the West. It occurs wherever incentives for bureaucrats cause their own interests and social interests to diverge (J. Baden and R. L. Stroup, *Bureaucracy Versus Environment: The Environmental Costs of Bureaucratic Governance* [Ann Arbor, MI: University of Michigan Press, 1981], pp. 217–18).

13. *East European Reporter* 2, no. 2 (1986): 5–7.

15. Ziegler (1987), pp. 51–52.

16. Quoted in RFE *Bulgarian SR* 1, no. 1 (3 February 1989). The state's ideological commitment to participation in the environmental sphere is also evident in the chapter on the GDR in G. Enyedi, A. J. Gijswijt, and B. Rhode, *Environmental Polities in East and West* (London: Taylor Graham, 1987), pp. 160–61. *The Hungarian National Concept and Requirements for National Policy* (1980) stated: "The active and permanent cooperation of the widest strata of society is an essential condition for a successful environment. It is promoted by the social and mass organizations" (M. Persanyi, "Gongos, Quangos, Blues and Greens (A comprehensive description of nongovernmental organizations in environmental protection in Hungary)," paper prepared for presentation at the Conference on Environmental Constraints and Opportunities in the Social Organizations of Space, Udine, Italy, 7–10 June 1989, p. 3).

20. This is the main argument of Vaclav Havel in his celebrated essay, "The Power of the Powerless." The power of the powerless is their ability to strike at the foundations of the facade of order by not playing the game and thus revealing the hollowness of the real state of society (see Vaclav Havel et al., *The Power of the Powerless* [London: Palach Press, 1985]).

21. Persanyi (1989), p. 17.

22. For example, the British Jan Hus Foundation, which supported the Czechoslovak opposition, sent Tom Burke of the Green Alliance in London to make contacts with Czech and Slovak environmentalists from 1986 onward.

23. RFE *Bulgarian SR* 10, no. 2 (4 November 1987); *Bulgarian SR* 13, no. 1 (25 November 1987); *Romanian SR* 5, no. 1 (29 March 1988); *East European Newsletter* 3, no. 1 (11 January 1989): 2.

24. *East European Newsletter* 3, no. 1 (11 January 1989): 1–3; 3, no. 11 (31 May 1989): 1–3; 3, no. 17 (28 August 1989): 4–6; 3, no. 18 (11 September 1989): 5–6; 3, no. 19 (October 1989): 6–7; RFE *Bulgarian SR* 2, no. 3 (9 March 1989); *Bulgarian SR* 4, no. 3 (22 May 1989); *East European Reporter* 3, no. 4 (Spring/Summer 1989): 26–28; 4, no. 1 (Winter 1989/90): 83–85.

25. Enyedi et al. (1987), pp. 66–67.

26. RFE BR/42 (20 March 1987).

27. RFE *Bulgarian SR* 10, no. 5 (5 December 1989).

28. The following three paragraphs are based on D. Fisher (August 1989), pp. 15–17; and D. Fisher, *Report on a Visit to Czechoslovakia* (London: Ecological Studies Institute, December 1989), annex 1.

29. The report is reproduced in *East European Reporter* 3, no. 3 (Autumn 1988): 26–30.

30. These are listed in Waller (1989), pp. 314–15.

33. DeBardeleben (1985), p. 79.

34. G. Kallenbach, "The Part of the Church in the Environmental Movement of the GDR," paper given at SEED Popular Forum, Bergen, Norway, 14 May 1990, p. 3.

42. Persanyi (1989), pp. 13–14; Waller (1989), p. 321; T. Fleischer, "The Blue Danube," *East European Reporter* 4, no. 2 (Spring/Summer 1990): 78.

43. Persanyi (1989), p. 14.

44. Ibid., pp. 15–16.

45. Ibid., p. 6.

46. Ibid., p. 9; L. Solyom, "Hungary: Citizens; Participation in the Environmental Movement," *IFDA Dossier* 64 (March/April 1988): 28–29.

47. The response to the Gabcikovo-Nagymaros Dam system is discussed in various documents: Fisher (August 1989), pp. 12–26; Solyom (1988), pp. 24–28.

48. See, for example, the comments of Persanyi (1989), p. 6.

49. This activity is described in Helsinki Watch (1987), pp. 79–80, 92–95.

50. Swedish-Polish Association for Environmental Protection, "Proceedings from SPM Seminar on Swedish-Polish Environmental Cooperation, February 23–24, 1988" (Upsala: Swedish Polish Association for Environmental Protection, 1989), pp. 69–73.

51. RFE *BR/42* (20 March 1987).

52. V. Sobell, "The Ecological Crisis in Eastern Europe," RFE, BR/5 (20 January 1988), pp. 12–13.

53. RFE *Poland SR* 1 (11 January 1989).

54. M. Sobelman, "New Objectives in the Area of Environmental Protection in Poland," *Environmental Policy Review: The Soviet Union and Eastern Europe* 3, no. 1 (January 1989): 22–27.

55. *Bloc* (November-December 1989), p. 14; Palach Press, *Uncensored Czechoslovakia: December 13, 1989,* p. 18; December 17, 1989, p. 13; December 19, 1989, p. 17; RFE *Czechoslovak SR* 19, no. 8 (20 September 1989).

56. Fisher (August 1989), pp. 19–20; Y. Golan, "Suspension of the Work on the Bos-Nagymaros Dam," *Environmental Policy Review: The Soviet Union and Eastern Europe* 3, no. 2 (July 1989); Persanyi (1989), pp. 8–9.

57. RFE *Hungarian SR* 16, no. 3 (28 October 1988).

58. From now on the established Western terminology will be used. The other vague term, nongovernmental organization (NGO), here represents the equivalent of more exact terms such as social movement or organization preferred by some social scientists, for example, J. D. McCarthy and M. N. Zald, "Resource Mobilization and Social Movements: A Partial Theory," in M. N. Zald and J. D. McCarthy, eds., *Social Movements in an Organizational Society* (New Brunswick, NJ: Transaction Books, 1987), pp. 15–42.

59. D. Fisher, *Report on a Visit to Bulgaria* (London: Ecological Studies Institute, February 1990), pp. 3–4.

60. The text may be found in Fisher (February 1990), annex 3.

61. Fisher (February 1990), annex 2.

62. *East European Newsletter* 3, no. 21 (October 1989): 6; RFE *Bulgarian SR* 0, no. 5 (5 December 1989); personal observation.

63. Ecoglasnost in Bulgaria, made up of about 90 local groups (Fisher [February 1990], p. 5); the Green Alliance in Croatia (D. Fisher, *Report on a Visit to Yugoslavia* [London: Ecological Studies Institute, May 1990], p. 15); the Green Movement in Serbia (Ibid., p. 5); the Green League in the GDR; the Green Circle in Czechoslovakia (Fisher [December 1989], p. 3); the Ecological Movement of Romania (D. Fisher, *Report on Two Visits to Romania* [London: Ecological Studies Institute, March/April 1990], p. 2).

64. In Czechoslovakia, the old leaderships of the Czech and Slovak Unions of Nature Protectors were dismissed, the Brontosaurus youth organization came out of the Socialist Youth Movement, and the Ecological Section of the Biological Society came out of the Academy of Sciences (Fisher [December 1989], pp. 2–3; *East European Newsletter* 4, no. 1 [January 1990], p. 4 [written by D. Fisher]); in Hungary the National Society of Nature Protectors began reforming itself and developing the already existing network of local groups around the country.

65. Bulgaria: The Bulgarian Green Party founded in December 1989 (Fisher [February 1990], p. 6; BBC Summary of World Broadcasts: EE/0654 B/2 [5 January 1990]); GDR: Founded in November 1989, with a founding congress in Halle in February 1990; Czechoslovakia: Numerous local parties formed in December 1989, which formed a federated Czech and Slovak Green Party in February 1990 (Fisher [December 1989], pp. 3–4; BBC Summary of World Broadcasts: EE/0662 B/8 [15 January 1990]; EE/0677 B/4 [1 February 1990]; EE/0692 B/5 [19 February 1990]; EE/0681 B/3 [6 February 1990]); Hungary: Green Party funded in November 1989 (*Manchester Guardian,* 20 November 1989); Poland: The first green party was founded in Cracow in December 1988. This has since split into a number of warring factions (A. Delorme, "Green Parties in Poland" [Cracow, December 1989]); Romania: There are several parties around the country, the most important of which was the Green Party of Romania (PER), founded in 1990 (Fisher [March/April 1990], p. 8); Yugoslavia: Bosnian-Hercegovinan Green Party founded in 1989 (*East European Newsletter* 4, no. 3 [February 1990], p. 6); Serbian Green Party founded in February 1990 (Fisher [May 1990]: 4); Slovenian Green Party founded in January 1990 (Fisher [May 1990]: 9).

66. White et al. observe the large nonvoting proportions of the electorate in Poland, Hungary and Czechoslovakia in a highly politicized situation (S. White, J. Gardner, G. Schopflin, and T. Saich, *Communist and Postcommunist Political Systems: An Introduction* [London: Macmillan, 1990], pp. 63–68).

67. V. Melucci, "Social Movements and the Democratization of Everyday Life," in J. Keane, ed., Civil Society and the State (London: Verso, 1988), p. 222; V. Melucci, *Nomads of the Present,* trans. and ed. by J. Keane and P. Mier (London: Verso, 1989), pp. 7–8.

87. Since the revolutions, the term "Eastern Europe" is being replaced by the term "Central and Eastern Europe."

88. The Ecological Studies Institute in London is currently undertaking a broad analysis of this issue.

89. A. Oberschall as cited in C. Tilly, *From Mobilization to Revolution* (Reading, MA: Addison-Wesley, 1978), p. 81; P. Lowe and J. Goyder, *Environmental Groups in Politics* (London: George Allen & Unwin, 1983), p. 47; McCarthy and Zald (1987), p. 34.

Chapter 12

2. The reference is to the administration of Flaviano Melo, elected in the November 1986 elections to serve as governor of Acre from March 1987 to March 1991. Flaviano represented the old local elite who controlled the rubber industry, and whose dominance was being challenged by a new elite of ranchers, mostly newcomers to Acre. He was also made aware at the beginning of his administration that Acre, the poorest and least important state in the Brazilian federation, could expect little financial support from the federal government in Brasília.

It therefore made good political and administrative sense to appear to respond sympathetically to many of the demands of the rubber tappers and their supporters. It would pay political dividends, appearing as an alliance of *Acreanos* (albeit of both exploiters and exploited) against newcomers. It was also attractive financially since, by subscribing to the principles of sustainable development demanded by grassroots organisations locally and being advocated internationally, the state government was able to become attractive to international organisations such as the World Bank and the International Tropical Timber Organisation who were willing to fund its development programmes.

State government publicity began referring to the 'ecological government of Acre', and promised to concentrate on promoting the rational use of forests rather than ranching. Controversial new roads and colonisation schemes were shelved. However, serious problems arose. Weak state governments have little capacity to withstand the political and economic superiority of the federal government; the power of the ranchers is increasing, as witnessed by the growth of the UDR in Acre; and above all, an opportunistic alliance between a decadent elite and its former subjects in the face of the challenge from a new elite has few long-term prospects.

3. *Seringueiros* trade brazil nuts using old 30 litre paraffin cans as the measure.

4. FUNTAC was set up to look at the problem of deforestation and the rational use of forest resources. It starts from the premise that Acre has a future in silviculture. FUNTAC is the agency responsible for the pilot forest management project approved by the International Tropical Timber Organisation. It is working on a plan for sustainably managed forests and local timber use, including the appropriate design of low cost housing for Rio Branco's growing population. It consults with Indians, rubber tappers, anthropologists, and other sectors of the state administration.

Part Three: The Prospects for International Environmental Cooperation

1. A classic work on barriers to cooperation is Mancur Olson, *The Logic of Collective Action: Public Goods and the Theory of Groups* (Cambridge: Harvard University Press, 1965). For a different perspective on similar questions, see Eleanor Ostrom, *Governing the Commons: The Evolution of Institutions for Collective Action* (Cambridge, England: Cambridge University Press, 1990).

2. For a summary of the objectives, scope, provisions, membership, and methods of these and other major international environmental agreements, see Helge Ole Bergesen, Magnar Norderhaug, and Georg Parmann, eds., *Green Globe Yearbook* (New York: Oxford University Press, 1992).

3. Benedick's chapter was written before the 1990 London meeting of parties to the convention substantially strengthened the agreement reached in 1987 in Montreal.

4. The problem of estimating the costs of responding to climate change is taken up in William R. Cline, *The Economics of Global Warming* (Washington, DC: Institute for International Economics, 1992).

5. To its credit, the World Resources Institute, which published the tables attacked by Agarwal and Narain, acknowledged the different ways of measuring national responsibility in a subsequent publication on the same theme. See World Resources Institute, *World Resources 1992–93* (New York: Oxford University Press, 1992), Box 13.3, p. 209.

Chapter 14

11. See, for example, Russell Hardin, Collective Action (Baltimore, MD: Johns Hopkins University Press, 1982); Mancur Olsen, *The Logic of Collective Action: Public Goods and the Theory of Groups* (Cambridge, MA: Harvard University Press, 1965); and Duncan Snidal, "Public Goods, Property Rights and Political Organization," *International Studies Quarterly* 23 (December 1979): 532–66.

12. Garrett Hardin, "The Tragedy of the Commons," *Science*, December 13, 1968, 1243–48.

15. Robert O. Keohane, *After Hegemony: Cooperation and Discord in the World Political Economy* (Princeton, NJ: Princeton University Press, 1984), 51–52.

16. Although in October 1990 negotiations were under way on a cooperative arrangement, experts believe that no convention or protocol will be signed before 1992.

17. In my work, I have reviewed the fields of regime analysis, international institutions and cooperation, game theory, economics, international political economy, and analyses of

empirical recounts of similar dilemmas of collective action (some of which I have mentioned in this article) and I have tried to synthesize this material in order to hypothesize the major factors for cooperation. They are the four "preconditions," which I examine here, along with six "catalysts" (hegemony, entrepreneurship, background international political system, transnational actors, international public opinion, and crises). These 10 factors form the basis of my ongoing research.

18. For total methodological accuracy, I should point out that these factors are not independent; they feed among themselves in a variety of directions. Thus some overlap necessarily exists among the four preconditions.

19. Robert Axelrod and Robert O. Keohane, "Achieving Cooperation Under Anarchy: Strategies and Institutions," *World Politics* 38, no. 1 (October 1985): 227.

20. These products included drugs used in inhalation therapy, certain insecticides, vaginal foam, and coolants in refrigerators and air-conditioning units. See "US Finalises Aerosol Ban," *New Scientist*, March 30, 1978, 839.

21. It is thought that only with the pressure of scientific evidence and the personal intervention of the emperor, was the possibility of substitutes finally entertained. See David Swinbanks, "Japan Supports Ban by the Year 2000," *Nature*, April 27, 1989, 694.

22. The Associated Press in Brussels, "Europeans Vow to Curb Ozone Killers," *The Citizen*, Ottawa, March 3, 1989, p. A6.

23. "US Finalises Aerosol Ban."

24. Unnamed executive quoted in Neil Kinnock, "The Holes in the Ozone Policies," *The Guardian*, London, March 4, 1989, p. 23.

26. Quoted in Richard North, "Scientists Urge Rapid Phase-Out of CFCs," *The Independent*, London, March 6, 1989.

27. Tim Radford, "80 Nations Agree to Phase Out CFCs by End of Century," *The Guardian*, London, May 3, 1989. This new consensus was strengthened at a meeting of the Parties to the Protocol in London in June 1990. See Nicholas Schoon, "Deal to Save Ozone Layer Agreed," *The Independent*, London, June 30, 1990.

28. For example, after the Montreal Protocol was signed in September 1987, 13 companies from seven different countries joined together to speed the testing of HFC123 and HFC134a—two possible alternatives to CFCs. Such cooperation among the international chemical companies was unprecedented. See Alun Anderson, "Depletion of Ozone Layer Drives Competitors to Cooperate," *Nature*, January 21, 1988, 201.

30. Robert O. Keohane, "International Institutions: Two Approaches," *International Studies Quarterly* 32 (December 1988): 379–96.

37. For example, Oran R. Young, "The Politics of International Regime Formation: Managing Natural Resources and the Environment," *International Organization* 43 (Summer 1989): 368–69.

38. Though India and China, in October 1990, had yet to sign the Montreal Protocol, representatives from both countries had indicated that they would.

39. See Article 5 of the Montreal Protocol.

41. Keohane, *After Hegemony*, 245.

42. It should also be noted that, apart from the obligation of states to report consumption data (Article 7), there is no specific reference to this consideration in the Montreal Protocol.

43. Stephan Haggard and Beth A. Simmons, "Theories of International Regimes," *International Organization* 41 (Summer 1987): 511.

44. Seyom Brown et al., *Regimes for the Ocean, Outer Space, and Weather* (Washington, DC: Brookings Institution, 1977), 235.

46. Mario J. Molina and F. S. Rowland, "Stratospheric Sink for Chlorofluoromethanes: Chlorine Atom-Catalysed Destruction of Ozone," *Nature,* June 28, 1974, 810–12.

49. John Maddox, "The Great Ozone Controversy," *Nature,* September 10, 1987, 101.

50. J. C. Farman et al., "Large Losses of Total Ozone in Antarctica Reveal CLOx/NOx Interaction," *Nature,* May 16, 1985.

51. For a clear, primarily nontechnical, discussion of the three theories, see Sharon L. Roan, *Ozone Crisis: The 15 Year Evolution of a Sudden Global Emergency* (New York: Wiley, 1989).

52. David Lindley, "Ozone Hole Deeper Than Ever," *Nature,* October 8, 1987, 473.

53. For an interesting discussion of this relationship, see the work of Peter M. Haas on "epistemic communities"—for example, Peter M. Haas, "Obtaining International Environmental Protection Through Epistemic Communities," *Millennium: Journal of International Studies* 19 (Winter 1990).

54. Svante Arrhenius, "On the Influence of Carbonic Acid in the Air upon the Temperature on the Ground," *Philosophical Magazine* 41 (April 1896): 237–76.

55. Measurements in Hawaii have recorded an increase in background carbon dioxide levels from 315 ppm (in 1958) to 348 ppm (in 1988).

56. The UK's Meteorological Office has discovered a rise of 0.5°C in global average temperature since 1900.

57. John Houghton, director general of the UK's Meteorological Office stated that: "It will be at least 10 years before anyone can be absolutely certain (and it might take as long as 30 years before indisputable evidence emerged)," quoted in Nicholas Schoon, "Greenhouse Effect 'Cannot be Proved until Next Century,'" *The Independent,* London, September 12, 1989, 5. Furthermore, Stephen Schneider noted that: "Another decade or two of observations should produce signal-to-noise ratios sufficiently obvious to enable scientists to agree as to the reliability of present estimates of global climatic sensitivity to increasing trace gases." Stephen H. Schneider, *Global Warming: Are We Entering the Greenhouse Century?* (San Francisco, CA: Sierra Club Books, 1989), 118.

Chapter 17

1. These figures and those used in the rest of the article are from UNCED Secretariat, "Facts and Figures on UNCED RIOCENTRO," UNCED/DPI/RIOCENTRO LSF/ICD (press release, 12 June 1992); UNCED Secretariat, NGO Unit. *In Our Hands* (Geneva: UNCED Secretariat, June 1992).

2. For studies documenting the increasing sophistication of international efforts for environmental protection, see P. M. Haas, *Saving the Mediterranean: The Politics of International Environmental Cooperation* (New York: Columbia University Press, 1990); P. M. Haas, R. O. Keohane, and M. A. Levy, eds., *Institutions for the Earth: Sources of Effective International Environmental Protection* (Cambridge, Mass.: MIT Press, 1993); and N. Choucri, ed., *Global Accords: Environmental Challenges and International Responses* (Cambridge. Mass.: MIT Press, 1993). For an approach that applies a similar process-based analysis to the study of progress in international relations, see E. Adler and B. Crawford, eds., *Progress in International Relations* (New York: Columbia University Press, 1991).

3. M. F. Strong, UNCED secretary-general, statement at opening of UN Conference on Environment and Development, Rio de Janeiro, Brazil, 3 June 1992. Texts that offer specific outcomes as criteria for UNCED's success include M. Khor, "Nine Key Tests for UNCED's Success," *Earth Island Journal,* June 1992, 4; and World Commission on Environment and Development, "Reconvened World Commission on Environment and Development" (London, 22–24 April 1992).

4. M. A. Levy, P. M. Haas, and R. O. Keohane, "Institutions for the Earth: Promoting International Environmental Protection," *Environment*, May 1992, 12; and Haas, Keohane, and Levy, note 2 above.

9. Here, the authors focus on new institutions narrowly construed as international organizations and constellations of international organizations. A broader definition of institutions would include any persistent and connected set of rules and practices that prescribe behavioral roles, constrain activity, and shape expectations. Of course, organizations may help establish and perpetuate this latter type of institution.

12. UN doc. A/CONF. 151/L.3/Add. 38, "Report of the Main Committee Addendum—Chapter 38: International Institutional Arrangements," 11 June 1992.

14. The argument that the organization of the Montreal protocol expert panels was essential to the protocol's success is made in E. A. Parson, "Protecting the Ozone Layer: the Evolution and Impact of International Relations," working paper no. 21-392-3 (Harvard University Center for International Affairs, Cambridge, Mass., 1992).

18. Although NGOs had hoped to present their reports formally to UNCED and make them part of the official conference record, they were unable to do so and thus no central clearinghouse exists for obtaining the reports or even an index of them. Approximately 15 NGO national reports were prepared for UNCED. Those in the authors' possession include "Bangladesh NGO Statement to the Earth Summit: Proceedings of the Workshop on Environment and Development" (Mohammadpur, Bangladesh: Center for Mass Education in Science, undated); "French NGO's Official Report for the Environment and for Development: To Work for an International Democracy" (Paris: Comité de Liaison des Organisations de Solidarité Internationales, undated); Alliantie voor Duurzame Ontwikkeling, "There Is an Alternative: The Netherlands National NGO Report with Regards to UNCED" (Utrecht, the Netherlands, undated); and Public Campaign on Environment and Development, "Citizens' Report on Environment and Development: Sri Lanka" (Sri Lanka, 1992).

19. "National Reports: The Next Step," *Network '92*, no. 17 (May 1992):1.

20. M. Valentine, "Twelve Days of UNCED," 2 July 1992, unpublished paper; available as "Network Final Report on Rio," Topic 1083, Econet conference en.unced.general.

21. OECD figures, reported in *The Economist*, 4 July 1992, 91.

22. The estimated need curiously represents both a rough doubling of present ODA and an increase to almost exactly 0.7 percent of OECD GDP. See World Bank, *World Development Report 1992* (New York: Oxford University Press, 1992), table 3.

26. UNCED Secretariat, NGO Unit, note 1 above.

27. Valentine, note 20 above.

28. A. Doherty, International Institute for Applied Systems Analysis, Laxenburg, Austria, personal communication with the authors, 29 July 1992.

32. In Rio, divisions were noted between developing-country NGOs, which were highly suspicious of working with their governments, and developed-country NGOs, which had had much lengthier, positive experiences in working with their governments.

33. UNCED figures are from the secretariat press conference, 11 June 1992. See UNCED Secretariat, note 1 above. For Stockholm, see UN doc. A/CONF.48/INF.6/Rev.1, 10 November 1972. For slightly different numbers, see A. Thompson Feraru, "Transnational Political Interests and the Global Environment," *International Organization* 28 (Winter 1974):31–60. Such numbers must be taken with a grain of salt because not all NGOs reported their attendance to the secretariat.

34. For instance, extensive links are drawn between the management of atmospheric and terrestrial ecosystems in the Climate Change treaty (article 4, paragraph f) and in

Agenda 21's chapters on protecting the atmosphere. See preparatory document UN doc. A/CONF.151/PC/42 for an early structure and organization of Agenda 21. The designers of the Stockholm Conference hoped to create a similar matrix of social and ecological interactions for international action, but such a sophisticated design was discarded during preparations for the conference.

Part Four: Institutions as Though the Earth Mattered

1. See Oran Young, *International Cooperation: Building Regimes for Natural Resources and the Environment* (Ithaca, NY: Cornell University Press, 1989), p. 32.

2. Young, *International Cooperation,* p. 32.

3. A similar argument is presented by former director of the U.S. Environmental Protection Agency William K. Reilly. See Reilly, "The Green Thumb of Capitalism," *Policy Review* (Fall 1990):16–21.

4. Jagdish Bhagwati, *Protectionism* (Cambridge, MA: MIT Press, 1989).

5. The campaign to change the Bank is described in Pat Aufderheide and Bruce Rich, "Environmental Reform and the Multilateral Banks," *World Policy Journal* 5, 2 (Spring 1988):301–321.

Chapter 21

2. *Our Common Future* (Oxford: Oxford UP, 1987). This report was prepared by the World Commission on Environment and Development, commonly referred to as the 'Brundtland Commission', during the period immediately preceding the decision to restructure the World Bank.

3. The Development Committee paper was prepared by Jeremy Warford, one of the leading architects of the Bank's environmental strategy, and was subsequently published under the title *Environment, Growth and Development* (World Bank, 1987). For the Address by President Conable to the World Resources Institute, Washington, DC, in May 1987, see *The Conable Years at the World Bank* (World Bank, 1991), 21–9.

4. E.g., Mauritius, Madagascar, and Lesotho, which pioneered the National Environmental Action Plan approach. A second group of countries in Africa (Rwanda, Ghana, Burkina Faso, and the Seychelles) has now completed the formulation of such Plans, and implementation will follow once they are approved. A further ten countries in Africa are now embarked upon the process, so this formula has become the dominant framework for the Bank's environmental activities in African countries. See *The World Bank and the Environment—A Progress Report* (World Bank, 1991), 29ff.

6. The level of staff effort in World Bank units is notoriously difficult to calculate, given the extensive use of consultant services. The First *Annual Report on the Environment* in 1990 gave a total of 30 professional staff and 15 consultants in the regions, with 24 professionals and 8 consultants in the Environment Department.

7. For a full discussion of the policy shift in this area, see World Bank, *Annual Report on the Environment,* 1991.

8. During 1991 the Environmental Assessment Sourcebook was published in three volumes to provide detailed guidelines on the application of the Directive. (World Bank Technical Paper No. 139—see in particular vol. i, ch. 1, for a full discussion of the Bank's procedures, and Fig. 1.1 for a representation of the concordance with the project cycle.) Category D was eliminated in the review of the Directive in 1991.

11. See also the 1990 *Annual Report on the Environment,* ch. 4, for a detailed description of primarily environmental projects, such as the $117 million loan to support the first

three years of Brazil's national environment programme and the $18 million Environment Management Project in Poland. In the 1991 *Annual Report on the Environment,* see p. 35 (Mauritius) and p. 43 (Philippines).

12. For a full description of both the Interim Multilateral Fund and the Global Environment Facility, as well as the technical assistance funds managed within the Bank for environmental purposes, see I. F. I. Shihata, *The World Bank in a Changing World* (Boston, Mass.: Martinus Nijhoff, 1991), ch. 4.

Part Five: The Sustainable Development Debate

1. For a view stressing the importance of paradigms in shaping global environmental futures, see Lester W. Milbrath, *Envisioning a Sustainable Society: Learning Our Way Out* (Albany, NY: SUNY Press, 1989).

2. This is the definition of sustainable development employed by Herman Daly; see Part Four.

3. World Commission on Environment and Development, *Our Common Future* (Oxford: Oxford University Press, 1987), p. ix.

4. WCED, *Our Common Future,* p. 43.

5. This argument is also presented in the statement of Malaysian Prime Minister Mahathir Mohamad at the 1992 Earth Summit; see Part Seven.

6. A similar criticism has been made of the "global change" discourse that became increasingly influential in environmental circles in the 1980s. See Frederick H. Buttel, Ann P. Hawkins, and Alison G. Power, "From Limits to Growth to Global Change," *Global Environmental Change* 1 (December 1990):57–66.

7. T. O'Riordan, "Future Directions in Environmental Policy," *Journal of Environment and Planning* 17 (1985):1431–1446.

Chapter 22

5. Based on data from World Bank, *World Development Report 1984* (New York: Oxford University Press, 1984).

7. FAO, *Fuelwood Supplies in the Developing Countries,* Forestry Paper No. 42 (Rome: 1983).

8. DIESA, *World Population Prospects,* op. cit.

9. Ibid.

11. W. Häfele and W. Sassin, "Resources and Endowments, An Outline of Future Energy Systems," in P. W. Hemily and M. N. Ozdas (eds.), *Science and Future Choice* (Oxford: Clarendon Press, 1979).

Chapter 23

1. Payer, C., 'Causes of the Debt Crisis' in B. Onimode (ed), *The IMF, the World Bank and African Debt: the Social and Political Impact,* Zed, London, 1989, pp. 7–16.

2. 'Action for Whose Common Future?' *Solidarity for Equality, Ecology and Development Newsletter* 1, 1989, Torggt. 34, N-1083 Oslo 1, Norway, pp. 6–7.

3. Wiebe, J. D., Vice-President, Globe 90, Executive Vice-President, Asia Pacific Foundation, in *Globe 90 Official Buyers' Guide and Trade Fair Directory,* p. 13.

4. Global Industrial and Social Progress Research Institute brochure, p. 3.

5. United Nations General Assembly, A/CONF 151/PC/2, 23 February 1990, p. 8.

Chapter 24

4. More precisely, there are ultimate limits to the stocks of material resources, the flows of energy resources, and (in the event of these being circumvented by a major breakthrough in fission/fusion technologies) to the environment's ability to absorb waste energy and other stresses. The limits-to-growth debate, while not conclusive as to specifics, appears to have effectively shifted the burden of proof about the absence of such fundamental limits onto the diehard "technological optimists" who deny the existence of such limits.

5. Of course, "meeting the needs" is a rather ambiguous phrase that may mean anything in practice. Substituting this phrase with "optimizing economic and other societal benefits" (Goodland and Ledec, 1987) or "managing all assets, natural resources and human resources, as well as financial and physical assets for increasing long-term wealth and well-being (Repetto, 1986a, p. 15) does not define the objectives of development more precisely, although the importance attached to economic benefits or wealth is rather obvious.

6. It is tempting to conclude that this nine-point formulation of SD is identical with the concept of "ecodevelopment"—the original term coined by Maurice Strong of UNEP for environmentally sound development (see Sachs, 1977 and Riddell, 1981). Certainly the differences are less obvious than the similarities. Nevertheless, some changes are significant—such as the dropping of the emphasis on "local self-reliance" and the renewed emphasis on economic growth.

8. Economists have responded by suggesting that currently used indicators of economic growth (GNP in particular) could be modified so as to somehow "build in" this correlation (e.g., Peskin, 1981). To what extent this is possible and whether it will serve more than a marginal purpose are, however, open questions (Norgaard, 1989).

9. Three other "social" usages of sustainability need to be clarified. Sustainable economy (Daly, 1980) and sustainable society (Brown, 1981) are two of these. The focus there, however, is on the patterns and levels of resource use that might be ecologically sustainable while providing the goods and services necessary to maintain human well-being, and the social reorganization that might be required to make this possible. The third usage is Chambers' definition of "sustainable livelihoods" as "a level of wealth and of stocks and flows of food and cash which provide for physical and social well-being and security against becoming poorer" (Chambers, 1986). This can be thought of as a sophisticated version of "basic needs", in that security or risk-minimization is added to the list of needs. It is therefore relevant to any paradigm of development, rather than to SD in particular.

Part Six: From Ecological Conflict to Environmental Security?

1. See, for example, "Redefining National Security," Worldwatch Paper no. 14 (Washington, DC: Worldwatch Institute, 1977); Jessica Tuchman Mathews, "Redefining Security," *Foreign Affairs* 67 (1989):162–177; Norman Myers, "Environment and Security," *Foreign Policy* 74 (Spring 1989):23–41.

2. This theme is also discussed by Mathews, "Redefining Security."

3. Vice President Albert Gore discusses this theme in his book on the global environment, *Earth in the Balance: Ecology and the Human Spirit* (New York: Houghton Mifflin, 1992).

4. Kent Hughes Butts, "Why the Military Is Good for the Environment," in Jyrki Käkönen, ed., *Green Security or Militarized Environment* (Aldershot, UK: Dartmouth, 1994).

5. Early examples include Fairfield Osborn, *Our Plundered Planet* (Boston: Little, Brown, 1953) and Harrison Brown, *The Challenge of Man's Future* (New York: Viking, 1954).

6. See, for example, Ken Conca, "In the Name of Sustainability: Peace Studies and Environmental Discourse," *Peace and Change* 19, 2 (April 1994):91–113.

7. Matthias Finger, "The Military, the Nation State and the Environment," *The Ecologist* 21, 5 (September/October 1991):220–225. See also, Seth Shulman, *The Threat at Home: Confronting the Toxic Legacy of the U.S. Military* (Boston: Beacon Press, 1992).

Chapter 25

1. Thomas Homer-Dixon, "On the Threshold: Environmental Changes as Causes of Acute Conflict," *International Security*, Vol. 16, No. 2 (Fall 1991), pp. 76–116.

2. The three-year Project on Environmental Change and Acute Conflict brought together a team of thirty researchers from ten countries. It was sponsored by the American Academy of Arts and Sciences and the Peace and Conflict Studies Program at the University of Toronto.

4. For example, see David Wirth, "Climate Chaos," *Foreign Policy*, No. 74 (Spring 1989), pp. 3–22; and Neville Brown, "Climate, Ecology and International Security," *Survival*, Vol. 31, No. 6 (November/December 1989), pp. 519–532.

5. Diana Liverman, "The Impacts of Global Warming in Mexico: Uncertainty, Vulnerability and Response," in Jurgen Schmandt and Judith Clarkson, eds., *The Regions and Global Warming: Impacts and Response Strategies* (New York: Oxford University Press, 1992), pp. 44–68; and Diana Liverman and Karen O'Brien, "Global Warming and Climate Change in Mexico," *Global Environmental Change*, Vol. 1, No. 4 (December 1991), pp. 351–364.

6. Peter Gleick provides a potent illustration of the effect of population growth on water scarcity in Table 3 of "Water and Conflict: Fresh Water Resources and International Security," *International Security*, Vol. 18, No. 1 (Summer 1993), p. 101.

7. The second and third types of scarcity arise only with resources that can be physically controlled and possessed, like fish, fertile land, trees, and water, rather than resources like the climate or the ozone layer.

8. Since population growth is often a main cause of a decline in the quality and quantity of renewable resources, it actually has a dual impact on resource scarcity, a fact rarely noted by analysts.

9. James Boyce, "The Bomb Is a Dud," *The Progressive*, September 1990, pp. 24–25.

10. Bernard Nietschmann, "Environmental Conflicts and Indigenous Nations in Central America," paper prepared for the Project on Environmental Change and Acute Conflict (May 1991); and Sergio Diaz-Briquets, "Comments on Nietschmann's Paper," ibid.

11. Jeffrey Leonard, "Overview," *Environment and the Poor: Development Strategies for a Common Agenda* (New Brunswick, N.J.: Transaction, 1989), p. 7. For a careful analysis of the interaction of population and land distribution in El Salvador, see chap. 2 in William Durham, *Scarcity and Survival in Central America: The Ecological Origins of the Soccer War* (Stanford, Calif.: Stanford University Press, 1979), pp. 21–62.

28. Arthur Westing, "Appendix 2. Wars and Skirmishes Involving Natural Resources: A Selection from the Twentieth Century," in Arthur Westing, ed., *Global Resources and International Conflict: Environmental Factors in Strategic Policy and Action* (Oxford: New York, 1986), pp. 204–210.

29. See Durham, *Scarcity and Survival.*

30. Peter Gleick, "Water and Conflict," Occasional Paper No. 1, Project on Environmental Change and Acute Conflict (September 1992); and Gleick, "Water and Conflict: Fresh Water

Resources and International Security," *International Security,* Vol. 18, No. 1 (Summer 1993), pp. 79–112.

31. In 1980, Egyptian President Anwar el-Sadat said, "If Ethiopia takes any action to block our right to the Nile waters, there will be no alternative for us but to use force"; quoted in Norman Myers, "Environment and Security," *Foreign Policy,* No. 74 (Spring 1989), p. 32. See also chap. 6, "The Nile River," in Thomas Naff and Ruth Matson, eds., *Water in the Middle East: Conflict or Cooperation?* (Boulder, Colo.: Westview, 1984), pp. 125–155.

33. See Thayer Scudder, "River Basin Projects in Africa," *Environment,* Vol. 31, No. 2 (March 1989), pp. 4–32; and Scudder, "Victims of Development Revisited: The Political Costs of River Basin Development," *Development Anthropology Network,* Vol. 8, No. 1 (Spring 1990), pp. 1–5.

34. Astri Suhrke, "Pressure Points: Environmental Degradation, Migration, and Conflict," Occasional Paper No. 3, Project on Environmental Change and Acute Conflict (March 1993).

35. Ibid.

45. Robert Repetto, "Balance-Sheet Erosion—How to Account for the Loss of Natural Resources," *International Environmental Affairs,* Vol. 1, No. 2 (Spring 1989), pp. 103–137.

46. This estimate does not include the economic costs of lost rooting depth and increased vulnerability to drought, which may be even larger. See Wilfrido Cruz, Herminia Francisco, and Zenaida Conway, "The On-Site and Downstream Costs of Soft Erosion in the Magat and Pantabangan Watersheds," *Journal of Philippine Development,* Vol. 15, No. 1 (1988), p. 88.

47. Ed Barbier, "Environmental Degradation in the Third World," in David Pearce, ed., *Blueprint 2: Greening the World Economy* (London: Earthscan, 1991), Box 6.8, p. 90.

70. Francis Wilson and Mamphela Ramphele, *Uprooting Poverty: The South African Challenge* (New York: Norton, 1989); George Quail, et al., *Report of the Ciskei Commission* (Pretoria: Conference Associates, 1980), p. 73.

71. See Mamphela Ramphele and Chris McDowell, eds., *Restoring the Land: Environment and Change in Post-Apartheid South Africa* (London: Panos, 1991); and Chris Eaton, "Rural Environmental Degradation and Urban Conflict in South Africa," Occasional Paper of the Peace and Conflict Studies Program, University of Toronto, June 1992.

72. World Resources Institute, *World Resources, 1992–93* (New York: Oxford University Press, 1992), p. 286.

73. Global Assessment of Soil Degradation, *World Map on Status of Human-Induced Soil Degradation,* Sheet 1, North and South America.

74. Thomas Weil, et al., *Haiti: A Country Study* (Washington, D.C.: Department of the Army, 1982), pp. 28–33.

75. Anthony Catanese, "Haiti's Refugees: Political, Economic, Environmental," *Field Staff Reports,* No. 17 (Sausalito, Calif.: Universities Field Staff International, Natural Heritage Institute, 1990–91), p. 5.

76. Elizabeth Abbott, "Where Waters Run Brown," *Equinox,* Vol. 10, No. 59 (September/October 1991), p. 43.

77. Marko Ehrlich, et al., *Haiti: Country Environmental Profile, A Field Study* (Washington, D.C.: U.S. Agency for International Development, 1986), pp. 89–92.

78. WRI, *World Resources, 1992–93,* p. 246.

79. Ibid., p. 272.

Chapter 26

1. This is not to overlook another environmental dimension to security concerns, in the form of damage done to the environment through, for example, Americans' defoliation in Vietnam or Saddam Hussein's torching of Kuwaiti oil wells [see A. Ehrlich and J. W. Birks,

eds., *Hidden Dangers: Environmental Costs of Preparing for War* (San Francisco: Sierra Club Books, 1990)].

2. J. Goldstone, *Revolution and Rebellion in the Early Modern World* (Berkeley, CA: University of California Press, 1990); R. D. Lipschutz, *When Nations Clash: Raw Materials, Ideology, and Foreign Policy* (New York: Ballinger, 1989); C. Ponting, *A Green History of the World* (London: Sinclair-Stevenson, 1991); G. Porter, "Post–Cold War Global Environment and Security," *Fletcher Forum of World Affairs*, 14, 2 (1990):332–344; W. Youngquist, *Mineral Resources and the Destinies of Nations* (New York: National Book Company, 1990).

4. J. W. Sewell and S. K. Tucker, eds., *Growth Exports and Jobs in a Changing World Economy* (New Brunswick, NJ: TransAction Books, 1988); J. W. Suomela, *The Effects of Developing Countries' Debt Servicing Problems on U.S. Trade* (Washington, DC: International Trade Commission, 1987).

6. F. C. Ikle and A. Wohlstetter, *Discriminate Deterrence: Report for the Department of Defense of the Commission on Integrated Long-Term Strategy* (Washington, DC: U.S. Government Printing Office, 1988).

Chapter 27

2. Lester Brown, *Redefining National Security* (Washington, DC: Worldwatch Paper, No. 14, October 1977); Jessica Tuchman Mathews, 'Redefining Security', *Foreign Affairs* (Vol. 68, No. 2, 1989), pp. 162–77; Michael Renner, *National Security: The Economic and Environmental Dimensions* (Washington, DC: Worldwatch Paper, No. 89, May 1989); and Norman Myers, 'Environmental Security', *Foreign Policy* (No. 74, 1989), pp. 23–41.

3. Richard Ullman, 'Redefining Security', *International Security* (Vol. 8, No. 1, Summer 1983), pp. 129–53.

4. Hal Harvey, 'Natural Security', *Nuclear Times* (March/April 1988), pp. 24–26.

5. Philip Shabecoff, 'Senator Urges Military Resources to Be Turned to Environmental Battle', *The New York Times*, 29 June 1990, p. 1A.

7. Quentin Skinner, 'Language and Political Change', and James Farr, 'Understanding Political Change Conceptually', in Terence Ball et al., (eds.), *Political Innovation and Conceptual Change* (Cambridge: Cambridge University Press, 1989).

8. For a particularly lucid and well-rounded discussion of security, the state and violence, see Barry Buzan, *People, States, and Fear: The National Security Problem in International Relations* (Chapel Hill, NC: University of North Carolina Press, 1983), particularly pp. 1–93.

17. Ronnie D. Lipschutz, *When Nations Clash: Raw Materials, Ideology and Foreign Policy* (New York: Ballinger, 1989).

19. H. E. Goeller and Alvin Weinberg, 'The Age of Substitutability', *Science* (Vol. 201, 20 February 1967). For some recent evidence supporting this hypothesis, see Eric D. Larson, Marc H. Ross and Robert H. Williams, 'Beyond the Era of Materials', *Scientific American* (Vol. 254, 1986), pp. 34–41.

20. For a discussion of authoritarian and conflictual consequences of environmental constrained economies, see William Ophuls, *Ecology and the Politics of Scarcity* (San Francisco, CA: Freeman, 1976), p. 152. See also Susan M. Leeson, 'Philosophical Implications of the Ecological Crisis: The Authoritarian Challenge to Liberalism', *Polity* (Vol. 11, No. 3, Spring 1979); Ted Gurr, 'On the Political Consequences of Scarcity and Economic Decline', *International Studies Quarterly* (No. 29, 1985), pp. 51–75; and Robert Heilbroner, *An Inquiry Into the Human Prospect* (New York: W. W. Norton, 1974).

22. Bernard Brodie, 'The Impact of Technological Change on the International System', in David Sullivan and Martin Sattler (eds.), *Change and the Future of the International System* (New York: Columbia University Press, 1972), p. 14.

23. For a particularly lucid argument that the nation-state system is over-developed relative to its actual problem-solving capacities, see George Modelski, *Principles of World Politics* (New York: The Free Press, 1972).

Part Seven: Ecological Justice

1. For a discussion of some of these issues prior to Stockholm, see United Nations, *Development and Environment: Report and Working Papers of a Panel of Experts Convened by the Secretary General of the UN Conference on the Human Environment.* Founex, Switzerland, June 4–12, 1971.

2. For a discussion of the links between ecology and social justice, see Alan S. Miller, *Gaia Connections: An Introduction to Ecology, Ecoethics, and Economics* (Savage, MD: Rowman and Littlefield, 1991).

3. Karen Warren, "The Power and the Promise of Ecological Feminism," *Environmental Ethics* 12 (Summer 1990):125–146; Wendy Harcourt, ed., *Feminist Perspectives on Sustainable Development* (London: Zed Books, 1994); Carolyn Merchant, *Ecological Revolutions: Nature, Gender and Science in New England* (Chapel Hill, NC: University of North Carolina Press, 1989); Irene Diamond and Gloria Feman Orenstein, *Reweaving the World: The Emergence of Ecofeminism* (San Francisco: Sierra Club Books, 1990). For a criticism of some variants of ecofeminism, see Janet Biehl, *Rethinking Ecofeminist Politics* (Boston: South End Press, 1991).

4. Warren, "The Power and the Promise of Ecological Feminism," p. 125.

5. See Biehl, *Rethinking Ecofeminist Politics.*

6. Susanna Hecht and Alexander Cockburn, *The Fate of the Forest: Developers, Destroyers, and Defenders of the Amazon* (New York: HarperCollins, 1990).

7. On environmental racism, see Robert D. Bullard, *Dumping in Dixie: Race, Class, and Environmental Quality* (Boulder, CO: Westview Press, 1990); Robert D. Bullard, ed., *Unequal Protection: Environmental Justice and Communities of Color* (San Francisco: Sierra Club Books, 1994); Karl Grossman, "From Toxic Racism to Environmental Justice," *E Magazine,* May/June 1992, pp. 28–35; Elizabeth Martinez, "When People of Color Are an Endangered Species," *Z Magazine,* April 1991.

Chapter 29

1. E. F. Schumacher, *Small Is Beautiful: Economics as if People Mattered* (New York: Harper & Row, 1973).

Chapter 31

1. This chapter is based on a longer article written for a collaborative project of the International Social Sciences Association, the Social Science Research Council, and Development Alternatives with Women for a New Era (DAWN) on 'Rethinking Population and the Environment'. I am grateful for comments on an earlier draft by Carmen Barroso, David Bell, Lincoln Chen, Adrienne Germain and Jael Silliman. The usual disclaimers apply.

2. The dissonance addressed in this chapter is between mainstream environmentalists from the North and women's health researchers and activists from both North and South.

3. My own position is that of someone who has come to these debates from a background of working on issues of gender and development, and this chapter will perforce tilt heavily

towards spelling out the positions taken from within the women's movements. I do not claim to be able to explicate how the mainstream of the environmental movement (especially in the North) has come to the particular definitions it has of 'the population problem'.

4. A different theoretical approach that takes better account of the shifts in patterns of inter-generational transfers, and therefore of age-based hierarchies, is contained in the work of Caldwell and Caldwell (1987).

5. Or, in the case of many parts of Europe, of population expansion through increased fertility.

6. For an influential early critique, see Mamdani (1974).

7. See Scott (n.d.) for a look at Norplant use in the contemporary United States.

8. Even rapid fertility decline may sometimes be indicative of a strategy of desperation on the part of the poor who can no longer access the complementary resources needed to put children's labour to use.

9. Examples of the former are Little (1992), Blaikie (1985); of the latter, Shaw (1989) and UN (1992). The latter argues, for example, that 'The failure to take fully into account the possible effects of other factors that might contribute to environmental degradation characterizes many analyses of population-environmental interrelationships at the national and global levels and thus limits their value in assessing the impact of demographic variables'.

10. An example is the well known Ehrlich-Holden identity, I = PAT, linking environmental impact (I) with population growth (P), growth in affluence/consumption per capita (A), and technological efficiency (T).

11. Personal discussion with V. Miller, co-founder of West Harlem Environmental Action in New York City.

About the Book and Editors

THIS CUTTING-EDGE COLLECTION brings together for the first time readings both classic and new on the theme of global environmental politics from a diversity of viewpoints and value orientations. In selections chosen for their authority and edited to preserve their integrity, *Green Planet Blues* speaks with many voices—from Garrett Hardin and Herman Daly to Petra Kelly and Gita Sen, and from the World Bank and the Brundtland Commission to the rubber tappers and indigenous peoples of the Amazon. North-South relations combined with an emphasis on class, race, and gender are leitmotivs threaded throughout the selections. The paradigms of sustainable development, environmental security, and ecological justice are used to explicate topics ranging from climate change, population growth, deforestation, the ozone layer, acid rain, and toxic dumping to transboundary pollution and the global commons.

The editors introduce the volume and each part using international relations concepts and frameworks such as sovereignty, transnationalism, international conflict and cooperation, and institutional reform. They help students make connections among the various readings and between environmental issues and political analysis. Indispensable as background reading, a stimulus for discussion, or a survey of the field, *Green Planet Blues* is an essential part of any course in environmental studies and international relations.

KEN CONCA is assistant professor of government and politics and MICHAEL ALBERTY and GEOFFREY D. DABELKO are doctoral students of government and politics at the University of Maryland at College Park.